Poem Unlimited

Buchreihe der ANGLIA/ ANGLIA Book Series

Edited by
Lucia Kornexl, Ursula Lenker, Martin Middeke, Gabriele Rippl, Daniel Stein, Hubert Zapf

Advisory Board
Laurel Brinton, Philip Durkin, Olga Fischer, Susan Irvine,
Andrew James Johnston, Christopher A. Jones, Terttu Nevalainen,
Derek Attridge, Elisabeth Bronfen, Ursula K. Heise, Verena Lobsien,
Laura Marcus, J. Hillis Miller, Martin Puchner

Volume 63

Poem Unlimited

New Perspectives on Poetry and Genre

Edited by
David Kerler and Timo Müller

DE GRUYTER

For an overview of all books published in this series, please see
http://www.degruyter.com/view/serial/36292

ISBN 978-3-11-076595-3
e-ISBN (PDF) 978-3-11-059487-4
e-ISBN (EPUB) 978-3-11-059266-5
ISSN 0340-5435

Library of Congress Control Number: 2019941339

Bibliographic information published by the Deutsche Nationalbibliothek
The Deutsche Nationalbibliothek lists this publication in the Deutsche Nationalbibliografie;
detailed bibliographic data are available on the Internet at http://dnb.dnb.de.

© 2021 Walter de Gruyter GmbH, Berlin/Boston
This volume is text- and page-identical with the hardback published in 2019.
Typesetting: Integra Software Services Pvt. Ltd.
Printing and binding: CPI books GmbH, Leck

www.degruyter.com

Contents

David Kerler and Timo Müller
Poetry and Genre: An Introduction —— 1

Canonic Genres Reconsidered

David Kerler
Genre and Archive Fever in Romantic Poetry: Percy Bysshe Shelley's "Ozymandias" and the Sonnet—— 17

Stefanie John
Contesting and Continuing the Romantic Lyric: Eavan Boland and Kathleen Jamie —— 31

Elena Furlanetto
Mystic Poetry Across the Ocean: Reconciling Persian Sufi Poetry and Walt Whitman's *Leaves of Grass* —— 47

Rainer Emig
The Dragon in the Gate: Modernism as a Challenge to Contemporary Poetic Genres —— 63

Patrick Gill
"Now it's failed": The Sonnet Form in the Poetry of Philip Larkin —— 83

The Politics of Genre

Pierre-Héli Monot
Possibilities, Responsibilities: On Poetic Genres and Political Poiesis —— 99

Astrid Franke
Murderous Minds: A Narratological Approach to Poems on Perpetrators —— 113

Ewa Kołodziejczyk
"I Have Always Aspired to a More Spacious Form": Czesław Miłosz's Reflection on Poetic Genres in American Exile —— 127

Kathrin Härtl
"They kept shifting shapes": Derek Walcott's *Omeros* and its Fluid Genre —— 139

Katharina Engel
Diversifying the Genre: Postmodern Strategies in Patience Agbabi's (Performance) Poetry —— 155

Annika McPherson
Resisting Genrefication: Gender and Genre in Jean 'Binta' Breeze's *The Fifth Figure* —— 171

Genre and Mediality

Michaela Hausmann
Crossing Genre and Media Boundaries: Poetry in Fantastic Literary Narratives and Their Film Adaptations —— 191

Jessica Bundschuh
Re-erecting Genre Distinctions?: The Sound Recordings of William Carlos Williams's *Paterson* and John Montague's *The Rough Field* —— 209

Timo Müller
Poetry to Music: Gil Scott-Heron's Intermedial Performance Aesthetics —— 227

Nassim Winnie Balestrini
The Intermedial Poetry of Rap: Words, Sounds, and Music Videos —— 239

Julian Wacker
Grime Poetry: Black British Rap Lyric(s) in the Twenty-First Century —— 255

Notes on Contributors —— 271

Index —— 275

David Kerler and Timo Müller
Poetry and Genre: An Introduction

When Polonius, in the second act of *Hamlet*, announces the theater company as the "best actors in the world, either for tragedy, comedy, history, pastoral, pastoral-comical, historical-pastoral, tragical-historical, tragical-comical-historical-pastoral, scene individable, or poem unlimited" (2.2.392–396), he raises several issues that have occupied scholarship on poetry and genre. While we continue to speak of poems and poetry, we have more or less deposed of the question of how poetry as a genre is defined, let alone the issue of its differing terminologies in various academic cultures (such as the differing meanings of the English *lyric*, the French *lyrique*, and the German *Lyrik*). By our very dismissal of genre as a subject of analysis we allow the old generic categories to persist unquestioned, and almost unchanged, in academic discourse. There is a need to subject traditional concepts of and attributions to such categories to informed scholarly analysis, particularly in studies of poetry, where they remain influential among critics and often exert formative influence on authors. This volume draws on a wide range of anglophone poetry to identify three areas where such critical analysis is particularly important: the contemporary discussion of traditional genres, the political implications of genre, and the relationship between genres and media.

Questions of genre, of its definition, subcategories, and functions, have been discussed controversially from Antiquity to our time. Persistent concerns revolve around inductive vs. deductive classification, singularity vs. collectivity, synchronic vs. diachronic approaches, and description vs. prescription, not to mention the question of what criteria for such distinctions have to and can be applied (Hempfer 1973; Michler 2015: 19–86): Does a genre exist as such, for example as an ideal entity in a Platonic sense, or is it a subjective (re)construction based on a selection of various concrete texts? What role does the individual reader's horizon of knowledge play in (re)constructing the genres within the act of reading; what cognitive processes come into play (Stockwell 2002: 28–35; Hallet 2007)? How many texts are needed to establish the conventions of a certain genre, what time period has to be considered, and do works from canonical authors have a stronger impact on this process? Finally, when and how does a descriptive construction of a genre itself become a prescriptive model for future (including retrospective) categorizations? These questions indicate the socio-historical, ideological embeddedness of genre concepts and the various discourses around them, which thus carry a potential for political and cultural conflict.

Ancient philosophers and writers already commented on the notion of genre, and they approached it from various perspectives and with different thematic interests. Aristotle, for instance, developed his famous definition of classical tragedy by contrasting the genre with epic poetry. In his *Poetics* he descriptively differentiates the genres by going through elements such as rhythm, content, structure, and representation. To a certain extent he also anticipates central elements of reader-response criticism as he distinguishes the subgenres of the tragedy (for example simple, ethical, or pathetic) by their respective impact on the audience (Culler 1999: 38). Originating from ancient thought, the classification of literature into poetry, drama, and prose became widely accepted over the course of the eighteenth and nineteenth centuries. The emergence of structuralism brought a renewed interest in genre and resulted in ever more differentiated taxonomies. Focusing on the novel and marginalizing poetry, Mikhail Bakhtin (1981) conceived genres as profoundly determined by their spatiotemporal configuration, or in his term, their usage of different 'chronotopes' – a concept that may be fruitfully applied to poetry as well. Northrop Frye (1957) and Gérard Genette (1979), in turn, tried to establish a genealogical, evolutionary model of genre that strived to reconstruct original forms (Hempfer 1973: 76–80).

The numerous structuralist approaches resulted in a variety of categories and classifications, but these were called into question by the new insights of poststructuralist theory by the end of the 1970s. This development was foreshadowed by the close readings of the New Criticism, which was in turn influenced by the nominalism of the Croce school in its valorization of the immanent individuality of the artistic work over external (generic) categories (Hempfer 1973: 38–41). To poststructuralists such as Jacques Derrida (2005), Roland Barthes (2002), or Julia Kristeva (1986), the attempt to distinguish different types of texts seemed to be tautological in view of a text's inherent intertextuality, its interwovenness within a *texte général*. As Derrida argues in his seminal essay "The Law of Genre" (1980), the concept of genre subverts itself in that it is based on the law of "purity" – "genres are not to be mixed" – that can never be fulfilled. In the logic of the language system, using – and thus citing – a specific genre is an act of repetition that brings about its "impurity, corruption, contamination, decomposition, perversion, deformation, even cancerization, generous proliferation, or degenerescence" (57). Finally, what definitions there are have been continually questioned by the literary experiments of the twentieth century and the new media of the twenty-first, most notably in the contexts of postmodernist genre hybridity, adaptation, intermediality, and performance poetry.

These reservations notwithstanding, generic categories remain in wide use in literary studies, as even a cursory glance at university course lists or publishers' catalogues attests. From poetics of postmodernist genre hybridity (Zymner 2003) and anthropological approaches (Göbel 2000) right through to debates on intermediality and adaptation (Elleström 2010; Hutcheon and O'Flynn 2013), performance (Novak 2011), cognitive theory (Duff 2000) and cultural memory (Erll and Seibel 2004; Humphrey 2005; Nünning, Gymnich, and Neumann 2007), interest in questions of genre has never really flagged in continental European scholarship. Numerous handbooks on genre and its theories have appeared there in recent years, most notably Dieter Lampig's *Handbuch der literarischen Gattungen* (2009), Rüdiger Zymner's *Handbuch Gattungstheorie* (2010), and Peter Scheinpflug's *Genre-Theorie: Eine Einführung* (2014). Interest is reviving in anglophone scholarship as well, as is attested by the appearance of John Frow's systematic survey in the Routledge New Critical Idiom series (2006), by the productive debates in journals like the triannual *Genre,* and by special issues of *NLH* (Cohen 2003b) and *PMLA* (Dimock and Robbins 2007). These publications have cleared the ground for extensions and reappraisals of the concept in specific critical contexts, including the spatial turn (Talley 2013) and postcolonialism, where the focus has been on cultural-imperialist implications of western genres (Crowley and Hiddleston 2011).

By including contemporary methodologies such as postcolonialism, gender studies, and media studies, the contributions in this volume aim at complicating existing approaches and situating them in their broader socio-cultural contexts. In so doing, they pursue a core question of literary studies – the definition and cultural uses of the concept of genre – from an interdisciplinary perspective that problematizes and extends the concept of genre itself. While the title of the volume title presupposes the existence of a genre describable as "poetry," some of the contributions challenge this position. They demonstrate the limitations of older concepts of poetry by exploring the boundaries of the concept and discussing hybrid forms such as hip hop. In all, the chapters discuss a wide range of poetic genres in conjunction with their theoretical, literary and socio-cultural appropriations.

The first section re-evaluates canonic genres from various cultural, ideological, and aesthetic perspectives across different literary epochs. The five chapters in the section go through two centuries of English, Irish, and American poetry to show that genres, on the one hand, constitute transhistorical models that are, on the other hand, actualized and thus modified within given socio-cultural and thus historical contexts. This interplay of continuity and discontinuity – an interplay characteristic of many literatures, especially perhaps British literature – results in subversive tensions that challenge and broaden the very notion of genre. The first chapter, by David Kerler, discusses the adaptation of the sonnet genre in Romanticism – his case study is Percy

Bysshe Shelley's "Ozymandias" (1818) – against the backdrop of the cultural and technological innovations between the late eighteenth and early nineteenth centuries, in particular the formative phase of the museum and the rapidly growing print culture. Drawing on Derrida's concept of archive fever, Kerler shows that Shelley employs the sonnet genre to critically engage with the proliferation of archives and archiving techniques of his age. Not only does "Ozymandias" mirror the epoch's desire to archive origins and originals, but it constitutes a metadiscourse on the archive and its precarious materiality, the latter extending from the emperor's statue onto the act of writing and eventually to the sonnet genre, which itself comes to function as archive.

The following chapter by Stefanie John, "Contesting and Continuing the Romantic Lyric," takes these issues to the contemporary period. Based on close readings of Eavan Boland's and Kathleen Jamie's uses of the lyric, John argues that contemporary actualizations of this genre break with Romantic notions of subjective transcendence in favor of an involvement with the plurality of modern identities and lives in the light of postcolonial, post-devolutionary and feminist agendas. Both poets draw on the aesthetic and ideological superstructure of the Romantic lyric, thus citing and subverting the very genre at the same time. They create a metalanguage that challenges the genre's boundaries – a self-reflexive duality that however stands in continuation with Romantic processes of self-questioning.

In the next chapter, Elena Furlanetto expands the question of Romantic (dis)continuities across the Atlantic as she traces the generic roots of American transcendentalist verse in Sufi poetry. Focusing on the construction and function of poetic persona in Walt Whitman's *Leaves of Grass* (1855) and the works of the thirteenth-century mystic poet Rumi, she discusses the ambivalent generic relation the transcendentalists established with their precursor and argues for a reconciliation of conflicting positions.

Rainer Emig's chapter "The Dragon in the Gate: Modernism as a Challenge to Contemporary Poetic Genres," takes the question of generic (dis)continuities to the twentieth century. It identifies three major tendencies in twentieth-century British and American poetry, ranging from continuity to discontinuity, that problematize the legacy of modernism: adhering to and subtly modifying the modernist program; sidestepping it through parody or by resorting to Romantic or Victorian forms; and critically engaging with its political implications. (Eavan Boland falls under the latter category, Emig notes in confirmation of John's findings.) While all of these tendencies seem to signal a departure from modernism, Emig concludes that they in fact update its agenda: by breaking with modernist rules, they continue its program of breaking with established patterns – a process in which genres mediate between the opposed yet closely intertwined poles of continuity and dissolution. Together with John's essay on the (dis)continuities of Romanticism, Emig's focus on the modernist legacy thus comprises a survey of the major influences on contemporary poetry and the fundamental role the concept of genre plays in these developments.

Patrick Gill's study of the sonnet in Philip Larkin rounds the section out with a case study that draws together insights from the previous chapters. Gill takes up the genre explored in the first chapter, the sonnet, and asks why its association with Renaissance and Romantic poetry did not undermine its popularity with twentieth-century poets. After all, the pessimistic empiricism of the Movement is diametrically opposed to the sonnet's characteristic resolution of conflicting ideas and its resulting sense of closure. Gill's analysis of Larkin's uses of the sonnet confirm Emig's point that many contemporary authors sidestep modernism by drawing on generic patterns from previous epochs. It shows that Larkin breaks with dualistic conceptions of openness and closure, replacing them with a lack of resolution, with stasis and doubt. Larkin's varied subversions of the sonnet form not only reflect his poetic development, Gill argues, but ultimately help him find his own poetic voice.

The political implications of these canonic revisions and reconsiderations come to the fore in the second section of the volume. The chapters in this section address four key political dimensions of genre: its interrelations with social class, the ethical implications of its epistemology (genre as a way of seeing), its entanglements with projects of colonization and decolonization, and the interrelations between genre and gender. The most prominent commentator on the first dimension, social class, has arguably been Fredric Jameson, who devotes the second chapter of *The Political Unconscious* (1981) to analyzing "The Dialectical Use of Genre" (103–50). Jameson seeks to recover genre criticism by exposing the social function of its putatively neutral categories. This approach makes such criticism a central tool in Jameson's project of tracing the interrelations between literary form and "the twin diachronic perspective of the history of forms and the evolution of social life" (105). While his case study in *The Political Unconscious* is romance, Jameson first tested his views in debates around science fiction, a genre that has inspired much class-based scholarship over the years (Bould and Miéville 2009; Mazierska and Suppia 2016; Cashbaugh 2016).

Poetry, by contrast, is rarely addressed by theorists of genre and class. One reason for this neglect, Hugh Grady suggests in "Notes on Marxism and the Lyric" (1981), may be the traditional poetic focus on the personal and the transcendent, which can appear "resistant to critical methods seeking to discover in the literary work the reflection of specific social conflicts and historical conjunctures" (544). If the realistic novel as theorized by Georg Lukács stages the "confrontation of bourgeois society with what it is," Grady argues, in lyric poetry "bourgeois society attempts to confront what it is not": the genre confronts "the substratum of human needs and yearnings, unfulfilled and unrealized within historical society" (551). The opening chapter of our section, Pierre-Héli Monot's "Possibilities, Responsibilities: On Poetic Genres and Political Poiesis," adds to the small body of scholarship on poetic genre and class but pursues a more positive line of inquiry. Rather than limiting poetry to bourgeois soul-searching, Monot explores the work of the American poet George Oppen, who returned to poetry after a quarter-century of working for the communist party. Reading Oppen's work against Cornelius Castoriadis' Marxist writing, Monot argues that "instituted poetic genres fulfill the crucial function of elaborating and clarifying the public deliberations of democratic societies." He arrives at this insight through an analysis of the style and voice of Oppen's poetry, which he locates in an American tradition shaped by Walt Whitman's socially conscious work.

Another way in which genre negotiates social class is perspective, as scholars are beginning to realize (Peak 2014). The epistemological dimension of genre is central to its political functions. Genre is a "way of seeing" (Lima 1993: 431), and scholarship on the politics of genre arguably needs to pay more attention to examine the perspectives particular genres privilege or occlude. The next chapter in our section takes an important step in this direction. Astrid Franke's "Murderous Minds: A Narratological Approach to Poems on Perpetrators" foregrounds the ethical implications of perspective by innovatively assembling poems narrated by people who committed or abetted violent crimes. Franke identifies the strategies poets use to establish an analytic distance to the minds of these perpetrators and to discourage affective responses such as admiration or pity. The chapter additionally contributes to genre criticism with its narratological approach, which makes accessible for the analysis of poetry a set of conceptual tools previously reserved for narrative texts.

Poets do not only manipulate perspective in their texts but bring a historically specific perspective to their subject matter – a perspective shaped by their social and textual environments. Ewa Kołodziejczyk's chapter on "Czesław Miłosz's Reflection on Poetic Genres in American Exile" examines these broader dimensions through a study of the Polish poet's exile in the United States. This experience opened up a new perspective on poetry and genre, Kolodziejczyk explains: it led Miłosz to reject traditional views of literature as separable into neat generic categories. Freed from the conventional expectations of his readership in communist Poland, Miłosz arrived at a more flexible conception of his work as an aggregate of various discourses, forms, and styles. Kolodziejczyk stresses the impact of contemporary American poetry, especially of Allen

Ginsberg, on this development. Her chapter thus adds an important transnational dimension to our exploration of anglophone poetry by positioning a foreign-language writer's engagement with and contribution to anglophone poetics.

Scholars of postcolonial and gender studies have contributed crucially to the transnationalizing of anglophone poetry studies, and they have taken a leading role in exploring the perspectivizing function of genre. In this process the very concept of genre has been drawn into question because of its alleged complicity with a white- and male-dominated view of literary history. The continuing prominence of the concept in postcolonial and gender studies, however, indicates the productivity of genre as both a creative and a critical category. Not only do many postcolonial and female writers employ traditional generic references, but as the chapters by John and Emig show, these writers revise the aesthetic traditions associated with these genres in creative ways. Scholars have risen to the challenge of identifying and discussing such creative revisions. This branch of scholarship reflects many of the larger emphases of postcolonial and gender studies, for example on speaking positions and perspectives, the role of literature in the social construction of reality, the cultural and historical specificity of aesthetic strategies, and the syncretism or hybridity of literary texts that draw from a variety of cultural contexts.

The very systems of coloniality and gender can be seen as "classification struggles" analogous with genre, as Peter Hitchcock has argued, which implies that "genre too is subject to decolonization" (2003: 301–302). One way of doing so, he suggests, is to introduce "difference," which links his decolonial project with Derrida's deconstructive one. Derrida turns to genre among other things because it oscillates between the natural and the symbolic, and because this conceptual oscillation continues in the discursive and social boundaries erected in the name of genre. Derrida draws an analogy with gender, a concept that shares the same signifier in French (*genre*) and the same disruptive in-between position in cultural debates (cf. Crimmins 2009). Feminist scholars of genre have drawn on this deconstructive approach but have complemented it with a more affirmative one that attends, among other things, to the politically empowering use of genre convention by women writers (Eagleton 2000). In postcolonial studies, a similarly affirmative approach can be found, for example in Margaret Cohen's contribution to the abovementioned special issue of *NLH*, where she points out that the very breadth of genre categories can serve political purposes by overcoming narrow cultural or national paradigms (2013: 481–499).

Genre criticism from postcolonial and gender studies has overwhelmingly focused on narrative genres such as the autobiography and the novel (Lima 1993; Erll and Seibel 2004; Hiddleston 2011). Few scholars seem to be aware of this potentially exclusionary focus. Those who are, for example Hitchcock, tend to argue that narrative genres have been paradigmatic for their fields because both colonial appropriation and revisionist accounts of (de)colonized lives and social contexts have relied on narrative (2003: 307). The last three chapters of our second section go beyond this relatively narrow focus and address the uses of poetry for self-assertion and intercultural negotiations in the multigeneric work of writers of color.

Kathrin Härtl discusses Derek Walcott's nuanced revisions of epic poetry in *Omeros* (1990), which is in many ways an epic poem in its own right but one that challenges both the imposition of European cultural standards on the Caribbean and the concept of genre itself. Katharina Engel positions the British performance poet Patience Agbabi in genre traditions that have long been associated with white poets. In portraying Agbabi as a decentered "nomadic subject" who evades limiting assumptions about the role of the black female poet, Engel also foregrounds questions of perspective, for example the tension between Agbabi's physical presence on the stage and the speaking voices she assumes in her poetry. Annika McPherson's chapter on the Jamaican dub poet Jean 'Binta' Breeze examines the thematic and aesthetic continuities that interconnect questions of genre and gender in the work of this transitional figure. It focuses on the collection *The Fifth Figure* (2006), which weaves poetry, memoir, and novelistic narrative prose into the structure of a Jamaican quadrille and traces the lives of five generations of women across the Atlantic. McPherson points out the challenge this approach implies to dominant notions of diaspora, and she raises the question of the genre(s) of diaspora – a question complementing that of the genre(s) of exile in Kolodziejczyk's chapter on Miłosz. What all chapters in the section share is the observation that poetic practice both defines and defies genre boundaries, and that this ambivalent role translates onto the political level, where poetry engages ideological boundaries and classification regimes.

In *Postmodernism, or the Cultural Logic of Late Capitalism* (1991), Jameson points out that this kind of analysis is increasingly undertaken in terms of media rather than genres. He welcomes this shift because it helps us understand that "older forms or genres" were also "media products" (67–68). Indeed, media studies have enriched the often abstract discussion of genre by foregrounding the material dimension of literary genres: book covers, typography, illustrations, but also the formative impact of transmission media such as magazines or the internet (Ritzer and Schulze 2016). This enriching effect has worked both ways. The vocabulary of genre analysis has laid the groundwork for typological discussions of media, and many media products, from western movies to digital poems, have been shaped by their adherence to older notions of genre. The existence of multimedial genres such as hip hop and of multigeneric media such as television casts further light on the manifold interconnections between the two concepts and areas of study.

Even these broad observations indicate that the word 'medium' can refer to different aspects of the communication process. Jameson distinguishes three aspects: medium as a "specific form of aesthetic production," a "specific technology," and "a social institution" (1991: 67). The media scholar Werner Wolf makes a similar distinction in his definition of media as "conventionally and culturally distinct means of communication, specified not only by particular technical or institutional channels (or one channel) but primarily by the use of one or more semiotic systems in the public transmission of contents" (2008: 19). The terminological shift from "aesthetic" to "semiotic" is characteristic of media studies and indicates an effort to disengage the conceptual tools of media analysis from aesthetic categories such as genre. The aesthetic dimension of media products has ensured the continuing relevance of such categories, however, and a closer look suggests that both the semiotic and the institutional aspects of medial transmission can be shaped and explained by notions of genre. The media theorist Siegfried Schmidt, for example, distinguishes conventionalized "media offers" from the semiotic, technological, and institutional levels alike and conceives these media offers in genre terms: his examples include "oral and written poetry," "book texts and hypertexts" (2000: 94–95, our trans.). Conversely, one of the few extended discussions of the relations of genres and media, Ansgar Nünning and Jan Rupp's "Media and Medialization as Catalysts for Genre Development" (2013), draws on the vocabulary of (inter)mediality studies to discuss the questions of how and why genres change over time.

Nünning and Rupp base their discussion on the genre of the novel, again illustrating the predominance of narrative fiction in genre studies (cf. Göbel and Schabio 2013). Another field that has generated scholarship on genre and media in recent years is the internet with its new forms of expression (Spooner and Yancey 1996; Wiggins and Bowers 2015; Taylor 2016). Conversely, there is a substantial amount of scholarship on the mediality of poems, from Marjorie Perloff's *Radical Artifice: Writing Poetry in the Age of Media* (1991) to recent examples like Paul Stephens' *The Poetics of Information Overload* (2015) and Andrew Burkett's *Romantic Mediations* (2016). There is a lack, however, of scholarship that discusses the generic and medial dimensions of poetry in conjunction. The chapters in our final section pursue this line of inquiry by examining various intermedial and intergeneric configurations: poetry embedded in novels and their film versions; recordings of poetry readings; poetry performed with music; and music modeled on poetry. Michaela Hausmann's "Crossing

Genre and Media Boundaries: Poetry in Fantastic Literary Narratives and Their Film Adaptations" examines the role of genre in the medial transposition of literature into film. In a close reading of the film adaptations of two popular novels for a young audience, J. R. R. Tolkien's *The Hobbit* (1936) and Suzanne Collins's *The Hunger Games: Mockingjay* (2010), Hausmann focuses on poems embedded in these novels and traces the changes in form, speech situation, and structural function as these poems are transposed into the film versions. The chapter differentiates previous models of medial transposition, which assume a generically homogeneous source medium, and at the same time explores the transgeneric and transmedial potential of embedded poems.

The following chapter, Jessica Bundschuh's "Re-erecting Genre Distinctions?: The Sound Recordings of William Carlos Williams's *Paterson* and John Montague's *The Rough Field*," offers a different perspective on this genre configuration. It also examines a medial transposition process (literature to reading), and once again the source medium is generically heterogeneous. In *Paterson* and *The Rough Field*, however, prose is embedded in poetry rather than the other way round. Starting from the observation that Williams tends to leave out the prose passages in his readings of *Paterson* while Montague incorporates them into his lyrical presentation style, Bundschuh discusses the question of whether audio performances undermine or reaffirm conventional genre boundaries. Whereas scholars of intermediality tend to assume that medial transposition is a complex process in itself, Bundschuh shows that it can either enhance or reduce the complexity of the work, and that both phenomena can occur in the same transposition process.

The concept of intermediality becomes itself the subject of discussion in the next two chapters. Timo Müller's "Poetry to Music: Gil Scott-Heron's Intermedial Performance Aesthetics" examines the work of poet, performance poet, and musician Scott-Heron, who works on the boundaries of genres (poetry and song) but also of media (the written and the spoken word, literature and music). Whereas many commentators on Scott-Heron's intermediality work with traditional notions of distinct media, Müller argues, his significance as an artist and as a case study for genre and media theorists lies in his continual blurring of such distinctions. Through contrastive readings of the records *Small Talk at 125th and Lenox* (1970) and *Reflections* (1981), Müller positions Scott-Heron's art in the conflictive yet creative space between poetry and music. Scott-Heron is often regarded as a crucial precursor of rap music, and this is where the next chapter takes up. Drawing on recent rap songs from the *Hamilton Mixtape*, Nassim Balestrini makes a case for analyzing rap music not just as poetry but as an intermedial poetic genre that draws on a variety of visual modes to spread its message and develop its aesthetics.

Rap music in its turn was an important inspiration for grime, a musical genre that emerged in black British contexts. In the concluding chapter of the volume, Julian Wacker accordingly positions grime as a poetic genre in many ways analogous to rap. Studying grime as poetry, he argues, widens our understanding of both forms of expression and especially of the increasingly intermedial shapes that poetry takes today. Taken together, the chapters of the mediality section can be read as a commentary on Marshall McLuhan's much-quoted assertion that "the medium is the message" (1964: 9). While media certainly influence and delimit the content they transmit, the chapters suggest, their message is shaped by various organizing principles that can be specific to one medium, operate transversally across media, or provide a basic pattern that reappears in several otherwise distinct media. Genre is one of the most powerful and pervasive of these organizing principles, and our volume demonstrates that research into the history, politics, and mediality of genres has lost none of its literary and cultural significance.

Works Cited

Aristotle. 1968. *Poetics*. Oxford: Clarendon Press.
Bakhtin, Mikhail M. 1981. "Forms of Time and of the Chronotope in the Novel". In: Michael Holquist (ed.). *The Dialogic Imagination*. Trans. Caryl Emerson and Michael Holquist. Austin: University of Texas Press. 84–258.
Barthes, Roland. 2002. "The Death of the Author". In: William Irwin (ed.), *The Death and Resurrection of the Author?* Westport: Greenwood Press. 3–7.
Bould, Mark, and China Miéville (eds.). 2009. *Red Planets: Marxism and Science Fiction*. Middletown: Wesleyan University Press.
Burkett, Andrew. 2016. *Romantic Mediations: Media Theory and British Romanticism*. Albany: State University of New York Press.
Cashbaugh, Sean. 2016. "A Paradoxical, Discrepant, and Mutant Marxism: Imagining a Radical Science Fiction in the American Popular Front". *Journal for the Study of Radicalism* 10.1: 63–106.
Cohen, Margaret. 2003. "Traveling Genres". *NLH* 34.2: 481–499.
Cohen, Ralph (ed.). 2003. "Theorizing Genres". Spec. issue of *NLH* 34: 2–3.
Crimmins, Jonathan. 2009. "Gender, Genre, and the Near Future in Derrida's 'The Law of Genre'". *Diacritics* 39.1: 45–60.
Crowley, Patrick, and Jane Hiddleston (eds.). 2011. *Postcolonial Poetics: Genre and Form*. Liverpool: Liverpool University Press.
Culler, Jonathan. 1999. *Dekonstruktion: Derrida und die poststrukturalistische Literaturtheorie*. Hamburg: Rowohlt.
Derrida, Jacques. 1980. "The Law of Genre". *Critical Inquiry* 7.1: 55–81.
Derrida, Jacques. 2005. "Différance". In: Julie Rivkin and Michael Ryan (eds.), *Literary Theory: An Anthology*. Malden: Blackwell. 278–299.

Dimock, Wai Chee, and Bruce Robbins (eds.). 2007. "Remapping Genre". Spec. issue of *PMLA* 122.5: 1370–1700.
Duff, David (ed.). 2000. *Modern Genre Theory*. Harlow: Pearson.
Eagleton, Mary. 2000. "Genre and Gender". In: David Duff (ed.). *Modern Genre Theory*. Harlow: Pearson. 250–262.
Elleström, Lars (ed.). 2010. *Media Borders, Multimodality and Intermediality*. Basingstoke: Palgrave Macmillan.
Erll, Astrid, and Klaudia Seibel. 2004. "Gattungen, Formtraditionen, kulturelles Gedächtnis". In: Ansgar Nünning and Vera Nünning (eds.). *Erzähltextanalyse und Gender Studies*. Stuttgart: Metzler. 180–208.
Frow, John. 2006. *Genre*. New Critical Idiom. London: Routledge.
Frye, Northrop. 1973. *An Anatomy of Criticism: Four Essays*. Princeton: Princeton University Press.
Genette, Gerard. 1979. *Introduction à l'architexte*. Paris: Seuil.
Göbel, Walter. 2000. "The State of Genre Theory, or, Towards an Anthropological Approach to Genre". *Symbolism* 1: 327–48.
Göbel, Walter, and Saskia Schabio (eds.). 2013. *Locating Postcolonial Narrative Genres*. New York: Routledge.
Grady, Hugh. 1981. "Notes on Marxism and the Lyric". *Contemporary Literature* 22.4: 544–555.
Gymnich, Marion, Birgit Neumann, and Ansgar Nünning (eds.). 2007. *Gattungstheorie und Gattungsgeschichte*. Trier: WVT.
Hallet, Wolfgang. 2007. "Gattungen als kognitive Schemata: Die multigenerische Interpretation literarischer Texte". In: Marion Gymnich, Birgit Neumann, and Ansgar Nünning (eds.). *Gattungstheorie und Gattungsgeschichte*. Trier: WVT. 53–71.
Hempfer, Klaus W. 1973. *Gattungstheorie*. Munich: Fink.
Hiddleston, Jane (ed.). 2011. *Postcolonial Poetics: Genre and Form*. Liverpool: Liverpool University Press.
Hitchcock, Peter. 2003. "The Genre of Postcoloniality". *NLH* 34.2: 299–330.
Humphrey, Richard. 2005. "Literarische Gattung und Gedächtnis". In: Ansgar Nünning and Astrid Erll (eds.). *Gedächtniskonzepte der Literaturwissenschaft: Theoretische Grundlegung und Anwendungsperspektiven*. Berlin: De Gruyter. 73–96.
Hutcheon, Linda, and Siobhan O'Flynn. 2013. *A Theory of Adaptation*. Oxon: Routledge.
Jameson, Fredric. 1981. *The Political Unconscious*. London: Methuen.
Jameson, Fredric. 1991. *Postmodernism, or, the Cultural Logic of Late Capitalism*. London: Verso.
Kristeva, Julia. 1986. "Word, Dialogue and Novel". In: Toril Moi (ed.). *The Kristeva Reader*. Southampton: Blackwell. 34–61.
Lampig, Dieter. 2009. *Handbuch der literarischen Gattungen*. Stuttgart: Kröner.
Lima, Maria Helena. 1993. "Decolonizing Genre: Jamaica Kincaid and the *Bildungsroman*". *Genre* 26: 431–459.
Mazierska, Ewa, and Alfredo Suppia (eds.). 2016. *Red Alert: Marxist Approaches to Science Fiction Cinema*. Detroit: Wayne State University Press.
McLuhan, Marshall. 1964. *Understanding Media: The Extensions of Man*. New York: McGraw-Hill.
Michler, Werner. 2015. *Kulturen der Gattung: Poetik im Kontext, 1750–1950*. Göttingen: Wallstein.

Novak, Julia. 2011. *Live Poetry: An Integrated Approach to Poetry in Performance*. Amsterdam: Rodopi.

Nünning, Ansgar, and Jan Rupp. 2013. "Media and Medialization as Catalysts for Genre Development: Theoretical Frameworks, Analytical Concepts and a Selective Overview of Varieties of Intermedial Narration in British Fiction". In: Michael Basseler, Ansgar Nünning, and Christine Schwanecke (eds.). *The Cultural Dynamics of Generic Change in Contemporary Fiction: Theoretical Frameworks, Genres and Model Interpretations*. Trier: WVT. 201–234.

Peak, Anna. 2014. "Servants and the Victorian Sensation Novel". *Studies in English Literature, 1500–1900* 54.4: 835–851.

Perloff, Marjorie. 1991. *Radical Artifice: Writing Poetry in the Age of Media*. Chicago: University of Chicago Press.

Ritzer, Ivo, and Peter W. Schulze (eds.). 2016. *Transmediale Genre-Passagen: Interdisziplinäre Perspektiven*. Wiesbaden: Springer VS.

Scheinpflug, Peter. 2014. *Genre-Theorie: Eine Einführung*. Berlin: LIT.

Schmidt, Siegfried J. 2000. *Kalte Faszination: Medien, Kultur, Wissenschaft in der Mediengesellschaft*. Weilerswist: Velbrück.

Shakespeare, William. 1982. *Hamlet*. Ed. Harold Jenkins. London: Arden Shakespeare.

Spooner, Michael, and Kathleen Yancey. 1996. "Postings on a Genre of Email". *College Composition and Communication* 47.2: 252–278.

Stephens, Paul. 2015. *The Poetics of Information Overload: From Gertrude Stein to Conceptual Writing*. Minneapolis: University of Minnesota Press.

Stockwell, Peter. 2002. *Cognitive Poetics: An Introduction*. London: Routledge.

Talley, Robert T. 2013. *Spatiality*. London: Routledge.

Taylor, Claire. 2016. "From the Baroque to Twitter: Tracing the Literary Heritage of Digital Genres". *Comparative Critical Studies* 13.3: 307–329.

Wiggins, Bradley, and Bret Bowers. 2015. "Memes as a Genre: A Structural Analysis of the Memescape". *New Media and Society* 17.11: 1886–1906.

Wolf, Werner. 2008. "The Relevance of Mediality and Intermediality to Academic Studies of English Literature". In: Martin Heusser, Andreas Fischer and Andreas H. Jucker (eds.). *Mediality/Intermediality*. Tübingen: Narr. 15–43.

Zymner, Rüdiger. 2003. *Gattungstheorie: Probleme und Positionen der Literaturwissenschaft*. Paderborn: Mentis.

Zymner, Rüdiger (ed.). 2010. *Handbuch Gattungstheorie*. Stuttgart: Metzler.

Canonic Genres Reconsidered

David Kerler
Genre and Archive Fever in Romantic Poetry: Percy Bysshe Shelley's "Ozymandias" and the Sonnet

Abstract: Using the example of Percy Bysshe Shelley's "Ozymandias" (1818), the essay scrutinizes the English Romantics' appropriation of poetic genres in the light of the epoch's proliferation of numerous archives and archival practices, most notably the increasing print culture. Drawing on Jacques Derrida's *Archive Fever* (1995), the essay argues that "Ozymandias" is a metadiscourse on cultural preoccupations with origins, originals, and (their) various archives, the latter also extending to its genre since the history of the sonnet is closely related to the history of its medium. A close reading of the poem together with a brief look at its cultural and material contexts will reveal that Shelley uses the sonnet genre to explore the epoch's desire to archive as well as the precarious nature of the archiving process and that of contemporary (material) archives.

Keywords: Romanticism, archive, materialism, deconstruction, Percy Bysshe Shelley

1 Genre, Archives, and Romanticism

In William Blake's "Introduction" to his *Songs of Innocence* (1789), we encounter a piper who is repeatedly urged by a child on a cloud to re-enact a song. During this re-enactment, the song is getting less and less spontaneous until the piper eventually writes it down in "a book that all may read" (line 14). As indicated by the piper's "rural pen" (line 17), with which he "stain'd the water clear" (line 18), and the vanishing of the child (who represents innocence) precisely at the point when the piper begins to write, the poem suggests that the very act of writing is inevitably bound to a loss of innocence. The metapoetic quality of Blake's poem ties in with the question of the poem as archive, that is, with the influence of aesthetics, genre, and language on the archived material and, not least, with the precarious materiality of the archive itself: the act of archiving is never "innocent" for as soon as the material is being archived it unavoidably becomes affected by the archive's power structures (including those of the chosen genre). In a wider context, the poem echoes the desire to archive and the related concerns regarding the proliferation of numerous archives during the Romantic

https://doi.org/10.1515/9783110594874-002

period, first and foremost the increasing print culture. What is alluded to in Blake's "Introduction" constitutes a major theme in Percy Bysshe Shelley's "Ozymandias" (1818). As I shall argue in the following, Shelley appropriates the sonnet genre to explore the epoch's desire to archive as well as the precarious nature of the archiving process and of contemporary archives. To this end, I will draw on the Derridean concept of archive fever, which allows me to consider the nexus between aesthetic, cultural, and material aspects of the archiving process at large.

In *Archive Fever: A Freudian Impression* (1995), Derrida conceives the archive largely in poststructuralist and psychoanalytical terms. On the one hand, he stresses the archive's textual and temporal structure: its openness for potentially unlimited supplementations and (the resulting) processes of de- and recontextualizations of the archive and its materials (1995: 14, 17–18, 22–23, 45). Not least, even the concept of the archive itself may be subjected to recontextualizations due to technological innovations, for example, which may also alter the archived material for "[a]rchivable meaning is also and in advance codetermined by the structure that archives" (1995: 18). As a result, the archive in the Derridean sense is fundamentally characterized by its paradoxical structure of simultaneous storage and effacement, of presence and absence, which threatens the very material it actually tries to preserve (1995: 13–14, 53–54). In short, it is characterized by a spectrality, to which the original French title *Le Mal d'archive* refers as *genitivus subiectivus* (the archive's sickness): "the structure of the archive is *spectral*. It is spectral *a priori*: neither present nor absent 'in the flesh,' neither visible nor invisible" (1995: 54). As *genitivus obiectivus*, on the other hand, Derrida considers the archiving subject to be suffering from a feverish desire to possess the (lost) object in its originality beyond the distorting effects of temporality – an archival fever that is at the same time kindled by an anxiety of the destructive effects of temporality:

> There would indeed be no archive desire without the radical finitude, without the possibility of a forgetfulness which does not limit itself to repression. Above all, and this is the most serious, beyond or within this simple limit called finiteness or finitude, there is no archive fever without the threat of this death drive, this aggression and destruction drive. (1995: 19; cf. 54, 57, 59)

This sense of (future) loss not only unleashes the fever to archive, but it also results in the creation of manifold archives that try to compensate for this lack. Literature plays a major role in reflecting and articulating these (partly unconscious) processes, thereby constructing its own archives. As Derrida notes, an archive would not be possible "without foundation, without substrate, without substance, without subjectile" (1995: 22). For the purposes of the present paper,

I consider the following places "of consignation, of 'inscription' or of 'recording'" (1995: 22–23) as possible archives: (imagined) spaces and objects, the lyrical I's subjectivity, the poem's genre, and ultimately (the materiality of) writing and the publication media.

A brief look at Derrida's essay "The Law of Genre" (1980) and a contextualization within his conception of the archive (fever) reveals how closely those two concepts are interrelated. Figuratively speaking, a genre functions as archive in that it frames or houses its materials. This metaphor is also inscribed in the word's etymology since *archive* derives from the Greek *arkhaion*: "initially a house, a domicile, an address, the residence of the superior magistrates, the *archons*, those who commanded" (Derrida 1995: 9). By the choice of a specific genre, thus, a new powerful archive is created, grafting its own structures on the respective materials and shaping them additionally.[1] Seen from the perspective of Derrida's 'archive fever,' this is the result of the "archontic power" of the archival act, its "functions of unification, of identification, of classification" (1995: 10). These basic operations also involve acts of consignation – that is, "*gathering together signs* [...] to coordinate a single corpus [...] in which all the elements articulate the unity of an ideal configuration" (1995: 10) – and the genre's general structuring principles, such as "resemblance, analogy, identity and difference, taxonomic classification, organization and genealogical tree, order of reason" (Derrida 1980: 81). In short, a genre performs a harmonizing function insofar as various elements are embedded in a synchrony that reflects the genre's received conventions and traditions. Finally, paratextual elements (such as titles, headings, prefaces, and annotations) can be added to this list as they may likewise fulfil a classificatory and/or evaluating function with regard to the main text and its genre (cf. Genette 1993: 11–13). Coleridge's preface to "Kubla Khan" (1816), for example, clearly locates his poem within the literary tradition of the fragment.

Up to this point, I have regarded literary genres as powerful archives that function as structural and semantic frameworks into which the respective material is inscribed. In addition to this, the very appropriation of these genres is simultaneously an archiving of their generic features: a case of intertextuality – what Genette calls architextuality (1993: 13–14) – with which a given genre and its literary tradition are preserved. At first glance, the use of conventional genres such as the sonnet in Romanticism might appear contradictory given its stress

---

[1] See Derrida 1995: 10–11; 14; 22–23 for the concept of "consignation" and the archive's shaping power in a general sense; and Derrida 1980: 56–57, 61, 74, 81 for the power structures a genre may graft on its objects.

on creative imagination and its programmatic break with petrified structures and existing (neoclassical) aesthetic norms and forms. Nevertheless, British Romanticism is not a movement that discards genres but rather a highly self-reflexive appropriation of genre traditions and their creative modification at the same time (Curran 1986; Duff 2009). This use of genres coincides with the peculiarities of the historical period, a period that was profoundly marked by (temporal) fragmentation and a general sense of loss. As Stuart Curran argues, the preceding Age of Enlightenment was characterized by "the failure of myth, the factionalism and proliferation of religious sects, the dissolution of iconographical knowledge"; put shortly, by a loss of "its past and all of its mythology" (1986: 205). As a result, British Romanticism is generally characterized by its re-imaginings of past and present in which traditional literary genres provide stable structures, repositories of cultural memory, to compensate for this lack (Curran 1986: 28, 205–206). In accordance with the ethos of Romantic aesthetics, however, literary genres were adopted in a creative and organic way. The Romantic movement involved a highly self-reflexive recovery and appropriation of existing genres and traditions (for example the ode, the sonnet, the ballad, or the romance) and their imaginative transformation at the same time – in other words, an ambivalent archiving of genre traditions and their simultaneous destruction, which overall characterizes the archive in the Derridean sense.[2]

2 "Ozymandias" and the Archive

When Shelley wrote on the subject of Ozymandias he might not have been aware that his take on the Egyptian emperor would also reflect the idea of the archive (fever) and its ambivalences. His sonnet, which was published in Leigh Hunts's *The Examiner* in 1818, very likely took its cue from Diodorus Siculus's *Bibliotheca Historica* (last century BC). Siculus relates the famous inscription on Ozymandias's statute reading "I am Osymandias, king of kings" (Griffiths 1948: 81), which inspired Shelley to reinterpret this sculptural demonstration of power as a warning statement on hubris and the transience of tyrants, empires, and power (Griffiths 1948: 80–81; Ferber 2007: 69; Stephens 2009: 155).

If we add another document to this archive of the poem's creation, further interesting interpretative layers can be revealed beyond its obvious political reading. In the seventeenth and eighteenth centuries Ozymandias was, as Walter

---

[2] See Duff 2009: VIII, 1–6, 10–11, 14–22, 19–22, 139–140, 201–211 and Curran 1986: 5, 13, 204–220 for Romanticism's relation to genre (theory).

Stephens shows, regarded rather as the "first founder of libraries than as hubristic despot" (2009: 160). This view can be traced back to the German scholar Burkhard Gotthelf Struve (1671–1738) and his influential study *Introduction to the Knowledge of Literature and the Use of Libraries* (1754), which was subsequently supplemented by other scholars and republished posthumously for decades. In this work, for Struve "as for generations of scholars before him, Ozymandias was synonymous with libraries and the attempt at preserving human memory through writing" (Stephens 2009: 158). This association primarily owed to the fact that Ozymandias was considered to have built the first library (though it probably was just a simple bookshelf) and to have placed the inscription "Healing-Place of the Soul" on it (see Stephens 2009: 158–160, 165–166).

By the choice of Ozymandias as subject, hence, Shelley's poem not only comments on a historical period that was profoundly marked by the sobering experiences of the French Revolution and the rise and fall of political powers, but also on a historical period that was concerned with historical origins and the idea of the archive. Especially in the context of Ozymandias as mythical founder of libraries, it is remarkable that the museum had its formative phase between the late eighteenth and early nineteenth centuries. The British Museum, for example, was founded in 1753, the Louvre in 1793, and the National Portrait Gallery in 1824 (Bennett 2002: 19; Underwood 2012: 238–239). The museum and its exhibited artifacts moreover belong to a material and visual culture characteristic of the period and its technological developments – a culture that prized "painting, print culture, book illustrations, visual media and technology, galleries, exhibitions, [...] picturesque tourism, and the Grand Tour with its emphasis on viewing and collecting objects abroad" (Thomas 2012: 88; cf. 87–97, 101–102). This transition into a visual culture was reflected, for example, in numerous ekphrastic poems such as "Ozymandias" or John Keats's "Ode on a Grecian Urn" (1820), depictions of picturesque landscapes such as John Clare's, or in Lord Byron's poetic travelogue *Childe Harold's Pilgrimage* (1812–1818) with its aestheticized portrayal of the poet's grand tour and of various historic sites and cultural artifacts.

From the mid-eighteenth century on, the museum's accumulation of the past was furthermore matched by a large number of increasingly professionalized historiographic studies and archaeological expeditions, which were, on the whole, the outcome of Europe's growing fascination with the past (Fricke 2009: 32–37; Underwood 2012: 229). The statue of Ozymandias that Diodorus may have referred to (though it did not have said inscription on it), for instance, was brought to the British Museum shortly after the poem's publication (see Stephens 2009: 164). Finally, these developments have to be seen within the wider context of the rapidly growing print culture of the time. There was substantial growth in printing and publishing from the late eighteenth century on (Belanger 1982: 6–7; Feather 2006: 98–99), which functioned as a material archive of these scientific advances and discoveries. Especially the increasing number of magazines and the countless periodicals further promoted the sciences and their professionalization by providing a medium for disciplinary discourse and making the results accessible to a broader audience (Flieger Samuelian and Schoenfield 2012: 72).

By exploring the precarious nature of the archiving process with the help of the sonnet tradition, Shelley's poem not only critically revises its own structures – a self-reflexivity that has always been typical for the sonnet genre (Wagner 1996: 72–73) – but also echoes contemporary archival concerns arising from this "new age of paper" (Stauffer 2006: para 8). As Andrew Stauffer argues, "[f]or the Romantics, the burgeoning culture of print led to two related archival troubles: the fragility of the material and the vast quantities of it" (2006: para. 14). While the sheer quantity of circulating paper can be seen as an excessive supplementation of the archive, which threatens archival practices rather than supporting them (Stauffer 2006: para. 3), the fears regarding the archive's materiality actually mirror the socio-economic and technological conditions of the time. In fact, there was a considerable discrepancy between the increasing quantity of paper due to technological evolution on the one hand, and the decreasing quality of printing and written paper over the course of the late eighteenth until the end of the nineteenth century on the other hand (Feather 2006: 87). "Ozymandias" thus mirrors Shelley's own archival desire – that is, "achieving immortality through print publication" (Marotti and Freiman 2011: 76) – in the light of an overall archival anxiety given the precarious materiality of paper and writing.

3 "Ozymandias" and Archive Fever

Given that Ozymandias was regarded as mythical founder of libraries, the poem's title – its inscription – already hints at an underlying metadiscourse on the contemporary preoccupation with origins, originals, and (their) various archives. This metadiscourse extends to genre since the history of the sonnet is also the history of its medium (Marotti and Freiman 2011: 66–75). The "Sonnet craze" (Duff 2009: 14) of the late eighteenth and nineteenth centuries has to be considered in the light of the period's rapidly emerging print culture and the related rise of a reading public – a materiality that affects Shelley's appropriation of the sonnet form and that is deeply indebted to the notion of archive fever.

From an intratextual point of view, "Ozymandias" originates in an archival fever manifesting itself in a desire to possess the object in its originality and to defy the destructive effects of temporality. This becomes evident in the poem's various narrative levels: firstly, within the embedded narrative of the traveller who relates of Ozymandias's destroyed statue. The latter constitutes a piece of art that was supposed to timelessly preserve (that is, spatially archive) the Egyptian pharaoh's power, but also to capture the essence of his character. That is, the sculptor strived for archiving the object in its originality beyond its mere physical appearance insofar as he "well those [Ozymandias's] passions read" (lines 5–6). Also noteworthy in this quote is Shelley's use of the verb "to read," which further unveils the discursive presence of the dominant print culture and its materiality. Secondly, the said archival fever can be seen in the framing narrative in which the traveller's tale is embedded, that is, its poetical archive. For this purpose, Shelley tellingly chooses the genre of the sonnet – a literary form that has been traditionally used to timelessly preserve its materials. Most notably within the context of Elizabethan love poetry and heavily influenced by Neo-Platonic ontology, the sonnet was thought to transcend the object's outer, physical appearance and to eternalize its essence. It therefore seems to provide the perfect frame for Shelley's ekphrastic depiction of the statue, in the course of which he tries "to make his words outlast their ostensible subject, to displace graphic representation with verbal representation" (Heffernan 1991: 311). Hence, the difference between framing and embedded narrative already alludes to an opposition between writing and visual art – an opposition that also extends to the difference between the framing/archiving genre and its object.

Notwithstanding this opposition, there are striking metapoetical similarities between the sculptor and the poet. Just as the sculptor "stamped on these lifeless things" (line 7) the aforementioned "passions" (line 6), the poet stamps the traveller's tale into the sonnet form (see also Fricke 2009: 179). With the verb "to stamp" Shelley again uses the language of materiality, which turns out to be revealing for his metadiscourse on print culture, the archive, and their relation to the sonnet genre. According to Derrida the notion of "impression" refers to the pivotal act of the archiving process, that is, to "the moment *proper* to the archive, […] the instant of archivization" (1995: 22), as it describes the very moment of the substrate's inscription. In other words, the sculpture is both a spatial archive of Ozymandias's power and a metaphor for the overall archiving process of the poem in which its genre and the image of the sculpture constitute tenor and vehicle respectively. And as the semantics of the sonnet form pass on the idea of eternalness (that is, as its generic tradition is architextually grafted on the object), Ozymandias's passions "yet survive" (line 7) within their spatial and poetic archive, both of them suggesting the archived material's presence.

These archives are, nevertheless, fragile constructions subjected to destructive forces. Ozymandias's presence is accompanied by a strong sense of loss. Not only is the materiality of the spatial archive (the sculpture) highly affected by the destructive forces of temporality, but its physical decay also leads to a re-contextualization of the archived material. What remains are only "[t]wo vast and trunkless legs of stone" and a "shattered visage" of the "colossal wreck" (lines 2, 4, 13). This decay stands in an ironic contrast to the hubristic inscription (the "king of kings" [line 10] and his works), the surrounding empty spaces of the desert ("The lone and level sands stretch far away" [line 14]) and, not least, to the larger scale of history proving the transience of Ozymandias's power.

The same is true for the statue's superordinated textual archive, the poem and its genre. At first sight one might be tempted to say that the textual wins over the architectural in that the statute is timelessly preserved in the present sonnet, the latter hence constituting "a poetic monument" to the monument (Janowitz 1984: 487; cf. 478–479, 487–489; Ferber 2007: 73). As a closer look reveals, however, the archived object is highly mediated and absent. First, there is the sculptor who "those passions read" (lines 5–6) and stamped them into the statue together with Ozymandias's words; second, the traveller, who discovered the statute, read the inscription, and narrates his tale to the speaker; and finally we have the poet, who grafts the sonnet form on this material (Heffernan 1991: 310–311; Bode 1994: 147; Wagner 1996: 71). As a result, the supposed presence of the archived object turns out to be a multiply deferred and fragmented one within this palimpsestic structure bearing traces of its different imprints or archival acts. With Derrida we can say that the iteration of the (linguistic) sign, its various de- and recontextualizations, inevitably leads to a break with its former communicative and semantic contexts, resulting in the aforementioned textual and contextual ironies in view of the monument's original message (cf. Derrida 2001: 26–29, 32, 34–35, 40, 184). What was originally intended as an epitome of Ozymandias power and achievement has been ironically inverted over the course of its various (textual) iterations and archivings (Janowitz 1984: 485–486; Heffernan 1991: 310–311; Bode 1994: 148).

Language turns out to be a highly precarious archiving medium since the sign's spatialization and temporalization via repetition constitute the source of its own effacement – a process that Derrida delineates with his concept of *différance* (cf. Derrida 1997: 6–18; Derrida 2005b; Derrida 2005a). With his emphasis on the temporal aspect Shelley revises the sonnet's characteristic mnemonic structure, that is, its being a "moment's monument" that aims at closure (Rossetti 1880: l. 1; cf. Wagner 1996: 71–74) – a sense of closure that we find, for example, in the Wordsworthian sonnet with its "longing to dwell, transcendentally or immanently"

(O'Neill 2011: 196). Instead the poem's archiving process, its medium, and its genre are marked by a fundamental incompleteness and openness for future recontextualizations. These characteristics do not only constitute the self-destructive aspect of the archive but also kindle the fever to archive. This archival fever manifests itself in the various attempts at permanently fixing the object, visually and in written (poetic) form – attempts that can be seen as supplements of the deficient archival act.

Beyond the outlined narrative instances we finally have Ozymandias himself, who speaks indirectly via the pedestal's inscription. But even his alleged quote is a problematic written archive since Shelley's material sources are themselves highly fragmented and deferred: Diodorus refers to Egyptian archives that, "if they ever existed, vanished long ago" (Stephens 2009: 163). And, as Stephens further shows, it is also questionable whether Shelley actually read Diodorus's book or just a fragment of it within the work of another author. Diodorus's *Bibliotheca Historica* was "for many centuries a *lost* library, containing shreds of even older losses" (Stephens 2009: 163), and up to this day many of its parts are still missing. Put differently, it is an archive that has been affected by its own precarious materiality. Moreover, the statue that was brought to the British Museum did not have the inscription (Stephens 2009: 163–164). Shelley hence might have been indeed inspired by various (incomplete) sources but primarily enriched them with his own imagination. The poem's critical history, however, is characterized by a downright fever to excavate and archive its origins, echoing the theme of the poem. As Christoph Bode notes, "[t]he critical history of 'Ozymandias' is almost exclusively the history of the quest for its sources, its origins, textual or extratextual" (1994: 143; see also Janowitz 1984: 478).

Turning back to the intratextual level of the poem, it is striking that even the sonnet structure decays similarly to the statue. On the one hand, the poem cites some of the sonnet's characteristic formal elements, such as its fourteen lines, the volta (though it is placed here after the eleventh line), or the Shakespearean sonnet's rhyme scheme (abab) at the beginning. On the other hand, the first quatrain is followed by an additional 'a' rhyme that eventually turns into terza rima (cdc ede fef). Via the dizziness of the terza rima and the various slant rhymes (for example *stone/frown, appear/despair/bare*) the poem's form figures the dissolution of its content. The ekphrastic depiction of the decaying statue likewise mirrors the decay of its poetical archive, its genre, further undermining the dominance of the textual over the visual. And just as Ozymandias's spatial archive inhabits a liminal position between memory and its destruction, the sonnet structure is present and absent at the same time, its structural traces loosely held together via alliterations, consonances, and assonances. The frequent use of fricatives (especially in lines 2, 4, and 7) evokes via their airflow onomatopoetically the trickling of the sands of time, that is, the temporality which affects both sculpture and text: "time will erode the traces not only of tyranny but also of art" (O'Neill 2011: 198). Seen from this perspective, the poem's paratext grafts another subversive context on the archived material similar to Ozymandias's quote on the statute's pedestal: read as founder of libraries, "synonymous [...] with the attempt to preserve human memory through writing" (Stephens 2009: 158), "Ozymandias" as the poem's title ironically comments on (and mocks) the poet's futile, maybe even hubristic, attempt at defying the destructive effects of temporality via poetic imagination and the sonnet genre.

4 Conclusion: "Ozymandias" and the Sonnet's Legacy

Shelley's "Ozymandias" inhabits a precarious position between the conflicting poles of (genre) memory, loss, and archival desire. It originates in an archival fever to timelessly possess the origin(al) and is followed by an ambivalent concurrency of the object's (re-)construction and its subsequent deconstruction. The destructive movements manifest themselves most notably in various forms of repetition (such as the highly mediated object within its various spatial and textual archives), the resulting de- and recontextualizations and, not least, the language system's differential structure emerging from the linguistic sign's spatialization and temporalisation in the course of its iteration. The same applies to Shelley's appropriation of the sonnet genre: As Derrida argues in "The Law of Genre," it is the act of iteration, that is, citing and thus archiving a specific genre, which brings about a genre's "impurity, corruption, contamination, decomposition, perversion, deformation, even cancerization, generous proliferation, or degenerescence" (Derrida 1980: 57). As a result, both the poem as archive and its archived object(s), including the generic tradition of the sonnet, are characterized by a paradoxical presence/absence, that is, by their spectrality. And it is precisely at this neuralgic point, the threshold between (genre) memory and its loss, between the archive and its destruction, between the fever to archive and the archive's fever, where the archive is constituted as such: "the archive [...] will never be memory or anamnesis as spontaneous, alive and internal experience. On the contrary: the archive takes place at the place of originary and structural breakdown of the said memory" (Derrida 1995: 14).

Finally, Shelley published "Ozymandias" not only within the context of a rapidly growing print culture and the related expansion of the reading public, but also within the epoch's revivification – headed by Charlotte Smith's

Elegiac Sonnets (1784) – of the sonnet form, which had been heavily marginalized since John Milton's death (Curran 1986: 29–30; Duff 2009: 15; Marotti and Freiman 2011: 74–76). In the light of the poem's theme, thus, Shelley's use of the sonnet genre might have been equally indebted to a further form of archival fever. As David Duff observes with regard to Romantic uses of genre, "[t]o use a literary genre was to render perceptible the sediment layers, to build up across time, which constitute that genre; to renew [...] the 'archaic elements' that lay buried within" (2009: 145). The numerous publications of sonnet anthologies – such as Leigh Hunt's *The Book of the Sonnet* (1867), William Sharp's *Sonnets of the Nineteenth Century* (1886), and Sir Arthus Quiller-Couch's *English Sonnets* (1897) – over the course of the nineteenth century testify that this archival fever regarding genres also had a lasting impact beyond the Romantic period (Duff 2009: 14–15; Marotti and Freiman 2011: 77–78). The construction of such archives played an important role in the formation of British collective identity[3] insofar as "the frequent appearance of English sonnet collections [...] throughout the British Empire with the sonnet as the epitome of English poetic form reflects a new confidence in the dominance of English national identity" (Marotti and Freiman 2011: 77–78). Against this backdrop, Shelley's "Ozymandias" retrospectively grafts a further ironic context on the sonnet form: read as epitome of British imperial self-confidence – a hubris metapoetically reflected in Ozymandias's "Look on my works ye Mighty and Despair" – the decaying sonnet form in Shelley's poem likewise mirrors Britain's loss of imperial power and dominance over the course of the following centuries.

Works Cited

Belanger, Terry. 1982. "Publishers and Writers in Eighteenth-Century England". In: Isabel Rivers (ed.). *Books and their Readers in Eighteenth-Century England*. Leicester: Leicester Univeristy Press. 5–25.
Bennett, Tony. 2002. *The Birth of the Museum: History, Theory, Politics*. London: Routledge.
Blake, William. 1988. "Introduction (*Songs of Innocence*)". In: David V. Erdman and Harald Bloom (eds.). *The Complete Poetry and Prose of William Blake*. New York: Anchor. 7.
Bode, Christoph. 1994. "'Look on my Works, ye Mighty, and despair!': Notes on the Non-teachability of Poetry". In: Manfred Beyer et al. (eds.). *Teachable Poems: From Sting to Shelley*. Heidelberg: Winter. 139–152.

---

[3] For the archive's relation to the constructions of (collective) identities see Lubar 1999: 14–16; Cook 2007, 8–12; Craven 2008: 169–181.

Cook, Terry. 2007. "Remembering the Future". In: Francis X. Blouin Jr. and William G. Rosenberg (eds.). *Archives, Documentation, and Institutions of Social Memory: Essays from the Sawyer Seminar*. Ann Arbor: University of Michigan Press. 169–181.
Craven, Louise. 2008. "From the Archivist's Cardigan to the Very Dead Sheep: What are Archives? What are Archivists? What do they Do?". In: Louise Craven (ed.). *What Are Archives? Cultural and Theoretical Perspectives: A Reader*. Burlington: Ashgate. 7–30.
Curran, Stuart. 1986. *Poetic Form and British Romanticism*. New York: Oxford University Press.
Derrida, Jacques. 1980. "The Law of Genre". *Critical Inquiry* 7.1: 55–81.
Derrida, Jacques. 1995. "Archive Fever: A Freudian Impression". *Diacritics* 25.2: 9–63.
Derrida, Jacques. 1997. *Of Grammatology*. Baltimore: Johns Hopkins University Press.
Derrida, Jacques. 2001. *Limited Inc*. Wien: Passagen.
Derrida, Jacques. 2005a. "Semiology and Grammatology". In: Julie Rivkin and Michael Ryan (eds.). *Literary Theory: An Anthology*. Malden: Blackwell. 332–339.
Derrida, Jacques. 2005b. "Différance". In: Julie Rivkin and Michael Ryan (eds.), *Literary Theory: An Anthology*. Malden: Blackwell. 278–299.
Duff, David. 2009. *Romanticism and the Uses of Genre*. New York: Oxford University Press.
Feather, John. 2006. *A History of British Publishing*. London: Routledge.
Ferber, Michael. 2007. "Ozymandias". In: Michael Hanke (ed.). *Fourteen English Sonnets*. Trier: WVT. 67–75.
Flieger Samuelian, Kristin and Mark Schoenfield. 2012. "Periodicals". In: Joel Faflak and Julia M. Wright (eds.). *A Handbook of Romanticism Studies*. Chichester: Blackwell. 69–86.
Fricke, Stefanie. 2009. *Memento Mori: Ruinen alter Hochkulturen und die Furcht vor dem eigenen Untergang in der englischen Literatur des 19. Jahrhunderts*. Trier: WVT.
Genette, Gérard. 1993. *Palimpseste: Die Literatur auf zweiter Stufe*. Frankfurt a. M.: Suhrkamp.
Griffiths, J. Gwyn. 1948. "'Ozymandias' and Diodorus Siculus". *Modern Language Review* 143.1: 80–84.
Heffernan, James A. W. 1991. "Ekphrasis and Representation". *New Literary History* 22.2: 297–316.
Janowitz, Anne. 1984. "Shelley's Monument to Ozymandias". *Philological Quarterly* 63: 477–491.
Lubar, Steven. 1999. "Information Culture and the Archival Record". *The American Archivist* 62.1: 10–22.
Marotti, Arthur F., and Marcelle Freimann. 2011. "The English Sonnet in Manuscript, Print and Mass Media". In: A.D. Cousins and Peter Howarth (eds.). *The Cambridge Companion to the Sonnet*. Cambridge: Cambridge University Press. 66–83.
O'Neill, Michael. 2011. "The Romantic Sonnet". In: A.D. Cousins and Peter Howarth (eds.). *The Cambridge Companion to the Sonnet*. Cambridge: Cambridge University Press. 185–203.
Rossetti, Dante Gabriel. 1880. "The Sonnet". *The Rossetti Archive*. http://www.rossettiarchive.org/docs/s258.texasproof.rap.html [accessed 29 May 2017].
Shelley, Percy Bysshe. 2012. "Ozymandias". In: Stephen Greenblatt (ed.). *The Norton Anthology of English Literature*. Vol. D. New York: Norton. 776.
Stauffer, Andrew. 2006. "Romanticism's Scattered Leaves". *Romanticism on the Net* 41–42. https://www.erudit.org/revue/ron/2006/v/n41-42/013155ar.html [accessed 23 March 2017].
Stephens, Walter. 2009. "Ozymandias: Or, Writing, Lost Libraries, and Wonder". *MLN* 124.5: 155–168.

Thomas, Sophie. 2012. "Visual Culture". In: Joel Faflak and Julia M. Wright (eds.). *A Handbook of Romanticism Studies*. Chichester: Blackwell. 87–103.
Underwood, Ted. 2012. "Historiography". In: Joel Faflak and Julia M. Wright (eds.). *A Handbook of Romanticism Studies*. Chichester: Blackwell. 227–244.
Wagner, Jennifer Ann. 1996. *A Moment's Monument: Revisionary Poetic and the Nineteenth-Century English Sonnet*. Madison: Fairleigh Dickinson University Press.

Stefanie John
Contesting and Continuing the Romantic Lyric: Eavan Boland and Kathleen Jamie

Abstract: The essay investigates the challenges and opportunities Romantic concepts of the lyric present to late twentieth-century poetry with a political cause. As women poets from Ireland and Scotland, Eavan Boland and Kathleen Jamie have addressed postcolonial and feminist matters. As a consequence, their poetry strives to overcome the subjective aesthetic of transcendence coined by English Romantic poets in order to create a contemporary, inclusive take on the lyric genre that gives expression to the plurality of modern identities and lives. Yet while Boland's and Jamie's poetry tussles with the ideological implications of the lyric, it also engages productively with Romantic precursors on the level of individual poems. The attempt to overcome what Boland calls a "Romantic Heresy" in the lyric tradition actually stands in continuation with processes of self-assertion and self-questioning devised by canonical Romantic poets from Wordsworth to Keats – a dialogue that is described as 'post-Romantic'. Boland's and Jamie's work exemplifies that the contemporary lyric remains a self-reflexive genre, even at those moments when it strongly evokes notions of authenticity and reality.

Keywords: Eavan Boland, Kathleen Jamie, Romantic lyric, post-Romantic, subjectivity

1 Introduction: Lyric as a Genre and the Question of Romantic Legacies

This essay investigates the challenges and opportunities Romantic concepts of the lyric present to late-twentieth-century poetry with a political cause. For the Irish poet Eavan Boland and the Scottish poet Kathleen Jamie, the Wordsworthian view of poetry as a "spontaneous overflow of powerful feelings" that "takes its origin from emotion recollected in tranquillity" (Wordsworth 2014: 92) bequeaths a paradoxical legacy. As women poets from Ireland and Scotland, Boland and Jamie have addressed questions of national identity and feminist matters, particularly in their work of the 1980s and 90s. As a consequence, their poetry strives to overcome the subjective aesthetic of transcendence associated with English

Romanticism. Eavan Boland describes the unique challenge posed by this inheritance for modern women poets in her essay "The Woman Poet: Her Dilemma," which was originally published in the magazine *Stand* in 1986 (see Maguire 1999: 58) and later reprinted in Boland's collection of critical prose *Object Lessons: The Life of the Woman and the Poet in Our Time* (1995). There she marks out a specific tension between a "new experience and an established aesthetic", between writing about the ordinary lives of Irish women and the influence of what she refers to as the "Romantic Heresy":

> Imagine, then, that a woman is going into the garden. She is youngish, her apron is on, and there is flour on her hands. It is early afternoon. She is going there to lift a child who for the third time is about to put laburnum pods into its mouth. [...] Now it begins. The first of these powerful, distracting voices comes to her. For argument's sake, I will call it the Romantic Heresy. It comes to her as a whisper, an insinuation. What she wants to do is write about the laburnum, the heat of the child, common human love – the mesh of these things. But where, says the voice in her ear, is the interest in all this? How are you going to write a poem out of these plain Janes, these snips and threads of an ordinary day? Now, the voice continues, listen to me, and I will show you how to make all this poetic. A shade here, a nuance there, a degree of distance, a lilt of complaint, and all will be well. (1995: 239–241)

For Boland, women's experiences in late-twentieth-century Ireland were incompatible with what tradition deemed appropriate subject material for poetry – a discrepancy she identifies as a legacy of English Romanticism. The shift of poetic content towards the poet's own subjectivity in that period led to

> a damaging division [...] between the perception of what is poetic on the one hand and, on the other, what is merely human. Out of this emerges the aesthetic which suggests that in order to convert the second into the first, you must romanticize it. (1995: 242)

Boland's programmatic essays call on women poets to overcome this romanticizing practice. The idea is to re-write the subjective lyric poem so that it takes account of the marginalized perspectives of women in Irish culture – moving them "out of myth into history," as she envisions it in her poem "Outside History" (2008: 188). Just as Boland strives to create an Irish poetic model that gives expression to women's experiences, Kathleen Jamie's work reconsiders mythified representations of Scotland. The poems in Jamie's collection *Jizzen* (1999) endorse feminist concerns and re-imagine Scottish landscapes and culture from a contemporary angle.

However, realizing such political critique proves to be a tricky affair – not least because of the impossibility of finding a language that unproblematically reproduces "history." Moreover, Boland's own sense that what she strives to overcome "is not romanticism proper, although it is related to it" (1995: 241) indicates the slippery nature of the legacy these poets seek to grapple with.[1] In the wake of New Historicist and political critiques of Romantic poetry, initiated by Jerome McGann's *The Romantic Ideology: A Critical Investigation* (1983), the term "Romantic" has often come to stand for an escapist conception of poetry, the idea that aesthetic forms can serve to displace 'actual' historical conditions. While Boland's and Jamie's poetry responds to such ideological implications, it also engages directly with Romantic precursors on the concrete level of individual poems – especially in regard to constructions of lyric subjectivity. Thus, the attempt to overcome a perceived "Romantic Heresy" in the lyric often actually stands in continuation with modes of self-assertion and self-questioning devised by canonical Romantic poets from Wordsworth to Keats.

Michael O'Neill describes lyrics as "shorter poems which devote heightened if often unostentatious poetic music to expressing the feelings of a real or imagined speaker" (2008: 281). This kind of poem still dominates British and Irish poetry publications. Such lasting popularity may well be due to the genre's versatility. Except for its relative brevity, there is no definite rhyme scheme, metre, or stanzaic structure that would classify a poem as lyric. Yet as Jonathan Culler reminds us, "genre is an abstract model, an account of a set of norms or structural possibilities" (2015: 48). Thus, the lyric is to a large extent defined by the individual realizations and transformations of such norms and possibilities across historical periods. The genre is given coherence less by any formal property than by the way lyric poems attribute a central role to the speaking and feeling subject – an element which is a crucial legacy of Romantic poetry and which is often emphasized in criticism of contemporary lyric poems. In an article on "Contemporary British Women Poets and the Lyric Subject," for example, Linda Kinnahan writes:

> With an emphasis upon the self's capacity for knowledge of itself and the world, through operations of the imagination, the Romantic aura of lyric authenticity assumes a poetic process in which individual, autonomous experience is transformed into the universal and transcendent voice of the poet. (2009: 177)

This tendency to elevate the personal out of its particularity lies at the heart of Boland's distinction between "the perception of what is poetic" and "what is merely human." Both Boland's and Kinnahan's comments exemplify the shifting values critics and poets have attached to the lyric and to its Romantic origins in particular. Jerome McGann's much-debated concept of "Romantic ideology"

---

[1] In Romantic studies the term is hardly used without mentioning its problematic ambiguity. For an exemplary overview of the critical history of the label "Romantic" that centres on the contrary positions of New Historicist Romantic studies and New Criticism, see Ferguson 1991.

epitomizes such meanings. According to McGann, major Romantic poems such as Wordsworth's "Lines written a few miles above Tintern Abbey" (1798) are "marked by extreme forms of displacement and poetic conceptualization whereby the actual human issues with which the poetry is concerned are resituated in a variety of idealized localities" (1983: 2).

Yet for Wordsworth such acts of imaginative "displacement" are counterbalanced by an active interest in "incidents and situations from common life" portrayed "in a selection of language really used by men" (2014: 78) – a dynamic that comes forth, for example, in one of the Lucy poems titled "Song" (1800): "She *liv'd* unknown, and few could know / When Lucy ceas'd to be; / But she is in her Grave, and Oh! / The difference to me" (2014: 114–115; lines 9–12; emphasis in original). The depiction of Lucy presents an instance of how women are rendered into idealized, yet passive poetic objects in lyrics by male (Romantic) authors – a practice that Boland's feminist poetics take issue with. But the poem also takes its impetus from the tension between abstraction and concreteness, captured by the juxtaposition of "*liv'd*" and "ceas'd to be," "unknown" and "known." The aesthetic design intensifies rather than transcends the particularity of subjectively felt human grief. Instead of dissolving the particular in universality, Wordsworth concludes by postulating subjectivity in terms of difference: "the difference to *me*," which is rhymed with "be" in the ninth line. Romantic lyrics can challenge notions of escapism, just as seemingly anti-Romantic contemporary poems, as I will show, may pursue more harmonizing perspectives than initially assumed.

Evidently, the Romantics' innovation of the lyric genre consisted not only in the elevation of subjective experience but also in scrutinizing the stability of notions of the self and the imagination.[2] In "Ode to a Nightingale" (1820) Keats construes an ambiguous lyric subject that relies on poetry to express individual desires, the fulfillment of which, however, consists in the erasure of selfhood, in merging with the external object to "dissolve, and quite forget" (line 21) its troubles via "the viewless wings of Poesy" (33). Such ambivalent positioning of the lyric subject, holding it in a state of "uncertainties, Mysteries, doubts" (Keats 2009: 109), can offer fruitful aesthetic points of departure for contemporary feminist and postcolonial poetry.

---

[2] For studies on subjectivity and self-consciousness in English Romantic poetry see e.g. Hartman 1970; O'Neill 1997; and more recently Bode 2008; Sandy and Wootton 2008; on 'alternative' models of Romantic selfhood see Curran 1988; Henderson 1996.

2 Eavan Boland: Contesting the "Romantic Heresy" in Irish Women's Poetry

Irish women poets throughout the twentieth century struggled not only with a male-dominated canon but also with a national poetic tradition that relied on patriarchal gender constructions and perpetuated, for example, the image of Ireland as the victimized "poor old woman" (Broom 2006: 111–112). Eavan Boland, who published her most recent poetry volume *A Woman without a Country* in 2014, has done much to challenge this tradition since the start of her career in the late 1960s. Boland's poetry repeatedly undermines marginalizing strategies as it strives to construct lyric subjectivities outside the "Romantic Heresy." Without downplaying the political significance of Boland's achievement, the tensions between aesthetic design and ideological critique in her work can be scrutinized to reveal its engagement with Romantic lyric practice.

"After a Childhood Away from Ireland" from the collection *Night Feed* (1982) illustrates how the strength of Boland's lyric vision often inheres in a seemingly simple, pared-down language that relies on imagery more than on musicality. In the poem Boland explores a divided sense of self, addressing the experience of exile in both national and gendered terms. Nine quatrains of short lines depict the speaker's homecoming voyage as a child through the traditional Wordsworthian mode of recollection in tranquillity. The opening lines introduce the events in a voice that comes across as personal and intimate: "One summer / we slipped in at dawn" (Boland 2008: 100). "One summer" manages to suggest that the events are selected from an individual life while also achieving a generalising force (in the vein of "Once upon a time"). Likewise, Boland's use of "we" rather than "I" as a personal pronoun does not diminish the effect of personal recollection but points toward concepts of community that are central to the poem. The "I" only takes over in the fourth stanza. Influenced by stories about returning emigrants, the speaker's teenage self has envisioned coming back to her native country as an emotionally overpowering event:

> Cobh.
> Coming home.
> I had heard of this:
> the ground the emigrants
>
> resistless, weeping,
> laid their cheeks to,
> put their lips to kiss.
>   (100)

Equating, by way of alliteration, a place with the idea of homecoming, the lines promote the sense of participating in a familiar and shared experience. But what the speaker actually experiences is a sense of alienation and exclusion from the "imagined community" (Anderson 1991) of the Irish nation – a rupture between private and public concepts of selfhood: "What I had lost / was not land / but the habit of land" (Boland 2008: 100). Now the island is a mere physical object, devoid of the higher meaning usually attributed to it through nationalist constructs of belonging.

Boland's descriptions of the coastal scene anticipate this loss of significance, as the speaker is welcomed by the "sloppy quiet" (100) at the port. Playing on the meanings of "sloppy," which indicates both rainy weather and foolish sentimentality, the line undermines clichéd ideas of Irish villages. Cobh – nowadays known as a quaint harbour town popular with tourists – appears as an uncanny presence, "an eerie / drawing near" (100). There is in the passage, too, a sense of frustrated expectation in regard to a specific lyric tradition: the poem partly activates and partly resists the "out-in-out process" developed by the "greater Romantic lyric," where an act of "memory, thought, anticipation, and feeling" occurs "closely intervolved with the outer scene" and leads to "an insight" or "resolves an emotional problem" (Abrams 2006: 197–198). To Boland's speaker, the arrival at the harbour, its "noiseless coming head-on / of red roofs, walls" (2008: 100), evokes a realization, but it is the realization that the "I" cannot form a connection with the land and its culture. This experience of rupture is only overcome – and then only partially – in the final two stanzas.

Crucial to the poem's proceeding is the shift from past to present tense and from outside world to interiority when it finally describes the speaker's present location in the nursery with her baby. Syntactical repetitions lay emphasis on the perceiving subject in the final two stanzas: "I climb / to your nursery. / I stand listening" (100) and "I bend to kiss you" (101). Only in the presence of the child in the domestic, feminine space of the nursery and only in retrospect can the grown-up speaker finally regain a sense of belonging, achieve a new sense of self, and thus experience the awareness that "Love is also memory" (100). Spatial imagery here serves to defend the relevance of human everyday lives against grander poetic visions: the intimacy of the nursery scene, where the speaker bends down to kiss her baby and embraces the atmosphere "of the summer's day ending" (101), contrasts with the unwelcoming, "eerie" (100) outdoor landscape described in the past tense in the earlier stanzas.

If an emphasis on women's ordinary domestic lives, symbolizing "common human love" (Boland 1995: 241), contests the gendered implications of the "Romantic Heresy" on an ideological level, "After a Childhood Away from Ireland" also necessarily takes up the twofold model of lyric subjectivity familiar from the poetry of English Romanticism. In the tranquillity of the nursery the speaker imaginatively recollects the split between her individual experience and public constructions of national belonging. Here Boland inevitably creates a new "myth" of harmonization, drawing on the scenario of imaginative retrospection laid out in Wordsworth's Preface to *Lyrical Ballads*. Thus, as the "brick pink" (Boland 2008: 100) color of the baby's cheeks points back to the "red roofs, walls" (100) depicted in the opening lines, the poem finally reconciles the categories of motherhood, exile, and Irishness, hinting at the creation of an alternative conception of self. This kind of selfhood incorporates ambiguities, such as "the dissonances // of the summer's day ending" (100–101), rather than striving to eliminate them. Free verse provides the formal opportunities to achieve this lyric vision: while the enjambment between the final two stanzas visually recreates rupture and "dissonances," this effect is offset by the penultimate stanza's repeated alternating of "I" and "to" at the onset of lines and by the harmonizing effect of internal rhymes in "ending" and "I bend," "brick" and "pink." Perpetuating a wish for self-assertion while simultaneously embracing the provisional quality of concepts of the self, their "dissonances," Boland here shapes a contemporary take on Keats's sense of the poetic productivity offered by negative states and uncertainties.

In "Mise Eire," from *The Journey* (1987), Boland directly attacks patriarchal myths of the nation. In line with its title, Irish for "I am Ireland," the speaker assumes the point of view of a personified Ireland, tackling established representations of its people: "I won't go back to it – // my nation displaced / into old dactyls" (2008: 128). Boland alludes to the Irish-language poem of the same title by the Easter Rising leader Patrick Pearse, who imagined Ireland as the lonely old mother of the mythic hero Cuchulainn: "I am Ireland / I am older than the Old Woman of Beare" (1998). But whereas Pearse draws on Celtic myth primarily to define a unique Irish national identity against England (Villar-Argáiz 2008: 122), Boland strives to turn Pearse's Ireland into a more human figure rooted in history and actual suffering. Both poems, however, foreground the originality and individuality of their vision.

In "Mise Eire," this emphasis on originality shows in the poetic form. Against Pearse's dactyls in "songs / that bandage up the history" (Boland 2008: 128), Boland sets her modernized free verse as the voice of womankind: "I am the woman – / a sloven's mix / of silk at the wrists, / a sort of dove-strut / in the precincts of the garrison" (128). To adapt Wordsworth's phrase, the poem speaks in a modern 'real language of women.' Its lively, clipped free verse breaks up the rhythms of traditional Irish poetry. The speaker writes Ireland's song anew, incorporating and speaking for a variety of female figures such as the garrison prostitute and the emigrant mother "on board the *Mary Belle*, / in the huddling cold" (128). If the speaker thus "chooses to inhabit these other voices in order to find her own," as Jody Allen Randolph puts it (2014: 83), the resulting sense of feminist unity stands in tension with the poem's emphasis on difference and individuality.

On the one hand, then, "Mise Eire" sets out to depart from the Irish tradition of "old dactyls" associated with a narrative of national history that ignores the voices of women or turns them into passive emblems, and instead depicts Ireland as a female poet who creates an aesthetic on her own terms, beyond the "Romantic Heresy." The statement-based syntax and accusatory tone marks a departure from the meditative, immersive style of "After a Childhood Away from Ireland." Boland here deploys the lyric genre to more polemically self-reflexive ends. At the same time, the way in which "Mise Eire" attaches universal relevance to one voice that speaks for many ("I am the woman") and its reliance on stable notions of poetic originality ("No, I won't go back") perpetuate Romantic notions of lyric innovation (128). It also reaches an awareness that the claim to represent an alternative historical narrative – a feminist one, in this case – can never be entirely saved from universalizing tendencies, especially not in the lyric genre, which tends to align persona and poet.

Continuity with Romantic lyric practice might not be surprising in a poem that draws on the first-person point of view to make a political claim, yet the significance of Boland's approach lies in its combination of idealistic assertiveness with meta-poetic reflexivity – what could be called the poem's post-Romantic knowledge. In its final stanzas the poem performs a crucial twist, culminating in a concluding statement that almost stands on its own. The Irish emigrant on the ship

>   neither
> knows nor cares that
>
> a new language
> is a kind of scar
> and heals after a while
> into a passable imitation
> of what went before.
>   (129)

The lineation visually sets off the woman from what she does not know or care about, just as meta-poetic reflection is detached from the more descriptive lines portraying the scene on the ship. Critics have explained the image of a scar left by the "new language" in terms of the emigrant's loss of the native Irish language (Schrage-Früh 2004: 58) and the notion that language can never fully heal the wounds of history (Burns 2001: 221), but the passage also intimates Boland's engagement with the poetic past, forever struggling with "imitation" and the textual "scars" of the male canon that gave rise to the "Romantic Heresy." This engagement is also implied in the way Boland constructs her lyric subject. The speaker's knowledge is superior to that of the other figures in the poem, denoting an authoritative and exceptional status attuned to the Shelleyan idea of poets as "unacknowledged legislators of the world" (Shelley 2006: 1199). Yet this visionary voice is won through the way it has earlier inhabited other perspectives, being equated with, almost dissolved into, ordinary women such as the prostitute and the emigrant "in the huddling cold, / holding her half-dead baby to her" (128–129). Speaking as poet and persona, Boland's post-Romantic subject enacts and reflects on her poetic and political cause at the same time.

The feeling of disconnection which triggers self-reflection in "After a Childhood Away from Ireland" already indicates Boland's sense of exclusion from an established masculine tradition as well as her position in between the Irish and English canons. Romantic poetry serves as a point of contention and orientation on the formal and conceptual levels. Boland's lyrics follow the contours of the "greater Romantic lyric," where contemplating a landscape or object triggers a process of self-questioning and self-invention , both as a point of orientation and in order to subvert it. The process is in tune with the way Boland's prose and poetry reiterates contentions about Romanticism as a poetic ideology: the risks of transcending historical truths through an aesthetic of egocentricity and "distance" from ordinary experience (Boland 1995: 241). Such developments also affect women poets of a more recent generation.

3 Kathleen Jamie's Post-Romantic Revision of Scotland

As Sarah Broom has noted, "concepts of nation and gender are often intricately intertwined, each participating in the construction of the other" (2006: 112). While Boland's work critically responds to such intersections in Irish culture, the pattern also recurs in other national and cultural contexts. The poetry of Kathleen Jamie tackles political themes in ways both similar and different from Boland. Jamie is most acclaimed for writing about nature and place from an angle that implies an environmentalist cause. Yet her interests – from the collections *The Queen of Sheba* (1994) and *Jizzen* (1999), published in the year of Scottish devolution, to *The Bonniest Companie* (2015), which appeared in the aftermath of the 'No' vote in the Scottish Independence Referendum – have long concerned both the non-human and the human inhabitants of her native

Scotland. Jamie's work from the 1990s often explores national and gendered identities. It is in this respect that her writing first faced the legacies of Romantic lyric as a challenge and opportunity.

The poems in *Jizzen* foreground birth and motherhood in a personal and political sense. "Jizzen," a note on the back cover of the volume explains, is Scots for "childbed." The opening poem "Crossing the Loch" has nothing to do with childbirth in the literal sense. But the title's allusion to Tennyson's "Crossing the Bar" (1889) already indicates a metaphorical purpose. In contrast to Tennyson's reflection on death, Jamie's poem heralds the birth of a poetic aesthetic that does away with nostalgic idealizations of Scotland, while also holding on to a unique sense of Scottish community and identity. "Crossing the Loch" traditionally describes a significant incident set in a picturesque landscape, yet the poem clearly makes a point of its Scotishness as something that exists in opposition to the English Romantic tradition.

Like Boland's "A Childhood Away from Ireland," the poem offers a memory. Four stanzas depict a group of young people embarking on a spontaneous boat trip. "Remember how we rowed toward the cottage / on the sickle-shaped bay / that one night after the pub" (Jamie 1999: 1), the first stanza opens, addressing the reader as though they were a companion. Similar to "After a Childhood Away from Ireland," the poem initially evokes a communal perspective, directing attention away from the individual persona, who is only introduced in the second stanza. More explicitly than Boland's, though, Jamie's setting alludes to encounters with nature in canonical Romantic poetry, especially to Wordsworth's boat-stealing episode in the first book of the 1805 *Prelude*: "The moon was up, the Lake was shining clear / Among the hoary mountains" (2014: 161–380; lines 386–387). For Wordsworth, recollecting the childhood experience of nature's sublimity leads to the realization of the unbridgeable difference between self and world, symbolized by "the huge Cliff" (412) that "[r]ose up between me and the stars" (413). This difference, the speaker apprehends, can only be overcome provisionally through the imagination.

The "hunched hills" (Jamie 1999: 1) in "Crossing the Loch" close in on the rowers in a similar manner to Wordsworth's imposing cliff. But Jamie's poem especially underscores the unreliability of subjective memory. Questions rather than assertions serve to portray the proceedings of recollection: "Who rowed, and who kept their peace?" (1). As Timothy Baker notes, "[t]he moment described is precise, but inaccessible" (2015: 65). Memories are blurred: when the "I" is introduced, it is to admit laconically, "I forgot who rowed" (Jamie 1999: 1). Here Jamie undermines the inclination to attribute utmost relevance to particular subjective experiences in the manner of Wordsworth's speaker in the *Prelude* who, after the boating episode, continues to feel haunted by "a dim and undetermined sense / Of unknown modes of being" (2014: 161–380; lines 422–423). Yet Wordsworth, too, often constructs scenes of subjective recollection only to question the possibility of accessing the past through the imagination. Thus the speaker of "Tintern Abbey" recognizes that memory requires mediation and he cannot experience nature in just the same way as when first visiting the Wye valley: "I cannot paint / What then I was" (2014: 65–70; lines 76–77). "Crossing the Loch" stands in continuation with such ambivalent lyric explorations of subjective memory, but it also intensifies the effect for its contemporary purposes.

Jamie contests the authority of the lyric subject more pronouncedly than Wordsworth, while anchoring the events described in a distinctly Scottish contemporary context. Her idea of Scotland includes the picturesque hills and bay as well as the threat of "ticking nuclear hulls" hidden in the water. It also manifests in Jamie's poetic wording: dialect words such as "loch" (1999: 1) and "blaeberries" (2) stand out amongst musical effects, including the onomatopoeic rendition of water lapping in "as though the loch mouthed 'boat'" (1). Free verse moreover replaces the blank verse frequently used by Wordsworth. Jamie's take on the nature lyric represents an effort to challenge the canonized English point of view, but the poem also foregrounds imaginative creation in traditional ways, for instance as it resorts to pathetic fallacy in its descriptions of "hunched hills" and "the cold shawl of breeze" (1). The speaker's initially vague perceptions become specific in envisioning sound and light effects, particularly the imagery of light and water:

> and who first noticed the loch's
> phosphorescence, so like a twittering nest
> washed from the rushes, an astonished
> small boat of saints, we watched water shine
> on our fingers and oars,
> the magic dart of our bow wave?
>
> (1)

The play with alliteration and vowel sounds around the central words "water," "boat," and "our" guides the reader towards a seemingly "magic" experience at the peak of the boating trip and of the poem. Associating light effects with nearsacred experience or a heightened state of mind, the passage evokes Coleridge's description of the water-snakes in "The Rime of the Ancient Mariner" (1798/1817), which move "in tracks of shining white" and emanate an "elfish light" (lines 274–275). Passages that most distinctly bring out Jamie's poetic artistry also place her closest to Romantic precursors.

If "Crossing the Loch" celebrates imaginative lyric vision at the same time that it emphasizes the difficulty of recreating subjective memory, these strategies do not cancel each other out. Rather, they exemplify a post-Romantic tension between restraining the control of the speaking subject over the poem and deploying its power to realize Jamie's specific perspective on Scotland. Picking up the casual, spoken manner of the opening stanza, the speaker finally acknowledges that it was "surely foolhardy, such a broad loch, a tide, / but we live – and even have children" (Jamie 1999: 1). In anticipation of the central motif of *Jizzen*, the poem impels the rebirth of the (Romantic) lyric as a genre that speaks for a contemporary post-devolutionary Scotland.

Jamie thus strikes a balance between what Eavan Boland calls "the perception of what is poetic" and "what is merely human" (1995: 242). Her poem aligns this difference with a sense of Scottish national belonging on the one hand and what Baker calls a "politics of difference" (2015: 62) on the other hand – a dynamic that also informs Jamie's stance on Romanticism. The focus on difference comes out especially in those lyrics that promote a feminist angle on nationhood. These poems imagine poetic history in a way that resonates with Boland's "Mise Eire." "Meadowsweet" has often been cited as one of Jamie's most powerful assertions of the female poetic voice and as a starting point for her ecopoetic vision (Severin 2011: 99). The poem's relationship to the Romantic lyric tradition and its modes of subjectivity have been given less thought – most of all because the poem does not feature a lyric "I" at all and thus less obviously makes itself available to being read along those lines. Still, the poem's approach to the lyric genre contributes importantly to Jamie's vision of reconciling Scottishness with women's poetry.

"Meadowsweet" describes the burial and metaphorical rebirth of a Gaelic woman poet. The poem's six short-lined tercets trace the re-emergence of this poet, buried traditionally face down (Jamie 1999: 49), by intertwining it symbolically with the growth of "summer seeds": the journey towards the surface made by "meadowsweet, bastard balm" becomes the journey of the woman poet towards creative fulfilment, culminating when she surfaces "mouth young, and full again / of dirt, and spit, and poetry" (49). This positive image of empowerment subverts Seamus Heaney's rendering of the passive "Bog Queen," who lies "waiting" to receive the "creeping influences" that will integrate her body into the natural cycle (1990: 66). "Meadowsweet" can be read more widely as a retort to a lyric tradition that has imagined women as idealized, yet silent and passive poetic objects, often equating femininity with nature or the land. In Wordsworth's "I travell'd among unknown Men" (1807), for example, England is gendered feminine and equated with the speaker's dead lover, Lucy: "Among thy mountains did I feel / The joy of my desire; / And She I cherish'd turn'd her wheel / Beside an English fire" (2014: 392–393; lines 9–12). In Coleridge's conversation poems silent female addressees, such as the unnamed "Lady" (line 24) in "Dejection: An Ode" (1817), serve as backdrops to the exploration of the speaker's interiority.

Rather than inhabiting the consciousness of the buried woman poet as speaker to contest such practices, Jamie assumes the third person point of view. She thereby distances her voice from Romantic lyric origins; at the same time, by situating "Meadowsweet" at the close of the volume that promotes a political and poetic renaissance, she also aligns her stance as a writer with the plight and cause of the buried poet. On closer inspection, the poem still focuses on the woman poet's subjective perception and self-assertion. Although the woman is not instated as the speaking persona, the verse moves from external observation ("they buried her") to tracing her perceptions (Jamie 1999: 49). Written in a single sentence that winds itself across the tercets, the poem aligns its perspective with the growth of the meadowsweet. Just after the liquid dripping off the corpse's lips "would seek its way down," the plants already begin "their crawl" upwards, "toward light" (49). Jamie creates a contemporary spin on Coleridgean organic form by combining the traditional outward-inward proceeding of the "greater Romantic lyric" with a movement downward and upward. As the corpse's hair is "slowly / unravelling" (49) in tune with the plants' slow growth, the verse unravels towards a concluding moment of revelation that brings forth, in Timothy Baker's words, "the promise of a new poem to come, a form of poetry that transcends individual experience and yet is rooted in immanent physicality" (2015: 69).

Baker unquestioningly postulates this "new poem to come," yet "Meadowsweet" also dramatizes the problems in realizing this vision – problems inherent to the lyric as a genre and, ultimately, to poetic aesthetics at large, which can never fully reproduce "immanent physicality." Dispensing with the lyric "I" to contest the Romantic practice of associating persona and poet also means keeping the Gaelic woman poet in the position of a signifier. She becomes a constitutive part of the post-Romantic "myth" of a feminist Scottish poetics, to use the terminology of Roland Barthes, who described modern myth as "a metalanguage" (2009: 138). This kind of language transforms a sign, "the associative total of a concept and an image," into the signifier of "a second-order semiological system" (137). Jamie's poem can only challenge the legacies of the Romantic lyric within the boundaries of such systems, by creating a metalanguage. When "dirt" and "spit" are put on equal level with "poetry" in Jamie's final line ("of dirt, and spit, and poetry"), which, by way of half-rhyme, brings to completion previous line endings on "slowly" and "already" (49), it is difficult to decide whether the poem negates or ironically expresses awareness of such complications.

All lyric poetry since the Romantics has engaged in a creative tussle with the literary past. Yet in contemporary women's poetry from Ireland and Scotland the need to innovate becomes an especially immediate concern: their "mobilising of the genre cannot but be political" (Dowson and Entwistle 2005: 241). As epitomized by

Boland's critique of the "Romantic Heresy," contemporary responses to the past do not solely consist in poet-to-poet exchanges described by traditional studies of influence (especially Bloom 1973) but can also comprise an awareness of genre history. Boland's and Jamie's work shows awareness both of the ideological risks and aesthetic potential of the subjective lyric coined in the Romantic period. Considering the ambiguity of Romantic period lyrics, which question their own terms against claims of escapism or idealism, it becomes clear that intertextual exchanges between the periods are multi-layered. Poets sometimes more readily embrace such continuities and the uncertainties and doubts they bring along, in the words of Keats's letter quoted above, than their critical readers[3].

Works Cited

Abrams, Meyer Howard. 2006. "Structure and Style in the Greater Romantic Lyric". In: Michael O'Neill and Mark Sandy (eds.). *Romanticism: Critical Concepts in Literary and Cultural Studies*. Vol. 1. London: Routledge. 197–224.
Anderson, Benedict. 1991. *Imagined Communities: Reflections on the Origin and Spread of Nationalism*. London: Verso.
Baker, Timothy L. 2015. "'An Orderly Rabble': Plural Identities in *Jizzen*". In: Rachel Falconer (ed.). *Kathleen Jamie: Essays and Poems on her Work*. Edinburgh: Edinburgh University Press. 62–70.
Barthes, Roland. 2009. *Mythologies*. Trans. Annette Lavers. London: Vintage Books.
Bloom, Harold. 1973. *The Anxiety of Influence: A Theory of Poetry*. New York: Oxford University Press.
Bode, Christoph. 2008. *Selbst-Begründungen: Diskursive Konstruktion von Identität in der britischen Romantik I: Subjektive Identität*. Trier: WVT.
Boland, Eavan. 1995. *Object Lessons: The Life of the Woman and the Poet in Our Time*. New York: Norton.
Boland, Eavan. 2008. *New Collected Poems*. New York: Norton.
Broom, Sarah. 2006. *Contemporary British and Irish Poetry: An Introduction*. Basingstoke: Palgrave.
Burns, Christy. 2001. "Beautiful Labors: Lyricism and Feminist Revisions in Eavan Boland's Poetry". *Tulsa Studies in Women's Literature* 20.2: 217–236.

---

3 "After a Childhood Away from Ireland". Copyright © 1982 by Eavan Boland, "Mise Eire". Copyright © 1987 by Eavan Boland, "Outside History". Copyright © 1990 by Eavan Boland, from NEW COLLECTED POEMS by Eavan Boland. Used by permission of W. W. Norton & Company, Inc.

"Crossing the Loch". Copyright © 1999 by Kathleen Jamie, "Meadowsweet" Copyright © 1999 by Kathleen Jamie, from JIZZEN by Kathleen Jamie. Reproduced with permission of the Licensor through PLSclear.

Coleridge, Samuel Taylor. 2006. "Dejection: An Ode". In: Duncan Wu (ed.). *Romanticism: An Anthology*. Malden: Blackwell. 673–677.
Coleridge, Samuel Taylor. 2006. "The Rime of the Ancient Mariner: In Seven Parts". In: Duncan Wu (ed.). *Romanticism: An Anthology*. Malden: Blackwell. 694–711.
Culler, Jonathan. 2015. *Theory of the Lyric*. Cambridge: Harvard University Press.
Curran, Stuart. 1988. "Romantic Poetry: The I Altered". In: Anne K. Mellor (ed.). *Romanticism and Feminism*. Bloomington: Indiana University Press. 185–207.
Dowson, Jane, and Alice Entwistle. 2005. *A History of Twentieth-Century British Women's Poetry*. Cambridge: Cambridge University Press.
Ferguson, Frances. 1991. "On the Numbers of Romanticisms". *ELH* 58.2: 471–498.
Hartman, Geoffrey. 1970. "Romanticism and Anti-Self-Consciousness". *Beyond Formalism: Literary Essays 1958–1970*. New Haven: Yale University Press. 298–310.
Heaney, Seamus. 1990. *New Selected Poems 1966–1987*. London: Faber & Faber.
Henderson, Andrea K. 1996. *Romantic Identities: Varieties of Subjectivity, 1774–1830*. Cambridge: Cambridge University Press.
Jamie, Kathleen. 1999. *Jizzen*. London: Picador.
Keats, John. 2006. "Ode to a Nightingale". In: Duncan Wu (ed.). *Romanticism: An Anthology*. Malden: Blackwell. 1395–1397.
Keats, John. 2009. "Letter to George and Tom Keats, December 21, 27?, 1817". In: Jeffrey N. Cox (ed.). *Keats's Poetry and Prose*. New York: Norton. 107–109.
Kinnahan, Linda A. 2009. "Contemporary British Women Poets and the Lyric Subject". In: Nigel Alderman and C. D. Blanton (eds.). *A Concise Companion to Postwar British and Irish Poetry*. Chichester: Wiley-Blackwell. 176–199.
Maguire, Sarah. 1999. "Dilemmas and Developments: Eavan Boland Re-Examined". *Feminist Review* 62: 58–66.
O'Neill, Michael. 2008. "Romantic Forms: An Introduction". In: Nicholas Roe (ed.). *Romanticism: An Oxford Guide*. Oxford: Oxford University Press. 275–309.
Pearse, Pádraic H. 1998. "I am Ireland". *CELT: Corpus of Electronic Texts: A Project of University College, Cork*. University College Cork. https://celt.ucc.ie//published/E950004-015.html [accessed 29 February 2016].
Randolph, Jody Allen. 2014. *Eavan Boland*. Cork: Cork University Press.
Sandy, Mark, and Sarah Wootton (eds.). 2008. "Modelling the Self: Subjectivity and Identity in Romantic and Post-Romantic Thought and Culture". Spec. issue of *Romanticism and Victorianism on the Net* 51. https://www.erudit.org/fr/revues/ravon/2008-n51-ravon2473 [accessed 5 July 2016].
Schrage-Früh, Michaela. 2004. *Emerging Identities: Myth, Nation and Gender in the Poetry of Eavan Boland, Nuala Ní Dhomhnaill and Medbh McGuckian*. Trier: WVT.
Shelley, Percy Bysshe. 2006. "A Defence of Poetry, or Remarks Suggested by an Essay Entitled 'The Four Ages of Poetry' (Extracts)". In: Duncan Wu (ed.). *Romanticism: An Anthology*. Malden: Blackwell. 1184–1199.
Severin, Laura. 2011. "A Scottish Ecopoetics: Feminism and Environmentalism in the Works of Kathleen Jamie and Valerie Gillies". *Feminist Formations* 23.2: 98–110.
Villar-Agáiz, Pilar. 2008. *The Poetry of Eavan Boland: A Postcolonial Reading*. Dublin: Maunsel-Academia Press.
Wordsworth, William. 2014. *Wordsworth's Poetry and Prose*. Ed. Nicholas Halmi. New York: Norton.

Elena Furlanetto
Mystic Poetry Across the Ocean: Reconciling Persian Sufi Poetry and Walt Whitman's *Leaves of Grass*

Abstract: As a fair amount of scholarship has suggested, Walt Whitman adapted tropes, atmospheres, and concerns of Sufi poetic genres such as Rumi's mystical lyrics. This essay addresses Sufi resonances in Whitman's "Song of Myself," "As I Ebb'd with the Ocean of Life," and "Out of the Cradle Endlessly Rocking," with particular emphasis on the construction of his poetic persona. The function of the poetic persona in Sufi verse –who assumes the identities of teacher, prophet, or even God himself – is one of the traits that most effectively characterizes this genre of mystic poetry. The male poet-figure who dominates Whitman's poetics and the narrating Selves of Sufi poetry are both invested in the construction of the poet as a borderless, permeable Self, positioned within a strongly connected spiritual-social network and present in several centers at once. The focus on parallels between the Sufi's poetic personas and Whitman's is beneficial in a number of ways. It explains a series of contradictions between the two poetics, such as between the Sufi aesthetics of placelessness and Whitman's American placedness, or between a poetic voice who hopes "not to cease until death" and the Sufi imperative to seek death before dying. It also complicates *Leaves of Grass*'s positioning in terms of genre and enables readings of Whitman through the prism of mystic poetry. The essay compares and reconciles the genre of Persian Sufi poetry and *Leaves of Grass*, arguing for the possibility of placing Whitman in a transatlantic tradition of mystic poetry. Most importantly, these parallelisms function as an incentive to lend more weight to the Islamic roots of American mystic poetry.

Keywords: Walt Whitman, Sufism, Transcendentalism, Romanticism, Islam

> "I never cease addressing myself about myself
> and returning in it to myself from myself."
> (Muhyiddin Ibn Arabi)

There is little doubt that Walt Whitman was acquainted with Sufi mystic poetry: he was an avid reader of Ralph Waldo Emerson and owned a copy of William Alger's anthology *The Poetry of the East* (1865), which he read and carefully annotated.[1] Unlike Emerson, Whitman did not openly pay homage to Sufism in his writings, but his contemporaries did not fail to notice that his poetry resonated with echoes of the Persian mystics. In 1857, Thoreau stated that *Leaves of Grass* sounded "wonderfully like the Orientals" (qtd. in Thomson 1910: 30). In 1866, Lord Strangford, an Orientalist scholar, commented on the "astounding affinity of *Leaves* in its spirit, content, and form alike, to Persian poetry" (Strangford qtd. in Farzan 1976: 573). The short poem "A Persian Lesson" (originally called "A Sufi Lesson") is the only direct tribute to Sufism in *Leaves of Grass* and it is often dismissed as "as isolated case, the reflection of a brief interest in Sufism" (Farzan 1976: 582). This claim, however, can be effectively disproved.

Ghulam Fayez and Massud Farzan, for example, highlight the striking similarities between Whitman and the thirteenth-century Sufi poet Rumi, casting the Sufi influence as one of the most incisive in Whitman's work. On a slightly different note, Arthur Ford reflects on Eastern imagery in *Leaves*, especially in "Salut au Monde," "Passage to India," and "A Persian Lesson," confirming the presence of references and tributes to Sufi thought. Ford adds that Whitman used Sufi images "unorthodoxly" and "to his own ends" (1987: 18); there is after all a series of fundamental contradictions between the Sufi model and his own. How could a doctrine of placelessness appeal to the man who sang America, the aspiring American poet? How can a poetic voice who hopes "to cease not till death" (Whitman 2002: 26) be compatible with the Sufi imperative of death before dying? As these interrogatives show, many of the problems concerning Whitman's adaptation of the Sufi genre revolve around the figure of the poetic persona, the poet-speaker that dominates "Song of Myself" and other prominent works of *Leaves*. By seeking to address and solve such incongruities, I compare and reconcile the genre of Persian Sufi poetry and *Leaves of Grass*, arguing for the possibility of placing Whitman in a transatlantic tradition of mystic poetry.

It is not in doubt that Sufi mystic poetry qualifies as a genre that subsumes various subgenres, although hardly canonizable. Michael Frishkopf, for example, is reluctant to classify it as folk, oral, or written literature, as Sufi poetry displays characters that belong to all of the above (Frishkopf 2003: 80). In "The Sufi Mystical Idiom in Alevi Aşık Poetry," however, Caroline Tee speaks of a "Sufi genre" (2013) and in her seminal book *As Through a Veil* (1982), Annemarie

---

[1] I would like to thank the editors and reviewers of this volume for their help in preparing my article for publication. I owe much to their insightful comments and accurate reading of my work.

Schimmel devotes a chapter to classical Persian mystic poetry and its subgenres. Among these, Schimmel enumerates the *mathnawi*, didactic lines in rhyming couplets, the allegorical novel in verse, the *divan*, the *ghazal*, the *qasida*, and many others. Although all these subgenres may differ in terms of form, Schimmel mentions that Persian mystic poetry relies on a range of standard topoi (Schimmel 1982: 56), and rhetoric devices that appear with different frequency in many of these subgenres, providing a thematic repertoire that allows us to speak of Persian mystic poetry as a category of its own. A few of these recurring tropes – which also resurface centuries and oceans apart in Whitman's poetry – include, for example, a language of intoxication and exhilaration conveyed by erotic metaphors that "almost always point to transcendent significance" (Martin and Tayob 2004: 527). As a result, Persian mystic poetry is populated by many a "Beloved," objects of desire both amorous and mystical and metaphors for God himself. The desire to die of literal or metaphorical death and be conjoined with God is also one of these recurring tropes, often appearing in combination with the desire of drowning in a divine ocean. The longing for an all-encompassing unity is also expressed through the celebration of pantheism, or the presence of God in all objects and beings, especially the Beloved.

This article will be mostly concerned with the function of the poetic persona: one of the conventional tropes that most effectively characterizes the genre of Sufi poetry. The persona assumes the identities of teacher, prophet, or even God himself. The combination of these didactic and messianic functions entails a specific understanding of poetry: J.R. LeMaster and Sabahat Jahan explain that the poet-prophet of Sufi mysticism "views poetry as his tool – rather, God's tool, and a vehicle with which to transmit God's message" (2009: 97). Like preachers, Sufi poet-prophets speak to a community of candidates for enlightenment – adepts or simple believers – but, like teachers, "are more concerned with encouraging their readers to question outmoded traditions and visible reality and to recognize the kinship between man and God as well as among all men" (LeMaster and Jahan 2009: 97). I turn my attention to all-encompassing and prophetic personas as a defining trait of both Sufi poetry and *Leaves of Grass*. The focus on poetic personas also allows me to clarify the series of contradictions mentioned above.

This paper will discuss three thematic areas that most clearly display these contradictions but also the conspicuous similarities between Whitman and Persian poetic personas, namely, their divinity, their wish for death or deathlessness, and their 'placedness' or 'placelessness.' I will resort to *Leaves of Grass* and the poetry of thirteenth-century mystic poet Rumi to show that Whitman's legendary egotism does not necessarily clash with the tenets of Sufi poetry that encourage the shedding of one's ego and the annihilation of the

Self. The two positions can in fact be reconciled insofar as Whitman's celebration of the Self coexists with some degree of self-dissolution. These parallels function as an incentive to reevaluate the resonance of Islam in the American literary canon, and they help positioning *Leaves of Grass*'s more precisely in terms of genre: although much scholarship classify Whitman's as mystical poetry, hardly any of them addresses its proximity to the Sufi imaginary.[2]

1 Divinity of the Poet-Speaker

One of the main stages on the Sufi spiritual path, according to Sufism scholar William Chittick, is the *fana'* or 'annihilation.' Since "man's self existence is not real," as there is no reality apart from God, "the illusion that it is real must be annihilated" by negating and eliminating the "I" (2005: 71). The annihilation of the impediments of mundanity and egotism, Chittick explains, allows the Sufi adepts to see that "they themselves had been nothing and still are nothing, because God alone has true reality" (2000: 42–43). To put it with Mahnaz Ahmad, the mystic's "individual ego, his contingent being, is irrelevant or illusory, and vanishes altogether in the great experience of self-extinction" (2014: 155). Chittick reports a passage from the *Masnavi* where Rumi celebrates the "non-existent" individual who, by achieving complete annihilation and "becoming selfless," has gained immortality and control over the physical and the spiritual realms.

> Such a non-existent one who has gone from himself (become selfless) is the best of beings and the great (one among them [men]). In passing away he really hath the life everlasting. All spirits are under his governance; all bodies too are in his control. (Rumi qtd. in Chittick 2005: 73)

The speaker of "Song of Myself," by contrast, affirms to "know perfectly well [his] own egotism" (Chittick 2005: 67), and his corporeal self seems far from vanishing. Whitman's speaker rejoices at whatever is immanent, treasuring the present moment's vibrant immediacy: "what is commonest, cheapest, nearest, easiest is Me, / Me going in for my chances [...], / Adorning myself to bestow myself on the first that will take me" (2002: 36). Similar to the Sufi adept in Rumi's lyric, the speaker of "Song of Myself" also aspires to governing spirits and bodies, but he does so from a vigorous self-centeredness as the human, the natural, and the celestial "tend inward to me, and I tend outward to them" (39). Whitman's speaker posits

---

[2] See, for example, Miller 1955; Walkington 1994; Kuebrich 1989; Farzana 2016.

a forcefully existing subject: as the Sufi adept who is dwelling in *fana'* becomes aware that he or she is nothing and God is the only existing reality, Whitman's Self does the opposite by establishing that the only existing reality is himself: "One world is aware and by far the largest to me, and that is myself" (42).

Furthermore, Whitman's speaker announces his own divinity with varying intensity. In section 5 of "Song of Myself," he sees himself as identical with and a continuation of God, affirming to know that "the hand of God is the promise of my own, / and the spirit of God is the brother of my own" (2002: 30). In section 24, he expresses his godlike nature along Christological lines, appropriating Jesus's famous utterance in the Gospel of Matthew: "the King will reply, 'Truly I tell you, whatever you did for one of the least of these brothers and sisters of mine, you did for me'" (Matthew 25:40). "Whoever degrades another degrades me," Whitman writes, "And whatever is done or said returns at last to me" (46). Later, the speaker elevates his body beyond religion, affirming that his head is "more than churches, bibles, and all the creeds" (46). Ultimately, the Self eclipses the gods of humanity, both historical and contemporary.

> Magnifying and applying come I,
> [...]
> Taking myself the exact dimensions of Jehovah,
> Lithographing Kronos, Zeus his son, and Hercules his grandson,
> Buying drafts of Osiris, Isis, Belus, Brahma, Buddha.   (42)

A comparison between Rumi's poetry collection *Masnavi* (ca. 1270) and "Song of Myself" shows that Whitman's human speaker imagines himself occupying the exact position that God occupies in Rumi's theology and poetics.

> The Prophet said that God has declared,
> "I am not contained in aught above or below,
> I am not contained in earth or sky, or even
> In highest heaven. Know this for a surety. O beloved!
> Yet am I contained in the believer's heart!"
>   (Rumi 2001: 60–61)

> Am not contain'd between my hat and boots,
> [...]
> I am not an earth nor an adjunct of an earth,
> I am the mate and companion of people, all just as immortal and fathomless as myself.
>   (Whitman 2002: 31)

Both Rumi's God and Whitman's poet-speaker declare that they exceed every tangible ("above or below"; "hat and boots") and intangible measure ("earth or sky, or [...] highest heaven" / "an earth or an adjunct of an earth"), but remain close and intelligible to human beings ("I am contained in the believer's heart"; "I am the mate and companion of people").

While the Selves of Sufi poetry yearn for extinction because they want to witness their humanity dissolve in the overpowering reality that is God, the poetic persona of "Song of Myself" repositions the individual as the all-feeling, all-seeing center of a world bursting with a myriad of realities. Yet, the principle of uncompromised self-assertiveness dominating Whitman's "Song of Myself" and the Sufi aspiration to selflessness are different sides of the same coin. There are in fact two ways to harmonize this apparent polarity. One is the principle of, as Rumi calls it, "becoming 'I am God'" (qtd. in Chittick 2005: 31); the other is the concept of the "Universal Man." These two aspects of Sufi doctrine contemplate the idea that the individual may be identical to God and they provide dialectical explanations for this possibility.

2 Glory to be Me: The "I am God" Principle

The paradox of these discrepant selves in Whitman's poetry can be solved via the "I am God" principle. The title "Song of Myself" is reminiscent of the famous utterance of the Sufi mystic al-Bastami, "Glory to be me" – an undeniably Whitmanesque statement. Bayazid-e-Bastami (d. c. 875.) and Mansur Al-Hallaj (d. 922) are central figures of Sufi theology that earned the title of "intoxicated Sufis" due to their visionary doctrine (Campo 2009: 90). Born in Persia to a Zoroastrian family, Bastami is especially remembered for his statement "Glory be to me," which he uttered in the course of ecstatic experiences of union with God. The religious authorities reacted with outrage at what they perceived as blasphemy, but the Sufi community defended Bastami, arguing that "he may simply have been quoting God" (Campo 2009: 107). Bastami's ecstatic utterance is comparable to the less fortunate Al-Hallaj's, who was put to death in 922, while Bastami is said to have escaped capital punishment by feigning madness (Copleston 1982: 97). Al-Hallaj's statement "I am the Truth" has been recorded as "the most extreme expression of mystical union with God in the history of Islamic mysticism" (Mason 2004: 290).

According to Sufi doctrine, not only would believers be fully justified in claiming that they are God, but they would be performing an act of extreme humility. As Rumi puts it,

> Take the famous utterance, "I am God." Some people think this is a great pretension, but "I am God" is in fact a great humility. Those who say, instead, "I am a servant of God" believe that two exist, themselves and God. But those who say, "I am God" have become nothing

and have cast themselves to the winds. They say, "I am God" meaning, "I am not, God is all. There is no existence but God. I have lost all separation. I am nothing." In this the humility is greater.

(Rumi 2000: 83)

In short, once the Sufi disciple has experienced *fana'* and extinguished his or her own Self, they abide in *baqa'*, or union in God. At this stage, the Self has completely dissolved in God and has therefore become God. The Sufi has acknowledged that reality is nothing but God, hence, since he exists, he must be God.

These famous utterances by intoxicated Sufis might constitute a precedent for Whitman's vociferous divine Self. A complete identification between the speaker and God occurs in "Song of Myself" too, where, according to Ford, the speaker is enraptured in an "ardent pantheism" that emerges, for instance, in the following lines (in section 5):

> And I know that the hand of God is the promise of my own,
> And I know that the spirit of God is the brother of my own,
> And that all the men ever born are also my brothers, and the women my sisters and lovers,
> And that a kelson of the creation is love.
>
> (Whitman 2002: 30)

The image of the Perfect Man or Universal Man is the second aspect of Sufism that contemplates the equalization of man and God. This principle of a single man (the microcosm) reflecting "all the perfect attributes of the macrocosm" (Ahmad 2014: 154) and containing "the universe in all its indefinite multiplicity" (Chittick 2005: 49–50) is one of the defining traits of Whitman's persona in "Song of Myself." He in fact claims to "contain multitudes" (2002: 77) and to be "possess'd" by and undistinguishable from "all [the] presences" he writes about, and to suffer the other's suffering as he finds himself in a "prison shaped like another man" (62).

Not only does Whitman's speaker contain and integrate the voices of his equals, men and women, he also incorporates less conscious and articulate forms of life. In the following passage from "Song of Myself," the speaker portrays himself as a primordial being, comparable to the Universal Man as "prototype," as Chittick describes him (2005: 49). Once again, the excerpt lends itself to a comparison with Rumi's *Masnavi*.

> I find I incorporate gneiss, coal, long-threaded moss, fruits, grains, esculent roots,
> And am stucco'd with quadrupeds and birds all over,
> And have distanced what is behind me for good reasons,
> But call any thing back again when I desire it.
>
> (Whitman 2002: 52)

> The spheres lag behind me in revolutions!
> Wine is intoxicated with me, not I with it!
> The world takes its being from me, not I from it!
> I am like bees, and earthly bodies like wax,
> I build up these bodies as with my own wax!
>
> (Rumi 2001: 48)

Not only do Rumi's and Whitman's Universal Selves contain, integrate, and reflect creation: they are in control of creation. They exert active and conscious power on the major and most intangible entities ("the spheres"; "what is behind me for good reasons") as well as on the minor beings populating creation ("bees"; "quadrupeds and birds"). Creation exudes from their physical bodies, the elements of stucco and wax bringing to mind the godlike process of molding life out of mundane materials such as clay and mud: they represent a microcosm that mirrors all the attributes of the macrocosm.

3 Cease Before Death? The "Sea Drift" Cluster

Sufi poetry understandably narrates the process of annihilation, extinction, obliteration of the Self through the metaphor of death. LeMaster and Jahan dedicate an extensive chapter to the Sufi's and Whitman's serene acceptance of death as a transformative experience rather than an ending (LeMaster and Jahan 2009: 172–202). The authors, however, focus on the physical death of the body, while I shall now turn my attention to *fana'* as a metaphorical death that the Sufi adept must achieve before dying. In Rumi's words,

> O you who possess sincerity, [...] choose death [...]. Not such a death that you will go into the grave, (but) a death consisting of (spiritual) transformation.
>
> (Rumi qtd. in Chittick 2005: 72)

The Sufi principle of "death before dying" appears to be in contradiction with Whitman's persona in "Song of Myself," who "hop[es] to cease not till death" (2002: 26) and professes to "know [he is] deathless" (42). Yet the Sufi's elaborate quest for spiritual death conflicts only with part of the numerous and variegated Selves contained in *Leaves*. Some of these Selves – the speaker of "Song of Myself" in particular – alternatively scorn, welcome, and serenely accept physical death; some "express a sense of despair and uncertainty and present a heightened focus on evil, abuse, and ugliness" (Morgan 1971: 41); others seek a metaphorical death in a way that brings to mind the Sufi path.

Farzan explains that in "Song of Myself," a "boisterous self-celebrating, self-singing 'I'" coexists side by side with a "modest, self-effacing, wondering 'I'" (1976: 578) who affirms that "no array of terms can say how much [he is] at peace [...] about death" (Whitman 2002: 75). It is also worth noting that "Song of Myself" ends with the literal dissolution of the speaker in nature, who vanishes in drafts and whirlpools, but not before alluding once more to a "spiritual pattern of physical death and rebirth" (Morgan 1971: 41).

> I depart as air, I shake my white locks at the runaway sun,
> I effuse my flesh in eddies, and drift it in lacy jags.
>
> I bequeath myself to the dirt to grow from the grass I love,
> If you want me again look for me under your boot-soles.
> (Whitman 2002: 77)

But while "Song of Myself" shows that the speaker may embrace death, it is not the best example to prove that a *cupio dissolvi* of the Sufi variety makes its appearance in *Leaves*. A more compelling "self-effacing" Self is to be found, in fact, in a section called "Sea Drift." The "Sea Drift" cluster – especially the opening poems "As I Ebb'd with the Ocean of Life" and "Out of the Cradle Endlessly Rocking" – stage a different Self than "Song of Myself": namely, a Self in crisis – a term that I intend to refer to a critical moment of passage and self-questioning. According to Charles H. Morgan, "As I Ebb'd" is the "lowest point" of the 1860 edition, its "nadir" (1971: 46): it marks the poet's "descent in the pattern of death and rebirth," nihilistic, hopeless, and "devoid of 'consoling moments'" (46). The reader is certainly faced with a lesser, more pensive Self than the "full declaratory voice" (Michael 2008: 193) of "Song of Myself." What is most relevant to our purposes, however, is that "As I Ebb'd" and "Out of the Cradle" richly resonate with Sufi echoes and themes.

In Sufi poetry, spiritual death is achieved through a symbolic drowning in the ocean or sea, which is a poignant metaphor for the dissolution of the human conscience into the vastness of God. Ibn Sina, Arab mystic and philosopher, visualizes the last stage of the believer's journey towards God (Union) as "a river that flows toward Divine-nature" and "a drop of water joining a river that returns it to an ocean" (Martin and Tayob 2004: 401). On a similar note, Chittick also resorts to drowning imagery when he explains that "when lovers find their Beloved present, [...] they are *drowned* in the sweet ocean of love's unity" (2000: 47). Drowning implies dying, but here Chittick uses a drowning metaphor to indicate dissolution in God, as love is always both erotic and transcendent. Consider the following passage from *Fihi ma Fihi* where Rumi visualizes the union with God through drowning imagery.

> Absorption is such that whoever enters it is no longer there. They make no more efforts, they cease to act and move. They are immersed in the water. No action is their action; it is the action of the water. But if they flail about in the water with their hands and feet, they are not truly submerged. If they utter a cry, "I am drowning," this too is not absorption. (2000: 83)

If for the Sufi the quest for union with God and attainment of the ultimate divine truth is often symbolized by death by drowning. "Sea Drift" also offers metaphorical drowning as a path to self-awareness: both in "Cradle" and "Ebb'd," immersion in water and death by drowning – either actual or merely imagined – also grants access to a more truthful Self and limpid poetic expression in the shape of "prismatic colors" (Whitman 2002: 214) or words "final, superior to all" (211).

In "Out of the Cradle Endlessly Rocking" the poet-speaker reminisces about the moment he became a poet – the moment when, as a child, he heard the heartbreaking lament of a mockingbird who had lost his companion. The text presents a variety of Sufi tropes, among them the loss of the Beloved, the resulting awakening to poetry, and the strange sympathy between a bird and a man who can understand the language of birds (cf. Furlanetto 2017). As the poem nears its end, the focus shifts from the mockingbird's pain to the poet-speaker's drowning fantasies. At the end of "Cradle" the ocean holds an irresistible, fatal attraction both erotic and poetic: the Atlantic Ocean whispers the word "death" and sensually lures the speaker to drown in its waters.

> Whereto answering, the sea,
> Delaying not, hurrying not,
> [...]
> Lisp'd to me the low and delicious word death,
> And again death, death, death, death,
> [...]
> Hissing melodious [...],
> But edging near as privately for me rustling at my feet,
> Creeping thence steadily up to my ears and laving me softly all over,
> Death, death, death, death, death.
> (Whitman 2002: 211)

The speaker abandons himself to a drowning fantasy where he softly becomes one with the ocean, which, as we initially established, is a recurrent trope of Sufi poetry symbolizing union and enlightenment.

Self-annihilation, however, is not particularly central in "Cradle," and is relegated to the coda of the poem, while the rest of the stanzas focus on the loss of the Beloved and the potential of this loss to awaken the poetic imagination. The connection between self-annihilation and death by drowning is more evident and poignant in "As I Ebb'd with the Ocean of Life," which marks an epiphany thanks to which the Self becomes aware of a fundamental splitting.

> Oppress'd with myself that I have dared to open my mouth,
> Aware now that amid all that blab whose echoes recoil upon me I had not once had the least idea of who or what I am,
> But that before all my arrogant poems the real Me stands yet untouch'd, untold, altogether unreach'd,
> Withdrawn far, mocking me with self-congratulatory signs and bows,
> With peals of distant ironical laughter at every word I have written,
> Pointing in silence to these songs, and then to the sands beneath.
> (Whitman 2002: 213)

The author of "all that blab" and "all the arrogant poems," the pre-epiphany "electric self" as the speaker calls it, is now confronted with the "real Me": a better man reminiscent of the "Perfect Man" of the Sufi tradition, unattainable, in his perfection "untouch'd" and "unreach'd." This dualism is strongly evocative of Rumi's 'two heads' doctrine, according to which men have two heads: the hidden and the manifest. The "original" head, the "pure head from heaven" is hidden under clay, while the "derived" head, who is incapable of seeing "the infinite universe," is manifest.

> In the head itself is nought, but ye have two heads;
> This head of clay is from earth, and that pure head from heaven.
> The many pure heads scattered beneath the clay,
> That thou mayst know the head depends on that other head!
> That original head hidden, and this derived head manifest,
> Forasmuch as behind this world lies the infinite universe.
> (Rumi 1992: 37)

In a similar way, Whitman's vociferous "electric Self" is the author of songs, poems, and "all that blab" (2002: 213) that result from an imperfect understanding of the world ("I perceive I have not really understood any thing, not a single object," 213). The "real Self," instead, remains untouched and unreached and expresses his disapproval through gestures rather than words ("pointing in silence to these songs, and then to the sand beneath", 213).

Towards the end of "As I Ebb'd," in a surprisingly Sufi gesture, the poet-speaker becomes one with the ocean:

> You oceans both, I close with you,
> We murmur alike [...]
> I too Paumanok,
> I too have bubbled up, floated the measureless float, and been wash'd on your shores,

> I too am but a trail of drift and debris,
> I too leave little wrecks upon you, you fish-shaped island.
> (Whitman 2002: 214)

His final drowning becomes unambiguous when he specifies, in brackets, "(See, from my dead lips the ooze exuding at last, / See, the prismatic colors glistening and rolling)" (214). These lines also show that the poet-speaker continues to talk after his death, which indicates, in the text's logic, that only one of his Selves has died while the other still lives and sings. The two lines visualize the "electric" Self's corpse after he drowned, while the "real Me" comments on this scene. The relieved, almost triumphant quality of this "at last" signals that the speaker welcomes death, which is paradoxically delivered by the "ocean of life." This is therefore "not such a death that you will go into the grave, (but) a death consisting of (spiritual) transformation" (Rumi qtd. in Chittick 2005: 72). The glistening "prismatic colors" oozing from the corpse's mouth, furthermore, suggest that the death of the electric Self has enabled a more layered, more luminous expression than his earlier, arrogant "blab" (Whitman 2002: 213), one that is comparable to the higher truth the Sufi adept achieves once the stage of *fana'* – his own drowning – is completed.

4 Placelessness vs. Placedness

By partially dissolving the substantial divergences between Whitman's poetic personas and the tenets of Sufi poetry, I do not intend to equalize the two. Therefore, this study ends by showing how Whitman has absorbed and substantially modified the Sufi notion of placelessness. Farzan claims that the lines from "Song of Myself" reported below were inspired by Rumi.

> Of every hue and caste am I, of every rank and religion,
> A farmer, mechanic, artist, gentleman, sailor, quaker,
> Prisoner, fancy-man, rowdy, lawyer, physician, priest.
> (Whitman 2002: 40)

> I am neither Christian, nor Jew, nor Gabr, nor Moslem.
> I am not of the East, nor of the West, nor of the land, nor of the sea.
> (Rumi qtd. in Chittick 2005: 76)

Both excerpts contain the aspiration to transcend the borders of ethnic ("not of the East nor of the West" / "Of every hue"), religious ("neither Christian not Jew" / "Of every religion"), and class ("nor Gabr nor Muslim" / "Of every caste") differences, to develop a mode of communication that is universal, and may encompass different realities and spaces. Furthermore Farzan notes that, "to the measure that the consciousness becomes emptied of its make-up (conditionings, prejudices, individual and racial memories, and the like), gradually the 'I' becomes nothing and everything" (1976: 579). It is precisely in this binary of "nothing" and "everything," however, that one of the main differences between Whitman and Rumi rests. While Rumi's speaker becomes nothing, Whitman's becomes everything.

In this text from his poetry collection *Divani Shamsi Tabriz* – where Rumi attempts to portray the condition of *baqa'*, or union with God – the anaphora of "I am not" mimics the process of annihilation of one's ego, during which the Self sheds the layers of his mundane attachments. Chittick explains Rumi's poetic choice in terms of "negative reality," namely, the attempt to define the illusory quality of reality by listing its limitations (Chittick 2005: 76). This "negative reality" becomes clearer when considering the poem in its entirety:

> *I am not* of nature's mint, nor of the circling heavens.
> *I am not* of earth, nor of water, nor of air, nor of fire;
> *I am not* of the empyrean, nor of the dust, nor of existence, nor of entity.
> *I am not* of India, nor of China, nor of Bulgaria, nor of Saqsin;
> *I am not* of the kingdom of Iraqain, nor of the country of Khorasan.
> [...]
> My place is the Placeless, my trace is the Traceless.
> (Rumi 1992: 125; emphasis added)

Compare Rumi's negative catalogue with the corresponding section of "Song of Myself":

> One of the Nation of many nations, the smallest the same and the largest the same,
> A Southerner soon as a Northerner, a planter nonchalant and hospitable down by the Oconee I live,
> A Yankee bound my own way ready for trade, my joints the limberest joints on earth and the sternest joints on earth,
> A Kentuckian walking the vale of the Elkhorn in my deer-skin leggings, a Louisianian or Georgian,
> A boatman over lakes or bays or along coasts, a Hoosier, Badger, Buckeye;
> At home on Kanadian snow-shoes or up in the bush, or with fishermen off Newfoundland,
> At home in the fleet of ice-boats, sailing with the rest and tacking,
> At home on the hills of Vermont or in the woods of Maine, or the Texan ranch.
> (Whitman 2002: 39)

The identity of Whitman's speaker is also devoid of affiliation. Yet the first major difference is that this rootlessness is articulated in the positive and not in the negative. If the abode of Rumi's Self is the placeless and the traceless,

Whitman's Self feels "at home" in multiplicity of American contexts at once. The second major discrepancy – and certainly the most profound – opposes Rumi's notion of placelessness to Whitman's obvious *placed*ness.

Rumi's lines sweep the political geography of thirteenth-century Asia, gradually renouncing affiliation with its nations. China, Bulgaria, Khorasan, India: none of the kingdom of men is fit to host the soul of the mystic confidently ascending to the vastness of God, which is alien to the human understanding and delimitation of space and thus placeless. In Whitman's case, we are presented with various components of the American landscape to which the speaker professes to belong. Hence, the dispersion of the self which is undoubtedly present in both Rumi and Whitman leads into two opposite directions: if Rumi's negative anaphora aims to shed the layers of the self by renouncing national affiliation, Whitman's affirmative catalogue does not discard the idea of national affiliation but intensifies it. Fayez claims that Whitman and Sufi poetry share a "dynamic, fluid, microcosmic and macrocosmic [Self], [who] can occupy infinite centers and overlap infinite centers at one time" (Fayez 1980: 18). Yet, the inclusiveness granted by a macrocosmic Self in "Song of Myself" mostly embraces a national experience. The speaker of "Song of Myself" affirms to be "One of the Nation of many nations," and he lists a series of American locations, declaring to feel at home in "the fleet of ice-boats, [...]/ on the hills of Vermont or in the woods of Maine, or the/ Texan ranch" (Whitman 2002: 39). One can conclude that Whitman's poetic persona is deeply anchored in the American reality and affirms himself as the transversal voice of his nation. He remains, in Ford's words, "loyal to his passion to be the most American of poets" (1987: 12).

The political relevance of a Sufi reading of Whitman is evident. Scholarship that connotes Whitman's *Leaves* as a work of mystic poetry does not characterize Whitman's mysticism as one of Sufi quality. In his review of David Kuebrich's 1989 *Minor Prophecy*, George Hutchinson notes that the book's main concern is to represent Whitman as the founder of a new American civil religion, but it does not take into account the "non-western religions which were the source of many of his ideas and techniques for representing ecstatic states" (1990: 104). More recently, Farzan has noted that a fair amount of research covered "Whitman's mystical poetry *qua* mystical poetry" and that this research has mostly focused on "Vedantic, Bhuddic, and Hindu classics" and less on Islamic mysticism (1976: 573). Harold Bloom has described Whitman as "the crucial celebrant of what I think we yet will call the American religion" and "forever [...] its poet-prophet" (2005). If this is true, then this new American civil religion is partly indebted to Islamic texts, and its literary expression owes much to the conventions that characterize the genre of Sufi mystical poetry.

Since the early 1990s, the United States has been experiencing an infatuation with Sufism, mostly thanks to Coleman Barks's popular re-translation of Rumi. This infatuation translated into what Amira El-Zein has called "the Rumi Phenomenon" (El-Zein 2000: 71), which entailed the employment of Sufi themes and figures in popular culture practices and a proliferation of works of literature on Sufi themes. In 1994, *Publishers Weekly* declared Rumi America's best-selling poet (Bihbihānī et al. 1999: 172). In spite of these recent developments, studies on Sufism and the Transcendentalists show that Sufi poetry runs deeper in American literary history. By concentrating on the figure of the poet-prophet in Rumi and Whitman, this article hopes to create greater awareness of the intimate connection between the American and the Islamic traditions of mystic poetry. In today's United States, where authorities view Muslim citizens with suspicion and relentlessly question their very right to walk on United States soil, it is crucial to remember that, to paraphrase the Koran, Islam may be closer to America than its jugular vein.

Works Cited

Ahmad, Mahnaz. 2014. "Whitman and Hafiz: Expressions of Universal Love and Tolerance". In: Mehdi Aminrazavi (ed.). *Sufism and American Literary Masters*. Albany: State University of New York Press. 153–162.

Alger, William Rounseville. 1865. *The Poetry of the East*. Boston: Roberts Brothers.

Bihbihānī, Sīmīn, Farzaneh Milani, and Kaveh Safa. 1999. *A Cup of Sin: Selected Poems*. Syracuse: Syracuse University Press.

Bloom, Harold. 2005. "Walt Whitman: America's Greatest Artist". *History News Network*. http://historynewsnetwork.org/article/13478 [accessed 28 July 2017].

Campo, Juan Eduardo. 2009. *Encyclopedia of Islam*. New York: Infobase Publishing.

Chittick, William C. 2000. *Sufism: A Short Introduction*. Oxford: Oneworld.

Chittick, William C. 2005. *The Sufi Doctrine of Rumi*. Bloomington: World Wisdom.

Copleston, Frederick. 1982. *Religion and The One: Philosophies East and West*. London: Continuum.

El-Zein, Amira. 2000. "Spiritual Consumption in the United States: The Rumi Phenomenon". *Islam and Christian-Muslim Relations* 11.1: 71–85.

Farzan, Massud. 1976. "Whitman and Sufism: Towards 'A Persian Lesson'". *American Literature* 47.4: 572–582.

Farzana, Shamsi. 2016. "The Theme of Mysticism in Walt Whitman and Emily Dickinson's Poetry". *European Journal of English Language and Literature Studies* 4.1: 1–15.

Fayez, Ghulam M. 1980. "Images of the Divine in Rumi and Whitman". *Comparative Literature Studies* 17.1: 33–43.

Ford, Arthur L. 1987. "The Rose-Garden of the World: Near East Imagery in the Poetry of Walt Whitman". *Walt Whitman Quarterly Review* 5.1: 12–20.

Frishkopf, Michael. 2003. "Authorship in Sufi Poetry". *Alif: Journal of Comparative Poetics* 23: 78–108.
Furlanetto, Elena. 2017. "Walt Whitman's 'Sea Drift' Cluster: The Encounter of Sufi and American Selves at Paumanok". In: Donatella Izzo and Vincenzo Bavaro (eds.). *Harbors, Flows, and Migrations: The USA in/and the World*. Newcastle: Cambridge Scholars. 95–110.
Hutchinson, George. 1990. Rev. of *Minor Prophecy: Walt Whitman's New American Religion*, by David Kuebrich. *Walt Whitman Quarterly Review* 8: 103–109.
Ibn Arabi, Muhyiddin. 2006. *The Universal Tree and the Four Birds: Treatise on Unification (al-Ittihad al-kawni)*. Trans. Angela Jaffray. Oxford: Anqa Publishing.
Kuebrich, David. 1989. *Minor Prophecy: Walt Whitman's New American Religion*. Bloomington: Indiana University Press.
LeMaster, J. R., and Sabahat Jahan. 2009. *Walt Whitman and the Persian Poets: A Study in Literature and Religion*. Bethesda: Ibex Publishers.
Martin, Richard, and A. I. Tayob (eds.). 2004. *Encyclopedia of Islam and the Muslim World*. New York: Macmillan.
Mason, Herbert W. 2004. "Hallaj, Al- (858–922)". In: Richard C. Martin (ed.). *Encyclopedia of Islam and the Muslim World*. Vol. 2. New York: Macmillan. 289–290.
Michael, Ann E. 2008. "Whitman's Paumanok Poems and the Value of Being 'Faithful to Things'". *Canadian Journal of Environmental Education* 13.2: 192–197.
Miller, James E. 1955. "'Song of Myself' as Inverted Mystical Experience". *PMLA* 70.4: 636–661.
Morgan, Charles H. 1971. "A New Look at Whitman's Crisis". *South Atlantic Bulletin* 36.2: 41–52.
Rumi, Jalalu-'d-din Muhammad. 1992. *Selected Poems from the Dīvāni Shamsi Tabrīz*. Trans. Reynold Nicholson. Cambridge: Cambridge University Press.
Rumi, Jalalu-'d-din Muhammad. 2000. *Discourses of Rumi (or Fihi ma Fihi)*. Trans. A.J. Arberry. Ames: Omphaloskepsis.
Rumi, Jalalu-'d-din Muhammad. 2001. *Masnavi i Ma'navi: Teachings of Rumi*. Trans. E. H. Whinfield. Ames: Omphaloskepsis.
Schimmel, Annemarie. 1982. *As Through a Veil: Mystical Poetry in Islam*. New York: Columbia University Press.
Tee, Caroline. 2013. "The Sufi Mystical Idiom in Alevi Aşık Poetry: Flexibility, Adaptation and Meaning". *European Journal of Turkish Studies*.
Thomson, James. 1910. *Walt Whitman: The Man and the Poet*. London: Ardent Media.
Walkington, J. W. 1994. "Mystical Experience in HD and Walt Whitman: An Intertextual Reading of 'Tribute to the Angels' and 'Song of Myself'". *Walt Whitman Quarterly Review* 11.3: 123–136.
Whitman, Walt. 2002. *Leaves of Grass and Other Writings*. New York: Norton.

Rainer Emig
The Dragon in the Gate: Modernism as a Challenge to Contemporary Poetic Genres

Abstract: The essay discusses modernism as a problematic ancestor of contemporary poetry. Its radical challenge to a coherent self, undermining of imaginary locations, and refusal of stable meanings are rejected by many later poems. When trying to trace them in a wide range of largely British poetry, three major positions emerge. A subtle sidestepping that, while following modernist generic features, subtly transforms them, for example abstract universal images into blatantly concrete ones. A rejection of modernism, either in the shape of parody or by returning to Edwardian, Victorian, even Romantic forms. Lastly a working through of the modernist agenda that confront its aesthetics with alternatives – for example of gender, ethnicity, class, and politics. According to many definitions of the postmodern, these responses represent postmodernism not as a farewell or safe distancing, but as a dialectic engagement that keeps modernism in poetry alive – paradoxically by exactly not succumbing to its rules.

Keywords: modernism, postmodernism, self, location, meaning

1 Introduction: Gatekeepers and Housebreakers

"[L]ike a great dragon folded in the gate to forbid all entrance" is the description that an exasperated Robert Bridges attached to Gerard Manley Hopkins's long poem *The Wreck of the Deutschland* (1875–76) when he tried to give Hopkins's poetry belated recognition by publishing a collected edition in 1918 (cf. Hopkins 106). By then Hopkins, who had only published a few poems during his lifetime, had been dead for twenty years. A Jesuit novice, Hopkins had been asked by his superior to commemorate the death of five Franciscan nuns, who had left Germany as a result of the *Kulturkampf*, in a shipwreck off the English coast in 1875. Clearly, Hopkins's superior had no idea what was coming when he received stanzas like the following one:

> Is out with it! Oh,
> We lash with the best or worst
> Word last! How a lush-kept plush-capped sloe
> Will, mouthed to flesh-burst,

> Gush! – flush the man, the being with it, sour or sweet,
> Brim, in a flash, full! – Hither then, last or first,
>   To hero of Calvary, Christ's feet –
> Never ask if meaning it, wanting it, warned of it – men go.
>   (Hopkins 1918: 14)

No one, Hopkins included, saw much space for such poetry at a time when Alfred Lord Tennyson had been Poet Laureate for 25 years and even his long and challenging poem on loss, *In Memoriam A.H.H.* (1849), was regarded by such influential voices as Queen Victoria as soothing and pleasing (cf. Rappaport 2003: 353). Indeed it is. A long elegy to Tennyson's friend Arthur Hallam, who died of a stroke at the age of only 22 in 1833, it cushions its tragedy in regular forms:

> Ring out, wild bells, to the wild sky,
> The flying cloud, the frosty light:
> The year is dying in the night;
> Ring out, wild bells, and let him die.
>   (Trilling and Bloom 1973: 460–461)

The comparison is a little forced, though. Hopkins's text is about a tragedy, and Tennyson's about mourning. Nonetheless, both deal with trauma, and *In Memoriam* subtly weaves images of storms, sea, and drowning into the superficially sedate and resolved meditations that appealed to Victoria after the unexpected death of her husband Albert in 1861. What the comparison highlights is that Hopkins's radical style, his sprung rhythm, his refusal to remain within established norms of the elegy genre (such as the regular rhyme scheme of Tennyson's poem), and his use of fragmented and newly coined words simply had no place and found no appreciative audience – or imitators – at the time of its composition. It is as if Tennyson himself had foreseen this when he wrote, also in *In Memoriam*:

> What hope is here for modern rhyme
> To him, who turns a musing eye
> On songs, and deeds, and lives, that lie
> Foreshorten'd in the tract of time?
>   (Trilling and Bloom 1973: 455)

Hopkins's poetry eventually found a different context. Its belated publication in 1918 associated it no longer with Victorian norms of poetic genres, but with the radical experiments of modernism. Eliot's *Prufrock and Other Observations* had just come out in 1917. Ezra Pound had been issuing volumes for years, including *Lustra* of 1916, in which the following much anthologised verses appeared:

> L'Art, 1910
> Green arsenic smeared on an egg-white cloth,
> Crushed strawberries! Come, let us feast our eyes.
> (Pound 1990: 118)

Imagism, to which this poem belongs, had already formulated its rules in 1913 and been practised by a range of poets. Hopkins's works seemed to fit neatly into this new aesthetics of direct treatment of the "thing" (Gould et al. 2005: 294) and abandoning of prescribed forms in favour of free verse. Some critics, including the present author, indeed regard Hopkins as a proto-modernist for exactly this reason (cf. Richards 1926: 195; Emig 1995a). Yet it is problematic to postulate a direct link, since, as we have seen, traditional notions of influence can hardly be claimed given the publication history of Hopkins's work. It rather seems as if Hopkins's oeuvre was one that his contemporaries and immediate successors ignored or circumvented. It was W. H. Auden who rediscovered Hopkins in formal and generic terms in the late 1920s and 1930s, at the very point when Auden tried to wean himself off the overwhelming impact of a model like Eliot's *The Waste Land* (1922).

For a scholar who has worked on modernism in poetry and on the impact of modernism on poems such as Auden's, but also on contemporary poetry in English, one of the questions that continues to be troubling is: did modernism in English poetry really have much of an impact on the way later poets wrote? This seems a silly or even blasphemous question at first glance. Do not all histories of English literature and overviews of poetry in English unanimously state that modernism was a decisive rupture that went hand in hand with the cultural rift of World War I? Literature responded and contributed to this rift with drastic experiments, and things could no longer be the same.

The present essay wishes to check whether this pronouncement is accurate. It will first describe the immediate aftermath of modernism in English poetry and then move forward to the present. It will read central aspects of the aesthetics of modernist poetry that are linked with genre conventions against examples from later periods. The conventions to be discussed in the following are the integrity of the lyrical I, the cohesion of the poetic setting, and the question of semantics – the poems' problematic meanings. How do all of these manifest themselves? In which typical or untypical forms? The essay will also consider related, more abstract issues such as self-reflexivity and the turning of the material (language) into the content of the poems. Do we find in modern and contemporary poetry in English responses to these modernist features or not?

One of the problems of this inquiry is, of course, the selection of poetic examples. In order to rely on a selection approved by a range of internationally recognised scholars, and one that is used in academic institutions worldwide, the essay draws on *The Norton Anthology of Poetry* as its guide through poetry in English until the mid-1990s, and adds some more contemporary authors toward the end.

2 Emulating Modernism

Modernism set itself strict rules. The famous Imagist ones often attributed to Pound, but also to F. S. Flint, are only one example:

1. Direct treatment of the "thing", whether subjective or objective.
2. To use absolutely no word that does not contribute to the presentation.
3. As regarding rhythm: to compose in sequence of the musical phrase, not in sequence of the metronome. (Gould et al. 2005: 294)

These rules are notoriously hard to interpret. What, for instance, is the "thing"? They are also very hard to follow. Who decides which words are necessary in a poem and which contribute (or do not contribute) to presentation? This is authoritarian, as is the way music is privileged over the regularity of the metronome (cf. Emig 1995b: 106–108). What is being attacked in all three rules are of course the conventions of established genres, such as fixed rhyme schemes, invocations in odes, lyricisms in lyrical forms, or clichéd speakers in dramatic ones (a form that Pound especially tried to modernise).

Few poets decided to subscribe to such a strict poetics among a group that – and this is one of modernism's paradoxes – wanted to break with rules in the first place. The American poet Marianne Moore continued to use modernist forms and images but already put an ironic twist on some of its radical assumptions. Her poem "Nevertheless" (1944) seems to be a response to poems like Pound's "L'Art, 1910" that takes up its radical imagery and radicalises its form even further in drastic enjambments:

> you've seen a strawberry
> that's had a struggle; yet
> was, where the fragments met,
> a hedgehog or a star-
> fish for the multitude
> of seeds. What better food
> than apple seeds – the fruit
> within the fruit – locked in
> like counter-curved twin
> (2005: 1334–1335)

The poem re-uses Pound's strawberry, takes up the challenge of fragmentation, both in imagery and form, but also undercuts it – for example by introducing a rhyming couplet at the end of each stanza. Its final image also shifts the poem's possible meaning in a very different direction from the self-enclosed, indeed almost aestheticist and decadent one of Pound's feast for the eyes:

> What sap
> went through that little thread
> to make the cherry red!
> (1335)

Sap and thread are seemingly harmless images for a big and contentious issue in literature: that of meaning and how it is established. Is it organic – like sap – or crafted like a thread (whose feminine implications are certainly a stab against the masculinist poetics of so many modernists)? Moore's poem ends in an exclamation mark, not a question mark. Meaning is triumphantly though perhaps also surprisingly established, and it is established through structure (cf. Cecire 2011: 84–85). What kind of meaning it is seems questionable – until one recognises the red cherry as an echo of a famous response by Gertrude Stein to the nagging questions about the meaning of her notorious sentence "A rose is a rose is a rose is a rose" (1913):

> Now listen! I'm no fool. I know that in daily life we don't go around saying "is a ... is a ... is a ..." Yes, I'm no fool; but I think that in that line the rose is red for the first time in English poetry for a hundred years. (Davis and Jenkins 2015: 264)

Red roses and cherries are no coincidences or tautologies, but puns on poetic clichés that are overcome by their very exhibition. Modernist strawberries, cherries, and roses are *read*, actively perceived that is, because they are defamiliarised in the way that the Russian Formalist Victor Shklovsky described in 1917 – at exactly the time when modernism was beginning to peak (cf. Shklovsky 1965). Moore's poem takes up modernist paradigms, but it also challenges, extends, and partly revises them – in line with its title, "Nevertheless."

Indeed many modernist innovations proved hard or impossible to imitate. The radical generic multiplication in *The Waste Land* and *The Cantos* (1925–1970), which makes it impossible to call these texts epic, lyric, or dramatic, proved attractive to young writers of the turbulent 1930s. In Cecil Day Lewis's *The Magnetic Mountain* (1933) the appeal of the long form leads to an unwitting imitation of Eliot's juxtaposition of learned references and modern ones. Lewis's left-wing politics take inspiration from Eliot's symbolism, but without recognising that in *The Waste Land* this symbolism does not fully add up – but then this has been true for many critics, too (cf. Wald 2002: 33–34).

Neither does *The Magnetic Mountain* trust the radical multiplicity of forms in *The Waste Land*, of which free verse is only one. Instead, it opts for quatrains, alternating rhymes, and regular tetra- and pentameters. The results is a disastrous attempt to look modernist, for instance by borrowing Hopkinsean images like the windhover or the carrion from "Carrion Comfort" (written 1884–1885) and pressing them into a form that is clearly more Tennyson than contemporary. Here is the poem's first stanza:

> Now to be with you, elate, unshared,
> My kestrel joy, O hoverer in wind,
> Over the quarry furiously at rest
> Chaired on shoulders of shouting wind.
> Where's that unique one, wind and wing married,
> Aloft in contact of earth and ether;
> Feathery my comet, Oh too often
> From heaven harried by carrion cares.
> (Day Lewis 1992: 135)

It does not help that the lines also feature Audenesque images, such as the quarry, and even echoes of A. E. Housman's *A Shropshire Lad* (1896).

Auden did a better job emulating *The Waste Land*'s epic yet fragmented model in *The Orators* (1936), a long and generically diverse poem that contains prose sections, regular poetic ones, but also graphics in a manner reminiscent of Pound's *Cantos*. Auden eventually decided that he could not stand the ambivalences he created in his long poem by following – not always entirely seriously – modernist diversification of form. He considered the poem's radical playing with political positions a failure and declared that *The Orators* could be read as proto-fascist – and some critics have decided to agree (cf. Worley 2013: 147–148). Yet radical ambiguity is also the price for following demanding models such as those of modernism (cf. Emig 1999: 52–79). The "Epilogue" poem in *The Orators*, the only part that has been repeatedly anthologised, shows an awareness of this in lines like "'O where are you going?' said reader to rider," once again a pun on rider/writer, or its concluding verse "As he left them there, as he left them there" (Auden 1991: 59).

3 Sidestepping Modernism

Most poetry written in Britain after World War II seems to bypass modernism altogether. It is American poets such as William Carlos Williams, Charles Olson, Lawrence Ferlinghetti, and Denise Levertov who take up the modernist torch. Poetry written in the British Isles instead seems to hark back to older traditions, such as Edwardian or even Victorian ones, when it comes to generic forms. Take the following verses as an example:

> Like a painting it is set before one,
> But less brittle, ageless; these colours
> Are renewed daily with variations
> Of light and distance that no painter
> Achieves or suggests. Then there is movement,
> [...]   (Thomas 2005: 1544)

This is certainly closer to Thomas Hardy than to the later Yeats, Eliot, or Pound. It is the beginning of "The View from the Window" by the Welsh poet R. S. Thomas, and it was written in 1958! It returns to a unity of poetic setting, it retains an unidentified but apparently coherent "we" in its finale, and although it does not provide a completely clear answer to its almost experimental aesthetic set-up, it insists that it asks a clear question: about seeing and making sense of what we see (cf. Thomas 2013: 74).

> Change, as slowly the cloud bruises
> Are healed by sunlight, or snow caps
> A black mood; but gold at evening
> To cheer the heart. All through history
> The great brush has not rested,
> Nor the paint dried; yet what eye,
> Looking coolly, or, as we now,
> through the tears' lenses, ever saw
> This work and it was not finished?
>   (Thomas 2005: 1544)

This is a beautiful poem and also a profound one. Yet it resorts to semantic elements that are traditional and thus alien to modernist aesthetics, such as history, the work of creation and/or art, and a moved but unified "we."

While R. S. Thomas looks beyond modernism to earlier periods, partly in order to devise his own troubled but ultimately coherent vision of Wales and Welshness, other post-World War II poets openly poke fun at modernism. The strange title of Henry Reed's poem "Chard Whitlow" (1946) – chard is a type of cabbage, and whitlow a sore on a finger – already indicates that it parodies several of Eliot's poems, including "Mr. Eliot's Sunday Morning Service" (1920), "The Boston Evening Transcript" (1920), and *Burnt Norton* (1936) from *Four Quartets* (cf. O'Neill 2013: 48):

> Chard Whitlow
> *(Mr. Eliot's Sunday Evening Postscript)*

> As we get older we do not get any younger.
> Seasons return, and today I am fifty-five,
> And this time last year I was fifty-four,
> And this time next year I shall be sixty-two.
> (Reed 2005: 1563)

The Waste Land's atmospheric and rather pathetic images of desolation in the desert and its invocations of Buddhism, and also the Christian prayer sequences of poems such as "Ash-Wednesday" (1930) are lampooned at the end of Reed's poem:

> Oh, listeners,
> And you especially who have turned off the wireless,
> And sit in Stoke or Basingstoke listening appreciatively to the silence,
> (Which is also the silence of hell) pray not for your selves but your souls.
> And pray for me also under the draughty stair.
> As we get older we do not get any younger.
> And pray for Kharma under the holy mountain. (1563)

There is, of course, serious criticism in all this lampooning. By invoking a radio audience, the poem indicates that figures like Eliot were established media personalities by the late 1940s. This stands in stark contrast to the impact of modernist publications in terms of popularity and sales. Eliot did not do badly with *The Waste Land*. In fact, all first editions combined (two in journals, an American book edition, and a British book edition by the Woolfs' Hogarth Press) brought in more than his regular annual salary as a clerk at Lloyd's Bank (cf. Rayney 1998: 82). Yet modernist publications never reached great popularity or significant circulation. They remained elitist not only in terms of form but also accessibility. Reed's poem also expresses a suspicion that the spiritual pathos of a text like *The Waste Land* might be merely a disguise for vacuity. Parody is, of course, also a sign of respect. We rarely poke fun at something that is neither popular nor respected, even when the parody intends to be critical. Modernist poetry, it seems, is an irritation to later poets like Reed. Its value is now in doubt, although its cultural status is not.

Much harder to categorise in this conundrum is Dylan Thomas's position towards modernism. In his own time, Thomas was frequently grouped among the "modern poets," a label that carefully avoided formal or stylistic identification, and indeed in many anthologies and poetry seminars he is simply added as yet another modernist. Yet a closer look at even his most frequently anthologised poems shows that this association is fraught with problems. The famous "The Force That Through the Green Fuse Drives the Flower" (1934), for instance, is subjective with a clearly identified lyrical I. It is neither fragmented nor particularly defamiliarising, although, admittedly, the "green fuse" is an odd image. Its thematic contents are also clear: youth, the organic, the creative, perhaps also the erotic, and their challenges and dangers.

> The force that through the green fuse drives the flower
> Drives my green age; that blasts the roots of trees
> Is my destroyer.
> And I am dumb to tell the crooked rose
> My youth is bent by the same wintry fever.
> (2005a: 1566)

Its poetic model is not so much modernist as proto-Romantic: Blake and his famous poem "The Sick Rose" (1794).

What is radical in Thomas's poem is its rhyme scheme – or apparent lack thereof. Parts of the poem display a very faint pattern of slant rhymes that are so off-kilter that half-rhyme is far too strong a term for them. The quoted first stanza has "flower," "destroyer," and "fever"; the second one "rocks," "wax," and "sucks," and perhaps also slant-rhymes "streams" and "veins." Yet the third stanza only has "pool," "sail," and "lime"; the penultimate one "head," "sores," and "stars." In short: the poem starts with an echo of a regular rhyme scheme and then seems to drift towards free verse. At the very point when no rhymes are visible any longer, the reader is confronted with a couplet, yet again one with a slant rhyme:

> And I am dumb to tell the lover's tomb
> How at my sheet goes the same crooked worm.
> (2005a, 1566)

In addition, all this rhyming irregularity is accompanied by a remarkable – and remarkably traditional – metrical pattern: iambic pentameter in the first lines of every stanza and in the couplet; another pentameter, though with a largely trochaic start, in the second lines; trochaic trimeter in the short third lines of each stanza; and two more iambic pentameters in lines four and five of each. Some significant freedoms have been taken over from modernism's radicalism, but they have been merged with decidedly non-modernist approaches to the lyrical I and poetic situation. This is also true for another famous Thomas poem, "In My Craft or Sullen Art" (1946):

> In my craft or sullen art
> Exercised in the still night
> When only the moon rages
> And the lovers lie abed
> With all their griefs in their arms,
> I labour by singing light

> Not for ambition or bread
> Or the strut and trade of charms
> On the ivory stages
> But for the common wages
> of their most secret heart.
>   (2005b)

Here we have the opposite of free verse: an intricate rhyming arrangement, a b c d e b d e c c a, that returns in slightly cropped form in the following stanza. The imagery, too, is far from modern – and certainly not modernist: labouring over one's art or craft at night, mention of trade and charms and ivory, and psalms and nightingales in the second stanza. These are echoes of medieval and Early Modern poems (cf. Goodby and Wigginton 2000).

Once again, if we apply the three tests for a residual modernism in poetry: fragmented or problematised lyrical I, setting, and semantics, Thomas's poem fails to tick any of these boxes. This is true for much post-World War II poetry, which presents itself as if modernist poetic experiments had never happened. A good example of a similar use of theme in a strikingly unmodernist form is "Strawberries" (1968) by the first Scottish Poet Laureate, Edwin Morgan:

> There were never strawberries
> like the ones we had
> that sultry afternoon
> sitting on the step
> of the open french window
> facing each other
> your knees held in mine
> the blue plates in our laps
> the strawberries glistening
> in the hot sunlight
> we dipped them in sugar
> looking at each other
> not hurrying the feast
> for one to come
>   (Morgan 2005: 1618)

His poem appears to confirm a common prejudice concerning modern poetry: that it is merely prose chopped up into verse. Yet its simultaneously coherent and fragmented pieces of narrative are the result of a clever use of enjambments that raises questions of coherence and cohesion, which in turn become questions concerning memory in the remaining verses. Again, however, the lyrical I, even though its relation to its own memory and the "you" that is addressed is challenged, is undoubtedly there. The same applies to the setting, even when it is perhaps a false memory. What the poem is about is also clear and does not evade the reader's critical inquiry. Morgan's strawberries, in short, are not read differently. Critical self-referentiality concerning its own structures and material, a typical sign of modernist poetics, is not what the poem is about (Nicholson 2002: 7, 65).

The return of narrative, even when its authority and authenticity are sometimes challenged, is another telling departure from modernist fragmentation, but also from its structural opposite: the creation, out of fragments, of a paradoxical impersonal myth that requires no narrative explanation. The unified visions of W. B. Yeats's "Byzantium" poems (1928–1932) and Eliot's *Four Quartets* (1943) are a far cry from what goes on in Donald Davie's reassessment of history in "Remembering the 'Thirties" (1955). The opening of Davie's poem may signal a certain scepticism but not loss of coherence and meaning, and it retains a unified "we":

> Hearing one saga, we enact the next.
> We please our elders when we sit enthralled;
> But then they're puzzled; and at last they're vexed
> To have their youth so avidly recalled.
> (Davie 2005: 1641)

Regular metre and rhyme scheme are also in evidence. When history is explicitly addressed, this happens neither in fragments nor in visions:

> The Anschluss, Guernica – all the names
> At which those poets thrilled or were afraid
> For me mean schools and headmasters and games;
> And in the process someone is betrayed.
> (1642)

There are, of course, modern English poets who do not tell poetic stories, reminisce about the past, or observe modern life critically or longingly, although many do. Geoffrey Hill could be listed among the storytellers, while Ted Hughes is famous for his shamanistic invocations of nature images for the very Romantic purpose of exploring creativity and the poetic imagination (Schuchard 2011). His famous poem "The Thought-Fox" (1957) resembles in this respect John Keats's "Ode to a Nightingale" (1819) more than any modernist poem, including Yeats's work, where nature and animal images are usually quickly unmasked as symbolic ciphers. The poem begins:

> I imagine this midnight moment's forest:
> Something else is alive
> Beside the clock's loneliness
> And this blank page where my fingers move.
> (Hughes 2005: 1810)

Regular though unrhymed quatrains contain a thickly clustered range of images that form metaphors. Some of these are not dissimilar to modernist ones. The "clock's loneliness," for instance, is not far from the animated objects and locations in Eliot's early poems. Yet where the poems in Eliot's *Prufrock* dissolve in mere potentialities and questions, and their speakers and protagonists echo away into nothingness, Hughes' poem ends triumphantly with the line "The page is printed" (1810).

4 (Post-)Colonial Modernism?

The preceding survey is a wide one, perhaps too wide. Yet still it contains an important omission. Modernism, especially in its so-called classical variety embodied by European and American writers of the first decades of the twentieth century, is a Western and in many ways a Eurocentric movement. In recent years a debate on the possible multiplicity of modernisms has started, and some have postulated a "Global Modernism" (Wollaeger and Eatough 2012) given the possibility of detecting modernist aesthetics and poetics in writers from colonial and postcolonial backgrounds. It would take a massive investigation of its own to engage with these ideas. Nonetheless, the selections in *The Norton Anthology of Poetry* indicate that these writers are now recognized as important voices in English-language poetry. This section will therefore examine how the prominent postcolonial poets R. K. Ramanujan from India and Edward Kamau Brathwaite and Derek Walcott from the Caribbean respond to the structural and generic challenges of poetic modernism.

Brathwaite appears to be the most radical of the three in formal terms. "New World A-Comin'" (1967) starts:

> Helpless like this
> leader–
> less like this,
> heroless,
> we met you: lover,
> warrior, hater,
> coming through the files
> of the forest
> soft foot
> to soft soil
> of silence:
> we met in the soiled
> tunnel of leaves.
>   (2005: 1803)

This is sparse and nonetheless complex poetry based on the seemingly simple distribution of what looks like prose into radically short poetic verses. No regular rhymes are in evidence, but a clear metrical pattern that amounts to a rhythm. The poem works with enjambments and radical semantic juxtapositions: what are "the files of the forest" or "soft soil of silence," and why is the "tunnel of leaves" soiled? While little poetic narratives could be found in the poetry of Larkin and others, here we have a poetic counter-narrative. Defamiliarisation takes place, but it takes place as a challenge by a plural lyrical speaker, a "we," to an implicit addressee, us, the readers. Similar to magical realism, we are confronted with a world that appears coherent but is clearly not ours. All of this is exciting, fascinating, and demanding. But it bears little resemblance to modernism's strategies of self-reflexion and fragmentation. Destabilisation of subject and meaning clearly occurs in Brathwaite's poem but targets specific cultural and political positions, not the allegedly universal (though of course Eurocentric) ones of modernist poetics (cf. Irele 1994: 720).

Walcott's poetry is just as colourful and indeed in some ways more pleasing to a European reader than Brathwaite's – exactly because it employs traditional generic patterns for its subversive messages (cf. Lee 2005: 117):

> A Far Cry from Africa
> A wind is ruffling the tawny pelt
> Of Africa. Kikuyu, quick as flies,
> Batten upon the bloodstreams of the veldt.
> Corpses are scattered through a paradise.
> Only the worm, colonel of carrion, cries:
> "Waste no compassion on these separate dead!"
> Statistics justify and scholars seize
> The salients of colonial policy.
> What is that to the white child hacked in bed?
> To savages, expendable as Jews?
> [...]   (2005: 1820)

Ramanujan is a further case in point. His "Self-Portrait" of 1966 is a radically short poem, unrhymed, using modern and tellingly unpoetic vocabulary:

> I resemble everyone
> but myself, and sometimes see
> in shop-windows
> despite the well-known laws
> of optics,
> the portrait of a stranger,
> date unknown,
> often signed in a corner
> by my father.   (2005: 1803)

We find, once again, radical enjambments and an ironic Oedipal Freudian twist at the end. But we also find a coherent lyrical I, a consistent setting, and one evident and clear question, all of which are signs of a departure from modernist models (cf. Prasad 1994: 14).

5 Working Through Modernism

Can we conclude from this investigation that modernism in poetry has proved a dead-end, that its impact on contemporary poetry is limited, and that poems taking up modernist positions do so ironically and critically? This is certainly a viable position. Modern poets like Geoffrey Hill relate their texts to Anglo-Saxon poems of the Early Middle Ages rather than the likes of Yeats, Eliot, and Pound (cf. Emig 2002: 42–46). Modern women poets like Fleur Adcock from New Zealand and the Poet Laureate Carol Ann Duffy from Scotland find their models in Victorian nonsense and children's poems rather than in the complex fragmented models of the modernists. Adcock's "The Ex-Queen Among the Astronomers" features a setting reminiscent of *Gulliver's Travels* (1726) and a fairy-tale protagonist. Duffy's "The Scottish Prince" (2003) is a modernised (and largely unrhymed) ballad, while "Mrs Midas" is a modernised, prose-like fairy-tale. The last things these poets are interested in, it seems, is form or the challenging of their own material. They investigate expectations, and they de-familiarise positions, but they do so relying on largely established and often very traditional models (cf. Smith 2003: 166). This is also true for Tony Harrison. In "A Kumquat for John Keats" (1981), Harrison addresses the importance and canonicity of the Romantic poet but does so in an ironic parody of Romantic poetic form. In his poems, the social and cultural investments within poetry and of poetry itself are at stake (cf. Rowland 2001: 92). His famous "Them & [uz]," for example, addresses the social distinction between so-called Received Pronunciation and regional dialect in Britain and how this distinction is reproduced by literature and people's attitude towards it:

> "Them and [uz]"
> (for Professors Richard Hoggart and Leon Cortez)
> αἴαι, ay, ay! ... stutterer Demosthenes
> gob full of pebbles outshouting seas –
> 4 words only of mi 'art aches and ... 'Mine's broken,
> you barbarian, T.W.!' He was nicely spoken.
> 'Can't have our glorious heritage done to death!'
> I played the Drunken Porter in Macbeth.
> 'Poetry's the speech of kings. You're one of those

> Shakespeare gives the comic bits to: prose!
> All poetry (even Cockney Keats?) you see
> 's been dubbed [ʌs] into RP,
> Received Pronunciation, please believe [ʌs]
> Your speech is in the hands of the Receivers.'
> [...]   (2005: 1873–1874)

All of this is presented in cleverly rhymed verses, even when they use defamiliarising phonetic transcription and colloquial and dialect forms. Fragmentation is used but to simulate an authentic oral speech situation. The poem punningly indicates in a term like "Receivers" the link between the linguistic, the economic, and the political. Modernist self-reflexion and its complicated fragmentations that generally refuse clearly identifiable messages are apparently irreconcilable with contemporary poetry's aim to assume critical positions in terms of gender, class, and others (cf. Deane 1994: 359–360).

But is this to be read as ignorance or failure, as a looking away from or a refusal to engage with modernist poetics of genre and form? When we recall the variety of what modern and contemporary poetry does – outside the rules of modernism – we realise that modernism's goal of a *tabula rasa*, a clean slate for a radically new aesthetics, has not come about. Perhaps it was a paradoxical idea from the start. Pound's radical dictum "Make it new" is, after all, a contradictory one (see North for its origins). What is the "it" that is to be made new if not tradition and existing forms and themes? Who is empowered to do this, and how? And still, postmodernist poetry in English has taken up the challenge. It has made poetry, its genres and their conventions, new. But in doing so, it has taken the modernist tradition as one of the "its" that were rife for remaking. Instead of a *tabula rasa* we get a *tabula plena*, a full board – perhaps also in the sense of a plentiful menu – or a *tabula lusoria*, a gameboard. In line with some of the more productive definitions of postmodernity and postmodernism, the "post" suggests not an abandoning, an overcoming, or a succession, but a critical working through, in our case of modernist forms and rules (cf. Welsch 2009: 193–206). In the departures, revisions, and even parodies of modernist genre norms this essay has examined, there is always also a critical engagement with them.

Think only of two important consequences of the demanding modernist challenges to genre and form that radicalise the characteristics discussed so far: impersonality, which radicalises the incoherent lyrical I, and the approximation of poetry to music or sculpture, which radicalises the fragmented settings and meanings of modernist poetry. Both of these ideas are paradoxical and ultimately impossible, although experimenting with them – the modernists would not enjoy the expression "playing," even though many of their postmodern heirs would – can produce challenging poetry. Eliot, who popularized the term "impersonality" in his essay "Tradition and the Individual Talent" (1919), indeed sees impersonality as grounded in tradition: not as the abandoning of the Romantic notion of creativity but as its radicalisation. He asks that writers be "judged" but "not amputated" by "the standards of the past," and describes the separation of the biographical personality of the author from the aesthetic creation he or she brings forth:

> poetry is not a turning loose of emotion, but an escape from emotion; it is not the expression of personality, but an escape from personality. But, of course, only those who have personality and emotions know what it means to want to escape from these things. (1975: 43)

None of this is antagonistic to the postmodern poetic examples analysed above. But, paradoxically, if modernist rules were followed to a T, they would make impossible exactly what they wish to prescribe. A totally impersonal utterance would not be one, since every form of communication requires a sender. A completely dissolved form just as much as a petrified one would contradict the metaphorical potential without which poetry cannot exist. Genre, the theme of the present volume of essays, is exactly what mediates between the contradictory tendencies towards dissolution and fixedness.

These points are illustrated by a poem by the female Irish writer Eavan Boland whose discussion will serve as a conclusion to this essay. Boland, who now teaches in the United States, writes poems that at first glance could not be further removed from modernist norms and rules. They are historical, often ostensibly subjective, and usually gendered. Neither impersonality nor poetry as sculpture is evident in them. And yet they take up the modernist challenges of form and impersonality, and they do so not by imitation, but by working and thinking through them. What could be more radical than establishing a speaking subject within a poem that yearns not to be confined to the poem, not to be forced to be a stable representation of a self? And what could be more of an affront to modernist hardness and reduction than to express these considerations in a subtle and beautiful lyrical form, in the most traditional setting of nature, yet a nature with a twist (cf. Emig 2015: 61–63)? Boland is not the only exponent of such an attitude, and it is perhaps no coincidence that one finds similar approaches in other often female poets from the so-called Celtic Fringe such as Medbh McGuckian from Ireland and Gillian Clarke from Wales.

In Boland's poem "A Woman Painted on a Leaf" (1994) an anonymous but clearly stable lyrical I finds the traces of another personality, or rather two: the fragile portrait of "A woman painted on a leaf" (Boland 1994: 69) painted by an equally anonymous artist. This discovery triggers a meditation on existence, art, and their limits, time and death, but also on the question of gender and objectification – something which has always assumed an ambivalent role in the arts, especially when women were the objects of representation. Rather than accepting an eternity frozen in an ideal form, the speaker of Boland's poem uses the leaf portrait to demand transience, a transience that will undo the art work and the represented women in the same way that time and death will undo the lyrical I. "I want a poem / I can grow old in. I want a poem I can die in" (69), the speaker says and thereby reverses modernism's demands of impersonality and the durability of sculpture not by contradicting them, but by extending them into their problematic taboo areas: desire and death. As a traditional lyrical poem about a meditating self that nonetheless takes this meditation into radical territories, and as a modern poem that takes the modernist inheritance seriously and at the same time beyond itself, "A Woman Painted on a Leaf" shows potential directions for postmodern poetry, in terms of gender and power but also of genre and form.

Works Cited

Auden, Wystan Hugh. 1991. *Collected Poems*. Ed. Edward Mendelson. London: Vintage.
Boland, Eavan. 1994. *In a Time of Violence*. New York: Norton.
Brathwaite, Edward Kamau. 2005. "New World A-Comin'". In: Margaret Ferguson, Mary Jo Salter and Jon Stallworthy (eds.). *The Norton Anthology of Poetry*. New York: Norton. 1803–1805.
Cecire, Natalia. 2011. "Marianne Moore's Precision". *Arizona Quarterly* 67.4: 83–110.
Davie, Donald. 2005. "Remembering the 'Thirties". In: Margaret Ferguson, Mary Jo Salter, and Jon Stallworthy (eds.). *The Norton Anthology of Poetry*. New York: Norton. 1641–1643.
Davis, Alex, and Lee M. Jenkins (eds.). 2015. *A History of Modernist Poetry*. New York: Cambridge University Press.
Day Lewis, Cecil. 1992. *The Complete Poems*. London: Sinclair-Stevenson.
Deane, Patrick. 1994. "The Occasion and Contexture of Speech in Contemporary British Poetry". *Contemporary Literature* 35.2: 343–364.
Duffy, Carol Ann. 2003. *The Good Child's Guide to Rock'n'Roll*. London: Faber & Faber.
Eliot, T. S. 1975. *Selected Prose*. Ed. Frank Kermode. London: Faber & Faber.
Emig, Rainer. 1995a. "Modernist Hopkins: Towards an Aesthetic of Self-Destruction". *Q/W/E/R/T/Y: Arts, Littérature & Civilisations du Monde Anglophone* 5: 185–196.
Emig, Rainer. 1995b. *Modernism in Poetry: Motivations, Structures and Limits. Studies in Twentieth-Century Literature*. London: Longman.
Emig, Rainer. 1999. *W.H. Auden: Towards a Postmodern Poetics*. London: Macmillan.
Emig, Rainer. 2002. "Lust in the Ground: The Erotics and Politics of the Soil in Contemporary Poetry". *Critical Survey* 14.2: 37–48.

Emig, Rainer. 2015. "Towards a Biodegradable Subjectivity: Two Women Poets from the Celtic Fringe". In: Cordula Lemke and Jennifer Wawrzinek (eds.). *Weeds and Viruses: Ecopolitics and the Demands of Theory*. Trier: WVT. 49–65.

Goodby, John, and Christopher Wigginton. 2000. "'Shut, too, in a tower of words': Dylan Thomas' Modernism". In: Alex Davis and Lee M. Jenkins (eds.). *Locations of Literary Modernism: Region and Nation in British and American Modernist Poetry*. Cambridge: Cambridge University Press. 89–112.

Gould Axelrod, Steven, Camille Roman, and Thomas Travisano (eds.). 2005. *The New Anthology of American Poetry: Modernisms, 1900–1950*. Vol. 2. New Brunswick: Rutgers University Press.

Harrison, Tony. 2005. "Them & [uz]". In: Margaret Ferguson, Mary Jo Salter, and Jon Stallworthy (eds.). *The Norton Anthology of Poetry*. New York: Norton. 1873–1874.

Hopkins, Gerard Manley. 1918. *Poems*. Ed. Bridges, Robert. London: Humphrey Milford.

Hughes, Ted. "The Thought-Fox". In: Margaret Ferguson, Mary Jo Salter and Jon Stallworthy (eds.). *The Norton Anthology of Poetry*. New York: Norton, 2005. 1810–1811.

Irele, Abiola. 1994. "The Return of the Native: Edward Kamau Brathwaite's Masks". *World Literature Today* 68.4: 719–725.

Lee, Clarissa. 2005. "Derek Walcott, Human Isolation, and Traditions of English Poetry". *Journal of Caribbean Literatures* 4.1: 109–122.

Moore, Marianne. 2005. "Nevertheless". In: Margaret Ferguson, Mary Jo Salter and Jon Stallworthy (eds.). *The Norton Anthology of Poetry*. New York: Norton. 1334–1335.

Morgan, Edwin. 2005. "Strawberries". In: Margaret Ferguson, Mary Jo Salter and Jon Stallworthy (eds.). *The Norton Anthology of Poetry*. New York: Norton. 1618.

Nicholson, Colin. 2002. *Edwin Morgan: Inventions of Modernity*. Manchester: Manchester University Press.

North, Michael. 2013. "The Making of 'Make It New': Ezra Pound's Slogan Was itself the Product of Histroical Recycling". *Guernica: A Magazine of Global Arts and Politics*. https://www.guernicamag.com/the-making-of-making-it-new [accessed 15 August 2013].

O'Neill, Michael. 2013. "The Thirties Bequest". In: Peter Robinson (ed.). *The Oxford Handbook of Contemporary British and Irish Poetry*. Oxford: Oxford University Press. 38–56.

Pound, Ezra. 1990. *Personae: The Shorter Poems of Ezra Pound*. Ed. Lea Baechler and A. Walton Litz. New York: New Directions.

Prasad, H.Y. Sharada. 1994. "A.K. Ramanujan: A Tribute". *Indian Literature* 37.4: 13–16.

Ramanujan, A.K. 2005. "Self-Portrait". In: Margaret Ferguson, Mary Jo Salter and Jon Stallworthy (eds.). *The Norton Anthology of Poetry*. New York: Norton. 1803.

Rappaport, Helen. 2003. *Queen Victoria: A Biographical Companion*. Santa Barbara: ABC-CLIO.

Rayney, Lawrence S. 1998. *Institutions of Modernism: Literary Elites and Public Culture*. London: Yale University Press.

Reed, Henry. 2005. "Chard Whitlow". In: Margaret Ferguson, Mary Jo Salter and Jon Stallworthy (eds.). *The Norton Anthology of Poetry*. New York: Norton. 1563–1564.

Richards, I.A. 1926. "Gerard Hopkins". *The Dial* 81.3: 195–203.

Rowland, Antony. 2001. *Tony Harrison and the Holocaust*. Liverpool: Liverpool University Press.

Schuchard, Ronald. 2011. "T. S. Eliot and Ted Hughes: Shamanic Possession". *South Atlantic Review* 76.3: 51–73.

Shklovsky, Victor. 1965. "Art as Technique". In: Lee T. Lemon and Marion J. Reis (eds.). *Russian Formalist Criticism: Four Essays*. Lincoln: University of Nebraska Press. 3–24.

Smith, Stan. 2003. "'What like is it?': Duffy's *Différance*". In: Angelica Michelis and Antony Rowland (eds.). *Choosing Tough Words: The Poetry of Carol Ann Duffy*. Manchester: Manchester University Press. 143–168.

Thomas, Dylan. 2005a. "The Force That Through the Green Fuse Drives the Flower". In: Margaret Ferguson, Mary Jo Salter and Jon Stallworthy (eds.). *The Norton Anthology of Poetry*. New York: Norton. 1566–1567.

Thomas, Dylan. 2005b. "In My Craft or Sullen Art". In: Margaret Ferguson, Mary Jo Salter, and Jon Stallworthy (eds.). *The Norton Anthology of Poetry*. New York: Norton. 1572.

Thomas, M. Wynn. 2013. *R.S. Thomas: Serial Obsessive*. Cardiff: University of Wales Press.

Thomas, R. S. 2005. "The View from the Window". In: Margaret Ferguson, Mary Jo Salter, and Jon Stallworthy (eds.). *The Norton Anthology of Poetry*. New York: Norton. 1544–1545.

Trilling, Lionel, and Harold Bloom (eds.). 1973. *Victorian Poetry and Prose. The Oxford Anthology of English Literature*. New York: Oxford University Press.

Walcott, Derek. 2005. "A Far Cry from Africa". In: Margaret Ferguson, Mary Jo Salter, and Jon Stallworthy (eds.). *The Norton Anthology of Poetry*. New York: Norton. 1820.

Wald, Alan M. 2002. *Exiles from a Future: The Forging of the Mid-Century Literary Left*. Chapel Hill: University of North Carolina Press.

Welsch, Wolfgang. 2009. *Unsere postmoderne Moderne*. Berlin: Akademie Verlag.

Wollaeger, Mark, and Matt Eatough (eds.). 2012. *The Oxford Handbook of Global Modernisms*. Oxford: Oxford University Press.

Worley, Matthew. 2013. "Communism and Fascism in 1920s and 1930s Britain". In: Tony Sharpe (ed.). *Auden in Context*. Cambridge: Cambridge University Press. 141–149.

Patrick Gill
"Now it's failed": The Sonnet Form in the Poetry of Philip Larkin

Abstract: While the sonnet may commonly be associated with particular literary periods such as the Renaissance or English Romanticism, few would think of the mid-twentieth century's Movement as a school with a pronounced affinity for this poetic form. After all, the Movement is generally associated with a sceptical empiricism and a degree of pessimism that does not seem to be overly compatible with the sonnet form. This essay investigates the way Philip Larkin's sonneteering developed, from late in the 1930s into the 1970s, and how it relates to his other poetry. Paying particular attention to Larkin's constant undermining of those structural properties that give the sonnet a positive and constructive outlook, the essay argues that from his earliest experiments with the form, Larkin's sonnet-writing was instrumental in developing his distinctive poetic voice.

Keywords: sonnet, Philip Larkin, Movement, pessimism, closure

Asked to suggest a list of prominent English sonneteers, few critics would be entirely in agreement, and yet some poets would probably be mentioned more than others: Thomas Wyatt and Henry Howard, Earl of Surrey for their pioneering work in introducing the form to England. Sir Philip Sidney and William Shakespeare for the prominence of their sonnet cycles and for their further development of the form as such. John Donne for his poetic innovations in the service of his religious convictions, and Milton as a last farewell to the form before its disappearance throughout most of the eighteenth century. Charlotte Smith for her prominent role in re-establishing the art of the sonneteer as an admirable pursuit, and of course Wordsworth for his further innovations in the form. In the twentieth century, it may well be the poets of the Great War that immediately spring to mind. One name unlikely to feature on many critics' lists, however, would be that of Philip Larkin.

Commonly identified with the mid-twentieth century's Movement, a school of poetry generally associated with "colloquial language as well as an anti-Romantic interest in urban themes" (Rostek 2015: 352), Larkin seems an unlikely champion of the sonnet form. The Movement poets' rejection of the elitist complexity of modernism along with their instinctual distrust of the "inflated romanticism" (Regan 2001: 209) so fashionable in the poetry of the 1940s led to their espousal of virtues such as "Common Sense," "clarity" and "verbal restraint" (ibid.), which suited the post-war reality of 1950s Britain. So did the fact that Larkin saw himself as a workaday pessimist in the tradition of Hardy and Housman rather than identifying with the unapologetic intellectualism of T. S. Eliot or the mystical exuberance of Dylan Thomas. But where Thomas's use of the sonnet could easily be aligned with his idea of poetry as a transformative power, Larkin's less ebullient stance and general pessimism seem at odds with a poetic form in whose very nature it is to ensure that "[e]motional problems [...] may actually be resolved" (Oppenheimer 1989: 3). It is a surprise, then, that the sonnet plays a central role in Larkin's development as a poet. So unlikely does this combination of the bespectacled poet from Hull and the sonnet form seem that it has been given no attention in critical discussions of Larkin's work. Where his sonnets are mentioned at all, they are simply read as instances of his poetry with little or no explicit reference to their use of the sonnet form.

It will be this essay's contention that throughout his career Larkin used the sonnet as a testing ground for his poetry. As his writing developed different nuances, his sonnets always laid the groundwork for his other poetry, foreshadowing the tenor of his published volumes. This is true of the young author of *The North Ship* (1945) as much as of the maturing voice behind *The Less Deceived* (1955) and the increasingly pessimistic poet of *The Whitsun Weddings* (1964). In fact, it is only in the writing of his final volume, *High Windows* (1974) that we see the trend reversed: instead of prefiguring the direction Larkin's poetry takes in that volume, the sonnets mimic the pattern established by the other poems in the book. Beyond the concrete concerns of Larkin's poetry, this case study provides a useful insight into the efficacy of literary form by showing how a poet's consistent engagement with a genre interested in productive and by and large optimistic outcomes helped him hone his skills in producing some of the most despondent and pessimistic English poetry of the twentieth century.

Rather than engaging with the various permutations of rhyme schemes and metrical patterns the sonnet has undergone in its long history, the primary objective of the present essay will be a delineation of Larkin's use of the modality, the logical progression and strategies, inherent in this "structured and argumentative form" (Müller-Wood 2015: 56). Oppenheimer, postulating that the sonnet is "the first lyric of self-consciousness, or of the self in conflict" (1989: 3), implicitly describes one of its most basic attributes: its dualistic conception. As Fuller explains: "The essence of the sonnet's form is the unequal relationship between octave and sestet. [...] This bipartite structure is one of observation and conclusion, or statement and counter-statement"

(1972: 2). And as Jost extrapolates from his observations on the work of a famous sonneteer:

> While Petrarch's samples illustrate the validity of various patterns, without constituting an exhaustive inventory for all time, they do establish the essential generic rules. Petrarch intended that the sonnet comprise fourteen lines. [...] These fourteen lines must be divided into two distinct portions which form two groups or systems of equal weight but unequal length. (1982: 228)

In terms of its argumentative structure, the sonnet utilises these two systems in order to represent "either a logical or a psychological division of the topic" (Jost 1982: 228), but this division is far from unbridgeable. It is much rather aimed at achieving some form of resolution between conflicting ideas or emotions (cf. Schlütter 1979: 9–10). This sense of closure offered by the sonnet is perhaps best summarised in the use of the closing couplet in English specimens of the form.

The present essay will continue to assess these two aspects of the argumentative strategy inherent in the sonnet form and how they are dealt with specifically in the sonnets of Philip Larkin: the representation of two distinct and separate systems of thought or argument and the capacity to offer however provisional a resolution of the conflict between them. Any poem that wants to make maximum use of the communicative efficacy of the sonnet form will have to employ these two basic tenets. That is not to say that it will of necessity have to adhere to them in the sense of a strict set of rules. In this regard, what Heather Dubrow says about the Petrarchan tradition in English poetry when she calls Petrarchism "the basso continuo against which arias in different styles and genres are sung" (1995: 7) is true of the sonnet in much more general terms as well: its form is effective in communicating even if not all the traditional expectations are met. Or rather, it is particularly effective where it deviates from standard expectations.

When Larkin's *Collected Poems* was published in 1988, editor Anthony Thwaite included twenty-four sonnets, eleven of which had remained unpublished throughout Larkin's life. Of the remaining thirteen, only eight had been printed in Larkin's original collections; and of these eight, five had appeared in Larkin's very first volume, *The North Ship* (1945). Thwaite's decision not to arrange the poems into clearly identifiable sections of previously published and unpublished material was vociferously attacked by Martin Amis in an extensive discussion of Larkin's posthumous reception published in the *New Yorker*:

> So instead of the three volumes of clearly finished work – *The Less Deceived* (1955), *The Whitsun Weddings* (1964), and *High Windows* (1974) – with all the other stuff tucked away at the back, we get a looser and more promiscuous corpus, containing squibs and snippets,

rambling failures later abandoned, lecherous doggerel, and confessional curiosities [...] (2001: 154)

The publication of Larkin's *Complete Poems*, edited by Archie Burnett,[1] in 2012 may not have been to Martin Amis's liking either. The latter seems generally biased against an inclusive editorial policy when he reminds his readers that "Larkin left a lot of good things out. His oeuvre (like his taste) was narrow, but it was crystallized" (Amis 2001: 154). Burnett's edition contains a total of thirty-two sonnets, nineteen of which were never published in Larkin's lifetime. By including these previously unpublished sonnets, Burnett's volume finally provides a reliable basis for an analysis of Larkin's use of the form and the impact it had on his career from the 1930s to the 1970s.

The most obviously remarkable aspect regarding Larkin's sonnets of the late 1930s and the 1940s is their sheer number. Between December 1938 and May 1949, Larkin wrote twenty-three of the total of thirty-two sonnets printed in Burnett's *Complete Poems*. Thwaite argues that "the earliest poems which strike [Larkin's] characteristic note and carry his own voice were written in 1946" (1988: xv). It thus seems a reasonable assertion that a significant portion of Larkin's sonnets were composed at a time when the poet was still finding his voice. There are two simple indicators of this: first of all, it is not difficult to see that some of Larkin's earlier sonnets appear highly derivative of other poets. Regan, for instance, remarks that Larkin "deftly catches Eliot's nocturnal landscapes" (2007: 148) in the sonnet "Street Lamps" of 1939 (Larkin 2012: 100). In contrast to this, "Flesh to flesh was loving from the start" of 1942 (Larkin 2012: 208–209) carries echoes of the poetry of the neo-romantic school of the New Apocalypse. The second, and perhaps more relevant indicator of Larkin's uncertainty regarding the direction his poetry was to develop in is to be found in his handling of the stanzaic organisation of his sonnets. Throughout the 1940s, Larkin's sonnets display a penchant for deviations from the standard formula of octave and sestet or quatrains and couplet. Of the twenty-three sonnets written in the 1930s and 40s, seven make a point of avoiding the traditional allocation of stanzas, opting instead for ostentatiously deviant forms such as the combination of septet, tercet, and quatrain in "Ultimatum" or the seven and a half lines followed by six and a half lines in "Unexpectedly the scene attained." As these experiments constitute less than a third of Larkin's sonnet output at the time, they may not seem overly relevant at first. However, taking into account the poems published in Larkin's lifetime,

---

[1] All dates given for the composition of poems are taken from Burnett's commentary in *The Complete Poems*.

an entirely different picture presents itself: of the seven sonnets experimenting with the allocation of lines that Larkin wrote in the 1930s and 1940s, he decided to publish six. Of the sixteen sonnets employing traditional sonnet stanzas, only four were published during the poet's life.

What the use of irregular stanzas offers the young Larkin is a means of signalling both the presence of standard expectations of the sonnet and an absence of complete adherence to them. Oddly numbered stanzas or isolated single lines remind the reader that there is a form to be considered while also indicating that the present sonnet deviates from that form. As a discussion of three of his early sonnets will show, the young Larkin used that tension most effectively to impede the sonnet's progress towards closure. Composed in September 1939, shortly after Larkin's seventeenth birthday, "Street Lamps" (Larkin 2012: 100) presents an urban evening scene. While the first portion of the sonnet is concerned with what regularly occurs in the time from dusk ("[w]hen night slinks, like a puma, down the sky") to dawn ("[u]ntil grey planes splinter the gloom at last"), the second portion describes a singular event the speaker witnessed "once:" a street lamp refusing to go out at the appointed time. The turning point between these two clearly separate portions is to be found in line nine, but rather than occurring at the beginning of the line, it falls into the middle of the line, which is then divided and set apart, so that the poem appears in the guise of eight and a half lines followed by five and a half lines. This is clearly done in aid of demarcating the transition between portion one (night, regularity, present tense) and portion two (morning, singular event, past tense), so even if it results in an unorthodox stanzaic organisation, it is done in order to emphasise a central component of the sonnet: its division "into two distinct portions which form two groups or systems of equal weight but unequal length" (Jost 1982: 228). Another central aspect, the sonnet's capacity to offer a resolution – however provisional – of the conflict between the two portions, is tested by "Street Lamps." The singular street lamp that "[v]ied the blue sky, and tried to rival it," that is, continued to glow after dawn, is implicitly shown to have failed when it "[t]ried to cast shadows contrary to the sun." No resolution or compromise is possible: the street lamp may try to continue casting light after dawn, but its efforts are futile when compared to the power of sky and sun.

A similar conceit of light and dark is also at work in the sonnet beginning "This was your place of birth, this daytime place" first published in 1942 and later printed as "II" in Larkin's first collection, *The North Ship* of 1945 (Larkin 2012: 6). As in "Street Lamps," the fact that the poem deals with diametrically opposed phenomena ("night"/"day") makes it easy to distinguish the two separate portions it consists of: a closing sestet concerned with "what the night will bring," and an opening stanza constructed around words such as "daytime," "glass," "light," and "sunbeams." However, said opening stanza ends after seven lines and is followed by an isolated line that serves as a transitional stage between day and night: "The clouds cast moving shadows on the land." So once more the division into distinct portions is emphasised by the unusual typesetting – but what does the poem offer in terms of a sense of closure? As in "Street Lamps," the young Larkin seems reticent to leave the reader with too conclusive a final statement, phrasing the entire closing sestet in the form of a series of questions:

> Are you prepared for what the night will bring?
> The stranger who will never show his face,
> But asks admittance; will you greet your doom
> As final; set him loaves and wine; knowing
> The game is finished when he plays his ace,
> And overturn the table and go into the next room?

An ostensibly more orthodox sonnet begun by Larkin in March 1940 is "Nothing significant was really said" (Larkin 2012: 178). This remained unpublished throughout Larkin's life but is rather typical of his early sonnets in that it also avoids the conveyance of a sense of closure. The most significant difference seems to be that the two arguments or stances on display are not kept entirely separate. The poem is concerned with the individual as private person and public persona. It describes a public speech given by a "brilliant freshman" much admired by the audience and contrasts this triumphant public appearance with the freshman's more private expressions of self-doubt. The division into separate portions is undermined in this sonnet, as the witness to the freshman's private unhappiness in the sestet ("remembered how / He'd found the genius crying when alone") is already introduced at the moment of the freshman's greatest triumph in the octave ("All but one declared his future great"). In terms of its lack of closure, "Nothing significant was really said" is in line with the other two sonnets of the 1930s and 40s discussed here, as it again ends on a question. But it is telling that the clear-cut separation into distinct arguments is undermined in Larkin's sonnets of this period as soon as he relinquishes his stanzaic tricks (half lines, isolated transitional lines) and adheres to traditional sonnet stanzas. This is a feature of Larkin's sonneteering that will resurface in the 1950s. What is most noticeable, though, is Larkin's disinclination to end his sonnets with any sense of closure or finality, instead ending them in questions, uncertainty or alternative choices.

Larkin's sonnets of the 1930s and 40s can be seen spanning the development from dutiful imitation to youthful experiment and a gradual awareness of the potential and limitations of the form. Given that the sonnet is preoccupied with ideas of logical progression and conflict, the mass of sonnets Larkin wrote between December 1938 and May 1949 is not just a sign of vernal prolificacy but of a need to test the waters of poetic form and readerly expectation on the part of the young Larkin. The true impact of Larkin's youthful experiments with the sonnet form would be felt much more keenly from the 1950s, particularly with the publication of *The Less Deceived* (1955). A closer consideration of the poems collected in that volume shows that many of them display the same predilection as Larkin's sonnets of the 1940s, particularly a tendency towards inconclusive endings, such as four poems ending in question marks, as well as closing lines such as "Not to prevent it is my will's fulfilment. / Willing it, my ailment" ("No Road" 34) or "Nothing, like something, happens anywhere" ("I Remember, I Remember" 41–42). And although these poems seem to have little in common with the sonnet, they tend to pose a problem and then resist univocal resolution, a skill Larkin honed in the 1940s when he first took up a poetic form ostensibly defined by its drive towards accommodation and closure.

The quantitative contrast between Larkin's career as a writer of sonnets in the 1940s and in the 1950s is stark. While the 1940s clearly marked his most productive period as a sonneteer, the 1950s saw him produce a grand total of only three sonnets. While they engage with radically different topics, they all follow a logical pattern which does not only stop short of providing closure as Larkin's earlier sonnets do, but instead drags the speaker into utter despair as he comes to recognise that his situation at the end of the poem is categorically worse than he suspected at its beginning.

"Autobiography at an Air-Station" of winter 1953 (Larkin 2012: 286) is a poem concerned with boredom and disappointment in the context of an unremarkable everyday experience. The poem is typographically divided into two stanzas: in the octave, the speaker surveys a group of passengers waiting for their delayed flight. The very first word of the poem, "Delay," which is repeated at the beginning of the second line, can be taken as programmatic of the goings-on presented in most of the octave: uncertain of the extent of this delay, "We," the waiting passengers, "amble to and fro, / Sit in steel chairs, buy cigarettes and sweets." This is a portrayal of a group of people united by a common fate. In the sestet, the pronoun "We" is replaced by "I," repeated four times in the space of six lines. What separates the two systems, then, seems to be clear: while the octave is concerned with a group of people, a community of travellers, the sestet focuses on the fate of a single person, the speaker. However, this clear-cut division into separate systems is undermined by the closing lines of the octave, when the speaker asks "Ought we to smile, / Perhaps make friends?" and comes to the conclusion that "in the race for seats / You're best alone. Friendship is not worth while." The idea of isolation is already present in the octave. The fact that it is also a predominant concern of the sestet means that the extent to which the two systems are indeed separated may not be in line with readerly expectations. Neither is the hope of some kind of resolution fulfilled in the sestet. Its second line may include a sentence sounding like acceptance, as the speaker considers that "if [he]'d gone by boat last night / [He]'d be there now." But his admission that "it's too late for that" underscores the perceived hopelessness of his situation, and his outlook rapidly deteriorates in the final lines of the poem, as he feels "[s]tupefied, by inaction – and [...] by fear." The real extent of his distress is only revealed in the closing statement of this sonnet: "I set / So much on this Assumption. Now it's failed." That this is far from "a resolution in the abiding peace of the soul itself" (Oppenheimer 1989: 3) is unmistakably expressed by the succinct sentence "Now it's failed," which offers very little leeway to any attempt at wresting something positive or conciliatory from the poem, especially as the title seems to suggest that this experience of fear, boredom, and failure is mirrored in the speaker's entire life.

While it may differ in its stanzaic structure from "Autobiography" in that its closing lines are arranged in two tercets, "Spring" (Larkin 2012: 40) follows a similar argumentative arc of a bad situation growing successively worse. As in "Autobiography," the octave starts with observations of a community of people, although this time it is concerned with people in a park rather than with frustrated air passengers: "The scene depicted in the first six lines is a confusion of humanity, artifacts, and nature; of young, old, animal, tree, cloud," Lolette Kuby states. "Propelled by verbals: 'set,' 'awakened,' 'sings,' 'flashing,' one image follows another with the speed of a kaleidoscope" (1974: 59). But as she points out, her comments concerning the lively scene depicted here are only applicable to the first six lines of the octave. The prepenultimate line already introduces a clear dichotomy by juxtaposing the previously mentioned "people," "children," "bird," "balls," and "dogs" with someone entirely out of place in this careless setting: "and me." In the line concluding what one would have expected to be a single, homogenous statement, the person of the speaker is described as "[a]n indigestible sterility," which expresses beyond doubt that the speaker's person cannot be accommodated by this scene. Apart from its univocal semantics, this line also stands out visually since the polysyllabic nature of "indigestible" and "sterility" means that the line's ten syllables take up significantly less space than those of any other line in the poem.

What follows in the two tercets is not a separate argument or train of thought, but a repetition of the contrast expressed in the octave. The first tercet is written in praise of spring and particularly in praise of spring's overwhelming fecundity. The second tercet turns again to the speaker and by extension to others like him who are equally incompatible with the season of "untaught flower" and "race of water." But instead of simply not belonging, their position is made even more unbearable in that they are described as those spring "has least use for" even though they "see her best." The lonely are thus described not just as having no active part in the lively spring scenery – they are seen as most aware of the beauty they are forever separated from. The tercets thus re-enact the conflict of the octave rather than resolving it and lead the reader to realise that the speaker's position is categorically more hopeless and isolated than expected.

The lack of separation of the two systems in Larkin's use of the sonnet form in the 1950s is consistent with his use of the same technique throughout the 1940s, but the outcomes he pursues are somewhat different: whereas in his sonnets of the 1940s the aim was to frustrate readerly expectations by not providing any conclusive outlook or verdict at the end, his sonnets of the 1950s cultivate not just a sense of paralysis or indecision but the "tenderly nursed sense of defeat" (Tomlinson 1957: 214) often associated with Larkin's poetry in general, and they do so against the conventions and expectations of what it is a sonnet is supposed to do. What should be a solution to a problem, or at least a working compromise, leaves the reader realising that no matter how badly things start, they can always get much worse.

Written in 1950, "Spring" is included in Larkin's 1955 collection *The Less Deceived*, and so it might seem reasonable to assume that Larkin's use of the sonnet form in that particular instance has a strong bearing on the poems in that volume. In actual fact, his use of the sonnet at this stage of his career tends to be one step ahead of his general poetic development, and so – rather than being seen in the context of *The Less Deceived* – "Spring" can be seen as a sign of things to come in Larkin's next volume, *The Whitsun Weddings* (1964). In very general terms, the poems collected in that volume are far less interested in the feelings of individual stasis as portrayed in *The Less Deceived* than in arcs or spirals of rapid deterioration. It may seem strange to link "Spring" with *The Whitsun Weddings*, not least because that volume does not include any sonnets whatsoever, but the structural parallel with a number of shorter poems taking the reader from an inauspicious premise to a conclusion far worse than was at first expected is noticeable. "Talking in Bed" (Larkin 2012: 61), "Take One Home for the Kiddies" (Larkin 2012: 59) and "Nothing to Be Said" (Larkin 2012: 50f.) perform the same argumentative sleight of hand on a similar scale, while a number of longer poems such as "Ambulances" (Larkin 2012: 63–64) and "An Arundel Tomb" (Larkin 2012: 71–72) avail themselves of a similar strategy for their endings.

Between the writing of "Autobiography at an Air-Station" in 1953 and the publication of *The Whitsun Weddings*, Larkin wrote another three sonnets that remained unpublished throughout his lifetime: "Hotter shorter days arrive, like happiness" (Larkin 2012: 301), "And now the leaves suddenly lose strength" (Larkin 2012: 301), and "January" (Larkin 2012: 302). These were all composed in a single cluster extending from October 1961 to January 1962. It would be idle to speculate why Larkin chose not to publish any of these three sonnets, but it is conspicuous that they all repeat certain strategies the reader of Larkin's poetry would already be familiar with, both in form and content. The next – and almost final – two sonnets Larkin composed do not repeat the themes of the turning of the seasons and aging, they do not work with half-lines to mark turning points, nor do they end in final statements driving home the rapid deterioration the speaker has undergone in the course of each poem. Instead of evoking the image of their speaker caught in an ever-diminishing space of individual hope and agency, these two sonnets open up vistas far beyond the speaker's immediate surroundings, and are thus clear deviations from Larkin's carefully crafted standard recipe. In terms of their dates of composition, it is conspicuous that they do not predate poems of similar design in the same volume, as was the case in all previous collections in Larkin's poetry. Instead, they follow other poems included in the volume in introducing enigmatic closing statements.

Written in 1970, "The Card-Players" (Larkin 2012: 84) is an ekphrastic poem based on a generic idea of a scene popularised by Dutch and Flemish painters of the seventeenth century: a group of men sitting around a table at an inn, playing cards, smoking, and drinking. Larkin's tone here is irreverent, as he gives the figures in his scene humorously Dutch-sounding names like "Jan van Hogspeuw" and "Dirk Dogstoerd." His main preoccupation seems to be with the depravity of these men as they urinate, "snore," "fart," and "gob" to their hearts' content. Any search for a clear-cut dichotomy or conflict in "The Card-Players" will soon settle on the apparent contrasts between the interior of the inn, in which the men enjoy each other's coarse company, and the outside world, which is described in terms of inclement weather. But all the elements represented by the weather ("rain," "mud," "gale") are also to be found inside, so that the relative comfort of the inn seems to hide its inherent kinship or comparability with the forces of nature raging outside. As far as the division into separate ideas is concerned, then, "The Card-Players" offers no clear-cut division. And after following what looks like a fairly traditional stanzaic organisation, it ends in an isolated closing line whose exact relation to what has come before is not entirely clear, given that it consists solely of exclamations rather than syntactically complete sentences: "Rain, wind and fire! The secret, bestial peace!" As in the poem itself, the two exclamations could form a contrasting pair where one represents external nature and the other the relative comfort of the inn, or they could be seen as belonging to a unified statement encompassing both internal and external scenes. In fact, the apparent disconnectedness of the line from the rest of the poem in syntactical, stylistic, and prosodic terms leaves it open to a variety of interpretations not previously encountered in Larkin's sonnets, which thus far tended either to achieve a univocally depressing ending or to leave the reader suspended between two clearly outlined ideas.

"Friday Night in the Royal Station Hotel" (Larkin 2012: 80–81) was written in 1966 and is also concerned with presenting a scene in a type of hostelry, but its closing statement is an even more enigmatic turn towards an expansive external reality. While the description of the scene in "The Card-Players" is enlivened by the presence of the rowdy drinkers, here the establishment is first and foremost distinguished by its emptiness: "empty chairs," "larger loneliness," "silence laid like carpet." The few figures who are mentioned by name are either static ("A porter reads / An unsold evening paper") or absent ("all the salesmen have gone back to Leeds"), and there is not even an "I," so that the empty building becomes the real subject of the poem. The two typographically marked portions of the sonnet consist of the first nine lines on the one hand and the concluding five lines on the other, although it is difficult to discern any striking difference between the two as far as theme or argument is concerned. What does stand out is the last line, or rather, the last line and the last word of the penultimate line: "*Now / Night comes on. Waves fold behind villages.*" Since the italics these words appear in indicate that they are what is written in the "letters of exile" mentioned before the colon introduces the final statement, they have to be read as a quote and can be understood as a turning inwards, a narrow focus on a particular. Given their content, however, these words seem to transcend the immediate world of the hotel and to open up vistas far beyond the building.

Both "The Card-Players" and "Friday Night in the Royal Station Hotel" were included in Larkin's final volume *High Windows* (1974). The poems contained in the volume were written between 1965 and 1974, and they comprise many different lengths, forms and styles. In terms of their ideas of logical or argumentative progression and the conclusions arrived at in their closing statements, several distinct groups of poems are discernible in the volume. However, it is the poems that take the persona through a concrete problem or situation almost banal in its everyday specificity, only to end in a highly symbolic and necessarily multivalent closing statement transcending the immediate horizons of the speaker, that are most characteristic of *High Windows* as they have no precedent elsewhere in Larkin's collections. The poem "Money" (Larkin 2012: 94) is one such example, as is "High Windows" (Larkin 2012: 80), the volume's title poem. In that poem, written in 1965 (and immediately followed by "Friday Night in the Royal Station Hotel" in the collection), Larkin explores his persona's jealousy of the sexual liberation of a younger generation. Observing those younger than him, he becomes aware of his jealousy, and then imagines what those older than him would have thought observing his behaviour in turn. The reaction to this ongoing battle of the generations is that of a multivalent image springing into the speaker's mind:

> Rather than words comes the thought of high windows:
> The sun-comprehending glass,
> And beyond it, the deep blue air, that shows
> Nothing, and is nowhere, and is endless.

This is the poetic voice also reflected in "The Card-Players" and "Friday Night in the Royal Station Hotel." And here, for the first time in the unfolding of Larkin's career, we can see the sonnets following rather than presaging the poetic trend as "High Windows" was written in March 1965 and "Friday Night in the Royal Station Hotel" in the following spring.

In the course of developing his trademark style, Philip Larkin intermittently engaged with the sonnet form. As a budding poet about to embark on a thirty-year career, the young Larkin produced a wealth of sonnets, few of which were published during his lifetime. But what even that early engagement with the sonnet form demonstrates is that Larkin was reluctant to follow the sonnet's tendency to produce neat outcomes. From the start, Larkin engaged with the logical structure of the sonnet by experimenting with the usual separation of two distinct arguments or perspectives and the sense of closure that is such a prominent feature of the form. By choosing this of all forms, he had to actively strain against not only the sonnet's most prominent structural features but also against the readerly expectations they engender in order to thwart the sonnet's drive towards resolution.

The first avenue he explored in order to counter the sonnet's tendency to resolve conflicts was to bring about uncertain outcomes. This produced a poetry "suspicious of its own claims, resisting its own rhetorical persuasiveness" (Swarbrick 1995: 2). The five sonnets he produced between 1949 and 1953 convert the sonnet as an expression of uncertainty, stasis, and doubt into a vehicle of deep pessimism: univocal conclusions await the reader at the end of the argumentative downward spiral Larkin's sonnets of that period inevitably form. And as this use of the sonnet form takes hold, it leaves its traces on the rest of Larkin's poetry, particularly on those poems collected in *The Whitsun Weddings*. The final stage of Larkin's sonneteering is the one that occurs between 1965 and 1974. The few resulting sonnets continue Larkin's experiments with the lack of differentiation between opposing stances or arguments, and when it comes to their closing lines, they inherit a new multivalence from earlier poems collected in *High Windows*.

Asked in an interview with Ian Hamilton in 1964 which poets he admired, Larkin expressed a clear preference for "people to whom technique seems to matter less than content, people who accept the forms they have inherited but use them to express their own content" (Larkin 2001: 19). What all of Larkin's experiments with the inherited form of the sonnet have in common is their primary interest in outcomes, perhaps best illustrated by Larkin's relentless focus on the closing lines of his sonnets. What matters most to Larkin is the impression his readers are left with at the end and the process through which they arrive at that impression. For maximum impact, Larkin can make use of the sonnet form to evoke a set of expectations in the reader that can in turn be used for effective communication by the poet. A sonnet that does not end with a satisfactory sense of accommodation is thus not in breach of some supposed set of rules – it simply draws particular attention to its lack of resolution. This is the spirit in which Larkin makes even his earlier sonnets "express [his] own content," and it is what makes them interesting reading in and of themselves. What the present essay has suggested, however, is that they not be seen in isolation but as testament to Larkin's continuous poetic development.

Works Cited

Amis, Martin. 2001. *The War Against Cliché: Essays and Reviews 1971–2000*. London: Cape.
Dubrow, Heather. 1995. *Echoes of Desire: English Petrarchism and Its Counter-discourses*. Ithaca: Cornell University Press.
Fuller, John. 1972. *The Sonnet*. The Critical Idiom 26. London: Methuen.
Jost, François. 1982. "Anatomy of an Ode: Shelley and the Sonnet Tradition". *Comparative Literature* 34.3: 223–246.
Kuby, Lolette. 1974. *An Uncommon Poet for the Common Man: A Study of Philip Larkin's Poetry*. Paris: Mouton.
Larkin, Philip. 1988. *Collected Poems*. Ed. Anthony Thwaite. London: Faber & Faber.
Larkin, Philip. 2001. *Further Requirements: Interviews, Broadcasts, Statements and Book Reviews 1952–85*. Ed. Anthony Thwaite. London: Faber & Faber.
Larkin, Philip. 2012. *Complete Poems*. Ed. Archie Burnett. London: Faber & Faber.
Müller-Wood, Anja. 2015. "English Poetry in the Sixteenth Century: Sir Thomas Wyatt, Henry Howard, Earl of Surrey, Anne Locke and the Petrarchan Sonnet Tradition". In: Sibylle Baumbach, Birgit Neumann, and Ansgar Nünning (eds.). *A History of British Poetry: Genres, Developments, Interpretations*. Trier: WVT. 55–65.
Oppenheimer, Paul. 1989. *The Birth of the Modern Mind: Self, Consciousness, and the Invention of the Sonnet*. Oxford: Oxford University Press.

Regan, Stephen. 2001. "The Movement". In: Neil Roberts (ed.). *A Companion to Twentieth-Century Poetry*. Oxford: Blackwell. 209–219.
Regan, Stephen. 2007. "Philip Larkin: A Late Modern Poet". In: Neil Corcoran (ed.). *The Cambridge Companion to Twentieth-Century English Poetry*. Cambridge: Cambridge University Press. 147–158.
Rostek, Joanna. 2015. "Poetry of the Fifties and Sixties Between Innovation and Tradition: Philip Larkin and the Movement". In: Sibylle Baumbach, Birgit Neumann and Ansgar Nünning (eds.). *A History of British Poetry: Genres, Developments, Interpretations*. Trier: WVT. 351–362.
Schlütter, Hans-Jürgen. 1979. *Sonett: Mit Beiträgen von Raimund Borgmeier und Heinz Willi Wittschier*. Stuttgart: Metzler.
Swarbrick, Andrew. 1995. *Out of Reach: The Poetry of Philip Larkin*. Basingstoke: Macmillan.
Tomlinson, Charles. 1957. "The Middlebrow Muse". *Essays in Criticism* 7.2: 208–217.

The Politics of Genre

Pierre-Héli Monot
Possibilities, Responsibilities: On Poetic Genres and Political Poiesis

Abstract: This essay discusses the recent renewal of interest in the political works of Cornelius Castoriadis (1922–1997) and in the poetic works of George Oppen (1908–1984). While Castoriadis produced one of the earliest substantial critiques of the emergence of a bureaucratic class under Stalinism and developed a theory of democracy as the production of political autonomy, George Oppen worked for the Communist Party USA for a quarter of a century, during which time he did not write any poetry. This essay discusses the implications of Oppen's return to poetry in the mid-1960s and suggests that the Whitmanian accents of his mature work presuppose a renewed consideration of the political possibilities of traditionalism in democratic societies. While academic discussions of poetic genres have often voided cultural history of its precarious relation to contextuality and practical ends, Oppen and Castoriadis both suggest that instituted poetic genres fulfill the crucial function of elaborating and clarifying the public deliberations of democratic societies.

Keywords: Cornelius Castoriadis, George Oppen, Walt Whitman, democracy, autonomy

1 Paideia, *humanitas*, "The People": The Genres of Political Community

> How curious! How real!
>
> (Walt Whitman, *Poetry and Prose* 176)

In his later essays, Cornelius Castoriadis frequently expounds on the idea that liberal, globalized capitalism remains dependent upon a number of cultural and political institutions and dispositions it cannot itself produce. Castoriadis speaks of these institutions and dispositions as "deposits" ("gisements") that are sedimented by and in history: deposits that are inherited from previous historical configurations and then drawn upon, evaluated, subjected to reasoned inquiry and to imaginative transformation, preserved or discarded by each succeeding era; yet also deposits that have been pillaged by capitalism since it has made the privatized, creative-destructive citizen its sole officially sanctified anthropological norm. Castoriadis takes the example of modern, European societies:

> The institutions in these societies include a strong democratic *component*. But the latter has not been engendered by human nature or granted by capitalism or necessarily entailed by capitalism's development. The democratic component is there as residual result, as the sedimentation of struggles and of a history that have gone on for several centuries. Among these institutions, the most important one is the anthropological type of the European *citizen*: a historical creation of a type of individual, unknown elsewhere, who can put into question the already instituted and generally religious representation of the world, who can contest existing authority, think that the law is unjust and say so, and who is willing and able to act to change the law and to participate in the determination of his or her own fate. This is what is, par excellence, not exportable, what cannot appear from one day to the next in another culture whose instituted anthropological presuppositions are diametrically opposed.[1]

These deposits, "anthropological types" ranging from the "upstanding Weberian civil servant" to "workers with at least a minimum of conscientiousness about their work" (1996: 79), rely on instituted and incorporated values that affirm and point towards a not-yet-achieved democracy that is deliberative, direct, and the object of both collective and individual responsibility. Here, Castoriadis is implicitly commenting upon Marx's and Engels's introductory definition of the "bourgeois regime" in the *Communist Manifesto*: "Constant revolutionizing of production, uninterrupted disturbance of all social conditions, everlasting uncertainty and agitation distinguish the bourgeois epoch from all earlier ones. All fixed, fast-frozen relations, with their train of ancient and venerable prejudices and opinions, are swept away, all new-formed ones become antiquated before they can ossify" (Marx and Engels 2012: 38). Where liberal capitalism posits personal interest both as its metaphysics and as its anthropological narrative, and always tends to its own de-historicization (notably through the affirmation of perennial Economic Laws), democracy, in Castoriadis's view, posits a high degree of historical self-consciousness: "Democracy is the self-institution of the collectivity by the collectivity, and it is this self-institution as *movement*" (79). Consequently, the kind of democracy propounded by Castoriadis rests on the transmission of an open set of political and cultural possibles instituted by a historically reflexive society, as well as on the transmission of historically constituted abilities and attitudes that allow this transmission itself to become the object of reflexive, deliberative democratic processes.

---

[1] The present translations are the work of a dedicated anonymous translator, offered online "as a public service in the hopes of encouraging reflection and action aimed at deepening, and realizing, the project of individual and collective autonomy on a worldwide basis in all its manifestations." The translation is accessible at <http://www.notbored.org/RTI.pdf>. The original is included in Castoriadis 1986: 134.

This, then, outlines one of the paradoxes of the institutional dimension of democratic reflexivity: the assessment and critique of the instituted schemes at work in a democratic society is predicated upon reflexive abilities that are instituted by this democratic society itself, notably through the collective task of education and its corresponding, specialized institutions (cf. Castoriadis 1999: 252–254). For all its obvious limitations, notably its neglect of heterosystemic or non-institutional forms of critique, Castoriadis's model mirrors the contingency, acknowledged and sanctioned by the pedagogues of Classical Antiquity, of the educational ideals of Ancient Greek παιδεία. As Werner Jaeger pointed out, participation in a deliberative democracy rested on the transmission of a set of abilities – analytical and rhetorical – that called a "universally valid model of humanity" into play, yet one that, crucially, had assimilated "every stage of its history and intellectual development" (1946: xxiv). Because it emerged out of a cultural move towards historical self-reflexivity, this anthropological ideal did not exclude the co-existence of its previous stages of development; as such, the universality of these ideals was predicated upon locally, historically and institutionally specific conditions of possibility: for the educator Isocrates, Universal Man was Greek, because the Greeks had predicated universality upon self-reflexivity.

Cicero, commenting on the works of Isocrates, and facing the difficult task of finding a rough equivalent for the political implications and cultural techniques enclosed in the word *paideia*, famously settled for the word *humanitas* as a suitable Latin signifier. Aulus Gellius's discussion of the implications of this translation, or transculturation, is worth quoting at length:

> Those who have spoken Latin and have used the language correctly do not give to the word *humanitas* the meaning which it is commonly thought to have, namely, what the Greeks call φιλανθρωπία ["philanthropy"], signifying a kind of friendly spirit and good-feeling towards all men without distinction; but they gave to *humanitas* about the force of the Greek παιδεία ["*paideia*"]; that is, what we call *eruditionem institutionemque in bonas artes*, or "education and training in the liberal arts." Those who earnestly desire and seek after these are most highly humanized. For the pursuit of that kind of knowledge, and the training given by it, have been granted to man alone of all the animals, and for that reason it is termed *humanitas*, or "humanity". (Gellius 1927: 457)

For Aulus Gellius, *humanitas*, with all its contingency, institutionality and technicity, is essentially a category of cultural politics. The normative image of the well-wrought man, passing its own contingency, institutionality and technicity on to the next generation, in turn secured an attitude towards tradition itself, that is, towards the institutional conditions of possibility of transmission. Plato's own metaphor for the well-wrought man in *The Republic* is that of "moulding" (πλάσις). "Bildung", from Old High German "*bildunga*", i.e. "image", "effigy", "creation", carries similar connotations. "Bildung" is, notably, also Jaeger's own translation of παιδεία into German. Henri Irénée Marrou's classic account of the educational ideals of Ancient Greek *paideia*, overdetermined as it is by the disarray of post-war France, insists on the political and metaphysical consequences of this doubly self-reflexive involution of tradition as culture and transmission: "Free, utterly free, faced by the crumbling walls of his city and abandoned by his gods, faced with a world with no end to it and an empty heaven, Hellenistic man looked vainly for something to belong to, some star to guide his life and his only solution was to turn in upon himself and look there for the principle of all his actions" (1956: 226). This passage has striking similarities with Whitman's poetic definition of American Pragmatism in *Democratic Vistas* – yet Whitman comes to a conclusion that is directly opposed to Marrou's: "How long it takes to make this American world see that it is, in itself, the final authority and reliance!" (Whitman 1982: 956; Rorty 1991: 178).

I understand Castoriadis's discussion of the institutionality of the conditions of possibility of criticism in democratic societies to be derived from Hellenistic pedagogy, and to be a critique of the slight misrepresentation of its consequences by modern, that is, pseudo-democratically socialized, *Altertumswissenschaftler* or classicists such as Marrou. Castoriadis's arguments in favor of a narrowly etymological reading of "democracy" can be understood, *ex negativo*, as a definition of what Castoriadis considers the common political system of contemporary Western societies: "liberal oligarchy" (Castoriadis 1997: 68). The permanence or historical stability of the anthropological types produced by Hellenistic education was something a democratic society could hold on to in spite of the demise of all other referential schemes. These anthropological types acted, to return to Castoriadis's term, as deposits that enable the *demos*, the people, to think about itself in terms of its responsibility for itself. On the scale of individual responsibility, Castoriadis's rephrasing of *paideia* as the crucial epistemic virtue of democratic citizenship echoes Rorty's conception of the "liberal ironist" as the ideal type of the post-Darwinian, post-metaphysical, and democratically attuned thinker: "The ironist spends her time worrying about the possibility that she has been initiated into the wrong tribe, taught to play the wrong language game" (Rorty 1989: 75). Compared to other historical schemes that describe historical transfers in terms of cultural and political continuities (culture, myth, custom), "deposit" is also remarkably literal: Castoriadis suggests, at times explicitly, that the plundering of functionally necessary anthropological types by liberal capitalism is, on the level of its ideological or "imaginary" content (Castoriadis 1987: 146), indistinguishable from the plundering of natural resources prevalent in modern industrialized (and, vicariously, post-industrial) societies, natural resources that are themselves the result of millenary accumulation.

If only in this respect, Castoriadis's critique of liberal capitalism might enable us to reframe the discussion of literary genres as an exercise in democratic "cultural conservationism": Literary forms, understood as cultural deposits, function as rhetorical ecosystems that imply an ethics geared towards their preservation and contestation along the lines of historically informed democratic practices. Indeed, scholars of literary genres and cultural taxonomy have generally failed to note that the contestation of such residual cultural forms has become thoroughly legitimate – almost to the point of exclusivity – as a critical position in the increasingly unified academic fields that deal with cultural history. The legitimacy of *dis-instituting* these sedimented cultural forms has given rise to a circular economy in which critical and academic orthodoxies in turn have become prescriptive in the production of literature: orthodoxies which, given academia's systemic need for "creative destruction," in turn reinstate these systemic needs as aesthetic norms (Schumpeter 2003: 81–86; Waters 2004: 13–41). This circular economy that articulates source material and critical commentary is predicated on the emergence, proliferation and constant renewal of a *Lumpenkommentariat* that only precariously benefits from the institutional or economic conditions of possibility that make institutional criticism viable – a learned class that, in an attempt at a strategic *imitatio prophetae*, at a strategic mimesis with those who more comfortably benefit from these conditions, tends to *introject* its precarious institutional situation, thus voiding cultural history of its own precarious relation to ideology and practical ends, be these ends democratic or not.

Following Castoriadis, we may consequently ask about the ideological conditions that have made the blanket contestation of residual, sedimented cultural forms a viable critical position on a more or less global, more or less transdisciplinary scale. More pointedly, and tentatively extending Castoriadis's notion of historically and locally constituted anthropological types to include their institutionalization or preservation in and as 'culture,' we can discuss the demises of the legitimizing effects of tradition upon cultural forms – 'genres' – in terms of the appearance of scholarly and artistic rationalities, rationalities that posit the contestation of established authority as their sole common denominator *while* neglecting to consider the fragile conditions of possibility, emergence and institutionalization of contestation.

2 On the Poetics of Democracy: George Oppen's "Of Being Numerous"

> One aspect of freedom is being ruled and ruling in turn.
> (Aristotle, *Politics* 1317b1)

Before 'genre' was constituted as an academic question of cultural taxonomy, a poetic genre, the long or lengthy American estuarial democratic poem – a simplistic, yet productive generalization akin to Golding's notion of the "American long poems" (Golding 1999: 86) – constituted itself as a political promise. I would like to suggest that George Oppen's serial poem "Of Being Numerous", included in his eponymous collection published in 1968, may be considered as the most recent major exponent of this poetic genre. As a poem, "Of Being Numerous" makes explicit a few of the alternative positions critics and readers alike may assume in the face of the univocal plundering of "cultural resources" that is symptomatic of the rebellious Adamism prevalent in current literary and cultural studies. As the last member in a relatively short lineage of American poets explicitly concerned with the development of a poetic form *and* of a total social fact – a lineage that includes Walt Whitman, Claude McKay and William Carlos Williams –, Oppen consistently drew upon the tradition of American poetry as one draws upon an idiom, i.e. as a set of aesthetic, philosophical and political possibilities. Whitman, McKay, Williams, and Oppen also appear to be related in a more teleological way, each successive generation making its relationship to socialist or proto-socialist thought both tenser and more explicit. While Whitman's admittance to the pantheon of the labor movement was only made official by his featuring in a British "Calendar of Socialist Saints" of the *fin de siècle*, Claude McKay wrote enthusiastically about the Soviet Union he had visited in 1922–1923, and William Carlos Williams, like Louis-Ferdinand Céline, drew upon his experience as a medical doctor to discuss the humanist dimension of modernism and socialism, and vice versa.[2]

Oppen's relationship to socialist politics was notoriously less ambiguous. After the publication of his first Objectivist collection in 1934, *Discrete Series*, Oppen stopped writing for nearly twenty-five years, dedicating himself to organizational work for the Communist Party USA. After an extended stay in Mexico, where his work as a carpenter shielded him from the increasingly inquisitive interest of the FBI for "his prior and current political commitments

---

[2] On Whitman see Harris 2013; on McKay see Tillery 1993; Cruse 2005: 47–49; on Williams and Céline see Jameson 2007: 51.

and activities," Oppen returned to writing poetry and published three collections of poetry, including *Of Being Numerous* in 1968, for which he was awarded the Pulitzer Prize (cf. Jennison 2012: 69). Oppen was a member of the Communist Party, a poet, and, crucially, never both at the same time.

With "Of being Numerous", Oppen wrote the most conspicuously Whitmanian poem of Late Modernism. Ranging from several explicit references to *Leaves of Grass* to a number of transparent Whitmannerisms (the ebb and flow of generations, the strident brotherliness), Oppen's poem reproduces in form and, to a large extent, in content the great Whitmanian tropes of the 1860s. Oppen remains attached to a number of disreputable, Whitmanian nouns and substantives ("truth", "universe", "happiness") – disreputable because they tended to elicit a particularly defensive and inflexible ontological scepticism from the critics contemporary to Oppen's later poetry, and to some degree still do up to the present day. In his superb study of Oppen's poetry, Michael Heller points to the kind of hesitant realism that makes "Of Being Numerous" a poem irreconcilable with the demands of any doctrinal, systematized thought style. In this, Oppen's opposition to hasty nominalism is akin to Orwell's anxieties about the "falsification" of words into "paraphrases" and of "men" into "chessmen" (Orwell 1968: 76):

> Oppen titles his poem 'Of Being Numerous' and not 'of humanity', because "humanity" is a word that culture has surrounded with communal sentiments, religious, social and political that obscure what the word denotes or points to. Put another way, the poem seeks to discover an actual substance to the word in the face of such loaded or debased terminology [...]. (Heller 2012: 52)

This exercise in terminological criticism can be rephrased, however, as an experiment in political foundationalism, sounding out these nouns as possible foundations upon which a discourse about individuality and community might be established. How is the experiment to be conducted? There are, as I will argue in what follows, two conditions of possibility for this question.

3 Epistemic Hope and Epistemic Humility

> I myself but write one or two indicative words for the future.
> (Walt Whitman, *Poetry and Prose* 175)

A collectivity, Oppen's "people of that flow," is encouraged to resolve its own contradictions by the means – that is, the attitudes in the face of tradition – handed down by three generations of poets engaged in a partly common poetic project.

How this collectivity might come to think of itself in terms of its responsibility *for* itself depends, for Oppen as much as for Whitman or McKay, upon a fundamental recognition both of individual destitution and of individual authority – and in this there lies no contradiction:

> For the people of that flow
> Are new, the old
> New to age as the young
> To youth
>   (Oppen 2008: 164–165)

The paradox is glaring: even though "We have chosen the meaning/Of being numerous" (166), the communal possibilities enclosed in this "meaning" can only be recovered through individual acknowledgement of individual perplexity in the face of the nouns the collectivity has chosen as means to think about itself. As the Genesis Rabbah, arguably one of the covert sources of the poem, puts it, albeit in the mode of a patriarchal lament: "No children, no adults; no adults, no disciples; no disciples, no sages; no sages, no elders; no elders, no prophets" (Freedman and Simon 1961: 342). There are no experts, there are no adults: as Castoriadis points out, deliberative discourse in a democracy is first and foremost doxic and opinion-laden, rather than epistemic. Cornell West has developed a similar argument with respect to the emergence of what he terms a "creative democracy" among early proponents of Pragmatism in the United States: "Emerson's swerve from philosophy [...] was an assertion of the primacy of power-laden people's opinion (*doxa*) over value-free philosopher's knowledge (*episteme*)" (West 1989: 212). Generally speaking, there is no such thing in Castoriadis's organon as a political science geared towards the deployment of concrete democratic practice, for the institution of autonomy by and for the *demos* lacks a referential, metaphysical frame beyond that of the constitutional provisions which, in theory at least, should guarantee the radical indeterminacy of the results of democratic deliberation. This, correlatively, entails the revaluing of literary tradition as the instrument with which the *demos* may hone its discursive, deliberative abilities. In the poem "That Land" from the short cycle "Five Poems about Poetry" (1965), a kind of metapoetic preface to "Of Being Numerous", "the certainties/Of place/And of time" leave man with "No hope of doubt" (Oppen 2008: 102–103). "Of Being Numerous" reverses this proposition, and returns to the theme of individual destitution and individual responsibility:

> We are not coeval
> With a locality
> But we imagine others are
>   (164)

And thus, Oppen suggests, our best "hope of doubt" might consist in the "curiosity" that is the only attitude towards tradition legitimized by tradition itself. Oppen concludes "Of being Numerous" with an extensive quote from a letter of Whitman to his mother (the paragraph break is Oppen's):

> The Capitol grows upon one in time, especially as they have got the great figure on top of it now, and you can see it very well. It is a great bronze figure, the Genius of Liberty I suppose. It looks wonderful toward sundown, I love to go down and look at it. The sun when it is nearly down shines on the headpiece and it dazzles and glistens like a big star, it looks quite
> curious ... (188)

The recovery of curiosity, or epistemic hope, as the horizon of communal participation is both an epistemological project and the attempt at remodeling our attitudes or dispositions towards what Oppen posits – or arguably: fetishizes – as textual material: a cultural deposit. The very first line of the poem is constative, "There are things", followed by a modified quotation from Robert Brumbaugh's *Plato for the Modern World* (1991) (Nicholls 2007: 85):

> There are things
> We live among 'and to see them
> Is to know ourselves.'
>   (Oppen 2008: 163)

Oppen's neo-platonic dictum is constative of the substantiality, or permanence, of the poetic tradition to which "Of Being Numerous" ostensibly seeks to belong. As an ontological and political theorem, however, the opening lines of the poem declare that this poetic tradition only exists when it is *possible* or, in other words, when it can be the object of continuation, contestation, criticism, and elaboration. Oppen's "Of Being Numerous" is commenting on its own democratic conditions of possibility, and previous totalitarian conditions of impossibility (cf. Castoriadis 1999: 252–254). The poem is, for instance, irreconcilable with the demands of the dialectical-materialist "Method" of socialist realism, whose tentacular colonizing of literature and philosophy during Stalinism – the historical and ideological present Oppen was coeval with – later triggered some of the most virulent criticisms of all dogmatic, doctrinal thought styles in modern poetry (Miłosz 1981: 217). In Oppen's case, it resulted in a poetic silence that lasted a quarter of a century. Does the "Intentional Fallacy" decreed by New Criticism (Wimsatt and Beardsley 1946: 468–488), Oppen's academic present, apply to works that do not exist?

4 "Not truth, but each other": On the Function of Literary Genres in Democracy

> Strange that the youngest people I know
> Live in the oldest buildings
>
> (George Oppen, *New Collected Poems* 176)

The recovery of curiosity, or epistemic hope, as the horizon of literary interpretation and political participation entails a reinvigorated sense of responsibility for the literary works that have made this recovery possible. Oppen's constative poem – "there are things" – is also constative of itself, in the sense that it requires of its readers the same kind of attention to the conditions of possibility of poetry as it paid to anterior versions of itself. This self-instituting circularity of poem and tradition is the most clearly patriarchal moment in Oppen's later poetry, although the Whitmanian undertones of the passage in question would possibly vouchsafe a non-gendered reading of "patriarchy" in this specific context, akin to the reading of patriarchal structures in the European juridical tradition propounded by Pierre Legendre (cf. Legendre 1999: 44). Oppen roughly quotes Kierkegaard's "He who will work shall give birth to his own father" (1983: 27; Oppen 2008: 172), and establishes the poetic precedent of Whitman as one that is instituted by the very acts of consideration and continuation.

Thus, Oppen's readers find themselves in a position analogous to that, described by Castoriadis, of the atavistic citizen of capitalist societies who faces exploitation and curiosity as the two irreconcilable attitudes towards the cultural sediments excavated by the production of learned commentary on a quasi-industrial scale. While Castoriadis draws attention to the absolute metaphor of sedimented geological layers in order to think of tradition from the perspective of its long historicity, general contingency and rapid plundering in industrial capitalism, Oppen explicitly rejects the possibility of a return to the other absolute metaphor of the Western scholastic tradition, the Porphyrian tree, as an alternative to the "the great mineral silence" of industrial commentary and its "irrelevant objects" (2008: 178–179): democratic deliberation cannot be articulated by anything other than "rootless speech" (2008: 173), for democracy, understood as an institutional system, remains foundational only insofar as its institutional foundations guarantee the radical indeterminacy of the products of the deliberations it makes possible. In this, Oppen shares with Simone Weil, whom he frequently discusses and quotes in his later works (cf. Nicholls 2007: 134), an interest in rephrasing "rootedness" as the "real, active and natural participation in the life of a community which preserves in living shape certain particular treasures of the past and certain particular expectations for the future" (Weil 2003: 43). In *Pascalian Meditations*, Bourdieu notoriously develops this critique of the devaluation of the practical ends and of the contextuality of cultural products into a critique of scholastic reason. The scholastic *lector*, he argues,

> is interested in texts, and in theories, methods and concepts that they convey, not in order to do something with them, not to bring them, as useful, perfectible instruments, into a practical use, but so as to gloss them, by relating them to other texts (under cover, on occasion, of epistemology or methodology). This reading thus sweeps away what is essential, that is to say, not only the problems that the concepts aimed to name and resolve [...] but also the space of theoretical and methodological possibles which led those problems to be posed, at that moment, and in those terms [...]. (2000: 62)

The "Scholastic Errors" described by Bourdieu in his critique of scholastic reason lead the academic reader to consider cultural products as naturalized objects of critical investigation instead of non-theorized or pre-theoretical, yet fully functional elements in the life-world these products evolved in. Oppen's critique of scholastic volubility ("They develop/Arguments in order to speak") leads to the recovery of, as Oppen has it in his collection *This in Which* (1965), a "substantial language/Of clarity, and of respect" (Oppen 2008: 156) which eschews both the kind of philological plundering that had become synonymous with New Criticism and the earliest forays into what would soon become Poststructuralism (2008: 170). Moreover, it confers a nomothetic function to poetry in a society that seeks to achieve autonomy, that is, self-limitation:

> Clarity, clarity, surely clarity is the most beautiful
> Thing in the world
> A limited, limiting clarity   (193)

Hence, Oppen's insistence on the functionality and value of poetic discourse in a democratic society runs counter to the central propositions of formalist literary studies: a poetry that is clear is so in virtue of its value as a useful, perfectible instrument, rather than in virtue of its use as what Genette ingenuously called a "pre-text" (1997: 396), that is, as a pretext for scholastic elucidation and the production of 'transparency' though learned commentary. Historically, Oppen's return to poetic utterance *through* Whitman is, I think, highly symptomatic of the ever tighter arrangement of literary production and literary criticism that was emerging at the time of the composition of

"Of Being Numerous", that is, at the cusp of an age predicated upon the sudden advent of a 'linguistic turn' decreed across the humanities and a depoliticization of philology – a depoliticization which became evident, for instance, with Kristeva's and Barthes' enthusiastic travels in, and infantile accounts of, Maoist China in 1974, shortly after the gruesome purges of the Cultural Revolution. The timely reprint of Simon Leys's essays on China and the "Mondanités Parisiennes" of fashionable Maoism gives a ferocious and exceptionally astute insight into this neglected chapter of recent intellectual history (cf. Leys 1998: 543–552). This depoliticization was to be denounced as mere legerdemain by the public outrage at Derrida's extravagant defense of Paul de Man's antisemitic wartime writings (cf. Derrida 1988: 220). Rather than playing out the anxieties of "belatedness" and "poetic misprision," concepts thanks to which the creative-destructive collages of the neoliberal era could be supported with the psychological and mythical great narratives it otherwise sought to undermine (Bloom 1997: xxviii), Oppen explicitly points out that the fate of poetry as raw material for industrial commentary must run counter to American poetry's originary, intended function as an instrument of doxological clarification, as a means of clarifying the numerous opinions upon which a democratic, non-foundational society must inevitably fall back in order to think about itself responsibly. Hence, the nomothetic function of poetry is coextensive with the democratic institution of limits *as well as* the democratic self-limitation of the nomothetic function of poetry – the achievement of "a limited, limiting clarity."

There is no "belatedness", then, in Oppen's neo-Whitmanian poem. The recent and simultaneous renewal of interest in Castoriadis's writings on democratic autonomy and in Oppen's later poetic work presages ways in which literary criticism might be encouraged to rethink its role in the social contract that binds it with the political community that supports it. The centrality of literary genres in this self-reflexive project can be substantiated both historically and theoretically. Historically, because it is through the regeneration and continuation of a specific poetic and discursive genre that poets like Oppen have attempted to institute a continuity with a self-reflexive democratic tradition that runs counter both to the main aesthetic strain of literary modernism *and* its often totalitarian political horizon. This is a fact of cultural history, and a significant one at that. Theoretically, because the institution of this political continuity consistently lays out its crucial condition of possibility: the recognition, continuation and development of a type of poetic discourse that should be coextensive with the lucid, self-reflexive discourse of any democratic political community.

Works Cited

Aristotle. 2013. *Politics*. Trans. Carnes Lord. Chicago: University of Chicago Press.
Aulus Gellius. 1927. *Attic Nights*. Vol. 2. Trans. J. C. Rolfe. Loeb Classical Library, Vol. 200. Cambridge: Harvard University Press.
Bloom, Harold. 1997. *The Anxiety of Influence: A Theory of Poetry*. Oxford: Oxford University Press.
Bourdieu, Pierre. 2000. *Pascalian Meditations*. Stanford: Stanford University Press.
Brumbaugh, Robert S. 1991. *Plato for the Modern Age*. Lanham: University Press of America.
Castoriadis, Cornelius. 1986. "Tiers Monde, Tiers-Mondisme, Démocratie". *Domaines de l'Homme: Les Carrefours du Labyrinthe*. Vol. 2. Paris: Seuil. 128–137.
Castoriadis, Cornelius. 1987. *The Imaginary Institution of Society*. Cambridge: Michigan Institute of Techonology Press.
Castoriadis, Cornelius. 1996. "Le Délabrement de l'Occident". *La Montée de l'insignifiance: Les Carrefours du labyrinthe*. Vol. 4. Paris: Seuil. 67–95.
Castoriadis, Cornelius. 1997. "The Pulverization of Marxism-Leninism". In: David Ames Curtis (ed.). *World in Fragments: Writings on Politics, Society, Psychoanalysis and the Imagination*. Stanford: Stanford University Press. 58–69.
Castoriadis, Cornelius. 1999. *Figures du Pensable: Les Carrefours du Labyrinthe*. Vol. 6. Paris: Seuil.
Cruse, Harold. 2005. *The Crisis of the Negro Intellectual*. New York: New York Review Books Classics.
Derrida, Jacques. 1988. *Mémoires pour Paul de Man*. Paris: Galillée.
Freedman, Harry and Maurice Simon (eds.). 1961. *Midrash Rabbah: Genesis*. Vol. 1. London: Soncino Press.
Genette, Gérard. 1997. *Paratexts: Thresholds of Interpretation*. Cambridge: Cambridge University Press.
Golding, Alan. 1999. "George Oppen's Serial Poems". In: Rachel Blau DuPlessis and Peter Quartermain (eds.). *The Objectivist Nexus: Essays in Cultural Poetics*. Tuscaloosa: University of Alabama Press. 84–103.
Harris, Kirsten. 2013. "The Labour Prophet? Representations of Walt Whitman in the British Nineteenth-Century Socialist Press". *Walt Whitman Quarterly Review* 30: 115–137.
Heller, Michael. 2012. *Speaking the Estranged: Essays on the Work of George Oppen*. Bristol: Shearsman Books.
Jaeger, Werner. 1946. *Paideia: The Ideals of Greek Culture. Archaic Greece: The Mind of Athens*. Vol. 1. Oxford: Blackwell.
Jameson, Fredric. 2007. "Céline and Innocence". *The Modernist Papers*. London: Verso. 45–51.
Jennison, Ruth. 2012. *The Zukofsky Era: Modernity, Margins, and the Avant-Garde*. Baltimore: The Johns Hopkins University Press.
Kierkegaard, Søren. 1983. *Fear and Trembling*. Ed. Howard V. Hong and Edna H. Hong. Princeton: Princeton University Press.
Legendre, Pierre. 1999. *Sur la Question Dogmatique en Occident*. Paris: Fayard.
Leys, Simon. 1998. *Essais sur la Chine*. Paris: Laffont.
Marrou, Henri Irénée. 1956. *A History of Education in Antiquity*. Madison: University of Wisconsin Press.

Marx, Karl, and Friedrich Engels. 2012. *The Communist Manifesto: A Modern Edition*. London: Verso.

Miłosz, Czesław. 1981. *The Captive Mind*. New York: Vintage Books.

Nicholls, Peter. 2007. *George Oppen and the Fate of Modernism*. Oxford: Oxford University Press.

Oppen, George. 2008. *New Collected Poems*. Ed. Michael Davidson. New York: New Directions.

Orwell, George. 1968. "New Words". In: Sonia Orwell and Ian Angus (eds.). *The Collected Essays, Journalism and Letters of George Orwell*. Vol. 1. London: Secker & Warburg. 3–11.

Rorty, Richard. 1989. *Contingency, Irony, and Solidarity*. Cambridge: Cambridge University Press.

Rorty, Richard. 1991. "Unger, Castoriadis, and the Romance of a National Future". *Essays on Heidegger and Others, Philosophical Papers*. Vol. 2. Cambridge: Cambridge University Press. 177–182.

Schumpeter, Joseph A. 2003. *Capitalism, Socialism and Democracy*. London: Routledge.

Tillery, Tyrone. 1993. *Claude McKay: A Black Poet's Struggle for Identity*. Amherst: University of Massachusetts Press.

Waters, Lindsay. 2004. *Enemies of Promise: Publishing, Perishing, and the Eclipse of Scholarship*. Chicago: Prickly Paradigm Press.

Weil, Simone. 2003. *The Need for Roots: Prelude to a Declaration of Duties Towards Mankind*. London: Routledge.

West, Cornell. 1989. *The American Evasion of Philosophy: A Genealogy of Pragmatism*. Madison: University of Cornell Press.

Whitman, Walt. 1982. *Poetry and Prose*. Ed. Justin Kaplan. New York: Literary Classics of the United States.

Wimsatt, William K. and Monroe Beardsley. 1946. "The Intentional Fallacy". *The Sewanee Review* 54.3: 468–488.

Astrid Franke
Murderous Minds: A Narratological Approach to Poems on Perpetrators

Abstract: This article argues for the usefulness of narratology for a specific body of ethically challenging poems that portray the minds of people who committed violent crimes or are at least complicit with them – a well-known example is Robert Browning's "My Last Duchess" (1843). A crucial aspect to be discussed with regard to ethics and aesthetics is the analytic distance to the murderous minds portrayed by the poems, and its relation to other, more immediate, perhaps affective responses such as admiration or pity. To describe the techniques achieving different effects, the article employs narratological terms such as interior, dramatic or narrated monologue, implied author and unreliability. Using Browning's poem as a starting point, the article proceeds to offer close readings of poems by Robert Hayden, Philip Metres, and Gwendolyn Brooks.

Keywords: unreliability, narratology, Robert Hayden, Philip Metres

One consequence of assigning a text to a genre is that it suggests a way of reading, and thus, to the critic, a number of adequate theories and approaches: When a text is considered to be a tools, few dare to apply drama theory; a poem is usually not approached with narratological tools. However, the functions and challenges of a text might create overlaps between genres and widening the horizon beyond the seemingly genre-appropriate approaches can be helpful. In that vein, Brian McHale's article with the deliberately presumptuous title "Beginning to Think about Narrative in Poetry" (2009) draws attention to a blind spot in contemporary narrative theory where the contribution of verse narrative to narratology is neglected (cf. also Hühn 2004). I would like to take a complementary approach here and demonstrate how the study of poetry, in turn, could benefit from narrative theory. I would like to illustrate this claim by discussing a body of poems that come into view for anyone interested in the broad research area of fiction and justice – an area dominated by investigations into novels by the likes of Martha Nussbaum, Winfried Fluck, and Wai Chee Dimock. Undoubtedly, poetry can also be part of this field: from claims of recognition in Whitman's "Song of Myself" (1855) to documentary poems such as Muriel Rukeyser's *Book of the Dead* (1938) to the various poems on the lynching of Emmett Till. My interest here lies in poems that explore and attempt to understand, perhaps even explain injustice by portraying its major agents and their minds. In contrast to the aesthetic challenges of giving victims a voice (such as presenting the unspeakable, finding words for trauma, render the dissolution of the body, etc.), presenting the speech or mind of a perpetrator seems at first to be primarily an ethical challenge. It may add insult to injury by silencing the victims one more time, it may engender sympathy or incite voyeurism, and an analytic attempt to *understand* an atrocity might be read as an attempt to *excuse* it. However, this ethical challenge is also tied to specific aesthetic challenges: How does a text steer a course between immersion into a murderous mind and distance to it? If there is a distance, is its effect judgmental, analytic and intellectual, or just visceral – like disgust, for instance? In other words: If there is a clear perspective onto the subject matter of the poem, how is this perspective created and how can we describe it?

Because we are dealing with texts most likely characterized by a clash of norms and values, we are thrown right into the middle of several lasting controversies in the field of narratology. They concern contested concepts such as unreliability and the implied author, literature as quotation, internal and external communicative frames, the terminology of describing the representation of speech and thought with varying degrees of explicit control over them, and, of course, the role of author and reader in forming or suspending moral judgment (cf. Shen 2017). It is no coincidence that the one poem most often discussed in narratological circles is Robert Browning's "My Last Duchess," which represents the speech of a man responsible for the murder of his wife and quite unrepentant about it. In the following, I will use this poem and its discussion in narratological scholarship to draw attention to some useful terminological distinctions. My goal is certainly not to go deeply into or even participate in the conceptual debates in this field; rather I would like to show what terms have been found helpful in analyzing and interpreting this particular poem with regard to what Booth called "Browning's portraits of moral degeneration" (2006: 338). I will then apply these terms to more recent examples of poems offering an insight into the minds of perpetrators by Robert Hayden, Philip Metres, and Gwendolyn Brooks, in order to demonstrate the variety of techniques, their effects, and their (ethical) implications. I hope to show how a study of these particular poems can benefit from research conducted typically in another genre.

"My Last Duchess" is usually called a "dramatic monologue," meaning that we get direct speech as in quotation marks, with the personal pronoun "I" referring to a speaker whom we do not assume to be the poet. As Dorrit Cohn has pointed out, the reference to drama is misleading: "This presence of a fictive speaker relates the dramatic monologue not only to soliloquy in drama, but also to fictional narrative in the first person [...] Viewed from this vantage point, all dramatic monologues are first-person narratives in verse form" (1978: 257). Thus, Browning's duke is related to Humbert Humbert from Nabokov's *Lolita* (1955), for instance, which has likewise been discussed with regard to the ethical implications of unreliable narration by a murderer: In both, poem and novel, a fictional figure addresses an audience internal to the fictional world. These figures are not themselves conscious of their fictionality but they are highly self-conscious speakers, that is, "conscious of facing an addressee" (Yacobi 1987: 337). Humbert Humbert addresses the "Ladies and Gentlemen of the jury" (Nabokov 1991: 9) while the duke, as we find out towards the end of the poem, speaks to an envoy of his next wife's family. The difference in the length of the texts and the size of the implied audiences create a number of effects which may balance each other out or even be countered by additional narrative means: In the course of reading the novel, the reader may come to feel directly addressed by Humbert because when not explicitly called "jury" the addressee seems indeterminate enough to comprise anyone ready to judge. In the poem, by contrast, the reader overhears a speech to a very specific but initially unknown addressee. Usually, as Yacobi has pointed out, the presence of "a separate, fictional receiver" (1987: 350) makes us aware of a "mediation gap" (1987: 335) between the fictional world rendered through the self-conscious speakers and ourselves, looking at both the speakers and their addressees. However, since we learn about the duke's listener so late, it is possible that readers may lose their distance and feel "overwhelmed" (Langbaum 1957: 83) by the duke just as the silent envoy is – perhaps to the point of identifying with the gifted rhetorician.

The reception histories of poem and novel confirm that, despite the difference in the size and the specificity of the implied audiences, the effect of the speaker vis à vis the external empirical reader has been quite similar: the fascination with the narrators arises from the crimes they reveal and from the manner in which they reveal them, given how obviously smart they are: jealousy, pride, coldness, power, and subtle cruelty all intermingle with a strong aesthetic sense, which links them to their creators. Both speakers have been said to take us in and make us complicit in their crimes, if only by reveling in their power, their language, and their power over language. Concerning "My Last Duchess," Langbaum, for instance, wrote that "we suspend our moral judgment because we prefer to participate in the duke's power and freedom, in his hard core of character fiercely loyal to itself" (1957: 83). This assessment, though often refuted since its publication in 1957, is useful here because its foundations reveal the reading procedures that may lead someone to recognize a tension between moral judgment and experiential empathy with a murderous mind, but then dissolve the former at the expense of the latter.[1] Langbaum assimilates the "dramatic monologue" into the Romantic tradition and assumes a predisposition to empathize or identify with the "I" of a poem, even more so when the speaker is so clearly a masterful and highly self-conscious rhetorician who thus acquires a certain similarity with the author. In other words, Langbaum downplays the mediation gap: the distance between the implied author and the fictional speaker, which can be discerned in the discrepancy between the speaker and the way he is constructed according to aims that cannot be his own but must be that of the implied author.

This is precisely where the confusing term 'unreliability' comes in (cf. Yacobi 1981: 113): Certainly the duke is not unreliable in the vernacular sense of not being likely to keep his word – quite the contrary. He is indirect, but his use of implication is easy enough to decipher and is meant to be deciphered by the envoy: the duke will not tolerate flirtatiousness in his next wife, no more than he did in his last one. For all we know about the character, this is a reliable message. In a technical sense, many conceptualizations of unreliability are available: with Phelan one might call the duke unreliable because he is "underreporting" with regard to his role in the death of his last duchess and "underevaluating," perhaps even "misevaluating," her behavior (2005: 34–37). As with Humbert Humbert, the duke's verbal art might lead to a certain degree of admiration and "bonding" in Phelan's terms, but the fact that the two men are murderers might be considered "warning signals" (2007: 232) against evaluative unreliability at least. This is tricky: The judgment passed in "She had / a heart – how shall I say? – too soon made glad, / Too easily impressed; she liked whate'er / She looked on, and her looks went everywhere" (Browning 1979: 58) may misrepresent the duchess out of jealousy and pride, but as we know from the ekphrastic part of the poem, at least one other person, the painter, also noted that the duchess was easily moved and excited by things. Is it necessary for us to feel that a husband should not criticize and be annoyed by his wife for being excited in order to evoke this type of unreliability on the axis of ethics? What about a male reader who has been socialized into gender expectations of a kind that lead him to promptly understand the duke's assessment and share it and who might not even be put off by the fact that he is a murderer? In order to focus on features of the text that might question the adequacy of a reading that bonds with the duke and through him with the implied author, it is advisable to first assert that there is indeed a gap between the transmission of the duke's narrated world (past and present) and the

---

[1] Amongst the critics are Wayne Booth 2006, Dorrit Cohn 1978, Ralph Rader 1976, and Tamar Yacobi 1987; my own use of Langbaum resembles Yacobi's (1987).

transmission of the world comprising the duke as created by the implied author. Even readers who share the duke's pride and misogyny may realize that the duke is created and manipulated by another entity. Thus the text spoken by the duke as quoted speech is open to the possible presence of different values and perspectives and hence to inner tensions we would have to deal with. This second step may lead to the detection of unreliability "as an inference that explains and eliminates tensions, incongruities, contradictions and other infelicities the work may show by attributing them to a source of transmission" (Yacobi 1981: 119). Inasmuch as these are based on moral norms, however, we cannot be sure that there are the same tensions and incongruities for every reader. Yet even for those entirely endorsing the duke, the poem still has the effect of framing a particular view, making it visible – exhibiting it like a portrait for others to peruse and judge.

In her discussion of Langbaum's reading, Yacobi touches upon aspects of the poem that should alert us to the way the speaker himself is framed and thus put in perspective (cf. Yacobi 1987: 344). Between the title and the beginning of the poem, we find the word "Ferrara," which clearly does not belong to the duke's discourse and for most readers, particularly educated ones who associate Italy and duchesses with the Renaissance, marks a distance in space and time: It suggests that the speaker and the duchess are historical figures and that the poem is set a long time ago. Besides, while the duke is responsible for the slow revelation of his message to the listener, he is not the one who creates our surprise in finding out the listener's identity. That masterful coup is the implied author's, for the duke knows all along who he has been talking to. Likewise, the "art of poetry," the iambic pentameter rhymed in couplets, is presumably not the duke's. Finally, Shifra Hochberg has argued that the portrait itself as it emerges through the ekphrasis of the poem constitutes a "countertext" (1991: 78), which subverts the duke's discourse. "As an emblem for female energy, self-empowerment, and erotic strength as enduring, timeless qualities, the portrait [...] comes to symbolize as well the function and power of art as the fulfillment of poetic desire" (1991: 78). Though the duke may have killed the duchess, art has immortalized her open show of desire and excitement, the famous "spot / Of joy" and "the smile" which the duke still has to come to terms with.

The discussion so far leads to two important points. First, both Langbaum's and Hochberg's readings demonstrate implicitly the importance of the reader's expectation and knowledge brought to the poem, partly through the ascription of genre. Langbaum attempts a historicizing reading based on assumptions about Romanticism and its reading habits. Hochberg places her reading in the context of feminist reassessments of Victorian poetry, Browning's in particular. What Langbaum and Hochberg bring to the text leads them to see varying degrees of Yacobi's "tensions, incongruities, contradictions and other infelicities" (1981: 119) and makes them argue for a wide or narrow distance between implied author and fictional figure. The overall effect of the poem as Langbaum sees it is a fascination with the duke as a gifted manipulator, despite the knowledge that it would be wrong to endorse his views. The effect Hochberg believes to be produced is a kind of *Schadenfreude*: the pleasure that arises from watching a proud, unsuspecting man become a vehicle in an unmasking of gender relations. That reading, however, depends to a large extent on a willingness to approve of a married woman's open show of sexuality.

The second point may explain these divergent readings and builds upon the above list of aspects framing the duke. That list also draws attention to how comparatively little framing there is. The implied author's main coup, as stated before, is the late revelation of the identity of the listener and thus the overall speech situation. Until then, it is only the inconspicuous "Ferrara" that hints at an implied author framing a speaker. Otherwise, the title, usually a place where the implied author's presence is felt, is given over to the duke: "*My* Last Duchess" – not "His Last Duchess" or "The Last Duchess." The pronoun immediately puts us into the speaker's place. And while the art of poetry is not the duke's, its specific means – the pentameter, the enjambments and the unobtrusive rhymes – all approximate natural speech and downplay the artifice of the text.

A comparison with other poets who give murderers a voice shows how daring Browning was. Muriel Rukeyser's *Book of the Dead*, Robert Hayden's "Middle Passage" (1941/1962), W. D. Snodgrass's *The Fuehrer Bunker* (1977/1995), or Philip Metres' *abu ghraib arias* (2011) all contain extended passages of thought or speech by men guilty of murder – interior or dramatic monologues – but all of them put the murderers' views into perspective. They frame these passages by means of titles, epigraphs, and typography; by versification and the arrangement of lines to intensify the sense of artifice; by frequent reference to musical genres; and more than anything, by juxtaposition with other voices, most notably those of the victims as in Rukeyser, Hayden, or Metres.

The question of genre influences our view of these poems. One could see many of them in the tradition of "documentary poetics" or "modern documentary" (Thurston 1999) and thus assume that they record and communicate a social and historical reality. This reading encourages research into the ways the poets use and alter documents. When focusing on the quoted voices of victims and thus on how the poet selects and frames their letters or testimonies, discussions often revolve around the danger of being condescending or sentimentalizing and around the challenge of preserving their dignity (cf. Thurston

1999). Yet another genre tradition in which these passages can be read, I will show in the following, is that of the dramatic monologue where we assume right away the construction of a speaker or writer for specific purposes.

In Robert Hayden's *Middle Passage* several direct speeches by white men involved in the slave trade are embedded in a longer poem. Some of these speeches are marked as quotes by quotation marks, while a religious prayer, excerpts from hymns, and a short narrative by a trader are not. Significantly, and in contrast to Metres' *abu ghraib arias*, the voices of the participants in the slave trade are juxtaposed not with the voices of victims but with one another. As the speakers are never accused directly, it is their bragging, their thinly hidden fear or guilt, and their defense against merely implicit accusations that undo them – all in all, the speakers effectively condemn themselves. An example may show how unreliability can thus be understood as ironic quote and the overall effect of the juxtapositions can be akin to dramatic irony where the external audience or reader knows much more than the participants of the internal speech situation:

> But for the storm that flung up barriers
> of wind and wave, The Amistad, señores,
> would have reached the port of Principe in two,
> three days at most   (Hayden 1985: 52)

The beginning of this testimonial establishes a self-aware speaker addressing a specific audience: that of a court having to decide on whether the slaves on board *The Amistad* should be returned to their Spanish owners, of whom the speaker is one, or be left free in the United States. His extended description of the mutiny is meant to demonize the Africans and evoke pity and solidarity from the members of a nation "whose wealth, whose tree of liberty/are rooted in the labor of your slaves" (Hayden 1985: 53). The reader, however, has encountered storms and other ominous signs of maritime dangers throughout the poem. This motif has become associated with Shakespeare's *The Tempest* (1610–1611) and by extension with another major motif, blindness and the loss of eyes. Together, these motifs alert us to recurring patterns in the rhetoric of whites involved in the Middle Passage: their tendency to see themselves as victims, their dehumanization of Africans, and their simultaneous blindness to their own inhumanity. Because the practice of throwing sick slaves overboard has been mentioned earlier, the following lines are a case of dramatic irony in that the speaker's condemnation of others comes back to him like a boomerang in the minds of the readers: "It sickens me / to think of what I saw, of how these apes / threw overboard the butchered bodies of / our men, true Christians all, like so much jetsam" (Hayden 1985: 53).

It would be tempting to use our obvious knowledge surplus at the end of the poem, accompanied perhaps by a feeling of moral superiority, to claim that these figures are blind and in their blindness make us see. Hayden does not allow us, however, to dismiss everything they say as unreliable. They also articulate some uncomfortable observations such as the complicity of African leaders in the enslavement of their enemies or the paradox that Americans, whose source of wealth lies in slavery, should defend the right of slaves to kill their masters in front of the Supreme Court. A dialectic of metaphorical blindness and insight, sickness and saneness, unconsciousness and consciousness runs through the poem and manifests itself in the formal features of those passages that provide insight into the minds of white slaveholders. The first two extended quotations in the poem are fictive diary entries, differing from the addresses by self-conscious speakers that follow. For Cohn, the diary entry is "a close relative – and an important ancestor – of the autonomous monologue" (1978: 208). As the diarist is presumably writing only for him- or herself, there is no assumed audience and thoughts can be formulated without too much concern for intelligibility. If this is pushed further into speech, we get an "autonomous monologue" such as Molly Bloom's, or an "unself-conscious interior monologist" such as Septimus in *Mrs. Dalloway* (1925) (Yacobi 1981: 123). Because these writers and speakers are unself-conscious, they are not concerned with hiding anything and give us the impression of witnessing "unhampered self-revelation" (Yacobi 1981: 123). However, just as Hayden's presumably self-conscious speaker in front of the court is curiously unself-conscious when it comes to his blindness towards things he "saw," so the presumably unself-conscious, private writer is actually quite self-conscious as he uses writing to quench his fears. This attempt segues into the beginnings of an acknowledgment of guilt:

> 8 bells. I cannot sleep, for I am sick
> with fear, but writing eases fear a little
> since still my eyes can see these words take shape
> upon the page & so I write, as one
> would turn to exorcism. [...]
>   Which one of us
> has killed an albatross?
>   (Hayden 1985: 49)

The writer is afraid of Ophthalmia, a highly infectious eye disease that leads to blindness and might leave the ship without anyone able to steer it. Using written language to fend off fear and assuring oneself of eyesight motivates a self-conscious way of writing and thus the art of poetry, which manifests in the perfectly regular iambic pentameter of the third line.

Yet, it is not obvious artifice that makes these voices stand out. On the contrary, what distinguishes the historical characters' language from that of the twentieth-century poet, apart from quotation marks, is its relative simplicity and accessibility, compared to the dense language of the poet in part III, for instance. This simplicity – of the prayers, a log-book entry, an eyewitness account, a narrative by a trader, and the speech by one of the slave masters of the *Amistad* – corresponds to a moral simplicity, a blind one-sidedness, which is countered by the implied author's and the reader's complex attempts to transform these passages into something one could learn from.

To put a murderer's mind into perspective is a complicated endeavor in both aesthetic and ethical terms. It highlights the overall power of poets vis à vis the voices they can manipulate for their own purposes. Hayden does this without imposing himself too strongly on his characters by making the characters illuminate one another – not by contrast but by their very similar blindnesses. Less complex juxtapositions may create strange effects. Consider the voices of American prison officials and guards in Philip Metres' *abu ghraib arias*, a long poem that juxtaposes victims and perpetrators in alternating order by the titles and the typography of their dramatic monologues. The victims' voices all carry the abstract title "(echo /ex/)" and disintegrate as the poem progresses, the last monologue consisting entirely of blank spaces and punctuation marks. The perpetrators' monologues, by contrast, are entitled "The Blues of ..." followed by individual names. An example is "The Blues of Charles Graner":

> the Christian in me
> knows it's wrong
> but the corrections
> officer in me can't
> help but love
> making a grown man
> piss himself
> (Metres 2011: 30)

By the time we read this poem, the name Graner or G has appeared several times in poems entitled "(echo /ex/)" that comprise reports of torture in which Graner plays a prominent role. He appears in another of these poems right after his own "Blues" and is mentioned again in "The Blues of Lynddie England." The contextualization introduces him as brutal and sadistic, independently of similar characterization in news coverage of the Abu Ghraib incidents or in Philip Gourevitch and Errol Morris' journalistic account of the infamous prison in *The Ballad of Abu Ghraib* (2009), which also contains the sentence quoted above. In Metres' poem, that sentence has been arranged into a perverse parallel construction in which the line "knows it's wrong" follows upon and is attributed to "the Christian" in Graner while the rhythmically echoing "help but love" follows upon and is attributed to "the corrections officer," rather than the other way around. Of course, love should be a defining characteristic of a Christian while to know what is wrong should be an attribute of a corrections officer.

The text is offered as a revealing self-reflection of someone who claims that his job is so much part of his personality that he "loves" to be sadistic even though another part of him knows that this is wrong. The most discordant element of the poem is its title. "Blues" does not refer to formal features here or elsewhere in the book. It originally refers to a major African American art form but may also more widely denote musical performances or texts that have their roots in oppression and serve as a means to survive, resist, or defy that oppression through wit, melancholy, and a zest for life despite disappointed hopes for love, work, recognition, and freedom. To call the monologues by the prison guards "Blues" is an attempt to set a mood and impose a moral vision. Similar to Gourevitch and Morris' "Ballads" the poetic genre suggests that the prison guards are also victims of oppression, the difference being that ballads traditionally narrated what white people do to other whites – this seems to me the more plausible and aesthetically and ethically satisfying choice of word.[2] In Metres's framing of Graner, we are led to deplore – or even assume Graner deplores – a kind of professional deformation that somehow associates him with the status of a black victim. In contrast to other poems discussed above, the discrepancy between the implied author's frame and the character's self-revelation cannot be dissolved by calling the character unreliable. The effect is a somewhat patronizing implied author who superimposes a meaning and evaluation onto the character's voice.

This is not to say that the voices of perpetrators cannot be used to challenge simple oppositions of good and bad, victim and perpetrator. This can be seen in Gwendolyn Brooks' poem "A Bronzeville Mother Loiters in Mississippi. Meanwhile, a Mississippi Mother Burns Bacon" (1960), whose lengthy title juxtaposes Mamie Till, mother of Emmett Till, with Carolyn Bryant, the woman who Emmett allegedly whistled at and whose husband murdered the fourteen-year-old boy. This poem serves as an example of yet another technique of making a fictional mind transparent – in this case to make us see the socializing forces shaping that mind, something the character herself does not fully understand.

---

[2] A number of writers mark their texts on murderous minds as musical genres: Charles Reznikoff subtitles his *Testimony: The United States, 1885–1915: Recitative*; Snodgrass has almost every poem in *The Fuehrer Bunker* followed by a "Chorus"; Metres calls his poems "Arias" and also "Blues."

This is how the poem begins, after the lengthy title has set the scene and introduced the main characters:

> From the first it had been like a
> Ballad. It had the beat inevitable. It had the blood
> A wildness cut up, and tied in little bunches,
> Like the four-line stanzas of the ballads she had never quite
> Understood – the ballads they had set her to, in school.
> Herself: the milk-white maid, the "maid mild"
> Of the ballad. Pursued
> By the Dark Villain. Rescued by the Fine Prince.
> (Brooks 1960: 61)

It is only through the personal pronoun in the fourth line that we realize we are witnessing the thoughts of a woman, and through the mentioning of ballads and school we understand that this is the white woman in Mississippi. Her socialization into the gender role of a Southern woman with the help of school and literature, insufficiently understood by herself, is cast as free indirect discourse, to use Genette's term, or "narrated monologue," as Cohn calls it (1978: 13). Her terminology helps to relate the narrative technique used by Brooks to the previously described technique of the "quoted monologue," (1978: 12) either dramatic as in Browning and Metres or silent and interiorized as in Hayden's diary entry. Understanding narrated monologue will help elucidate the effect and achievement of the poem.

We are to assume that Carolyn Bryant is speaking to herself, saying, as in quoted dramatic monologue: "It has been like the ballads I have never quite understood – the ballads they set me to, in school." In the poem, however, her voice and that of the poet blend into each other, not least because of the third-person pronoun and the past tense, which distinguish the passage from dramatic monologue. By imitating rather than quoting the way a figure may speak to herself and "leaving the relationship between words and thoughts latent, the narrated monologue casts a peculiarly penumbral light on the figural consciousness, suspending it on the threshold of verbalization in a manner that cannot be achieved by direct quotation" (Cohn 1978: 103). The result is ambiguity and uncertainty as to who we are listening to and to what extent any insight is really the woman's. As the reception history of the poem shows, this is exactly what critics have argued about (cf. Kent 1981; McKibbin 2011). But this weaving in and out of a person's consciousness also alerts us to the unconscious effects of socialization the female accomplice of a murderer has undergone. She is both an active participant in and a passive product of the power structures of race and gender that led to Emmett Till's murder.

I would like to mention one last example, again by Robert Hayden, where the distinction between a murderer's mind and a surrounding frame is blurred – but by a different technique and to a different effect. The poem "Night, Death, Mississippi" (1966) opens with an alternation of interior monologue by an unself-conscious thinker, a sick old man who may be speaking to himself, and an interrupting narrative voice talking about that man in the third person in the present tense:

> A quavering cry. Screech-owl?
> Or one of them?
> The old man in his reek
> and gauntness laughs –
> One of them, I bet –
> and turns out the kitchen lamp,
> limping to the porch to listen
> in the windowless night.
> (Hayden 1985: 15)

It takes the reader a while to understand the situation prompting the thoughts and actions of the old man: He is listening to a lynching but is not entirely sure whether the sounds he hears come from an owl or a human being. He starts to reminisce nostalgically about past times when he himself participated in lynchings and tortured someone. The personal pronoun "I" marks the old man's thought, but there are expressions such as "A quavering cry" with which the poem opens, or later "White robes like moonlight / In the sweetgum dark" that segue into or come out of the man's mind (1985: 15). They blur the border between the old man's mind and his environment that is rendered in a language with distinctive poetic qualities such as alliteration or the unusual composites that are a specialty of the narrator's voice: "windowless night," sweetgum dark," and, in part II, "*rawhead and bloodybones night*" (Hayden 1985: 16). In Brooks' poem, the foregrounding of mental activities through verbs like "understood," "remember," or "think" (Brooks 1960: 61–63) and the "narrated monologue" serve to provide a perspective both inside and outside the mind of a guilty woman who does not fully understand her own position in the matrix of race and gender. In Hayden's poem, by contrast, the old man is not trying to understand or think; in his preoccupation with his body and the memory of others he is as unself-conscious as the animals he and his family frequently mention. What is startling is how easily his mind thus blends with his surroundings. Like the "windowless night" there is no clear outside or inside. This is frightening because it suggests that the mood and mindset of the old man are all-encompassing, deeply inscribed into the 'nature' of the South, nature so clearly including not only trees and animals but human beings, language, and culture. Only religious incantation, set off in italics, seems to provide a clear difference – clearer, at least, than the subtleties of unusual composites.[3]

There are various ways in which writers can create transparent murderous minds. A crucial question for the ways in which ethics and aesthetics are intertwined has been the distance between speaker and implied author and the presence of another evaluative frame. This is of course not the only way of approaching evil through portrayals of evil-doers. Poetry, like narrative, seems to be well suited for an analytical perspective, for trying to understand not necessarily *why* but *how* murderous minds work the way they do. But a wider scope in terms of genre would have to include the means of comedy to make us laugh at murderers, for example, or the use of satire to imagine ways of correction. One may well wonder whether that, too, can be achieved by poetry.

Works Cited

Booth, Wayne C. 2006. "Control of Distance in Jane Austen's *Emma*". In: Walter Jost (ed.). *The Essential Wayne Booth*. Chicago: University of Chicago Press. 34–53.

Brooks, Gwendolyn. 2005. "A Bronzeville Mother Loiters in Mississippi: Meanwhile, a Mississippi Mother Burns Bacon". In: Elizabeth Alexander (ed.). *The Essential Gwendolyn Brooks*. New York: Library of America. 61–67.

Browning, Robert. 1979. "My Last Duchess". In: James F. Loucks (ed.). *Robert Browning's Poetry: Authoritative Texts, Criticism*. New York: Norton. 58–59.

Cohn, Dorrit. 1978. *Transparent Minds: Narrative Modes for Presenting Consciousness in Fiction*. Princeton: Princeton University Press.

Franke, Astrid. 2010. *Pursue the Illusion: Problems of Public Poetry in America*. Heidelberg: Winter.

Franke, Astrid. 2015. "Poetry and (In)Justice". In: Jiří Flajšar (ed.). *New Perspectives on American Poetry: From Walt Whitman to the Present*. Olomouc: Palacký University. 37–52.

Franke, Astrid. 2017. "Satin-Legs Smith and a Mississippi Mother: Dissections of Habitus in Two Poems by Gwendolyn Brooks". In: Christa Buschendorf (ed.). *Power Relations in Black Lives: Reading African American Literature and Culture with Bourdieu and Elias*. Bielefeld: Transcript. 35–54.

Hayden, Robert. 1985. *Collected Poems*. Ed. Frederick Glaysher. New York: Liveright.

Hochberg, Shifra. 1991. "Male Authority and Female Subversion in Browning's 'My Last Duchess'". *LIT* 3: 77–84.

Hühn, Peter. 2004. "Transgeneric Narratology: Application to Lyric Poetry". In: John Pier (ed.). *The Dynamics of Narrative Form: Studies in Anglo-American Narratology*. Berlin: De Gruyter. 139–158.

---

3 I have offered more extensive interpretations of the poems by Hayden in Franke 2010 and Franke 2015, and by Brooks in Franke 2017. I wrote these, however, without fully realizing how helpful narratological tools could be.

Kent, George E. 1981. "Aesthetic Values in the Poetry of Gwendolyn Brooks". In: R. Baxter Miller (ed.). *Black American Literature and Humanism*. Lexington: University Press of Kentucky. 75–94.

Langbaum, Robert. 1957. *The Poetry of Experience: The Dramatic Monologue in Modern Literary Tradition*. London: Chatto & Windus.

McHale, Brian. 2009. "Beginning to Think About Narrative in Poetry". *Narrative* 17.1: 11–30.

McKibbin, Molly Littlewood. 2011. "Southern Patriarchy and the Figure of the White Woman in Gwendolyn Brooks's 'A Bronzeville Mother Loiters in Mississippi. Meanwhile, a Mississippi Mother Burns Bacon'". *African American Review* 44.4: 667–685.

Metres, Philip. 2011. *Abu Ghraib Arias*. Denver: Flying Guillotine.

Nabokov, Vladimir. 1991. *The Annotated Lolita*. Ed. Alfred Appel. London: Penguin.

Phelan, James. 2005. *Living to Tell About It*. Ithaca: Cornell University Press.

Phelan, James. 2007. "Estranging Unreliability, Bonding Unreliability, and the Ethics of *Lolita*". *Narrative* 15.2: 222–238.

Rader, Ralph. 1976. "The Dramatic Monologue and Related Lyric Forms". *Critical Inquiry* 3.1: 131–151.

Shen, Dan. "Unreliability". In: Hühn, Peter et al. (ed.). *The Living Handbook of Narratology*. Hamburg: Hamburg University, 2017. http://www.lhn.uni-hamburg.de [accessed 20 April 2017].

Snodgrass, W. D. 1995. *The Fuehrer Bunker: The Complete Cycle*. Brockport: BOA Editions.

Thurston, Michael. 1999. "Documentary Modernism as Popular Front Poetic: Muriel Rukeyser's 'Book of the Dead'". *Modern Language Quarterly* 60.1: 59–83.

Yacobi, Tamar. 1981. "Fictional Reliability as Communicative Problem". *Poetics Today* 2.2: 113–126.

Yacobi, Tamar. 1987. "Narrative Structure and Fictional Mediation". *Poetics Today* 8.2: 335–372.

Ewa Kołodziejczyk
"I Have Always Aspired to a More Spacious Form": Czesław Miłosz's Reflection on Poetic Genres in American Exile

Abstract: The article discusses the ways Czesław Miłosz's perception of genres evolved starting from his early literary career in Poland (1934–1945) until the year 1968 in California, when his famous manifesto *Ars poetica?* appeared. In this poem, he ultimately rejected a traditional perception of literature, defined as texts distinguished for their specific features or as a repertoire of norms in favor of literature aggregating all possible discourses, forms and styles. The paper demonstrates how his acquisition of Hebrew and Greek as well as his encounter with Allen Ginsberg's poetry influenced his understanding of genres and his literary goals. The intellectual solitude of the exilic poet freed him from the thematic and formal expectations of his audience in communist Poland, where literature was being censored and émigré authors were the only voices of the voiceless. Not only did Miłosz avoid being a political voice, but he used circumstances of his life to absorb twentieth-century discourses in order to provide a literary testimony to his epoch.

Keywords: Czesław Miłosz, exile, genre, American literature, Allen Ginsberg

This paper examines Czesław Miłosz's conception of poetic genre in the light of his famous poem *Ars poetica?* written in Berkeley, California, in 1968. It positions the poem as an important stage in Miłosz's reflection on aesthetic norms and their roles in contemporary poetry. The first section briefly demonstrates how the poet's approach to poetic genres evolved in response to major aesthetic changes in the literature of the twentieth century, to historical and political events in Europe, and to his individual situation in between the Polish and American audiences. The second section examines Miłosz's engagement with Walt Whitman, Allen Ginsberg, and the California counterculture of the 1960s to demonstrate that his approach to literature cannot be dissociated from his exile in the United States. The third section offers a close reading of *Ars poetica?* that reveals its disruptive effect on Miłosz's perception of poetic genre and elucidates his independent and unique position in twentieth-century thinking on the poetic process.

https://doi.org/10.1515/9783110594874-009

1 Miłosz's Poetic Genres

The problem of genres was a significant issue in Czesław Miłosz's poetry. In his early writings *A Poem on Frozen Time* (1933), *Three Winters* (1936), *Rescue* (1945), *Daylight* (1953), and *Treatise on Poetry* (1957), he constantly experimented with the Polish and European literary traditions. His poems were entitled hymns, songs, ballads, treatises, toasts, albums, sentences, prayers, notes, dithyrambs, odes, letters, chronicles, and so forth. Even in this stage, however, a tendency to mingle poetic genres with those from epic and drama as well as from the non-literary spectrum is clearly visible. As a modernist poet, Miłosz played with genres by filling the frames provided by these genres with intellectual and emotional contents that either transcended or subverted them. By the 1950s, although the poet lived outside Poland, he drew on parody and pastiche of the didactic genres of the Enlightenment in order to discredit directives of socialist realism imposed on Polish literature and art in the years of Stalin's terror (cf. Nycz 2000).

Later, his approach to genres evolved towards thematizing them in poems like those in the volumes *City without a Name* (1969) and *From the Rising of the Sun* (1974), and ultimately towards rejecting traditional perceptions of literature as a body of texts distinguished for their specific features or as a repertoire of norms and rules (cf. Nycz 1996: 55–84). As they could no longer serve for describing "the unattainable earth," as the title of his poetry volume from 1986 puts it, Miłosz explored all possible forms of writing: maxims, anecdotes, meditations, crumbs of worldly wisdom, introspections, and records of dreams. One can argue that he made use of a sort of postmodern freedom to blur boundaries of genres and discourses. In California, having weak response from both the Polish and international literary audience, Miłosz might have liberated himself from genres with greater ease.

After Miłosz had defected to the West in 1951, publishing his literary writings was prohibited in the communist Polish People's Republic. Only in 1980, when he was awarded the Nobel Prize in literature, did the first edition of his poetry appear on the official Polish market.

In the United States, he remained almost exclusively known for one book, *The Captive Mind*, translated into English in 1953. As Bogdana Carpenter points out, he attained "reputation as a scholar, critic, translator and brilliant essayist, but not as a poet" (2003: 46). Paradoxically, the intellectual solitude of the exilic poet freed him from the obligations and expectations of the literary audience, especially the one he might have encountered in Poland. Marc Robinson generalizes: "Unfettered by old obligations, unswayed by cultural assumptions, blissfully unheedful (at least for a moment) of the customs of the country, the most energetic exiles have the opportunity to see things from an unvisited perspective – to enjoy a degree of sensitivity and acuity unavailable to most non-exiles" (1994: xvi–xvii).

Between 1968 and his death in 2004, Miłosz introduced many new forms of writing into his poetry. He entitled his poems incantations, readings, lectures, confessions, invocations, parables, diaries, meditations, biographies, dialogues, notebooks, and prescriptions. Some of them relate to the rhetoric tradition, some have obvious connections with melic poetry; others indicate the absorption of non-literary forms into his oeuvre. The aged poet invented new literary genres and gave them unexpected names, "road-side dog" being the most famous one and serving as a title of his volume of writings from 1997. The name of the genre alluded to the poet's viewing himself as an observer of everyday life. Simultaneously, however, and with equal frequency he employed standard classic forms like the haiku. This attitude to genre explains mature Miłosz's preference for the device of collage and his strong attachment to multi-voicedness in his poetry. In the broader context of twentieth-century European literature, this shift may be seen as fairly typical, though it also has many individual facets.

2 Miłosz and American Poetry

Written in 1968, *Ars poetica?* is a prelude of Miłosz's further crusade against conceptions of genre based upon strict norms and rules. As Ryszard Nycz argues:

> Seen from this perspective, the "more spacious form" of Miłosz's design is essentially a project of conceiving poetry as the *koine* [the common language] of the twentieth-century experience. It is a development of a poetic discourse that connects literary genres, the lyric, the epic, the dramatic, the reflexive, as well as distinct sociolects and discursive registers. It is also a poetry that becomes not a passive carrier, but an active bearer of the "spirit of the times," lending shape and crucial meaning to the problems of the shared and individual experience of man. This, then, in brief, is the project of a "poetry [that] is a palimpsest that, when properly decoded, provides testimony to its epoch". (2011: 24–25)

Situated in such a perspective, *Ars poetica?* indicates an important stage of Miłosz's search for the optimal mode of his own literary speech. In a poem that traditionally explains "the art of the poetry" or meditates what poetry is, Miłosz challenges modernist notions that poems should be written for their own sake.

One of the most famous lines in the poem, "I have always aspired to a more spacious form that would be free from the claims of poetry or prose" (2005:

240–241),[1] introduces a problem of genre. Miłosz frequently synonymized the terms genre and form as he regarded the latter as a far broader concept relating to all rules of writing. The line was written on Grizzly Peak, California, eight years after Miłosz had been offered a professorship in the Slavic Languages Department at Berkeley University. As early as the 1940s, while serving as cultural attaché in the United States, he had understood that he could not write poems in a language other than his mother tongue. Yet despite the constraints that it might impose on him, writing letters, essays, and literary criticism in English enabled him to recover some linguistic freedom of expression too. Even at the time of his diplomatic service in the 1940s, he was well acquainted with English-language poetry. During World War II he had been translating William Shakespeare, William Blake, and T. S. Eliot into Polish. After 1945, he had been working on his anthology of English poetry including John Donne, John Milton, Robert Browning, W. B. Yeats, and Thomas Traherne. In the United States, having read Walt Whitman in the 1930s, he would also read William Carlos Williams, Carl Sandburg, Ezra Pound, and E. E. Cummings. He had commented on his meetings and conversations with Robert Frost, Robert Lowell, and Robert Shapiro. From behind the Iron Curtain he had contributed articles on Wallace Stevens, Marianne Moore, Robinson Jeffers, Edgar Lee Masters, Vachel Lindsay, Hart Crane, Archibald MacLeish, Conrad Aiken, Theodore Roethke, Edwin Markham, and Hilda Doolittle to Polish literary magazines. After his defection in 1951, the decision to write in his mother tongue seemed to doom him to obscurity. In Berkeley in 1968, this early decision, along with his deep intellectual solitude, anticipated an emblematic fate of the twentieth-century European poet in exile. Bożena Karwowska argues that making their own houses out of writing is one of exilic writers' strategies to cope with their situation. They

> find their home in language – either their native tongue or the tongue of their new country. [...] Exile (regardless of its reasons and category) increases the value of language as a sustaining link to old and new worlds. The exile's biggest fear is loneliness, but solitude is a condition immanent to the exilic fate, and it accompanies emigrants regardless of their frequent attempts to form groups or literary circles. (2011: 89)

---

[1] Unless otherwise indicated, the English translations of Miłosz's poems are taken from the 2005 edition *New and Collected Poems 1931–2001*. They are referenced in the main body by indicating the number of the page and the relevant lines in brackets. It is interesting that in the above-quoted line the Polish verb 'tęskniłem' ('I longed for') was translated as 'aspired,' which may disclose the poet's manner of creating his image in the international settings.

According to Marc Robinson, "[w]hatever language exiles favor, writing offers them territory that they alone can legislate. The page becomes one of the few spaces where others aren't telling them how to behave" (1994: xvii). This also describes Miłosz's perception of poetry as space, especially in California, where poetry was a lonely territory for articulating his self in his mother tongue. He did not, however, apply a strategy of numerous émigré writers who would treat their life abroad as a chance to nurture their marginality and a way of intensifying their personal alienation (cf. Stephan 2003: 10).

Miłosz made use of his existential condition in many ways. In the 1960s and 1970s it spurred him to translate numerous texts into Polish, including those of the biblical *Five Megillot, Book of Job, Psalms, Gospel According to Mark*, and *Revelation of St. John* (cf. Haven 2006: 178). His endeavors as a translator were not, however, a "surrender to a 'myth of the past' or indication of the norms that were binding in the past" (Nycz 2011: 22). For the poet critical of modern alienation in "the land of Ulro," as William Blake named a secular state of mind (Blake 2001: 34), translating the Bible was an instrument of spiritual renewal. It was also a literary project, not merely a religious one. His endeavors, which required the acquisition of Hebrew and Greek, subtly influenced his self-perception as a poet and his understanding of literary genres. By these translations Miłosz wanted to integrate the Bible with his own poetics, to fuse biblical verse with his own stanza, and, more broadly, to create a new language for Polish contemporary poetry and to amplify its scope. His interest in the Bible paralleled his extensive readings of Walt Whitman's poetry. He emphasized the links between biblical, Whitmanian and his own lyrical verse. In his opinion, they all stemmed from a similar understanding of the word, which by nature is spatial and makes room for reality. Consequently, as poetic genres are spatial structures as well, Miłosz expands and transcends them in a way, so they might serve for better representing the contemporary world.

In the 1960s in California, he also witnessed the origins of counterculture, which he critically commented on in his *Visions from San Francisco Bay* (1969). This collection of essays commences with a story of the Spanish conquest of California in the eighteenth century, which he judges as demonic. Even back in the 1940s, Miłosz had described American civilization in demonic terms, pointing to its loss of memory, secularization, alienation of individuals, and lack of metaphysical imagination or reasoning in transcendent categories. His engagement with American culture and the discrepancy between the medial and the unmediated image of the country make him a spiritual ally of many early-twentieth-century American writers such as Henry Miller, John Steinbeck, and Theodore Dreiser, as well as a precursor of multiethnic American literature written from immigrant stances.

In the 1960s, being a voracious reader of American contemporary poetry, he initially adopted Allen Ginsberg's *Howl* (1955) as a negative point of reference in his literary assessments. His attitude to Ginsberg evolved and became more nuanced with time. In his letters to Zbigniew Herbert, he admitted *Howl* was a very important poem. He also came to associate Ginsberg with the Whitmanian tradition of poetry, and Whitman was the American poet he himself valued the most. Broadly speaking, there are three reasons why the Polish poet favored Whitman: firstly, the inner freedom that enabled him to achieve "a more spacious form" that was also inspired by biblical verse and cadence; secondly, the poet celebrating his self was still a witness to history; and thirdly, his poetry was inhabited by numerous speakers. In Miłosz's later view Ginsberg was a lone inheritor of Whitman, with a parallel efficiency that revolutionized lyrical verses.

At the same time, Miłosz was aware of being under the constant influence of the culture he inhabited. He depicts his dilemma in the dialectics of home and open space, which is the core of the imagery in the poem: "for our home is open, there are no keys in the doors, / and invisible guests come in and out at will" (2005: 240, lines 29–30). The question, "What reasonable man would like to be a city of demons, who behave as if they were at home?" (2005: 240, lines 14–15), puts this issue in the most direct way. In the Polish version, "a city of demons" is "a state of demons" ("państwo demonów"). Surely, this meaningful change in Lillian Valle's translation, authorized by the poet, was not accidental. In the American translation Miłosz alludes to the bloody history of California in eighteenth century, which makes the name of the major Californian city Los Angeles highly problematic.

To be just, however, Miłosz also presents the poet's mind as vague, far from angelic innocence: "It's hard to guess where that pride of poets comes from, when so often they're put to shame by the disclosure of their frailty" (2005: 240, lines 11–12). The quest for a 'more spatial form' is articulated in spatial metaphors, and the opposition of home and city in the poem indicates the poet's problems in finding his own place in the intellectual landscape of the United States, where poetry is perceived merely as a private activity in whose "egocentricism lay its universality" (Cavanagh 2009: 244). Should the exilic poet enclose himself in a solipsistic circle of personal experiences or transform these experiences so "that they become universal, accessible to all" (Miłosz 2002–2009: IV, 31)? What community and tradition might he represent and address, especially by writing in Polish, which to the Americans is as remote as "one of the lesser-known African dialects" (Miłosz 2002–2009: III, 146)?

The metaphor of home resonates with another of Miłosz's famous poems, "My Faithful Mother Tongue," also written in 1968 and placed in the same volume, *City without A Name*. Here the exilic poet equates his home with his mother tongue: "You were my native land; I lacked any other" (2005: 245, line 7); "But without you, who am I? Only a scholar in a distant country, a success, without fears and humiliations. Yes, who am I without you? Just a philosopher, like everyone else" (2005: 245, lines 20–24). Also, the metaphor refers to T. S. Eliot's meditations on tradition from his essay "Notes Towards the Definition of Culture," where he employs an image of home to describe legacies of particular civilizations and to discuss the dynamic relationship members of culture maintain with their past.

3 Space and Genre in *Ars poetica?*

In *Ars poetica?*, 'home' is a metaphor of inherited tradition and cultivated particularity, but also an enclave of intimacy, protective of external influences depicted as one-off visitors and alien intruders. It represents the want of order and form that can be turned against chaos and nothingness. It introduces the tension between private and public, local and global, individual and collective, and finally the tension between matter and spirit. Such a position brings into memory Kazimierz Wyka's observation that this poetry relies on numerous antitheses (Kwiatkowski 1985). In Miłosz's specific experience of modernity, this attitude can be viewed as an opposition of the postmodern fluidity as defined by Zygmunt Bauman. Yet Miłosz sees the limitations of such a binary, overly geometrical picture, and so he develops and complicates Eliot's notion of tradition visualized in the American poet's image of home. First of all, he acknowledges human inner creative forces with some reservations:

> In the very essence of poetry there is something indecent:
> a thing is brought forth which we didn't know we had in us,
> so we blink our eyes, as if a tiger had sprung out
> and stood in the light, lashing his tail.
> (2005: 240, lines 5–8)

The image of a tiger, which embodies dark and low drives in human psyche, accentuates Miłosz's suspicions regarding the nature of the artistic act. Some may argue that the image of the tiger alludes to William Blake's poem from 1794. Although Miłosz commenced translating his poetry as early as in the 1940s, he also admired the eminent Polish poet Bolesław Leśmian, who offered a famous image of a panther symbolizing the senses, sexuality, and the dark drives of human nature.

Miłosz's further reflections on poetry as "dictated by a daimonion" (2005: 240, line 9) complement his line. In this part of the poem, Miłosz demonstrates his fidelity to his former recognition of what poetry and who poets were. From his early youth he believed in a mysterious communion with invisible force that led his mind and hand. As early as in the 1930s, he deplored secular avant-garde literary manifestos with arguments he took from the European intellectual past. Much later he would repeat his views: "I suppose, looking back, that everything was dictated to me, and I was just a tool. Of what I don't know. I would like to believe that I am a tool of God, but that's presumptuous. So I prefer to call whatever it is my '*daimonion*'" (Haven 2006: 159–160).

He argued that being a poet was similar to prophetic vocation, and so a poet was a medium of some higher power, an instrument in the service of transcendence. Such statements were of Socratic origins, which Miłosz underlined by using a term "daimonion." Also, they recalled the Romantic tradition, which favored transcendent aspects of creation against norms and patterns. His voice, however, as one may read in *Ars poetica?*, is not solely of an angelic kind, and so the home of the poet's mind cannot be perceived either as an asylum protective from external chaos or as an oasis of inner order. By introducing such contradictions, the poem renews a discussion on the legacy of Classicism and Romanticism, the tension between tradition and avant-garde, ethics and poetics in contemporary literature. It also demonstrates the poet's dramatic attempt to reconcile his classical pursuit of moral discipline with the unpredictable eruption of the imagination as theorized by the Romantics. Bożena Karwowska interprets his attachment to this image of the poet as a strategy of forming his exilic identity. She argues that with time "it became obvious that his professional identity, based on the model of the poet-prophet, was closer to the idea of a loner than a group member" (2011: 86).

Miłosz complicates his own conception of the poet's mind by referring to modern psychology and philosophy, challenging traditional categories of man's integrity. In the words, "how difficult is to remain just one person," (2005: 241, line 30) the poet harks back both to his own experience being transformed by the culturally alien environment in exile and to the process of constant reinterpretation of the past. In such circumstances, how can a poet shape this realm in a single and steady 'form' or genre if this realm is not under his full control or can be hardly spotted as elemental experience of temporality? As the title of the poem *Ars poetica?* suggests, these are incompatible actions. *Ars poetica* defined as a treatise on poetry or poetics no longer offers sufficient rules to twentieth-century writers; therefore, the poet appends the title by a question mark.

To Miłosz, the poet's awareness anticipates all possible ways of literary expression. Therefore, Miłosz transforms a discussion of literary forms and genres, which the title of his poem might have suggested, into a meditation on the poet's existence. In *Ars poetica?* he does not put the capacity of speech (perceived in a biblical sense as a power of denominating reality) above conventions of poetics and rhetoric yet, but in *My Faithful Mother Tongue* he definitely does. He writes:

> Every night, I used to set before you little bowls of colors
> so you could have your birch, your cricket, your finch
> as preserved in my memory.
> (2005: 245, lines 3–5)

For Miłosz, speech is too rich to be fitted in the Procrustes' bed of genres. Also, the categorization implied by genre too much resembles of the natural order of species. Whereas the natural world is finite, our speech may create worlds that transcend and go beyond these limits. This is why speech as such exceeds all instances of its usage and becomes a mighty instrument in the poet's hand. To Miłosz's speaker in *Ars poetica?*, however, writing poems is an existential act that imposes great responsibilities:

> as poems should be written rarely and reluctantly,
> under unbearable duress and only with the hope
> that good spirits, not evil ones, choose us for their instrument.
> (2005: 240, lines 34–36)

That is why Ginsberg is a negative yet hardly visible character of the piece. In *Visions from San Francisco Bay*, where Miłosz critically commented on the American counterculture, Ginsberg was merely a prophet foreshadowing the coming of Moloch's era, a figure which both in John Milton's *Paradise Lost* and in *Howl* stood for a demand of very costly sacrifice. He symbolized everything that Miłosz rejected: mental disorder in its clinical and metaphorical sense; the Beatniks' bravura, self-destruction, irrationalism, indefinite mystical inclinations, leftist immaturity, and infantile search for utopia; as well as a style that was characterized by excess, empty talk, and exaltation (cf. Jarniewicz 2011: 142). Ginsberg made his mental disorder a stylistic frame of his howl, excusing his inconsistency of speech by his disease. Miłosz emphasizes his distance to such acts of writing, his distaste for literature as an expression of intimate privacy. He dismisses all forms of alienated poetry, preoccupied either with itself or articulating merely introspective anxieties.

For Miłosz, Ginsberg was an example of the fall of public man, which Jürgen Habermas defines as usurping the social scene through the private psyche to the detriment of both individual and society (Habermas 1991). His poetry fails to exceed personal interest and, more problematically, is ahistorical. It is worth noting that the single voice of the lyrical 'I' from the first part of the poem is replaced here with the collective 'us,' referring not only to the community of poets but more generally to people whose voice is heard in public. That is why Miłosz, instead of uncontrolled extraversion, commends 'silent integrity' (2005: 241, line 27) to earn the respect of relatives and neighbors. This concept alludes to his postwar poems, where he presented his imperative of salvation through art and literature:

> What is poetry which does not save
> Nations or people?
> A connivance with official lies,
> A song of drunkards whose throats will be cut in a moment,
> Readings for sophomore girls.
> That I wanted good poetry without knowing it,
> That, I discovered late, its salutary aim,
> In this and only this I find salvation.
> (2005: 7, lines 14–21)

In 1968, his aesthetic program articulated twenty-five years earlier remains valid and comes down to the necessity of producing "wise books" (2005: 240, line 21), which demonstrates his nostalgia for the biblical, that is to say sacred and didactic perception of word and speech. Interestingly, he does not elaborate on the aesthetic value or on formal aspects of wise books in the poem. Rather, he emphasizes that they come about in houses visited by good spirits more willingly than in psychiatric clinics (cf. 2005: 240, lines 23–24).

Wisdom is a virtue often achieved in interaction. If, as Miłosz believed from his youth, various events burden a whole community, they touch poets in a most intimate manner and inspire their writings so that the poets are no longer alienated. This in turn puts poetry at the intersection of private and public, giving it specific tasks and obligations:

> for our home is open, there are no keys in the doors,
> and invisible guests come in and out at will.
> (2005: 241, lines 31–32)

Such a position benefits the development of poetic genres in numerous ways. As Georg Simmel claimed in his sociology of borders,

> only a man has the faculty of binding and unbinding, and in this specific manner: that one is always a presupposition of the other. By disengaging two things from the undisturbed state of nature, in order to designate them "separate," we have already related them to each other in our awareness. We have differentiated them both, together, from

everything that lies between them. And vice versa: we experience as connected only what we previously isolated in the same way. Things first have to be separated from each other so as to be united later on. [...] In an immediate just as in a symbolic sense, in a physical as well as a spiritual sense we are, at each moment, the ones who separate what is connected and connect what is separate. (1994: 5)

Simmel conceived a door as an exceptional point in space, where a man unites with infinity he previously disengaged from by maintaining the borders of home. In Miłosz's poem, the image of open door symbolizes the situation of the exilic poet disengaged from his own culture who decides to open up to influences of American culture. At a door we free ourselves from the limitations of closed spaces, giving our lives to infinite directions. By opening the door we annihilate the division between interior and exterior, which also plays a significant role for Miłosz attempting at synthetizing powers of consciousness and subconsciousness. Numerous possibilities expressed by the poetic imagery of an open door partially calms the exilic poet's anxiety of losing his identity under external influences and increases his aspiration of making poetry more spacious.

What consequences does this approach bring about? Having refused the aesthetic isolation of lyric poetry and its perception as an antisocial genre taken out of the flux of history, Miłosz transcended genres and commenced binding different texts and traditions as well as favoring social heteroglossia and linguistic diversity. Perceiving literature "as the art of articulating public issues, a medium and avenue for the organization of intellectual life in the public sphere" (Nycz 2011: 24), he started absorbing many possible verbal ways of denominating the world. He exercised a specific kind of impurity as opposed to the concept of pure or non-contextual poetry: his poetic language absorbed prosaic, everyday speech as well as discourses of contemporary humanities – history, sociology, philosophy, theology, and others. Having liberated himself from obligations of a political bard, the heavy load of responsibility that Central and Eastern European poets were expected to shoulder, in the United States, Miłosz did not lose his close engagement with society and history. To the contrary, in California, he was proving the lyric poem was a historical and social genre, a vehicle poets may navigate to enter all public spheres. Not only did his poems lingered on many lips and engaged with life conducted in actual time allow Miłosz crossing out the chalk circle of an exilic poet writing in a little known dialect. They gave him an unchallenged position of the most important poet writing in the United States, and sealed his reputation as an essential American poet.

Works Cited

Blake, William. 2001. *Milton: Poemat w dwu księgach. Zaślubiny Nieba i Piekła.* Trans. W. Juszczak. Kraków: Towarzystwo Autorów i Wydawców Prac Naukowych "Universitas".
Carpenter, Bogdana. 2003. "The Gift Returned: Czesław Miłosz and American Poetry". In: Halina Stephan (ed.). *Living in Translation: Polish Writers in America.* Amsterdam: Modern Humanities Research Association. 43–75.
Cavanagh, Clare. 2009. *Lyric Poetry and Modern Politics: Russia, Poland, and The West.* New Haven: Yale University Press.
Habermas, Jürgen. 1991. *The Structural Transformation of the Public Sphere: An Inquiry into a Category of Bourgeois Society.* Cambridge: MIT Press.
Haven, Cynthia L. (ed.). 2006. *Czesław Miłosz: Conversations.* Jackson: University Press of Mississippi.
Jarniewicz, Jerzy. 2011. "*Niepotrzebna opona na skraju drogi, czyli Miłosz rozlicza się z Ginsbergiem*" ["A Discarded Tire by the Road, or Miłosz Settles Up with Ginsberg"]. *Przekładaniec* 25: 142–154.
Karwowska, Bożena. 2011. "Reading Miłosz in Exile". In: Stanisław Latek (ed.). *Czesław Miłosz: Multiple Worlds, Game of Forms.* Kraków: Oficyna Wydawniczo-Drukarska "Secesja". 77–95.
Miłosz, Czesław. 2005. *New and Collected Poems 1931–2001.* London: Penguin Books.
Miłosz, Czesław. 2002–2009. *Wiersze.* 5 vols. Kraków: Wydawnictwo Literackie.
Nycz, Ryszard. 1996. *Sylwy współczesne.* Kraków: Universitas.
Nycz, Ryszard. 2000. *Tekstowy świat. Poststrukturalizm a wiedza o literaturze.* Kraków: Universitas.
Nycz, Ryszard. 2011. "Twentieth-century Poet in the Public Space". In: Stanisław Latek (ed.). *Multiple Worlds, Games of Forms.* Kraków: Oficyna Wydawniczo-Drukarska "Secesja". 19–33.
Robinson, Marc (ed.). 1994. *Altogether Elsewhere. Writers on Exile.* Boston and London: Faber & Faber.
Simmel, Georg. 1994. "Bridge and Door". Trans. Mark Ritter. *Theory, Culture and Society* 11: 5–10.
Stephan, Halina (ed.). 2003. "Introduction: The Last Exiles". *Living in Translation: Polish Writers in America.* Amsterdam: Modern Humanities Research Association. 7–29.
Wyka, Kazimierz. 1985. "Ogrody lunatyczne i ogrody pasterskie". In: Jerzy Kwiatkowski (ed.). *Poznawanie Miłosza: Studia i szkice o twórczości.* Kraków: Wydawnictwo Literackie. 15–41.

Kathrin Härtl
"They kept shifting shapes": Derek Walcott's *Omeros* and its Fluid Genre

Abstract: The essay examines Derek Walcott's reappropriation of the epic as a genre, with its strong connections to imperial power and the formation of national myths. Walcott's negotiations of the epic as Caribbean literary form reframe the genre for his own poetics, a project that is most persuasive in his meta-poetic discussions of generic concepts in his epic poem *Omeros* (1990). The essay aims to analyze the self-reflexive accounts of uncertainty and indeterminacy regarding genre in *Omeros* as both a postcolonial Caribbean poetics of resistance and a manifestation of Caribbean intertextuality. After a brief discussion of Walcott's position on genre and tradition in his critical essays, the essay argues that his 'epic' poem deals with the question of genre not by introducing distinctive, stable generic attributes. Instead, *Omeros* expresses the floating character of genre, especially in postcolonial and Caribbean contexts. Through its use of oscillating narrating voices and maritime imagery, it discloses and dismisses normative conceptions of the epic as a Eurocentric imperial strategy.

Keywords: Derek Walcott, epic, *Omeros*, intertextuality, postcolonial

I

In 1992, Derek Walcott opened his Nobel lecture "The Antilles: Fragments of Epic Memory" with an account of a visit with American friends to Trinidad for the annual performance of the Hindu epic *Ramleela* by descendants of indentured Indian cane cutters in the small village Felicity:

> [T]his Saturday afternoon *Ramleela*, the epic dramatization of the Hindu epic *Ramayana*, was going to be performed, and the costumed actors from the village were assembling on a field strung with different-coloured flags, like a new gas-station, and beautiful Indian boys in red and black were aiming arrows haphazardly into the afternoon light. Low blue mountains on the horizon, bright grass, clouds that would gather colour before the light went. Felicity! What a gentle Anglo-Saxon name for an epical memory. (1998: 65)

The *Ramayana*, the epic as a genre, and its role in Caribbean culture are key elements of Walcott's argument in his Nobel lecture. Initially, he perceives himself in the position of a tourist watching a foreign, exotic festive play. He is impressed by the "beautiful Indian boys" and by the performance appealing to all senses, but he provides an external perspective when describing his lack of knowledge and uncertainty about the plot and the figures, which appear on stage: "Princes and Gods, I supposed – What an unfortunate confession! 'Gods, I suppose' is the shrug that empties our African and Asian diasporas" (1998: 66). Although *Ramleela* is an annual festivity on Trinidad, Walcott's knowledge about the text and its performance is surprisingly limited. His expertise on the *Odyssey*, on the other hand, is quite extensive.

> I had no idea what the epic story was, who its hero was, what enemies he fought, yet I had recently adapted the Odyssey for a theatre in England, presuming that the audience knew the trials of Odysseus, hero of another Asia Minor epic, while nobody in Trinidad knew any more than I did about Rama, Kali, Shiva, Vishnu, apart from the Indians, a phrase I use pervertedly because that is the kind of remark you can still hear in Trinidad: "apart from the Indians." (1998: 66)

The constellation of Walcott's poor knowledge of Indian tradition and his excellent "Epic Memory" (1998: 65) of the *Odyssey* provides a prototypical example of the entanglements of various literary traditions and their conflicts produced by colonial history. The numerous influences of different colonizing parties as well as different diasporic peoples in the Caribbean diversify and hybridize the literary tradition on these islands. Although Walcott compares the ignorance of the Caribbean audience concerning the *Ramayana* with the British ignorance of the *Odyssey*, the status of these epics in Caribbean literary discourse is distinctly different and the relation between these epics and their global reception is more complex.

Colonial education, which brought for example George Chapman's translation of the *Odyssey* into the Anglophone colonized world, is one reason why in some parts of the Caribbean the story of Odysseus and his trials may be more widely known than the story of *Ramleela*. In "Homecoming: Anse La Raye" (1969), Walcott ironically comments on the journey of the 'classics' into the colonial classroom and contrasts it with the erasure of the history of the Middle Passage: "Whatever else we learned at school, / like solemn Afro-Greeks eager for grades, / of Helen and the shades of borrowed ancestors, / there are no rites for those who have returned" (2013: 110). By the term "Afro-Greeks" Walcott foreshadows the highly disputed research on *Black Athena* (Bernal 1987) that tried to undermine the cultural authority of Greek culture and show the influence and hegemony of African cultures in Antiquity. Walcott takes up this critical perspective on European culture and its role in the Caribbean in the juxtaposition of the *Odyssey* and *Ramleela* at the beginning of his speech. Thus, he seemingly exemplifies how the impact of European literary traditions on Caribbean culture correlates with neglecting the role of other literary traditions in the Caribbean. In the course of his speech, however, Walcott re-evaluates his own position on Caribbean literature and develops a poetics of mimicry that is explicitly linked to the genre of epic poetry regarding not only European classics but also the Hindu epic *Ramayana* and its cultural function in Caribbean literature.

This essay aims to describe and analyze the self-reflexive accounts of uncertainty and indeterminacy regarding genre in Walcott's *Omeros* (1990) as a postcolonial Caribbean poetics of resistance. After a brief discussion of Walcott's position on genre and tradition in his essays, I argue that his 'epic' poem deals with the question of genre not by introducing distinctive, stable generic attributes. Rather, *Omeros* expresses the floating character of genre, especially in postcolonial and Caribbean contexts. By its use of oscillating narrating voices and maritime imagery, it discloses and dismisses the normative strategy of genre in the case of the epic as Eurocentric imperial strategy.

Walcott's choice of the epic to underscore his argument on Caribbean literature is not by chance. Not only form, style, and its cast define the epic, but its strong connection to an ideology of imperialism. The genre, as Peter Hulme observes, served well for European and specifically English imperialism during the nineteenth century.

> As the European nations, especially England, took on their imperial roles, the classical world of the Mediterranean grew in importance as a repository of the images and analogies by which those nations could represent to themselves their colonial activities. (1986: 35)

The story of English exploration and imperialism has often been told in narratives, tropes, and rhetoric of ancient epics such as the *Iliad* and the *Aeneid*. References to both texts legitimized English colonization of the Caribbean in prose and poetry from the sixteenth century: notably *The Tempest*, which contains clear allusions to Virgil's text (Merten 2004: 69–70).

This specific use of Classical Greek epics culminates in J. A. Froude's travelogue *The English in the West Indies Or, the Bow of Ulysses* (1888), in which he evokes the *Iliad* as an image for the political system of imperialism in the Caribbean:

> If ever the naval exploits of this country are done into an epic poem – and since the Iliad there has been no subject better fitted for such treatment or better deserving it – the West Indies will be the scene of the most brilliant cantos. (Froude 2010: 10)

Reframing the political reality in the English colonies with the narrative structure of the epic not only legitimizes colonial presence in the Caribbean, but already implies and determines the presumably successful result of the heroic narrative which only requires an English hero in the tradition of Odysseus to 'come home.' More than a mere capitalist investment, Froude argues that the 'West Indies' are part of the myth of 'Britannia' and laments a possible loss of the colonies:

> For England to allow them to drift away from her because they have no immediate marketable value, would be a sign that she had lost the feelings with which great nations always treasure the heroic traditions of their fathers. When those traditions come to be regarded as something which concerns them no longer, their greatness is already on the wane. (2010: 10)

Thus, the epic is not only a classical genre that Walcott reflects on, but he considers the tradition of the epic as a mode of story-telling that often takes side with the triumphant winners (Quint, 1993: 9). Froude's use of the epic to legitimize colonization is not an uncommon strategy. Hulme describes how European explorers and colonizers tried to trace back the roots of uncanny observations in the 'New World' to ancient knowledge. The re-analysis of lexical items like 'hurricane' or 'cannibal' provided them with Latin roots and thus dismissed any non-European influence on the English language (Hulme 1986: 100–101)

In his analysis of the "epical memory" (1998: 65) in the Antilles, Walcott self-critically assesses his own position towards these various influences on his literary writings:

> They believed in what they were playing, in the sacredness of the text, the validity of India, while I, out of the writer's habit, searched some sense of elegy, of loss, even of degenerative mimicry [...]. I was polluting the afternoon with doubt and with the patronage of admiration. I misread the event through a visual echo of History. (1998: 67)

Walcott's questioning of his perspective on the performance focuses on what he regards as wrong understanding of history and textual influence: one that treats history and literary tradition as stable concepts that can only be looked at with nostalgia and the yearning for a lost past and that understands the transfer of genres into a different cultural environment as "degenerative" imitation. However, Walcott claims that the performance of the *Ramayana* is not a nostalgic re-enactment of Indian traditions in the Diaspora but "like a dialect, a branch of its original language, an abridgment of it, but not a distortion or even a reduction of its epic scale" (1998: 68). Caribbean culture reframes various literary traditions and Walcott thus states that neither rewriting nor repetition of the literatures of the colonizer or the diaspora is a reduction, distortion or abridgment, but instead creates something new.

With reference to the *Ramayana*, Walcott develops the concept of mimicry he had described extensively in his essay "The Caribbean: Culture or Mimicry?" (1974). He underscores that "these forms originated in imitation if you want, and ended in invention" (1998: 9). This concurs with his general assessment of literary traditions, which he describes by using maritime imagery in his essay "The Muse of History" (1974):

> one acknowledges not an exchange of influences, not imitation, but the tidal advance of the metropolitan language, of its empire. [...] It is the language which is its empire, and great poets are not its vassals but its princes. (1998: 51)

In the image of "tidal advance," Walcott pursues a reciprocal relation between colonial history and Caribbean literary strategies that is not reducible to ideas of secondary or belated imitations of a former and supposedly superior literary tradition (Härtl 2019: 185–186). This statement demonstrates that, although often accused of being euro-centric, his evaluation of various literary influences in Caribbean poetry takes not only European epics into account but also various intertexts such as the *Ramleela*. What is more, it introduces a strong argument about genre in general. Genre as a normative strategy is subject to ideological functions resulting in discourses of fidelity or originality – categories that are not in the focus of Walcott's critical assessment of his own poetics. In Rei Terada's study of Walcott's poetry she remarks: "If Walcott did not exist, theorists of influence would have had to invent him" (1992: 43). Numerous studies deal with Walcott's exuberant use of intertextual references from Homer to Shakespeare, Dante, Jonson, Donne, Yeats, Joyce, and Pound. Accordingly, these studies also reflect on his treatment of various canonical genres, such as the epic or the sonnet, for example in the sonnet sequence "Tales of the Island" from the 1962 collection *In a Green Night* (Müller 2012).

Walcott's long poem *Omeros* is one of his most complex and multi-layered texts regarding various literary influences. Far from concealing these intertexts, it displays them prominently. However, there are not only references to European epic texts: Fumagalli claims that the beginning of *Omeros* also alludes to Caribbean poetry, for example poems by Brathwaite, Nichols, and Césaire (2000: 17). Supporting this observation, Farrell shows links to African epic texts and demonstrates that the epic is not only a Western European tradition but can be found in various parts of the world:

> Walcott's construction of Homer not as a participant in an exclusively European scribal culture but as a singer of folktales whom one might find just as readily in an African or Afro-Caribbean context as in that of archaic Greece. (1997: 254)

In a similar vein, Walcott calls the *Odyssey* "another Asia Minor epic" in his Nobel lecture, thus implying that the borders of the European tradition are indistinct and underlining that genre is not only a category which needs to be revised within its formal structures but also regarding its position within the system of national literatures.

The discussion of whether *Omeros* can or should be labelled as 'epic' started directly after its publication (cf. Farrell 1997: 272–273). Walcott (maybe consciously) remained ambivalent on this question. Thus, his reflections on *Omeros* are deeply affected by his skeptical attitude towards definite categorization, since he suspects ideological or cultural politics behind these attributions, as he subsequently argues:

> So the book is really not about a model of another poem; it is really about associations, or references, because that is what we are in the Americas: we are a culture of references, not of certainties. (Walcott 1997: 239)

As a Caribbean postcolonial writer, Walcott is necessarily acutely aware of the problems of comparison to and recycling of supposed European traditional genres. The danger of colonizing Caribbean literature by a focus on the epic and other genres extends to the literary critics as well:

> The fact is that – everywhere in the myriad traditions outside ancient Greek – 'the epic' is an analytic rather than an indigenous concept and label, and in applying it uncritically to long narrative forms from other cultures we run the risk of unintentionally colonizing their verbal art. (Foley 2004: 173)

Omeros can be seen as a literary testing ground for Walcott's poetics of mimicry, which is always in danger of perpetuating European genres and ideologies while actually aiming to subvert them. Thus, *Omeros* chooses to comment on its own structure and imagery instead of just resisting imperialist structures of the epic as the following analysis of the varying narrating voices will show. It first and foremost questions the strategy of using rigid concepts of genre that exclude ideas of rewriting and cultural appropriation.

II

As far as form is concerned, *Omeros* plays excessively with generic conventions. Although the verses are mainly in loose *terza rima* and therefore allude to epic predecessors such as Dante's *Divina Commedia*, the verse scheme is interrupted by various other forms, for example dramatic dialogues or verses that resemble the interplay of question and answer of the Christian catechism (Hofmeister 1996: 538). The text consists of seven books and 64 chapters, thus oscillating between the genre of the novel with regard to its use of chapters and the epic with regard to its stanzaic design (Merten 2004: 177). Three main storylines are inextricably interwoven in the course of the text. One strand centers on the Caribbean people of St. Lucia, with special focus on the love triangle between Achille, Hector, and the beautiful Helen. Philoctete, a fellow fishermen, is afflicted by a wound (like his Greek namesake) and will be healed by Ma Kilman, a Caribbean obeah woman. The obvious epic allusions in the names of the Caribbean cast in this storyline can be read as self-reflexive rewriting of the Classical Greek epics in its own right. Even more momentously, they reflect the use of the epic as an imperialist strategy as slaves in former British colonies were often given names of epic heroes as a pejorative act of colonial power (Van Sickle 1999: 8). Further comparisons to epic form have been made on different levels, for example the Dantesque topos of the poem as a journey and the journey as a poem (Fumagalli 2000: 20). The poem's expansiveness on a structural level has also been regarded as epic (Hofmeister 1996: 541).

On the other hand, the cast of the poem does not, with exception of the names, resemble typical heroes and their actions. This is one reason why Walcott hesitates to call it an epic:

> I do not think of it as an epic. Certainly not in the sense of epic design. Where are the battles? There are a few, I suppose. But 'epic' makes people think of great wars and warriors. That isn't the Homer I was thinking of; I was thinking of Homer the poet of the seven seas. (qtd. in Bruckner 1993: 396)

Walcott is not interested in the rewriting of ancient battles. His focus lies on the act of narration and representation, which he sees epitomized in the figure of Homer. This is the reason why *Omeros* not only abounds in allusions to epic figures and plots but above all concentrates on self-reflexive accounts of storytelling, which is far more insightful as far as the category of genre is concerned. This meta-poetic strategy is especially used in connection with three figures who are known as or perform as bards and storytellers in addition to the anonymous first-person narrator of *Omeros*: Major Plunkett, Seven Seas, and Homer/Omeros. Each of them mirrors in different ways the modes of representation of St. Lucia and its repercussions for generic concepts of the epic.

The English expatriate and owner of a pig farm Major Plunkett and his Irish wife Maude are the main characters of the second storyline. Plunkett, who is established as an author figure, aims to write a historical account of St. Lucia by using Helen as his protagonist: "Helen needed a history, / that was the pity that Plunkett felt towards her" (1990: 30). The reference to Helen is not only a consideration of the Greek epic as the role model for Walcott's historiography. Rather, it stresses the euro-centric recycling of this tradition by English explorers and colonizers, who referred to St. Lucia as "Helen of the West Indies":

> the island was once
> named Helen; its Homeric association
> rose like smoke from a siege   (31)

In addition to Plunkett's questionable reason for writing about St. Lucia and Helen at all – his unfulfilled desire for Helen – his problematic way of representation becomes evident in his treatment of Caribbean history: he is counting the number of cannons used in historical battles and recites "every billet, regiment, / of the battle's numerological poetry," thereby "flattening an ocean / to paper diagrams" (95). Thus, for Plunkett seascape functions as a metaphor for history where each mode of representation inevitably leads to reduction. He does not use the Caribbean seascape as a figurative space for the complex historical entanglements of Imperial forces and diasporic people, as for example Édouard Glissant describes it:

> We are the roots of a cross-cultural relationship. Submarine roots: that is floating free, not fixed in one position in some primordial spot, but extending in all directions in our world through its networks and branches. (1989: 67)

Rather, Plunkett narrows the seascape to a blank sheet of paper that only reproduces data of Imperial battles. Thus, his interest in statistics and "Homeric repetition" (Walcott 1990: 96) simplifies the description of Helen and by proxy the island.

This process epitomizes Walcott's first misinterpretation of the *Ramayana* in Trinidad in his Nobel lecture. However, similarly to Walcott's essay, the narrative in *Omeros* self-reflexively shifts its perspective. Only in the course of the text does the first-person narrator come prominently into view. His role and perspective on the epic and Caribbean mode of representation are more complex and seem to be set in opposition to Plunkett's attempts of representing St. Lucia. The allegorical journeys of the first-person narrator into the past as well as his journeys to other countries frame and connect the different narratives of the poem. Plunkett's unsuccessful task mirrors the project of the anonymous narrator, who himself continuously questions his mode of representation concerning the choice of the epic as a point of reference. His critique of Plunkett's use of Homeric allusions leads him to reflect on his contention: "Didn't I prefer a road / from which tracks climbed into the thickening syntax / of colonial travelers, the measured prose I read / as a schoolboy?" (227). The narrator presents himself as a diligent reader of the colonial literary canon yet simultaneously questions this literary tradition. This doubt is comparable to the reading experience described in Walcott's poem "Sea Grapes" (1976): "The classics can console. But not enough" (2013: 197). Ultimately, the narrator tries to evade the "Homeric shadow" in *Omeros*: "when would it stop / the echo in the throat, insisting, 'Omeros'; / when would I enter that light beyond metaphor (271). However, to abandon metaphors is an impossible task in poetry. Thus, neither the poem itself nor the persona present a solution in the text. Instead, in the last chapters of the poem the metaphor and similes that are used are striking and paradox. They once again take up maritime imagery by using the double meaning of 'craft':

> Like Philoctete's wound, this language carries its cure,
> its radiant affliction; reluctantly now,
> like Achille's, my craft slips the chain of its anchor
> (323)

The "craft," which signifies the ship as well as the act of writing, serves as an empowering vehicle for the narrator, enabling him to break away from the stable bonds to the land as well as from the literary traditions represented by the anchor in this stanza.

While Plunkett serves as a character in Walcott's poem, the twin figure of Seven Seas and Omeros is used in a more meta-poetic way. Omeros as well as Seven Seas come into view in the same moment as the first-person speaker of the poem appears. Seven Seas sits in front of his house in the morning sun and looks, although he is blind, at the lagoon:

> Except for one hand he sat as still as marble,
> with his egg-white eyes, fingers recounting the past
> of another sea, measured by the stroking oars. (12)

The sea is not only present in the name of the bard figure, but he is tapping rhythmically while reciting the past: He is presented telling the past story of another sea that might be the Mediterranean. This blind black man is therefore presented as a Homeric epic singer, obliged to the oral tradition of story-telling. The description by the first-person narrator of this "black fisherman," who "scanned the opening line / of our epic horizon" (13), contains a summoning of Omeros:

> O open this day with the conch's moan, Omeros,
> as you did in my boyhood, when I was a noun
> gently exhaled from the palate of the sunrise.
> [...]
> Only in you, across centuries
> of the sea's parchment atlas, can I catch the noise
> of the surf lines wandering like the shambling fleece
> of the lighthouse's flock.   (12–13)

The first-person narrator who introduced Seven Seas now appeals to Omeros, who is put in the role of a Muse, and the influence of this Muse on the narrator is overwhelming. Maritime imagery is used to express poetry, especially its textual and material character: the surf lines equal the line of a poem written on the sea's parchment atlas and the sound of these poems (its metrical as well as its rhythmical quality) can be heard in the noise of the sea.

Traditionally, the invocation of the Muse is part of the opening of an epic, comparable to the invocation of the muses in the *Odyssey* or the *Iliad*. It introduces the anonymous first-person narrator of *Omeros* as a singer or bard in tradition of the oral performance of epics. However, while Seven Seas as a figure alludes to the epic tradition, the sea itself resists any "epic memory":

> The ocean had no memory of the wandering of Gilgamesh,
> or whose sword severed whose head in the Iliad.
> It was an epic where every line was erased
> yet freshly written in sheets of exploding surf.
> [...] It never altered its metre
> to suit the age, a wide page without metaphors.
> Our last resort as much as yours, Omeros.   (295–296)

Just as the narrator desires to express the Caribbean without a "Homeric shadow," the sea resists any usurpations of epic narratives. The maritime image serves as a metaphor for a liberating space that provides an ever-changing pool of literary opportunities. While the sea figures as a poem that forms "lines," is "written down," and follows metrical rules ("it never altered its metre"), it does not function as an archive for epic memories such as the *Iliad* or the Gilgamesh epic. Walcott extends the metaphor by presenting the sea not only as a space of erasure, but also as a space in which genre as an act of name-giving obtains another quality.

III

The Janus figure of Omeros and Seven Seas is most noticeable in a beach scene in Book Seven, Chapter 56. In the first canto the transfiguration of the bard figure is presented in detail. The uncertain shape and form of the figure that emerges from the sea can be read as a metaphor for genre and poetics that is not interested in the normative act of generic terms, but in the mechanisms and processes generic terminology relies on as soon as it emerges in a different cultural environment. The narrator persona takes a stroll along the beach and notices some flotsam in the sea. Initially, the indeterminacy of object and subject features prominently: is it a "driftwood log," a "bust," or a "coconut shell" (279) that is washed ashore? The vastness of the ocean and the perspective from the beach only allow speculations at first. But the object turns out to be a person emerging from the sea:

> I knew
> that the floating head had drifted here. The mirrors
> of the sky were clouded, and I heard my own voice
> correcting his name, as the surf hissed: "Omeros."
> The moment I named it, the marble head arose,
> fringed with its surf curls and beard, the hollow shoulders
> of a man waist-high in water with an old leather
> goatskin or a plastic bag, pricking the dog's ears,
> making it whine with joy. Then, suddenly, the weather
> darkened, and it darkened the forked, slow-wading wood
> until it was black, and the shallows in that second
> changed to another dialect as Seven Seas stood
> in the white foam manacling his heels. (279)

At the beginning of this scene the persona seems to be just a spectator without agency. This changes immediately as soon as the object is named: the marble bust is named "Omeros" by the sea itself. However, the persona does not take this name for granted but corrects it. This ambiguous moment can be read in two ways. The modification of the name may refer to a shift in pronunciation from Ancient Greek to Modern Greek, from Ô-meros to O-méros (Dougherty 1997: 336). By the change of accentuation the persona, figuring as a beachcomber, claims power over the bust of Homer. This shift does not only call for a modernization of the epic – to 'make it new' – but also concentrates on the oral character of the epic as a shared feature not only with the Caribbean oral tradition but with epics from all over the world.

On the other hand the change of name also relates to the shape-shifting that takes place in the following verses. It is initiated by the act of naming, which turns the first-person narrator into an Adamic figure. "Adam's task of giving things their names" (2009: 152) is an essential part of Walcott's masculine trope for the processes and tasks of his general figuration of the author. The act of naming and its power are presented here in an extraordinary way because it is this very act that brings the bust into life and makes it emerge from the sea. The naming process can be seen as an act of authority and authorship: the author (as a spectator) gives his creatures the proper and their 'own' names. The flotsam that is washed ashore is shape-shifting, and the active act of name-giving by the first-person narrator become tropes for Caribbean culture. Walcott develops these tropes in various essays, for example in "The

Figure of Crusoe" (1965), and in poems such as *Another Life*, where he establishes the paradoxical image of "the virginal unpainted world" (2009: 152) on the one hand and the image of "flotsam" in *Omeros* on the other. Walcott's mimicry as strategy relies on this double image that is remarkably a colonialist strategy and is reflected for example in the terms "Old World" and "New World." Not only does he re-use colonial strategies, Walcott also repeats a Romantic tradition of the author as a male genius who creates by the power of naming: "the artist's Adamic task of renaming creates an image of the artist that, despite its cultural specificity, recalls the Romantic concept of the artistic genius" (Boeninger 2011: 475).

This double move is expressed in the transfiguration process that starts after this emergence. It is not only indeterminacy in the moment of perception that resembles the question of generic attribution, but also the plaster of the bust develops a life of its own. It transfigures again from a Crusoe figure (alluded to by the goatskin) into a darkening figure until it becomes the black bard figure Seven Seas. Again Walcott appropriates a colonial figure, Robinson Crusoe, in order to subvert the master-slave narrative, which is not only essential in historical discourse but also in terms of intertextuality:

> We are Crusoes: as poets, as novelists, as playwrights, we survey islands, and we feel they belong to us – not in a bad, godlike manner, but with that sense of exhilaration, of creative possession. (Walcott qtd. in Hirsch 1996: 63; cf. Terada 1992: 78)

However, the process the bust undergoes by emerging from the sea is not linear. The white marble bust of Homer as a signifier of the European literary tradition does not simply change into a new shape. Rather, it remains in an oscillating state:

> They kept shifting shapes, or the shapes metamorphosed
> in the worried water; no sooner was the head
> of the blind plaster-bust clear than its brow was crossed
> by a mantling cloud and its visage reappeared
> with ebony hardness, skull and beard like cotton,
> its nose like a wedge; no sooner I saw the one
> than the other changed and the first was forgotten
> as the sand forgets a shadow in widening sun,
> their bleached almond seeds their only thing in common
> (280–281)

The sea serves as a pool for cultural artefacts, whose forms are interchangeable and can be the source for mimicry. The "plaster-bust" of Homer serves as reference to European residues of cultural influence whose shape is remodeled by the sea and therefore can be appropriated in Seven Seas, the Caribbean version of Homer.

Elizabeth DeLoughrey describes the spatial features of the sea as particularly productive for these intertextual connections:

> Focusing on a seascape rather than landscape as the fluid space of historical production allows us to complicate the nation-state, which encodes a rigid hierarchy of race, class, gender, religion, and ethnicity for its representative subjects. Because the surface of the ocean is unmarked by its human history and thus cannot be monumentalized in the tradition of colonial landscapes, a turn to the sea as history can produce an equalizing effect. (2007: 21)

Referring implicitly to Deleuze's concepts of the smooth and the striated (2004: 523–551), DeLoughrey claims that the surface of the ocean, in contrast to landscapes, is not marked by colonial power and thus serves as an equalizer. Homer's bust as representative of a Western tradition can easily be perceived as a coconut shell or a log, and therefore as a regional and typical part of the Caribbean flora and fauna. Indeed, the fluid character of the sea has an equalizing character because it prevents genealogical assumptions: in the ocean of texts anything can possibly end up as flotsam and jetsam. Tobias Döring argues that the idea of beachcombing is an "autopoetic" reflection, the author functioning as a collector and writing as bringing together these different artefacts or texts found at the beach (2015: 118). Concerning genre, *Omeros* goes even further. "Homer" is not only washed ashore and collected by the artist as beachcomber. Rather, "Homer" as a metonym for the European literary tradition of the epic turns out to be a shape shifter, and the form of the epic, supposedly stable, becomes something else as soon as the beachcomber becomes Adam and names the flotsam. The emergence of Seven Seas is only made possible by the new name and the appropriation of power implied in the act of name giving.

The metaphorical function of the sea is substantial for the transfiguration processes the figure emerging from the sea goes through. The indeterminacy of the shape seems to be produced by the ocean itself at the beginning ("They kept shifting shapes," 280). It is a categorizing problem or a matter of perspective, which is problematized by the lack of orientation or coordinates at sea. For the mapping of the sea is not only a descriptive act of natural orientation points, but also a formative act. This is as exemplified by the definition of the Prime Meridian, which is also discussed in Omeros: "Once the world's green gourd was split like a calabash / by Pope Alexander's decree" (191). Walcott is referring to the Treaty of Tordesillas in 1494, when the imperial authorities Spain and Portugal introduced a meridian to solve conflicts about colonies in the New World. The meridian is therefore exemplary of a normative act of categorization that the imperial powers performed. This is what Walcott subverts by the indistinctness of the maritime imagery and the new meridian he defines for himself, because after this first moment of perception and misperception – a rather passive moment – the act of naming does not help to determinate this figure conclusively, but the narrating figure keeps on shifting shapes.

Omeros uses the sea as a spatial expression of transnational generic transpositions as being flotsam at the beach and not immediately recognizable. Epic allusions are only recognizable as long as the coordinates or the map are at hand, as soon as it is flotsam at the beach it can be seen as almost everything. *Omeros'* proposition, hence, is to see genre as a discursive construct closely related to space and culture. The Caribbean Sea makes conventional readers of canonical epics turn their reassuring gaze from land to sea and accordingly leads to a subversion of traditional conventions. The sea is the metaphorical space that is used in a self-reflexive account of *poeisis*, thus also of writing in the Western tradition, including the epic and other poetic constructs. The poem does not erase the Western genre but renders generic categories fluid. It thus comments on genre on a structural level and in terms of cultural politics, questioning the conventional notion of epic as a genre of the powerful.

Works Cited

Bernal, Martin. 1987. *Black Athena: The Afroasiatic Roots of Classical Civilization*. New Brunswick: Rutgers University Press.

Boeninger, Stephanie Pocock. 2011. "'I Have Become the Sea's Craft': Authorial Subjectivity in Derek Walcott's *Omeros* and David Dabydeen's 'Turner'". *Contemporary Literature* 52.3: 462–492.

Bruckner, D. J. R. 1993. "A Poem In Homage To An Unwanted Man". In: Robert D. Hamner (ed.). *Critical Perspectives on Derek Walcott*. Boulder: Lynne Rienner. 396–399.

Deleuze, Gilles, and Félix Guattari. 2004. *A Thousand Plateaus: Capitalism and Schizophrenia*. Trans. Brian Massumi. London: Continuum.

DeLoughrey, Elizabeth. 2007. *Routes and Roots: Navigating Caribbean and Pacific Island Literatures*. Honolulu: University of Hawai'i Press.

Döring, Tobias. 2015. "Caribbean Beachcombers". In: Ursula Kluwick and Virginia Richter (eds.). *The Beach in Anglophone Literatures and Cultures: Reading Littoral Space*. Aldershot: Ashgate. 107–119.

Dougherty, Carol. 1997. "Homer after Omeros: Reading a H/Omeric Text". In: Gregson Davis (ed.). *The Poetics of Derek Walcott: Intertextual Perspectives*. Spec. issue of *The South Atlantic Quarterly* 96.2: 335–357.

Farrell, Joseph. 1997. "Walcott's Omeros: The Classical Epic in a Postcolonial World". In: Suzanne Wofford, Margaret Beisinger, and Jane Tylus (eds.). *Epic Traditions in the Contemporary World: The Poetics of Community*. Berkeley: University of California Press. 247–273.

Foley, John M. 2004. "Epic as Genre". In: Robert Fowler (ed.). *The Cambridge Companion to Homer*. Cambridge: Cambridge University Press. 171–87.

Froude, James Anthony. 2010. *The English in the West Indies or The Bow of Ulysses*. New York: Cambridge University Press.

Fumagalli, Maria Cristina. 2000. "Derek Walcott's *Omeros* and Dante's *Commedia*: Epics of the Self and Journeys into Language". *The Cambridge Quarterly* 29.1: 17–36.

Glissant, Édouard. 1989. *Caribbean Discourse: Selected Essays*. Charlottesville: University Press of Virginia.

Härtl, Kathrin. 2019. *The Common Bond of the Sea. Derek Walcott und Joseph Conrad*. Paderborn: Fink.

Hirsch, Edward. 1996. "An Interview with Derek Walcott". In: William Baer (ed.). *Conversations with Derek Walcott*. Jackson: University Press of Mississippi. 50–63.

Hofmeister, Timothy P. 1996. "The Wolf and the Hare: Epic Expansion and Contextualization in Derek Walcott's 'Omeros'". *International Journal of the Classical Tradition* 2.4: 536–554.

Hulme, Peter. 1986. *Colonial Encounters: Europe and the Native Caribbean, 1492–1797*. London: Methuen.

Merten, Kai. 2004. *Antike Mythen – Mythos Antike: Posthumanistische Antikerezeption in der englischsprachigen Lyrik der Gegenwart*. Munich: Fink.

Müller, Timo. 2012. "Transnationalism in Contemporary Black Poetry: Derek Walcott, Rita Dove, and the Sonnet Form". In: Udo J. Hebel (ed.). *Transnational American Studies*. Heidelberg: Winter. 249–268.

Quint, David. 1993. *Epic and Empire: Politics and Generic Form from Virgil to Milton*. Princeton: Princeton University Press.

Terada, Rei. 1992. *Derek Walcott's Poetry: American Mimicry*. Boston: Northeastern University Press.

Van Sickle, John B. 1999. "The Design of Derek Walcott's 'Omeros'". *The Classical World* 93.1: 7–27.

Walcott, Derek. 1974. "The Caribbean: Culture or Mimicry?". *Journal of Interamerican Studies and World Affairs* 16.1: 3–13.

Walcott, Derek. 1990. *Omeros*. New York: Farrar, Straus and Giroux.

Walcott, Derek. 1997. "Reflections on *Omeros*". *The South Atlantic Quarterly* 96: 229–246.

Walcott, Derek. 1998. *What the Twilight Says: Essays*. London: Faber & Faber.

Walcott, Derek. 2009. *Another Life*. Boulder: Lynne Rienner.

Walcott, Derek. 2014. *The Poetry of Derek Walcott: 1948–2013*. New York: Farrar, Straus and Giroux.

Katharina Engel
Diversifying the Genre: Postmodern Strategies in Patience Agbabi's (Performance) Poetry

Abstract: This paper focuses on meta-poetic reflections in the work of the contemporary British poet Patience Agbabi. In close readings of selected texts and performances from her four published collections, three interlinked postmodern strategies are identified by means of which Agbabi unsettles poetic conventions and questions the politics of the genre from "ex-centric" positions (Hutcheon): Agbabi puts equal value on the written and the spoken word; she plays with the tension between herself as "poet-performer" (Novak) and her constructions of poet(ic) personae; and she engages in postmodern experiments with traditional forms. Thus, Agbabi creates an image of the postmodern poet as a decentered "nomadic subject" (Braidotti) and subverts limiting assumptions about what characterizes a Black female performance poet and her work to diversify the genre.

Keywords: contemporary Black British poetry, performance poetry, postmodernism, ars poetica, genre

Poetry can be seen as a restrictive and restricting genre in the UK. Explicit and implicit expectations carried by the label "poetry" decide who gets published, read, reviewed, and studied while other voices remain unheard or marginalized. When it comes to representing the diversity of ethnicities, genders, and sexualities as well as a diversity of forms, poetry as a business and as a field of literary studies can still be male dominated, white, and heterosexual as well as focused on the page (cf. Moore 2013; Anaxagorou 2016; Kean 2016; Salzman and Wack 2008: 7–17). Since Patience Agbabi was chosen as one of the Poetry Society's New Generation Poets in 2004 – with only one other BAME (Black, Asian, and Minority Ethnic) poet, Moniza Alvi, on that prestigious list of twenty – she has been regarded as an influential voice at the center of the contemporary British poetry scene. She is often grouped with the few Black female voices of her generation in the poetry mainstream, such as performance poets SuAndi and Dorothea Smartt, dub poet Jean 'Binta' Breeze, or the page poets Jackie Kay and Bernardine Evaristo. Agbabi has been called an Oxford-educated "formalist" (Novak and Fischer 2016: 361), a "tireless ambassador for spoken word poetry" (Evans-Bush 2013), and "a thoroughly modern postmodernist" (Murphy 2010: 81) whose poetry

https://doi.org/10.1515/9783110594874-011

for the page and for the stage is as much indebted to the British canon as it is to popular culture. With her provocative and playful poems, Agbabi questions any "rigid preconceptions about what [a poet] should produce, [which are] based on superficial categories such as race, sexuality, ethnicity, politics, nationality and gender" (Ramey 2009: 311).

Over the past few years, Agbabi's publications have received considerable scholarly attention. Catherine Murphy (2010) provides a thorough reading of her first three collections that analyzes the "public and private dimensions of poetry and the concomitant obligations of the poet" (68) as reflected in Agbabi's postmodern poetics and identity politics. Her work is compared with that of other Black British performance poets, for example by Lauri Ramey (2009) who discusses SuAndi's and Agbabi's diverse influences focusing on Agbabi's creative engagement with the English canonical tradition. Manuela Coppola (2016) contrasts Agbabi's and Jean 'Binta' Breeze's takes on Chaucer's "Wife of Bath," employing the postcolonial concept of "transnationalism" (305). An earlier publication from Coppola links Black diaspora studies and queer studies to argue that Agbabi "queers the sonnet form" (2015: 369). Andrea Sand and Merle Tönnies discuss Agbabi's work as an example of a development "from the 1990s onwards" in which Black British performance poetry "engages constructively with writing and written traditions" instead of keeping an "exclusive focus on orality" (2010: 105). In their most recent publication, Sand and Tönnies still discuss Agbabi's translations of orality into writing and vice versa, but with a focus on how the poet-performer Agbabi becomes a unifying center behind the text (Tönnies et al. 2016).

Taking insights from these various approaches to Agbabi's oeuvre, this paper conducts close readings of her meta-poetic texts and performances from all four of her published collections. This paper clarifies how Agbabi, as a self-declared "poetical activist" (Agbabi 2003), challenges conventions and unsettles dominant conceptions of the genre poetry and its sub-genres. Using feminist postmodern theory combined with Julia Novak's method of analyzing performance poetry, this paper identifies three interlinked strategies by means of which Agbabi works towards a "radical diversification" of contemporary poetry (Broom 2006: 1): she equally values the written and the spoken word to heal "the chasm between page and stage" (Agbabi 2003); she deliberately plays with the tension between herself as Black female poet-performer and her constructed fictive selves in the poems, thereby foregrounding that identity is performative and unfixed; and she engages in postmodern experiments with traditional forms. All of this presents Agbabi's readers and audiences with highly sophisticated, yet accessible poetry that conducts "cultural critiques [...] with a smile" (Arana 2007: 4–5).

1 Page Poetry *and* Performance Poetry

Agbabi's focus on the performability of poetry is a refusal to regard the written word as superior to the spoken word and an attempt at bridging the page-stage divide that still haunts contemporary poetry. Having started her career in the nineties as a performer at open-mic events and slams in London, Agbabi seems to be particularly aware of the effect of her "verbal acrobatics" (2000: 9, line 41) on audiences as well as on readers. In her manifesto-like "Prologue" to her second collection *Transformatrix*, Agbabi makes the (performance) poet's love for language and her seductive skill with words the topics of the poem (2000: 9–11). As a statement on the intersections between both forms of (her) poetic expression, she positions the poem on a "continuum between orality and writing that facilitates the transition from the page to the stage" (Tönnies et al. 2016: 302) and vice versa. Hence, it is very fitting that Agbabi uses an alternative title when she performs the poem: On stage, the "Prologue" becomes "Word."

Agbabi starts her playful reflection on the respective advantages of spoken word and page poetry by focusing on the sensual experience of using language. Directly addressing the audience and readers, the poet-speaker asks them: "[g]ive me a word / any word / let it roll across your tongue / like a dolly mixture" (lines 1–4) to feel "each syllable vibrate" (line 7) when they "say it loud" (line 5) and "say it again again again again again / till it's a tongue twister / till its meaning is in tatters / till its meaning equals sound" (lines 9–12). Replete with repetitions, alliterations and consonances of "l" and "t" sounds, these onomatopoetic opening lines remind recipients of the delicious sensation of mouthing words, which naturally involves heavy use of the tongue and highlights the mind-tickling effect of listening to them.

The video recording of Agbabi performing "Word" at a *London Liming* event in June 2013 (Tilt Spokenwd 2013) underlines how the sensuality and musicality of language are as central to her poetry as the meaning of the words. In this performance, which is exemplary of her style, Agbabi plays with intonation and unexpected breaks, sometimes pauses between syllables, and frequently changes the pace of her delivery. Her hand gestures and upper-body movements take up the rhythm of the "rap attack" (line 57). Agbabi's facial expressions – most notably smiles and raised eyebrows – give emphasis to her cunning wordplay and help her keep and guide the audience's attention. Her body language thus ties in with her reaching out to the audience: "Does this inspire? / Is your consciousness on fire? / Then let me take you higher" (lines 19–21).

However, "Prologue" pays just as much attention to readers of the word on the page: In the first stanza, the poet-speaker encourages the addressee through sentences that echo the previous lines of spoken word to "now write [the word] down, / letter by letter / loop the loops / till you form a structure. / Do it again again again again again / till it's a word picture" (lines 13–18). As with the performative instructions on how to "say" (line 6) a word, via frequent repetitions that do indeed form a "word picture," the written lines again describe their own effect (line 18). Moreover, the printed version of "Prologue" is a lesson in how Agbabi's three-minute performance can be conveyed to the readers of her three-page poem. They are pressed to take up a fast rhythmic pace as the poem rushes through a plethora of repetitions, consonances, and assonances, along with full and half rhymes. The interconnectedness of writing and orality is further underlined by the frequent omission of punctuation and the use of slang words such as "cos" (lines 25, 48, 56, 62) or "wanna" (lines 54, 91). Combined with directly addressing the reader throughout the poem, the text too constructs an audible voice: a tangible speaker on the 'stage' of the page.

The poem's call and response structure, which is created by the poet posing questions and repeatedly requesting "give me ...," establishes a link to elements of audience participation in dub poetry and could be read as "conspicuously convey[ing] a sense of 'African orality'" (Tönnies 2008: 92). Conversely, audiences might be reminded of being quizzed in school. They are treated like students who "only gotta pay attention" (line 29) as they "sit back, relax" (line 30) to be introduced to the poet's aesthetics, which are metaphorically described as "[m]y school of mathematics / [that] equals verbal acrobatics" (lines 40–41). The speaker invites them to reflect with her on her poetic process and, in particular, on her approach to the two interlinked performative spaces of page and stage. As part of the poetic "mission" (line 25) to (re)connect orality and writing, she mixes references to writing poetry to be published as a text (e.g., "give me Word for Windows" (line 60)) with references to poetry that works in performance and "express[es] in excess / the M I X / of [her] voice box" (lines 86–88). With the audience as well as the readers as her witnesses, the Black poet proves that she has "more skills than [she] got melanin" (line 52) in manipulating language in both fields.

At the climax of the captivating performance – the second to last couplet on the page – the speaker once more presents poetry in its spoken and written form as parallel projects that influence each other: "Give me a stage and I'll cut form on it / give me a page and I'll perform on it" (lines 97–98). The conceptual chiasmus of atypically associating the stage with form and the page with performance interlinks the two sub-genres and proves them equally effective in terms of expression for the Black poet. This ties in with Kwame Dawes's "Considerations" on Black British performance poetry: "If we can accept that the page is as much a performance space as is the stage, we may begin to find ways to speak about poetry without some of [the] prejudices. A poet ought to be able to choose her own 'performative space'" (2005: 284). Agbabi's poetry speaks to her acting on and advocating for the (Black) poet's freedom to choose both performative spaces. Hence, by embracing the "page-stage continuum" (Tönnies et al. 2016: 304), Agbabi also counters "literary ghettoization" (Ramey 2004: 111) as she asks to overcome segregating and confining stereotypes about white page vs. Black stage poetry. When asked about this ethnic dimension to the page-stage dichotomy in the UK, Agbabi recently confirmed that for Black British poets "there is definitely an issue in publishing still." However, she sees the performance scene now as "quite mixed" in terms of poets' ethnicities and states that the boundaries between performance poetry – still sometimes seen as "more black" – and page poetry "are being more blurred. It's slow but it's starting to happen" (Novak and Fischer 2016: 359–60).

2 The Post-Modern Poet and the Poet(ic) Persona

The analysis of "Prologue"/"Word" proves that Agbabi writes fictionalized versions of herself into her texts to explore the complexity of her identity and to discuss the role(s) of the postmodern Black female performance poet within the genre of poetry. Creating such a poet(ic) persona for the page and repeatedly performing this I (-dentity) on stage allows Agbabi to regard her fictive self from a distance and as a constructed role. This perspective on Agbabi's performance poetry suggests a notion of identity that ties in with Judith Butler's poststructuralist concept of identity as "a performative accomplishment": identity is the effect of "a stylized repetition of acts" resulting in "*an appearance of substance*" (1990: 140–141). However, as Julia Novak argues in her work on live poetry, to realize "the conceptual split of author/speaker" on which a recognition of the constructedness of Agbabi's I (-dentity) rests "is much harder for the audience" (2012: 359) when these poems contain "many instances of an 'I'" and show a "noticeable overlap of character traits and biographical facts between poet-performer and fictive speaker in the text" (2011: 192–93). The audience feels encouraged to conflate the real poet, Patience Agbabi, with the self she performs on stage, her "performance self." As a further result of this "identifying effect" of live poetry and similar to the effect achieved in confessional poetry, the readers of the printed performance poem are also likely to identify Agbabi with the poetic persona on the page (Novak 2011: 187–188, 192). To underline that Agbabi relies on the appearance of sameness, Merle Tönnies, Joana Brüning, and Andrea Sand describe the recurring lyrical I in these texts as her "lyrical Self," "an extension of and addition to [Novak's] 'performance self'" (2016: 314).

The final poem of Agbabi's first collection *R.A.W.* with the fitting title "Rappin It Up" (1995: 61–63) tackles the poet's persona's difficulties with the English canon of poetry. In this humorous rap poem, Patience Agbabi's lyrical I, goes by the initials "*PA*" (line 35) and tells her audience how she rebuffed Wordsworth and Milton, who tried to "get it going" (line 53) with her in a bar, boasting about their dull "master poem[s]" (line 67). She also proudly relates how she told "the King of Noise" (line 79) Shakespeare to "[g]et off the stage" (line 88) in a disco because there was "not a spark / originality" (lines 84–85) in his performance. PA's unpleasant encounters with the (self-)important white English poets literally and metaphorically enact the critical and "ironic dialogue with the past" (Hutcheon 1996: 4) that Linda Hutcheon discusses in *A Poetics of Postmodernism* as the main concern of postmodern fiction. The female poet persona cannot evade confrontations with "the Great Tradition" (line 99) even though she would rather enjoy "the beauty / of [her] own imagination / happy jus being / alone in [her] head" (lines 26–29). PA is "annoyed" (line 40) by the metaphorical "hot sweaty fingers" (line 42) of the "pawing" (line 65) dead poets who are pushing their "obsolete" (line 93) poetry on her. PA self-confidently introduces herself as "poetess" to the male poets, reclaiming the belittling label.

Telling her(-)story and writing back to a white, male dominated canon is "a political act" (line 122), just as the Black lyrical I claims in the monologue "R.A.W." from the same collection (1995: 48–50). For this "poet provocateur" (Murphy 2010: 73), performing rap poetry is a means of "taking our languages back / using our own black words / and being heard" (lines 119–121). The fighter for Black peoples' rights introduces herself: "I am a poet / it's a four-letter word" (lines 29–30). In both poems the marginalized poet's perspective on poetry and her alternative way of expressing herself in the genre come into focus: the persona in "R.A.W.," who declares that Black "*rhythm and word*" (line 8) is "*WAR*" (line 18), and PA, who is 'rappin up' tradition, both work unconventionally with slang-infused, rhythmic (spoken) words that "communicate right from ya / head down to ya feet" ("Rappin It Up", lines 94–95).

PA draws her inspiration for this poetry that is "alive" (line 90) from listening and dancing, "jivin' and writhin" (line 38), to "the ska-beat" (line 62) and "the hip hop" (line 73); hence her (stage) name PA, which is also a play on the abbreviation for public address system. The poet in "R.A.W." similarly emphasizes that her performance poetry is heavily influenced by Black music, from "gospel" (line 62) and "the Black blues / 'n' soul" (lines 82–83) to "belowthebeltjellyrocknrolljazzfunk" (line 84), whereas the lyrical I in "Word" underlines the diversity of her influences by referring to her mother who "fed [her] rhymes through the umbilical" (line 73) and mentioning that she was "raised on Watch with Mother / The Rime of the Ancient Mariner and Fight the Power" (lines 75–77). In typical postmodern fashion, Agbabi's poems celebrate "the erosion of the older distinction between high culture and so-called mass or popular culture" (Jameson 2000: 2), with performance poets as personae who "*don't give a fuck*" ("Rappin It Up", line 100) about the genre's supposedly superior status and traditional conventions in (page) poetry. All three poems present conflicts with the white, male-dominated tradition as part of the postmodern poet's predicament, yet, ironically, they also illustrate how the poets of the past, who are "felt to be the establishment and the enemy – dead, stifling, canonical" (Jameson 2000: 2), nevertheless provide inspiration for the contemporary Black female performance poet.

Coming back to the "ambiguous relation between poet-performer and fictive speaker" (Novak 2012: 367), Agbabi's lyrical selves in "R.A.W.", "Rappin It Up" and "Word" share – with themselves and with Agabi – that they are witty and intelligent Black female performers, who have strong opinions and are determined to make themselves heard. Their monologues "refer back to Agbabi's own work and sound like hidden advice on how to 'read' her poetry" (Tönnies et al. 2016: 315). In Agbabi's later, less performance-oriented poems, like some of her sonnets in *Transformatrix* (2000) and *Bloodshot Monochrome* (2008) which will be discussed in detail below, she creates similarly innovative poets as lyrical Is, and while the personae are not always as explicitly marked as Black and/or female or even given the author's name, the poems can be read as part of a continuing poetic meta-commentary on the image of the poet and on Agbabi's approach to poetry as a genre. Hence, Merle Tönnies, Joana Brüning, and Andrea Sand convincingly propose that "the 'lyrical Self' [...], to some extent, equips [...] Agbabi's work with underlying (meta-textual) instructions or recommendations on how to read and understand [her] poetry" (2016: 314). From these observations they come to the conclusion that the lyrical Self "becomes a means to implement the re-introduction of the author-figure" which includes "re-introducing the formerly banned intention and opinion of the literary author-figure into the creation and reception process" (2016: 314, 316). Or, in other words, the lyrical Self is an "approach to re-constructing a center" (2016: 318) after postmodernists proclaimed "the death of the author" (Barthes 1990: 142).

However, one should stress that Agbabi's lyrical selves on the page – like her performance self on stage – always remain constructions that can only provide fictionalized images of an author-figure. Accordingly, it is more fitting to speak of 'lyrical selves' in the plural than of one 'lyrical Self' (in the singular and with a capital 'S') that indicates an author(ity) as center behind the texts. The fact that Agbabi creates multiple similar and yet different selves – often with a good amount of self-irony – underlines that she actually does not even appear to "pretend that there is no 'conceptual split' between the performer and the lyrical I" (Tönnies et al. 2016: 316). Agbabi seems intensely aware, and seems to want her readers and audiences to be aware, of how she plays with the "ambiguous relation between poet-performer and fictive speaker" (Novak 2012: 367). Thus, Agbabi's multiple lyrical selves can rather be read, similar to "intensely self-reflexive" narration in postmodern fiction, as a means of self-consciously reflecting on her status and role after 'the death of the author.' As Hutcheon reminds us, 'the death of the author' needs to be understood as the death of the unified and coherent author-subject who writes with god-like authority based on "humanist notions of originality and universality," not the death of the author-subject as the producer of the text (1996: 192). She further stresses that postmodernist discourses "do not deny the individual, but they do 'situate' her/him" (1996: 46). Hence, instead of reading Agbabi's lyrical selves as a recourse to a "traditional author-figure" and the reconstruction of "a center" (Tönnies et al. 2016: 318), they can be seen as a medium through which Agbabi – often ironically – comments on her sense of being situated in and by dominant literary discourses and voices her resistance to fixed labels.

The lyrical selves thus function as a postmodern means of critically, even subversively deconstructing centers and re-situating herself and her poetry within the genre discourse. Agbabi invokes binaries like Black/white, male/female, tradition/innovation only to ultimately move away from "an old either-or" to an "and-also of multiplicity and difference," thus evoking an image of the "ex-centric" postmodern author (Hutcheon 1996: 62, 12) that can be best described, in Braidotti's terms, as a "nomadic subject" (1994: 4). By employing the metaphor of the traveler who "never takes on fully the limits of one national, fixed identity," Braidotti proposes, like Hutcheon, "a situated, postmodern [...] understanding of the subject" that takes into account that identity is always multiple and changing, so that it is only graspable in retrospect as "what we have already ceased to be" (1994: 33, 4, 14). Thus, "the nomad stands for movable diversity" as opposed to "one, sovereign identity" (1994: 14). As "a form of intervention on the debate between feminism and the postmodernist crisis of values and representations of the subject," Braidotti claims, the "figuration of the nomad" stresses that the dynamic postmodern subject engages in a "subversion of set conventions" and "resists settling into socially coded modes of thought and behavior" (1994: 28, 5).

The dramatic monologue "Ufo Woman (Pronounced Oofoe)," published in Agbabi's second collection *Transformatrix*, perfectly illustrates the "nomadic mode" (Braidotti 1994: 1) and "the liberating effects of moving from the language of alienation (otherness) to that of decentering (difference)" (Hutcheon 1996: 62;

Agbabi 2000: 15–17). Agbabi creates a female alien as lyrical Self, a poetic persona with "space-hopper-green / slingbacks, iridescent sky-blue-pink skin / pants and hologram hair cut" (lines 2–4). "Ufo Woman" was even made into a short film for Channel Four in 1998, and Agbabi herself appears in this film as the diasporic space traveler. She is dressed up as "Ufo Woman" with silver-blue face paint, an outsize Afro wig and a bright blue full-body suit, but still plainly recognizable as the poet herself. This shows that she encourages the audience to create the connection between herself and the poetic persona. Especially if the audience knows that Agbabi was born to Nigerian parents but fostered by a white English family in rural England, they will read the story of the alien woman with her "bold wild skin color" (line 56) who suffers "retroactive spacism" (line 76) as a fictionalized representation of Agbabi's experience.

The "Ufo Woman's" journey, parallel to Agbabi's biography, takes the her from the center, London, where she gets off her space ship and where her passport is stamped "ALIEN" (line 10), to the periphery in Sussex, where people also "stare with flying saucer eyes" (line 24) and call her names. She travels on to a second(ary) center, Lagos in Nigeria, where she is "oyinbo" (line 64), the "outsider, other" (line 66) again – now because her way of speaking and of presenting herself is seen as "white" (line 66). The alien(ated) woman finally returns to London, "raw" (line 68) from the hurtful experiences of being other(ed) in the centers as well as on the margins. However, Agbabi's lyrical self overcomes her pain and in an act of resistance and self-empowerment renames herself "Ufo Woman" (lines 69–72). The three letters had been used as a pseudo-acronym of 'you fuck off' to insult her, but now "Ufo" is re-claimed as "a blessing" (line 70): as a name for a nomadic subject who celebrates her unidentifiable status. Embracing her ex-centric difference, "Ufo Woman" eventually decides to surf "the galaxy" (line 83) instead of staying on earth in backward societies that are still based on binary hierarchical structures, such as Black/white, female/male.

"Ufo Woman" and the other poems that feature a fictionalized version of Agbabi as poetic persona are embedded in a greater number of her texts that "[contain] many instances of an 'I'" (Novak 2011: 192) but work against a conflation of the poet-performer and the fictive speaker by providing explicit markers of difference between the two. In her most recent publication *Telling Tales* (2014), a rewriting of Geoffrey Chaucer's *Canterbury Tales* (1387–1400), Agbabi, as the author of the collection, seems to step as much into the background as possible. That *Telling Tales* is a rewriting to begin with, and of a medieval text, which in itself mostly consists of rewritings, again reflects the postmodern image of the decentered author who is seen to "write in tandem with others" and whose "art is considered not the product of original genius" (Hutcheon 1996: 191) but of intertextual practices. In contrast to Chaucer,

Agbabi does not even choose to appear as a fictionalized author-figure in her "remix" (Agbabi 2014: 2, line 34) but tries to disappear behind her characters.

However, Agbabi's poems still foreground her preference for poets as poetic personae because her present-day pilgrims all take the role of poetry slam performers. Agbabi translates Chaucer's frame narrative of the storytelling contest into the twenty-first century by turning it into a poetry slam that "MC" Harry 'Bells' Bailey initiates on a bus journey from London to Canterbury among the diverse group of 24 travelers. When performing a selection of the tales on stage, Agbabi informs the audience that her aim is to be invisible behind the contemporary pilgrim-slammers who are telling their own tales in their unique voices. Thus, the poems display a great variety of different forms and styles on the page-stage continuum "from the grime to the clean-cut iambic, / rime royale, rant or rap" (Agbabi 2014: 1, lines 27–28). In the collection, the pilgrims' modernized names are given with the poem's title as if they were actual authors of their tales. Furthermore, fictive "Author Biographies" (115–120) in the back of the book support the illusion that they are real poets. In performance, Agbabi reads these clichéd bios out to the audience before she launches into the poem proper. Thus, she stresses that the fictive poets take center stage despite the fact that she lends her voice to them. For a "Telling Tales Slam" (RenaissanceOne 2016) hosted at The Albany, Deptford in May 2014 by Apples and Snakes, England's leading organization for curating performance poetry events, Apples and Snakes even commissioned other authors to perform Agbabi's texts and thus took her wish to "not [be] present" to a new level (Novak and Fischer 2016: 360).

But whether Agbabi constructs speakers that appear to be versions of herself or whether she creates characters that are explicitly marked as different from herself, this reading of Agbabi's poetry foregrounds that her diverse personae are part of Agbabi's postmodern aesthetic strategy: The literary (page) and literal (stage) performances of diverse complex identities can be read as Agbabi's poetic means of establishing decentered positions of "ex-centricity" (Hutcheon 1996: 62). In line with this, the fictionalized versions of Agbabi herself introduce an image of the poet-subject as a nomad who is, contrary to a traditional author figure, a "multiple entity" (Braidotti 1994: 36) at the same time inside and outside of the dominant literary discourses of poetry.

3 Agbabi's Postmodern Play with Poetic Form

On her mission as a "poetical activist" (2003), Agbabi also uses the genre's own conventional weapons – that is, traditional forms – to attack gendered or raced assumptions about forms and the history of poetry. "Transformatrix," for example, contradicts traditional associations of the sonnet with a male poet-speaker who reflects on love, language, and the object of his desire, his female muse. Agbabi's sonnet compares the writing process to an erotic lesbian power play between the poet(ic) persona, who is implicitly gendered female, and her dominatrix.

> I'm slim as a silver stiletto, lit
> by a fat, waxing moon and a seance
> of candles dipped in oil of frankincense.
> Salt peppers my lips as the door clicks shut.
> A pen poised over a blank page, I wait
> for madam's orders, her strict consonants
> and the spaces between words, the silence.
> She's given me a safe word, a red light
> but I'm breaking the law, on a death wish,
> ink throbbing my temples, each vertebra
> straining for her fingers. She trusses up
> words, lines, as a corset disciplines flesh.
> Without her, I'm nothing but without me
> she's tense, uptight, rigid as a full stop.
>
> (Agbabi 2000: 78)

The sonnet deals with an erotic ritual that taps into female, mystical sources of artistic inspiration. This is highlighted in the opening lines by the comparison of the speaker's "slim" (line 1) body to a "silver stiletto" (line 1), the epitome of aggressive female sexiness; by putting the poem under the sign of the major symbol of femininity, the "fat, waxing moon" (line 2); and by describing the arrangement of candles as "seance" (line 2). With ink taking the place of blood and with the dominatrix/muse "discipline[ing]" (line 12) the self-imprisoned poet, writing poetry becomes a physical, sexual act performed between the two women. While the traditional association of the sonnet with love and eroticism is kept, Agbabi does not perpetuate a male-dominated, heteronormative image of the poetic process, but links inspiration and creativity to lesbian desire. This programmatic "breaking [of] the law" (line 9) is, for Manuela Coppola, a sign of Agbabi's "queering" (Coppola 2015) of the sonnet form because Agbabi's move away from heterosexuality to queer sexuality mirrors the "step beyond the safe boundaries of literary conventions" (Coppola 2015: 381). Instead of depending on the "silencing of woman [...] through figuring her as muse [...] – the mute, gazed-upon object mirroring back to the masculine I his essential identity and significance" (Kinnahan 2009: 181), Agbabi's sonnet suggests that a female I speaks about the significance of her powerful muse and about how her writing depends on their exclusively female, exciting, and existential exchange.

If the dominatrix-muse is understood as a personification of poetry, the strict rules and the sensual pleasure that she offers capture how the poet faces the formal restrictions and conventions of the genre, which she might both enjoy and at the same time struggle to express herself in. Like "a corset that disciplines the flesh" (line 12), traditional forms such as the sonnet provide a strict framework that however proves fruitful for productive creation. As Agbabi stresses when asked about "Transformatrix" by Lauri Ramey, "I wanted to subvert the [negative] feminist vision of the sonnet as corset: I think constriction can give you freedom" (Ramey 2004: 132). Hence the concluding couplet of the sonnet: Without a relationship to tradition the (female) poet is "nothing" (line 13). And without female poets entering a daring, passionate exchange with tradition, the genre of poetry remains, like the dominatrix on her own, "tense, uptight, rigid" (line 14) and comes to a "full stop" (line 14). Choosing "Transformatrix" as the title of the collection implies that Agbabi herself can be regarded as a transformatrix, a dynamic and innovative female poet who frees herself from the thought that traditional forms have to be limiting and that the genre is gendered male.

The sonnet sequence "Problem Pages" in *Bloodshot Monochrome* takes up and expands the theme of presenting critical perspectives on the history of the genre and its conventions that runs through all four of Agbabi's poetry collections. The 14 prose poems each consist of 14 lines and display "the proposition-resolution-dynamic of the Petrarchan sonnet" (Jenkins 2011: 126). The octave is a fictitious letter, supposedly written by a famous dead sonneteer, in which s/he complains in a conversational tone about a problem s/he has in her/his private or public life as a writer. The troubled poets (seven male, seven female) cover the whole history of the sonnet and range from the white male Renaissance founders of the English sonnet tradition, Henry Howard, Earl of Surrey, and William Shakespeare, to the Black female modern sonneteers June Jordan and Gwendolyn Brooks. By painting an exaggerated image of their character, Agbabi gives each poet a unique voice that functions like a caricature, and the issues she invents for the poets help provide an ironically distorted perspective on their lives. To further heighten the sequence's level of parody, the letters are all addressed to "Dear Patience," implying that the canonical poets seek advice from Patience Agbabi, who takes the role of agony aunt and replies to each poet's desperate inquiry in the sestet.

This rough outline of "Problem Pages" already indicates that the sequence combines the postmodern strategies that this paper identified in Agbabi's poetry: Agbabi "bridg[es] the gap between élite and popular art" (Hutcheon 1996: 20) as she merges the sonnet form with the advice column. This results in a sequence of 14 hybrid prose poems that share the same fixed layout on the page. The poem's text is arranged in full justification with the title in capital letters and the octave in bold style followed by the sestet as a second paragraph, which meets expectations of the sonnet as a visibly regular, crafted 14–line form. The poem titles are each an intertextual reference to a sonnet of the poet who writes in the octave. But, contrary to the expectations that the titles create, the style of the prose is as conversational as in a popular magazine or even a personal conversation, which, typical for Agbabi, stresses the link between writing and orality. For the "call and response" (Murphy 2010: 79) of letters to and from agony aunt Patience, Agbabi strategically uses her lyrical self to literally and metaphorically enter a conversation with the poets of the past. By foregrounding their struggles, she dethrones the glorified canonical writers and ironically puts her lyrical self in the superior position of being able to give advice to these alleged geniuses. Hence, the humorous agony aunt-scenario suggests that "Patience" has a hand in their success stories. Moreover, the instructive and encouraging replies of Agbabi's alter ego contain a series of statements about poetry and being a poet that also function as self-reflexive commentary on Agbabi's own experiences and poetic practice.

Agbabi makes a case for the equal significance of performance and written poetry when she, as Patience, suggests to Surrey, "Craft your discipline on the page *and* the stage" (33, line 11), or empathises with Shakespeare's anger at being "typecast a performance / poet" (34, lines 2–3). She underlines that, for her, entertainment and high-brow art are not mutually exclusive when she reminds Robert Frost that "[m]eticulously crafted poetry can appeal / to the élite and the masses if accessible" (42, lines 11–12). She supports feminist canon revision when she encourages the disheartened Lady Mary Wroth and expresses hope that her poetry, "may / [...] receive due critical attention" (35, lines 13–14). She corrects Wordsworth who claims that it is his "friend" S. T. Coleridge "to whom [his] intellect / is most indebted" (38, lines 2–3) by reminding him: "Your intellect is equally indebted to your sister" (38, line 9). As if making a comment about Agbabi's own embrace of traditional forms, Patience claims that the poet can find "freedom in form" (42, line 9), which should be an end in itself regardless of public reception: "Love form not fame" (42, line 14). Politics in the poetry business are repeatedly addressed when poets "suspect homophobia/racism" (34, line 8), for example in Claude McKay's complaint about racism in international publishing and Gwendolyn Brooks's despair concerning discriminatory debates against "black poets using / traditional white forms" (45, lines 5–6). Patience answers Brooks in two simple equations that ring true for the contemporary poetry business and can be seen to apply to the reception of Agbabi's poetry collections as well: "some say poetry + politics = propaganda" (45, line 9) and "blackpoet + sonnet = sellout" (45, line 10).

"Problem Pages" clearly functions as an *ars poetica*. It takes up the case made in "Rappin It Up," "Word"/"Prologue," and "Transformatrix" for both performance and page poetry, for a Black feminist politics, and for the use of traditional poetic forms. However, because of the postmodern playfulness and irony of the advice-column scenario, the conventional seriousness and significance of *ars poetica* poems are undermined. Not only does Agbabi rob the canonical poets of their status as flawless geniuses, but her use of an agony-aunt self to voice metapoetic opinions equally ridicules a traditional notion of the author figure as an authority offering universal truths. Agbabi's sequence rather foregrounds "that there is no one author and no one poem," as Murphy states (2010: 79). The premise that each sonnet consists of the writing of two poets makes it clear in the first place that any belief in unity or perfection is dispelled. The advice-column sonnets further stress that being a poet asks for a continuous process of self-reflection and of re-situating the self, which is a private as well as a public affair. Agbabi underlines the insecurities, the disappointment, despair, and anger this entails in the all too human poets. Thus, the letters also comment on how little changes about the way poets and poetry are judged, labelled, and limited by dominant conceptions of genre. While similar experiences and sentiments bridge the gap between writers of all times, including herself, and create a sense of continuity between past and present, the diversity of poets and problems suggests that there cannot be one solution that fits all: Patience provides many different points of exit underlining the variety of poetic responses that are possible within the genre. She makes a strong case for the genre's openness to diversity. The rhetorical question Patience poses in her reply to Shakespeare underlines this: "When will people stop categorizing / and embrace the page-stage, black-white, / heterosexual-homosexual continuum?" (34, lines 9–11).

Agbabi's poetry, and especially those poems which feature her ex-centric lyrical selves, affirms that critical engagement with categorizations proves productive for the genre's development towards more diversity. She fufills the full page-stage continuum as her poems shift between performance poetry and page poetry, continuously "inviting [poetry's] past to meet its future" (Ramey 2009: 321) as she invokes the classics and often chooses to present her poetry in tight poetic forms but equally draws on popular culture as an important influence on her practice. Hence, Agbabi is not as desperate as Patience's clients in "Problem Pages." Completely in her element as a postmodern 'transformatrix,' she draws strength and inspiration from conversations with her poetic ancestors – strength that she uses to "question [poetry's] relationship with the categorical costumes of the past and present in order to explore what is politically and poetically possible in [the genre's] future" (Murphy 2010: 67). Thus, to employ Braidotti's spatial metaphors again, Agbabi's poetry can be read like the map of the travels of the postmodern nomadic author-subject, whose "movable diversity" is not restricted by "a triumphant *cogito* supervising the contingency of the self" (1994: 14). With a positive "lack of inhibitions regarding the Western literary tradition" (Murphy 2010: 68), Agbabi takes alternative paths that diversify the genre. She seems to heed the credo that Harry 'Bells' Bailey voices in the last piece, the "Back Track" of *Telling Tales*, one that sounds like a promise for Agbabi's future projects: "all that's written is written to inspire us" (2014: 113, line 16).

Works Cited

Anaxagorou, Anthony. 2016. "From the Back of the Bus: The Significance of BAME Writers". *Pen Transmissions*. English Pen. www.englishpen.org/pen-atlas/from-the-back-of-the-bus [accessed 10 March 2017].
Agbabi, Patience. 1995. *R.A.W.* London: Gecko Press.
Agbabi, Patience. 1998. "Ufo Woman". *LitPop Identity*. Dir. Sonali Fernando. Channel Four.
Agbabi, Patience. 2000. *Transformatrix*. Edinburgh: Payback Press.
Agbabi, Patience. 2003. "Author Statement". *British Council Literature*. British Council. www.literature.britishcouncil.org/writer/patience-agbabi [accessed 12 March 2017].
Agbabi, Patience. 2004. *Bloodshot Monochrome*. London: Gecko Press.
Agbabi, Patience. 2014. *Telling Tales*. Edinburgh: Canongate.
Arana, R. Victoria (ed.). 2007. *"Black" British Aesthetics Today*. Newcastle: Cambridge Scholars.
Barthes, Roland. 1988. "The Death of the Author". *Image – Music – Text*. Trans. Stephen Heath. New York: Noonday Press. 142–148.
Braidotti, Rosi. 1994. *Nomadic Subjects: Embodiment and Sexual Difference in Contemporary Feminist Theory*. New York: Columbia University Press.
Broom, Sarah. 2006. *Contemporary British and Irish Poetry*. Basingstoke: Palgrave Macmillan.
Butler, Judith. 1990. *Gender Trouble: Feminism and the Subversion of Identity*. New York: Routledge.
Coppola, Manuela. 2015. "Queering Sonnets: Sexual and Transnational Identity in the Poetry of Patience Agbabi". *Women: A Cultural Review* 24.4: 369–383.
Coppola, Manuela. 2016. "A Tale of Two Wives: The Transnational Poetry of Patience Agbabi and Jean 'Binta' Breeze". *Journal of Postcolonial Writing* 52.3: 305–318.
Dawes, Kwame. 2005. "Black British Poetry: Some Considerations". In: Kadija Sesay (ed.). *Write Black, Write British: From Post Colonial to Black British Literature*. Hertford: Hansib. 282–299.
Evans-Bush, Katy. 2013. "Patience Agbabi". *Poetry International Rotterdam: The Poetry International Foundation*. Poetry International Web. www.poetryinternationalweb.net/pi/site/poet/item/23548/29/Patience-Agbabi [accessed 10 March 2017].
Hutcheon, Linda. 1996. *A Poetics of Postmodernism: History, Theory, Fiction*. New York: Routledge.
Jenkins, Lee M. 2011. "Interculturalism: Imtiaz Dharker, Patience Agbabi, Jackie Kay and Contemporary Irish Poets". In: Jane Dowson (ed.). *The Cambridge Companion to Twentieth-Century British and Irish Women's Poetry*. Cambridge: Cambridge University Press. 119–135.

Kean, Danuta. 2016. "Writing the Future: Black and Asian Writers and Publishers in the Market Place". London. *Spread the Word*. www.spreadtheword.org.uk/writing-the-future [accessed 12 March 2017].

Kinnahan, Linda A. 2009. "Contemporary British Women Poets and the Lyric Subject". In: Nigel Alderman and C. D. Blanton (ed.). *A Concise Companion to Postwar British and Irish Poetry*. Chichester: Blackwell Publishing. 176–199.

Moore, Fiona. 2013. "Big Five Poetry Publishers in the UK: A Gender Audit". Web blog post. *Displacement*. Displacement. http://displacement-poetry.blogspot.de/search?updated-max=2013-06-29T20:58:00%2B01:00&max-results=10&start=58&by-date=false [accessed 10 March 2017].

Murphy, Catherine. 2010. "Performing, Transforming, and Changing the Question: Patience Agbabi – Poet Enough!". In: Emily Taylor Merriman and Adrian Grafe (eds.). *Intimate Exposure: Essays on the Public-Private Divide in British Poetry Since 1950*. Jefferson: Mc Farland. 67–84.

Novak, Julia. 2011. *Live Poetry: An Integrated Approach to Poetry in Performance*. Amsterdam: Rodopi.

Novak, Julia. 2012. "Performing the Poet, Reading (to) the Audience: Some Thoughts on Live Poetry as Literary Communication". *Journal of Literary Theory* 6.2: 358–382.

Novak, Julia, and Pascal Fischer. 2016. "On the Interface Between Page and Stage: Interview with Patience Agbabi". *Zeitschrift für Anglistik und Amerikanistik* 64.3: 353–363.

Ramey, Lauri. 2004. "Contemporary Black British Poetry". In: R. Victoria Arana and Lauri Ramey (eds.). *Black British Writing*. New York: Palgrave Macmillan. 109–136.

Ramey, Lauri. 2009. "Performing Contemporary Poetics: The Art of SuAndi and Patience Agbabi". *Women: A Cultural Review* 20.3: 310–322.

RenaissanceOne Stories. 2016. "Telling Tales Slam". *YouTube*. The Albany. www.youtube.com/watch?v=OhEXl7yHf4g [accessed 6 December 2018].

Salzman, Eva. 2008. "Introduction." In: Eva Salzman and Amy Wack (eds.). *Women's Work: Modern Women Poets Writing in English*. Bridgend: Seren. 7–17.

Sand, Andrea, and Merle Tönnies. 2010. "The Features and Meanings of Orality in Black British Performance Poetry". In: Jörg Helbig and René Schallegger (eds.). *Anglistentag 2009 Klagenfurt: Proceedings*. Trier: WVT. 105–114.

Tilt Spokenwd. 2013. "Tilt Presents London Liming: Patience Agbabi Performs "Word"". *YouTube*. Tilt and Rich Mix. www.youtube.com/watch?v=5Z530jow2DA [accessed 12 March 2017].

Tönnies, Merle. 2008. "Translating African Traditions and Identities: Black Poetry in Contemporary Britain". In: Klaus Stierstorfer and Monika Gomille (eds.). *Cultures of Translation*. Newcastle: Cambridge Scholars. 87–104.

Tönnies, Merle, Joana Brüning, and Andrea Sand. 2016. "The Duality of Page and Stage: Constructing Lyrical Voices in Contemporary British Poetry Written for Performance". *Zeitschrift für Anglistik und Amerikanistik* 64.3: 301–320.

Annika McPherson
Resisting Genrefication: Gender and Genre in Jean 'Binta' Breeze's *The Fifth Figure*

Abstract: Jean 'Binta' Breeze is most frequently labeled Jamaica's 'first female dub poet.' The discussion of her work to date exemplifies the difficulty of determining the genre boundaries not only of dub poetry, but also of poetry more generally. Thematic continuities and aesthetic overlaps show the interconnection of questions of gender and genre throughout Breeze's poetry. Especially *The Fifth Figure* (2006) both illustrates and transcends classificatory desires in that it weaves poetry, memoir, and novelistic narrative prose into the structure of a Jamaican quadrille. In its musical, temporal, and spatial layering of the narrative dances of five generations of women across the Atlantic, the text also challenges dominant notions of diaspora.

Keywords: dub poetry, sound studies, gender, diaspora, translocal Caribbean

Jean 'Binta' Breeze joined the circle around the well-known dub poets Michael Smith and Oku Onuora at the Jamaica School of Drama in the late 1970s. She first performed on stage with Mutabaruka, who also produced the first recordings of her poetry. Breeze is often referred to as the "first female dub poet in [a] male-dominated field" (qtd. in Breeze 1996: 498). In 1985, following an invitation by Linton Kwesi Johnson to the *International Book Fair of Radical Black and Third World Books*, she moved to England and subsequently taught Theatre Studies at Brixton College. In 2012 she was appointed Member of the Order of the British Empire (MBE). Her fellow poet Benjamin Zephaniah had famously refused his Officer of the Order of the British Empire (OBE) appointment in 2003 with the following statement in *The Guardian*:

> Me? I thought, OBE me? Up yours, I thought. I get angry when I hear that word "empire"; it reminds me of slavery, it reminds of thousands of years of brutality, it reminds me of how my foremothers were raped and my forefathers brutalised. It is because of this concept of empire that my British education led me to believe that the history of black people started with slavery and that we were born slaves, and should therefore be grateful that we were given freedom by our caring white masters. It is because of this idea of empire that black people like myself don't even know our true names or our true historical culture. I am not one of those who are obsessed with their roots, and I'm certainly not suffering from a crisis of identity; my obsession is about the future and the political rights of all people. Benjamin

> Zephaniah OBE – no way Mr Blair, no way Mrs Queen. I am profoundly anti-empire. (Zephaniah 2003)

Unlike Zephaniah, and in spite of her own stated aversions to the "British Empire thing," Breeze accepted the medal awarded to her for her services to literature:

> I have always said that I was not going to accept such an award if it was offered to me, but when it was offered, I felt a certain amount of delight. I thought "how lovely." [In addition], I have always had a kind of soft spot for the Queen because I see her as a mother figure in a big family trying her best to keep the kids in line [...]. So I said on that basis, I will accept. (qtd. in Cummings 2012)

Breeze's iconic status as the "first female dub poet" has tied her work to questions of gender both on the personal level as well as based on the content and performance of her work. In "Can a Dub Poet Be a Woman?" (1990) she points out three comments on her poetry that made her more aware of her gendered position and reception within the field: first, that her poem "Aid Travels with a Bomb" (1983) was supposedly "much more suited to a male voice" – the implied suggestion being that "it was more masculine to achieve [...] distance from the subjective or personal"; second, statements to the effect "that a radical dub poet should not be 'wining up her waist' on the stage as it presented a sexual image rather than a radical one; and, third, that her work "was becoming far too personal" (Breeze 1996: 499). These comments provide the critical junctures for the following exploration of the interconnection of questions of gender and genre across Breeze's poetry in general and *The Fifth Figure* (2006) in particular.

Breeze's work has consistently questioned the boundaries not only of dub poetry, but also of poetry more generally. Especially *The Fifth Figure* both illustrates and transcends classificatory desires in that it weaves poetry, memoir, and narrative prose into the structure of a Jamaican quadrille. Its musical, temporal, and spatial layering of the narrative dances of five generations of women across the Atlantic also challenges dominant notions of diaspora. There are, however, significant thematic continuities and aesthetic overlaps between Breeze's earlier 'dub' poetry and *The Fifth Figure*. Against the backdrop of a genre discussion, these overlaps will be explored in comparison to poems such as "Dreamer" (1987/1988) and "A Song to Heal" (1990/1992), as well as the widely circulating "Riddym Ravings" (1988).[1]

---

[1] Most of Breeze's poems have been (re-)released on several compilations and published in various collections. The album *Riddym Ravings* featuring "Dreamer" and "Riddym Ravings"

1 Riddim, Sound, and Performance in and beyond Dub Poetry

Dub poetry relies heavily on the sounding of what Kamau Brathwaite has called "nation language" to emphasize "the African aspect of [the] New World/Caribbean heritage," in opposition to the "pejorative overtones" of designations such as "dialect" or "creole English" (1993: 265–266). In her discussion of Jamaican popular culture, Carolyn Cooper asserts the necessity "to cross the divide between Slackness and Culture, between Jamaican and English, between the oral and the scribal traditions" in theoretical writing as well (1993: 12). Building on Cooper's influential work, Mimi Sheller invokes the notion of "transgressive 'oraliteracy'" (2003: 187). Yet, she points out that, due to "the deep layering and reiteration of [exoticist] representations of the Caribbean," the reception of such linguistic practices outside of their cultural context can also "feed into the consumer's appetite for the racialised/sexualised other" and related fantasies that are deeply inscribed in colonial history (Sheller 2004: 107). I refer to this global commodification process, which can severely impinge upon forms of creative resistance, as the 't®opicalization' of the Caribbean. The frequently implicit assumption that Caribbean cultural production is by default resistant, however, can equally feed into such patterns of 't®opicalization.'

In his review of Christian Habekost's influential study *Verbal Riddim* (1993), G. A. Elmer Griffin describes dub poetry as

> a highly developed, politically charged rhythmic art form which merges local musical folk idioms (initially reggae) with political commentary and analysis. It combines the values of poetry, the properties of voice as instrument, and the power of the vernacular, spoken in the context of political resistance and identity assertion. It places itself subtly and elusively between political speech, dramatic recitation, and song. (1995: 60)

While the musical dimensions of dub poetry were crucial to early delineations of the genre, the complexity of the sonic has consistently defied clear definitions. As Cooper points out in her review of *Verbal Riddims*, the "forceful Jamaican Creole aphorism 'Word Soun' 'Ave Power' (word-sound has power) is toned down in [Habekost's] distorted English translation 'Word Sound and Power'" (1997: 151), which has nevertheless become a frequently cited shorthand for dub poetry's engagement with the sonic (*Word Soun' 'Ave Power:*

---

was released in 1987 and the print collection *Riddym Ravings and Other Poems* in 1988. Similarly, "A Song to Heal" appeared on the album *Tracks* in 1990, while it was published in print in the collection *Spring Cleaning* in 1992.

Reggae Poetry is also the title of the 1983 compilation produced by Mutabaruka which features Breeze's "To Plant" and "Aid Travels with a Bomb"). 'Word Sound and Power' as a linguistic practice is often invoked within the context of Rastafari (e.g. Pulis 2003). In and beyond Rastafari 'Dread Talk' (Pollard 2000), the use of language in the Caribbean as a site of struggle, resistance, and transformation constitutes an epistemic shift that highlights the divesting of colonial linguistic and cultural power in the sense of what Walter Mignolo calls "epistemic de-colonial de-linking" (2009: 2).

Cooper also reprimands Habekost for his categorization 'women's dub poetry' instead of more substantial interrogations of masculinity and femininity through the category of gender (Cooper 1997: 152). Habekost's comments on Breeze's statements in her 1989 newspaper article "Where Have All the Dub Poets Gone?" in *Voice* further entrenched the notion of a division of "dub practitioners" at the time into

> two camps: one group (especially Benjamin Zephaniah, Levi Tafari, Oku Onuora, Desmond Johnson, and Lillian Allen and her fellow-Canadians) who unequivocally supported and promoted the term 'dub poetry'; [and] another group (Linton Kwesi Johnson, Mutabaruka, Jean Breeze) who rejected the term, claiming that dub was only one particular style in their repertoire, although they still allowed the increasing popularity of the label to further their careers. (Habekost 1993: 44)

This typology and the controversy on the genre label notwithstanding, Breeze – in reference to the influence of the famous Jamaican poet and folklorist Louise 'Miss Lou' Bennett – has asserted the importance of the voice as her instrument for attempting to produce "work so simple in its truth and in its details that it becomes as big as the universe," while at the same time criticizing dub poetry for "not enough experimentation with the form and [for] becoming as constraining in its rhythms as the iambic pentameter" (1996: 498).

More recently, Michael Bucknor has placed dub poetry as a postmodern art form that "exploded onto the literary scene" out of a "crucible," the most common ingredients of which include Walter Rodney's ban from Jamaica, the Caribbean Artists Movement, Miss Lou's influence, reggae music, and Yard Theatre poetry performances (2011: 255). Bucknor describes the "aesthetics of dub" in terms of its

> reliance on musical support and sound techniques, its use of a demotic language – creole speech, dread talk, 'nation language' – its exploitation of speech rituals and resources of the oral tradition – warning, prophesy, name-calling, cursing, call and response – and by allusiveness, proverbial wisdom and verbal wit. (2011: 255)

Imbued with the "ideological, counter-discursive pressure points from black consciousness, decolonization, Garveyism, Rastafarianism, Marxism/socialism to anti-colonial nationalism" (Bucknor 2011: 255–256), dub thus emerged as a decolonial cultural practice.

However, there are also critics of the underlying assumption of dub as a necessarily resistant sonic and textual practice. Kei Miller, for example, in "A Smaller Sound, A Lesser Fury: A Eulogy for Dub Poetry" accuses dub of a "fetishizing" containment of the revolution by the protest poets in what he calls its "minstrel show 'youth' phase" (2013). Whether or not to classify a poem as 'dub,' then, and how to place it in relation to questions of resistance, to some extent appears to be in the ear and mind of the beholder. In his eulogy, Miller also states that dub "taught us that there is a time to be angry, to be furious, and that this fury can be composed and become a thing of eloquence" (2013). What is striking regarding the lingering 'echo' of dub, however, is that the critical discussion of musical and poetic dub has become somewhat disconnected. Whereas there are extensive studies on the soundscapes of dub reggae (e.g. Veal 2007; Partridge 2010), critical reading practices of music and poetry often ignore each other. As the critical discussion of dub traced above has emphasized, the power of the spoken word, the power to represent, is inextricably entwined with sounds. Hence the attempt at correspondence between sound and meaning in Rastafari linguistic practices aims to overturn colonialist power structures and to phonically embody, as it were, resistance to colonial categorizations. Julian Henriques has traced this in relation to reggae sound system culture in *Sonic Bodies* (2011). Thinking *through* (rather than *about*) sound he attempts to reflect the embodied ways of knowing and alternative epistemologies that can also be aligned with decolonial thought more broadly (2011: 275–276).

While some dub poetry certainly has on its agenda to "dub out the isms and scisms," as Oku Onuora has famously phrased it (qtd. in Morris 1997: 66; see also Bucknor 2011: 257), attempts at categorical definition have consistently failed to capture the variety of poetic expression covered by artists operating under or rejecting the label. Some of these challenges are indeed based on the question of how to define dub in this context, but they equally apply to the wider notion of poetry that is invoked in these debates. Beyond attempts at delineating the origins of dub, tracing its shifting definitions, or reading it through a postmodern lens, it is important to stress that techniques such as 'versioning,' 'riddim,' and mixing (see e.g. Welsh 2001: 86–87) exceed academic desires for classification. Similarly, the 'postcolonial' frame of reference is frequently not the primary choice within Caribbean criticism, but is more often applied from without. This is arguably also the case with 'diaspora' – at least if one wants to follow Derek Walcott's argument that "diaspora is not a Caribbean word" and that the attributions of "dispossession" and "displacement" it invokes are problematic in their overgeneralized application (2012: 0:30:00). While Veal describes the mixes of dub music as "reflecting the ruination of an idealized African past, or as the harbingers of an as-yet-unarticulated cultural formation" (2007: 218), I would argue that dub poetry in the wider sense articulates precisely this cultural formation and that overgeneralized notions of diaspora contribute to the containment of this formation in colonialist rhetoric. Such a containment also includes simplistic invocations of resistance which urgently need to be re-theorized if they are to avoid the further commodification of dub poetry as "anthems of resistance" (Habekost 1993: 57).

Beyond neat compartmentalization, dub poetry more broadly can encompass "riddim poetry" as well as "sound poetry" and "reggae poetry" or "performance poetry" (Habekost 1993; Morris 1997; Welsh 2001). In an adaptation of Veal's observations on dub in the continuum of Jamaican music (2007: 26), I thus refer to dub as a *performance-to-print continuum* and to Breeze as a poet of what I call the 'translocal' Caribbean rather than the Caribbean diaspora. The 'translocal' emphasizes the mobility as well as multiple rootedness and situatedness of many Caribbean writers and artists, while also connoting the simultaneity of localized and globalized themes and contexts across much of their work (e.g. Munkelt et al. 2013).

2 Sound, Sight, and Dance in Breeze's Poetry

Many of Breeze's poems lead multiple lives, as it were: on the stage, on the page, and across various recordings. On the album *Tracks* (2000), for example, "Dreamer" features a basic reverb or echo technique, while "A Song to Heal" is voiced over a reggae beat that aligns it with more conventional notions of dub poetry. One of Breeze's most widely anthologized poems, "Riddym Ravings," was also released in several recorded versions – most recently as "Mad Woman" on the album *Eena Me Corner* (2009), with a distinct bass line and rhythm.[2] Given the many performance versions with lyrical and other variations, for example in intonation, rhythmic delivery, or accompanying beat, "Riddym Ravings" is one of Breeze's most versatile poems. All three mentioned poems feature women speakers and, as many others across her compilations and collections, relate to questions of gender and sexuality, while especially "Riddym Ravings"/"Mad Woman" also addresses mental health. In 2011, a BBC

---

[2] Further versions include e.g. the recording as "Riddym Ravings" on the 1987 cassette album *Sister Breeze: Riddym Ravings*, in print in Breeze 1988; as "Riddym Ravings (The Mad Woman's Poem)" in Breeze 1993; and in Brown and McWatt 2005: 308–311.

Radio 4 interview with Breeze by Irish poet Matthew Sweeney for *Out of the Vortex* was prompted by a study that stated that "poets are thirty times more likely to undergo a depressive illness than the rest of the population, and twenty times more likely to be committed to an asylum" (Breeze 2011b). In the interview Breeze discusses how the voices on the radio she listened to at the time influenced "Riddym Ravings" and how she has lived with schizophrenia since her early twenties, as a result of which she "weaves her experience of illness into her poems." In this instance, sounding constitutes a technique of articulation and a coping mechanism that further complicates notions of subjectivity and the personal within Breeze's poetry beyond simplistic autobiographical assumptions.

While the interpenetration of sound and word is at the heart of any spoken or performed poetry, it can at times also come to life silently in the reader's mind across the performance-to-print continuum. Although Breeze's *The Fifth Figure* at first sight seems to steer away from dub, it likewise illustrates and transcends classificatory desires. It is described in its blurb as

> A book-length sequence mixing poetry and prose which chronicles the lives of five generations of Caribbean and Black British women of mixed ancestry.
> Part novel, part poem, part family memoir, its structure is based on the Jamaican quadrille, a hybrid version of the dance brought from Europe by the island's former colonial masters. Beginning in the late 19th century with her great-great grandmother's first quadrille, Breeze tells a many-layered tale of love and betrayal, innocence and suffering, hardship and joy over a hundred years as each mother sees her daughter join a dance which shapes her life. (Breeze 2006)

Interweaving the narratives and dances of five generations of women across the Atlantic into a "dramatic monologue" (Breeze 2006: blurb), *The Fifth Figure* clearly defies singular genre classifications.

Its title image by Agostino Brunias, *Villagers Merry Making in the Island of St. Vincent* from the 1770s, is very telling as to the origins and legacies of 't®opicalization.' It ties in with another well-known Brunias painting, *Dancing Scene in the West Indies* (Myrone 2013). The Italian-born Brunias came to England at the age of 28 and left for the West Indies with William Young as the government official's personal artist.[3] His romanticized genre paintings of idyllic 'leisure-time' life on the islands are prime examples of active historical misrepresentation. They "represented to London viewers 'exotic' and culturally distant performances which testified to the relative barbarism of their participants," while the "pristine attire" of the merry-makers "matches contemporary accounts promoting a positive

---

3 See "Comments". Image Reference: Bilby-5. www.slaveryimages.org.

image of life in the slave-plantations" (Myrone 2013), which supported pro-slavery lines of argument. Yet, as Beth Fowkes Tobin argues, despite the "status as objects of a natural history inquiry" of those represented, such pictures "did not succeed entirely" in erasing a subject's personhood (1999: 18) because

> Brunias's paintings and prints of African Caribbeans, both freed and enslaved, bear traces of the struggle for personhood, and in his representations of clothing we can see both the suppression and presence of narratives of self-actualization for the subjects of his paintings. Brunias's paintings and prints, in recording the quotidian cross-cultural encounters of the 'sugar' islands, capture the contradictions inherent in the colonial slave societies of the West Indies, contradictions having to do with the African Caribbean struggle for agency within a slave society that was also a market economy. (1999: 144)

The sonic and the visual spheres of representation overlap in the history of the quadrille. The courtly quadrille formation dance from which Breeze's structure takes its inspiration was popular across late-eighteenth- and nineteenth-century Europe and made it to the colonies via France and England (Kassing 2007: 135–137). Depending on location and variation, it consisted of four to six, sometimes eight parts or set figures with a certain order of recurring 8-measure themes in each figure, in either 2/4 or 6/8 time (Clarke and Crisp 1981: 96–98).

As Caroline Muraldo points out, the quadrille was practiced in the colonies by European descendants on their holidays (2013). It was subsequently adapted in music and style from the "great house dancing" (Lewin 2000: 132), with distinct forms and versions as well as different costumes across the islands. The formal Jamaican Quadrille, which today is a cultural dance signifying folk tradition, has four figures and in the ballroom version "retains formal dress and deportment," leaving little room for improvisation, while the so-called camp-style quadrille "uses couples in various formations and [features] far more spontaneous and improvised music and movements based on the particular dance figure" (Lewin 2000: 132). Until the mid-twentieth century, quadrilles "were a lively part of village life" during "community fairs, picnics and holiday celebrations," where "they were kept alive at regular sessions arranged by elderly enthusiasts. If instruments were short, voices and clapping sufficed" (Lewin 2000: 132). According to dance instructor Pat Powell, when dancing the quadrille "you can always learn something else. You're learning about yourself, you're learning about each other and the working together, the coming together of people and [...] you can use it in so many different ways to help yourself," which is why for her, the main task is "keeping the tradition and looking at how our ancestors had survived – used the quadrille to survive – and the lessons that they taught us and how *we* can use the quadrille to survive" (qtd. in

Breinburg 2013). In Breeze's quadrille text there are five figures and a 'bridge' between the fourth and the fifth figure. In quadrille dance, Lewin calls the fifth figure "the most original and typically Jamaican one" out of the possible eight figures, as it is "danced to mento music" (2000: 132). Mento, "Jamaica's indigenous dance, song, and instrumental style," accentuates the last beat of each bar (Lewin 2000: 103). Similar to dub's voicing of nation language as a decolonial practice across the performance-to-print continuum, the articulation of the sonic and the body in mento song and dance add further layers of meaning to the genre palimpsest of the quadrille in *The Fifth Figure*.

3 Genres, Figures, and Re-Memory in *The Fifth Figure*

Breeze has traced quotidian lives and private as well as social crises of Caribbean women vis-à-vis cultural and political expressions of hegemonic masculinity throughout her performances, recordings, and publications. In *The Fifth Figure* she follows those further down historical and ancestral lines. The genre and stylistic shifts both within and from one figure and dance to the next express the painful continuities and ruptures across the generations. While the women's stories move forward in a linear manner from one generation to the next, the issues they face recur in a non-linear fashion reminiscent of Toni Morrison's notion of re-memory. In *Beloved* (1987), Morrison uses "the signals of 'telling' as a survival strategy – dialect, narrative recursion, suspension of time and place" through articulation of characters' voices as a "prosopopeic (re)memory" which blends and collapses voice and text into one another, resulting in an "introspective that enfolds the dimensions of both the mind and history in a visually rich and dazzling projection of a revisioned time and space" (Holloway 1990: 518). The word thus becomes "a dynamic entity that (re)members community and connects it back to the voices from which it has been severed, effectively forcing it out of its silence" (Holloway 1990: 523, fn. 3). Although *The Fifth Figure* marks these processes of voicing through different genre registers and styles rather than through a collapsing of voice and text, recurrent motifs also connect the figures in a prosopopeic function across time and space, reconnecting them to their previously unarticulated heritage.

Emmeline in "Figure One" joins her Anglican missionary brother James in Jamaica after their parents' death and upon arrival feels "eaten up by green" and "overwhelmed by colour" in visceral response to its climate and vegetation (7). "In one of the first free villages / in the hills above the cane," which James likens to Zion, he aims to dissociate himself from the vices of the recently abolished system of enslavement, not least through his "private vow of poverty" (7–8). Equally appalled and fascinated by the village's "illegitimate children the plantation owners had fathered with slave women" (8), Emmeline's moralizing and exoticizing gaze is initially conveyed in narrative stanzas. She recounts how she falls for the housekeeper Nana's green-eyed son Gobi and how his rich half-brother Charles – "Gobi, but with blue eyes" (10) – tries to teach her the first figure of the quadrille when she is invited to the great house. Running the plantation estate in the valley, Charles would be a good catch, but Emmeline does not develop desires for him but for Gobi. Plagued by feelings of sin, she blames "the magic of the hills, the spirits in the bush" for dancing with Gobi instead (11). His dance is "almost the same as the quadrille" (12) but of a different beat, invoking the difference between the ballroom and the village variations of the dance where, "[i]f instruments were short, voices and clapping sufficed" (Lewin 2000: 132).

The village in the hills is a space marked by the power dynamics of the plantation, embodied by the half-brothers and the villagers, whom James refers to as "the rainbow people" (8). These dynamics cast their shadow into post-Emancipation times, so that the invocation of *"Jubilee, Jubilee, / this is the year of Jubilee / Queen Victoria set we free, / Queen Victoria set we free"* marks but a moment of utopian hope (13). In the song and dance surrounding the celebrations, Emmeline gives in to her desire for Gobi. The syntax completely breaks up in Emmeline's recollections of their physical encounter and of James's killing his half-brother when finding them together (14). Capitalizing on the power differential and his white privilege, James is let off as the jurisdiction determines that Gobi raped Emmeline. Since even "freedom couldn't change that verdict," the empty spaces surrounding "he was black / and I was white / nothing had changed really" (14) both visually and as breaks in the rhythmic structure, mark the unspoken and unspeakable barrier of the discourse of 'miscegenation.'

Succumbing to her pain, Emmeline blames "the bushes / black magic in the bushes" and is unable to face or take care of her girl child, the "[b]ush baby" (14–15). Determined to "not let the bush in" and to fight it back with a machete (15), her rejection of the child becomes symptomatic for the inability to face her position in the colonial power differential and the trauma of racialized violence. The bush thus becomes a recurrent motif of mental instability throughout the generations to follow. Believing that "[t]he bush wants to take back the child" and that it is her who would bring about the child's demise (15), Emmeline finally determines that she cannot fight but "must make peace with the bush." She has to "be a wife to the bush," that is, silently submit to its will (18) and accept her position on the perpetrators' side of the colonial divide through her complicity of "white blood" (17). For Emmeline, this acknowledgement of white privilege comes at the price of mental instability and the loss of the possibility of a motherly bond, which is displaced onto the grandmother Nana instead – who, however, significantly is not given a voice of her own.

Emmeline's daughter Susan, called Susu, thus is "born of bush" (19) and cannot relate to her mother. She refuses to go to school with the girls whose privilege is marked by "pasty skin and long straight hair" (19). Susu chooses the carpenter's son, whom she calls Son Son, to dance with and thus learns the second figure of the quadrille – again not the formal ballroom type taught in school, "but the dip and sway of the villagers" (20). In contrast to her mother, her agency is underlined by her choice of partners to fulfil her desire for children. When Son Son fails her through infidelity, she chooses Woody as her next partner. Although her agency is curtailed by his physical abuse, when Woody falls off a mule and is paralyzed, Susu attributes this to divine intervention (25). Susu's dance focuses on her agency vis-à-vis men that is enabled by her economic stability, as well as on her relationship to Nana and to her children. Conveyed entirely in longer prose passages, her figure reflects the continuities in the colonial system of racialized hierarchies on the island.

"Figure Three," Susu's and Woody's daughter Amanda, "could pass anywhere for white" (26) but feels "drab and colourless" (30) in the company of the black girls in her school. Amanda's narrative is full of colorist terminology, and in her self-perception she is "not black enough" to fit in (32), turning the narrative of privilege into one of feeling excluded. She has a close relationship to her father, whom everyone else seems to neglect, but a troubled relationship with her mother, although she takes up sewing to financially support her. When finishing a wedding dress Amanda meets "her Solomon" Max, from the German village across the mountains, who "looked just like the prince in the story books" and with whom she dances three figures of the quadrille as payment for her sewing at one of the village's mento yards (30–34). Her mother's "woman to woman talk" comes too late, though, and Max – "already betrothed to a fellow German girl from his own village" – does not acknowledge their child, whom Amanda names Sheba, although she "was white, even whiter than us, [looking] German like Max and his family" (37). At the age of six, Amanda sends Sheba off to live with Mrs. Hull, who "wanted a companion for her son [John] who would not look out of place in the home" (37). Amanda's narrative is marked more clearly by the language of memoir, adding another genre layer to the palimpsest while retaining the reflective style of the previous figures.

Indicative of another continuity in the social politics of the island, Sheba, "Figure Four," thus grows up with "Mommy Hull" as another substitute mother figure. At festivities she learns all four figures of the formal quadrille but – unlike her ancestors – makes sure "not to dance like the servants" (39). Upon John's departure for Cambridge Sheba is sent back to Amanda. Alienated from her birth mother, she wonders: "Why won't this other woman look at me instead of standing like a servant by the buggy?" (40) and, when requested to help with the planting of the small remaining lot sub-divided through the generations, tells her that where she – in denial of her origin – ostensibly comes from, "only black people were sent out to work the land" (41). When Susu dies, Sheba is "most afraid" of the ancestral graves in the yard (42), feeling their presence like a repressed memory pointing to the trauma of enslavement and racialized identity. On her eighteenth birthday at a village dance, Sheba has to rethink the quadrille as she has learned it, as a fifth figure is introduced by the mento band. Curry explains to her that "they didn't dance the ballroom way" because "when you worked hard all the time and just had one night to dance, it seemed silly to stand still and wait or just dance four figures when you could add more" (43). Curry stops coming to the dances when he finds out that Sheba is pregnant, although he does support their daughter Sarah, "a bouncing white baby" who, as Amanda says, "resembles the Germans" (45). Like other women of Hillside have begun to do, Sheba eventually transgresses the colorist hierarchy and marries "Black Fred," but has no further children with him.

The generational dance continues in the figure titled "Take Me to the Bridge," with Sarah as the literal bridge to the current generation. A bridge in music theory describes a melodically contrasting unique section within a song.[4] In the structure of Breeze's quadrille, this bridge is an insertion or interlude that stylistically resonates with Canadian-based dub poetess Lillian Allen's 1986 "feminist 'war-poem'" "Nelly Belly Swelly," which Habekost calls "one of the most haunting pieces of women's dub poetry" (1993: 206), as it topicalizes the rape and ensuing pregnancy of 13-year-old Nellie by a man from her neighborhood. The focus of Breeze's bridge, however, is on Sarah's ambitions to get out of Hillside and attend nursing school. Unlike the previous figures' narrative memoirs, hers is rendered in third person and condensed into a single stanza/verse, dramatizing the transition to the fragmented style of the final figure.

The fifth figure remains unnamed. According to an interview with Jane Dowson, Breeze's family memoir as told to her by her aunt Vida, based in turn on *her* grandmother's recollections, inspired *The Fifth Figure* (Breeze 2011b: DVD), which is also implied in the blurb. This would make Breeze the fifth

---

[4] In lyrics and in melody the title of the fourth figure features prominently in James Brown's 1970 "Get Up (I Feel Like Being a Sex Machine)". "Take Me to the Bridge" is also a 1980 disco song performed by Vera.

figure by genealogy. Yet the palimpsest of genre and style complicates a simplistic autobiographical reading and instead suggests a prosopopeic function of this figure. A long poem in its own right, this part returns to a more dub-oriented style and language. It features versions of the chorus "come, come, chile, / let we sing the song again" (Breeze 2006: 47), invoking the grandmother's and the ancestral voices as giving advice through Sheba's redemptive song, as it were. Stylistically this figure resonates with Breeze's poem "Testament": "sing girl / sing / dere's more to you / dan skin" (2011b: 54). Curry and his daughter stick out in the community of Hillside, 'whitened' across the centuries, for he looks "like him come over here from Guinea" (48). With Sarah away at nursing school in Kingston, the poem introduces the common themes of rural-to-urban migration and reinforces the theme of the absent mother figure. Rendered as a dialogue between the grandmother's advice and the child's thoughts, the various mother-daughter relations, with their respective idiosyncratic complications tied back to Emmeline's and Gobi's tragic foundational story, reverberate across time in prosopopeic re-memory style.

Sarah returns as a qualified midwife and attempts a new life in one village after the other. Upon being found exploring her body with the neighbor Peter, the speaker invokes Emmeline's ancestral fear of the bush in lines like "I must pray that the bush don't come and hold me," thus bringing the narrative full circle to the first figure (53). The last figure is filled with painful episodes of abuse by a caretaker, being sent to stay with her tyrannical father, being molested by the schoolmaster, and the constant threat of too early childbearing that also runs through the generations. The mandate "[t]o stay out of the bush" (Breeze 2006: 54) furthermore signifies a disdain for rural life and aspirations for ostensibly better livelihood in the city, which are common themes in Caribbean literature. However, rural-to-urban migration often results in the loss of community and spiritual balance. The disillusionment of urban life and the concomitant loss of mental stability is also a key theme invoked in the haunting sonic articulation and dub beat of Breeze's "Riddym Ravings."

But there are also joyful memories of returning to Granny Sheba during the school holidays and of her soothing voice, "We going to laugh till the whole nation / Think we gone insane / So run, come chile / Let we sing the song again" (63). Song and dance again are presented as relief and spiritual coping mechanisms: "The church could not compete / with the mento beat" (66). While liberation discourse seeps in as a promise, it is again experienced with the full blow of contradictions imposed onto the ambiguously racialized body in a colorist society. Claiming her "Arawak heritage," the speaker states: "I belonged to this island / I belonged to the bush," yet she remains "too white to speak" as head girl for her school during the time of black power rallies (70).

After a tragic accident that killed a child, "[d]eath, bush and blood" take over the prosopopeic dub poet's rhymes (Breeze 2006: 72). Denied by her father for living with a Rastafarian, and diagnosed with schizophrenia, she is visited by voices both creative and painful: "I would turn on the radio to soothe me / And do whatever the radio said / So the reggae entered my veins / The drums of mento and rastafari [sic] / Joined up in every refrain" (75), furthering the intertextual link to "Riddym Ravings." The invitation to perform poetry on stage provides a sense of home, and poetry becomes a new way of dancing (76). Living in diaspora enables the speaker's development of a sense of 'Caribbean' identity, while a trip to South Africa, which does not live up to the promise of the search for a home on the continent, stifles a Pan-African identification. Instead, it is Granny Sheba's songs that provide grounding and consolation. From the mento-supported quadrille dance to the sonic realm of dub poetry, the speaker becomes empowered through the existential necessity and sonic enactment of ancestrally inspired "Word Sound and Power." However, this empowerment remains curtailed by the deep-seated ancestral trauma, the pains of racialization and colorism, and by gendered violence enacted on the female body and mind.

4 Dubbing out Genre through 'Sonic Delinking'

The cultural practices and soundscapes of 'Word Sound and Power' that have come to be identified with Rastafari invoke a similar kind of "reality-shift" as the one that Partridge attributes to the technologies of dub music (2010: 82). Rather than considering these technologies a manipulation and distortion of reality (Williams in Partridge 2010: 82), a decolonial reading emphasizes the dimension of alternative knowledge production. Johannes Ismaiel-Wendt shifts the focus of the study of music within postcolonial studies from an illustration of worldviews to an epistemological system. Against territorialized thinking and perception in the form of *topophilia* (the desire for localization) in the study and analysis of music, he suggests *topophobia* as a theoretical concept (2013: 90–95). He considers the fundamental contingency between polymorphic, movement-generated music and its localization to be a consequence and instrument of colonialist thinking and action in representational systems. What he calls "tracknowlogy" in turn sees the track as a productive concept escaping the compulsion for localized cultural representation. Sound synthesizing as a de-naturalizing strategy and tracks as independent epistemological systems require a different kind of hearing and close listening, which Ismaiel-Wendt calls "sonic delinking" (2013: 104). While the "body- and geopolitics" of racist classification and the third-worldization of the recently re-branded Global South feature in the metropolitan consumption of dub as well, sonic delinking, in turn, means disobedience against the burden of "acoustic representation, liability, and belonging" activated by musical forms (Ismaiel-Wendt 2013: 102). This aligns it with the "de-colonial epistemic shift" outlined by Mignolo in the sense of foregrounding "other epistemologies, other principles of knowledge and understanding and, consequently, other economy, other politics, other ethics" (2007: 453).

In a productive dialogue between the current study of dub music and poetry, sonic delinking would involve attuning the ear to the echoes of history that reverberate across *The Fifth Figure* and the Atlantic world, and that challenge our notions of diaspora. In Breeze's text, the generations enter into a complex dance, at the end of which we arrive in a present inextricably entwined with the preceding centuries through re-memory and embodied knowledge, with all its complexities and contradictions that are expressed across a range of genres and poetic soundscapes. 'Word Sound and Power,' in music and in poetry, as well as in the continuum that is dub, has shaped and continues to produce decolonial culture. Whether we take up the epistemic challenge of what Anthony Bogues, in reference to Bob Marley's "redemptive poetics," has called "symbolic insurgency" (2003: 199) is ultimately up to us and not to the poetry nor to questions of genre.

Works Cited

Allen, Lillian. 1986. "Nelly Belly Swelly". *Revolutionary Tea Party*. Verse to Vinyl/World Records. MP3.
Bogues, Anthony. 2003. "Get Up, Stand Up: The Redemptive Poetics of Bob Marley". *Black Heretics, Black Prophets: Radical Political Intellectuals*. London: Routledge. 187–206.
Brathwaite, Edward Kamau. 1993. "History of the Voice: 1979–1981". *Roots*. Ann Arbor: University of Michigan Press. 259–304.
Breeze, Jean Binta. 1988. *Riddym Ravings and Other Poems*. Ed. Mervyn Morris. London: Race Today.
Breeze, Jean Binta. 1993. "Riddym Ravings (The Mad Woman's Poem)". *Critical Quarterly* 35. 1: 85–88.
Breeze, Jean Binta. 1996. "Can a Dub Poet be a Woman?". In: Alison Donnell and Sarah Lawson Welsh (eds.). *The Routledge Reader in Caribbean Literature*. London: Routledge. 498–500.
Breeze, Jean Binta. 2000. *Tracks*. LKJ Records. CD.
Breeze, Jean Binta. 2006. *The Fifth Figure*. Highgreen: Bloodaxe Books.
Breeze, Jean Binta. 2009. "Mad Woman". *Eena Me Corner*. Arroyo. CD.
Breeze, Jean Binta. 2011a. Interview by Matthew Sweeney. *Out of the Vortex*. BBC. https://www.bbc.co.uk/programmes/b00y6qtj [accessed 23 December 2018].

Breeze, Jean Binta. 2011b. *Third World Girl: Selected Poems*. Highgreen: Bloodaxe Books. Includes *Live at the Y Theatre, Leicester*. DVD.

Breinburg, Ken. 2013. "Exploring Cultural Dance: Quadrille: Pat Powell Discusses the Impact of Jamaican Quadrille". *YouTube*. https://youtu.be/GbqkUM56rBk [accessed 23 December 2018].

Brown, Stewart, and Mark McWatt (eds.). 2005. *The Oxford Book of Caribbean Verse*. Oxford: Oxford University Press.

Brunias, Agostino. 1770–1780. *Villagers Merry Making in the Island of St. Vincent, with Dancers and Musicians, a Landscape with Huts on a Hill*. Oil paint on canvas. National Library of Jamaica, Kingston.

Bucknor, Michael. 2011. "Dub Poetry as a Postmodern Art Form". In: Michael Bucknor and Alison Donnell (eds.). *The Routledge Companion to Anglophone Caribbean Literature*. London: Routledge. 255–264.

Clarke, Mary, and Clement Crisp. 1981. *The History of Dance*. New York: Crown.

Cooper, Carolyn. 1990. "Words Unbroken by the Beat: The Performance Poetry of Jean Binta Breeze and Mikey Smith". *Wasafiri* 5.11: 7–13.

Cooper, Carolyn. 1993. *Noises in the Blood: Orality, Gender, and the 'Vulgar' Body of Jamaican Popular Culture*. Durham: Duke University Press.

Cooper, Carolyn. 1997. "Review: *Verbal Riddim: The Politics and Aesthetics of African-Caribbean Dub Poetry* by Christian Habekost". *NWIG: New West Indian Guide / Nieuwe West-Indische Gids* 71.1–2: 151–153.

Cummings, Mark. 2012. "Jamaica's First Female Dub Poet Honoured by the Brits". *Jamaica Observer*. http://www.jamaicaobserver.com/westernnews/Jamaica-s-first-female-dub-poet-honoured-by-the-Brits_11981575 [accessed 6 December 2018].

Forbes, Curdella. 2009. "Jean 'Binta' Breeze". In: Victoria R. Arana (ed.). *Dictionary of Literary Biography: Twenty-First-Century 'Black' British Writers*. Detroit: Thomson Gale. 84–94.

Griffin, G.A. Elmer. 1995. "Word Bullets. Review of *Verbal Riddim: The Politics and Aesthetics of African-Caribbean Dub Poetry* by Christian Habekost". *Transition* 66: 57–65.

Habekost, Christian. 1993. *Verbal Riddim: The Politics and Aesthetics of African-Caribbean Dub Poetry*. Amsterdam: Rodopi.

Henriques, Julian. 2011. *Sonic Bodies: Reggae Sound Systems, Performance Techniques, and Ways of Knowing*. London: Continuum.

Holloway, Karla F. C. 1990. "*Beloved*: A Spiritual". *Callaloo* 13.3: 516–525.

Ismaiel-Wendt, Johannes. 2013. "Track Studies: Popular Music and Postcolonial Analysis". In: Jana Gohrisch and Ellen Grünkemeier (eds.). *Postcolonial Studies across the Disciplines*. ASNEL Papers 18. Amsterdam: Rodopi. 88–107.

Kassing, Gayle. 2007. "Dances of the 19th Century". *History of Dance: An Interactive Arts Approach*. Champaign: Human Kinetics. 135–140.

Lewin, Olive. 2000. *"Rock it Come Over": The Folk Music of Jamaica*. Kingston: University of the West Indies Press.

Mignolo, Walter D. 2007. "Delinking: The Rhetoric of Modernity, the Logic of Coloniality and the Grammar of De-coloniality". *Cultural Studies* 21.2–3: 449–514.

Mignolo, Walter D. 2009. "Epistemic Disobedience, Independent Thought and De-Colonial Freedom". *Theory, Culture and Society* 26: 1–23.

Miller, Kei. 2013. "A Smaller Sound, A Lesser Fury: A Eulogy for Dub Poetry". *SX Salon* 14. http://smallaxe.net/sxsalon/discussions/smaller-sound-lesser-fury [accessed 5 December 2018].

Morris, Mervyn. 1997. "A Note on 'Dub Poetry'". *Wasafiri* 13.26: 66–69.
Munkelt, Marga, et al. 2013. "Introduction: Directions of Translocation: Towards a Critical Spatial Thinking in Postcolonial Studies". *Postcolonial Translocations: Cultural Representation and Critical Spatial Thinking*. ASNEL Papers 17. Amsterdam: Rodopi. xiii-lxxix.
Muraldo, Caroline. 2013. "Exploring Cultural Dance: Quadrille: Caroline Muraldo & Members of her Dance Groups Talk Quadrille". *YouTube*. Ken Breinburg. https://youtu.be/wfN3prgkTD0 [accessed 5 December 2018].
Myrone, Martin. 1764–1796. "Agostino Brunias: *Dancing Scene in the West Indies*". *Tate*. http://www.tate.org.uk/art/artworks/brunias-dancing-scene-in-the-west-indies-t13869#endnote_back_17 [accessed 5 December 2018].
Partridge, Christopher. 2010. *Dub in Babylon: Understanding the Evolution and Significance of Dub Reggae in Jamaica and Britain from King Tubby to Post-Punk*. London: Equinox.
Pollard, Velma. 2000. *Dread Talk: The Language of the Rastafari*. Montreal: McGill-Queen's University Press.
Pulis, John W. 2003. "'Word-Sound-Power': Language, Social Identity, and the Worldview of Rastafari". In: Richard K. Blot (ed.). *Language and Social Identity*. Westport: Praeger. 243–260.
Sheller, Mimi. 2003. *Consuming the Caribbean: From Arawaks to Zombies*. New York: Routledge.
Sheller, Mimi. 2004. "Oraliteracy and Textual Opacity: Resisting Metropolitan Consumption of Caribbean Culture". *Language and Intercultural Communication* 4.1–2: 100–108.
Tobin, Beth Fowkes. 1999. *Picturing Imperial Power: Colonial Subjects in Eighteenth-Century British Painting*. Durham: Duke University Press.
Veal, Michael E. 2007. *Dub: Soundscapes and Shattered Songs in Jamaican Reggae*. Middletown: Wesleyan University Press.
Walcott, Derek. 2008. Interview by Harrlett Gilbert. BBC World Book Club. BBC. https://www.bbc.co.uk/programmes/p02r7n8v [accessed 18 December 2018].
Welsh, Sarah Lawson. 2001. "The Literatures of Trinidad and Jamaica". In: Albert James Arnold (ed.). *A History of Literature in the Caribbean: English- and Dutch-Speaking Countries*. Vol. 2. Amsterdam: John Benjamins. 69–96.
Zephaniah, Benjamin. 2003. "'Me? I thought, OBE me? Up yours, I thought'". *The Guardian*. https://www.theguardian.com/books/2003/nov/27/poetry.monarchy [accessed 5 December 2018].

Genre and Mediality

Michaela Hausmann
Crossing Genre and Media Boundaries: Poetry in Fantastic Literary Narratives and Their Film Adaptations

Abstract: While poems are usually considered self-contained pieces of literary art, this essay investigates how embedded poems may be conducive to narrative mediation in the written medium of literature and the audiovisual medium of film. For this purpose, two ballads from fantastic novels and their respective film adaptations will be analysed as case studies: "Misty Mountains" from J.R.R. Tolkien's *The Hobbit* and Peter Jackson's *The Hobbit: An Unexpected Journey*, and "The Hanging Tree" from Suzanne Collins's *The Hunger Games: Mockingjay* and Francis Lawrence's *The Hunger Games: Mockingjay, Part 1*. By comparing the novels' and the film adaptations' treatment of the respective ballads in terms of form, speech situation, and functions, the analysis will provide insights into the transgeneric and transmedial potential of embedded poems.

Keywords: embedded poems, narrative mediation, ballads, literature, film adaptations

"I always think [Tolkien] used songs as a third voice. You have dialogue. You have a narrator. And you have these songs that sort of give you another window into that world" (Adams qtd. in "Songs" 2015). What Doug Adams says about Tolkien's songs in relation to his narratives seems to attest to the importance of embedded songs and poems in relation to the narratives for the overall mediation of the story. On par with dialogue and the narrator's voice, the songs and poems are not simply decorative elements but engage with these other forms of discourse and contribute to the overall aesthetics of the narrative. This paper will investigate how this engagement is realised in two popular novels and their respective film adaptations. Due to the constraints of literature as a medium, the ballads – the main focus of this paper – are solely represented by their lyrics in the novel, so that only the words and, sometimes, a vague description of the mood of the song are mediated, but not a musical and thus audible dimension. These constraints do not apply to film as a medium, where the written lyrics from the novels can be endowed with a musical quality so that the ballads can actually be represented as songs. Therefore, for the purpose of this paper, I use the overarching term 'poetry' to refer to the poetic form of the

https://doi.org/10.1515/9783110594874-013

ballads' lyrics as the central objects of analysis. The differentiation between the literary and cinematic representations of the ballads will be made transparent during the analysis, thus shedding light on the intergeneric and intermedial potential of embedded poetry in novels and films.

Two exemplary ballads will be scrutinised with regard to their form, their speech situation, and their functions for the overarching written and audiovisual narrative: "Misty Mountains" from J.R.R. Tolkien's novel *The Hobbit* (1936) and Peter Jackson's film *The Hobbit: An Unexpected Journey* (2012), and "The Hanging Tree" from Suzanne Collins's novel *The Hunger Games: Mockingjay* (2010) and Francis Lawrence's film *Mockingjay, Part 1* (2014). The choice of the poetic genre of ballads allows for increased comparability, and the ballad's association with song and music (cf. Baldick 2008: 71) exemplifies the problem of mediality in novel and film because both examples are merely described as songs in the narratives but rendered audible musically in the film adaptations. Specifically, the two film/novel pairs and their ballad examples share a number of parallels. Both examples are integrated as part of the novels' and films' diegeses, not as paratexts. Therefore, a main focus of the analysis will lie on the ways the hypodiegetic plot and themes of each ballad are aligned with the overarching narratives. Another parallel is that both novels include fantastic elements – "fantastic" being used in the wider sense of containing impossible elements (cf. Attebery 1992: 11; Clute and Grant 1999: 335)[1] – so they seem particularly suitable for the integration of ballads, whose own stories often comprise supernatural or impossible elements (cf. Baldick 2008: 73). A fantastic setting may moreover enable the representation of ballads as part of an imagined poetic tradition and therefore turn poems into windows onto these fantastic worlds. Finally, both film adaptations were big-budget blockbusters released in the course of a few years, suggesting a similar level of cinematographic techniques and developments, and providing a sufficiently concise time frame for the analysis.

---

1 In this chapter, the term 'fantastic' is not used in the restricted Todorovian sense but as a broader term that accommodates several non-realistic genres such as fantasy, science fiction, etc. According to Todorov the "fantastic is that hesitation experienced by a person who knows only the laws of nature, confronting an apparently supernatural event" (1975: 25). This hesitation must remain unresolved in a text, otherwise the text would have to be allocated to "a neighbouring genre, the uncanny or the marvelous" (1975: 25). As this definition only applies to a very narrow body of texts, Todorov's approach is unsuitable for this analysis. Instead, Attebery's (1992) and Clute and Grant's (1999) conception of the fantastic as a mode of literature that includes impossible phenomena will be employed because it enables the inclusion of heterogeneous texts such as *The Hobbit*, which would actually classify as fantasy, and *Mockingjay*, which is a science-fiction dystopia.

1 Theoretical and Terminological Considerations

The embedding of poetry in a larger narrative precludes any notion of poetry as a hermetically sealed genre but nevertheless requires sufficient distinction from other genres such as novels. While classical notions of genre were traditionally interpreted as static and historically stable typologies, the Romantic period attempted to establish "a philosophical theory of genre as distinct from a purely descriptive account of individual genres," of which Goethe's *Naturformen* or 'natural forms' of poetry – epic, lyric and dramatic – are among the most influential (Duff 2000: 3–4). During the twentieth century, however, more radical configurations of genre emerged. Derrida famously deconstructed the notion of genre entirely, since "the marks by which a work inscribes itself within a genre paradoxically do not belong to that genre; and hence the generic boundary is dissolved at the very moment when it is established" (Duff 2000: 5). As a combination of these conflicting theories, many genre theorists have consequently adopted a cognitive concept of genre because it provides a system and a certain degree of classification, but also accounts for generic change and for Derrida's point that a literary work does not belong to a genre, but can participate in several genres. Hence, it is a descriptive rather than a philosophical concept.

According to this cognitive concept, genres are prototypically organized mental constructions with central and peripheral theoretical features and also concrete members (texts, films, games etc.). Genres are in constant flux because they can be modified by every new member that is incorporated. They are slightly different for each and every person and have fuzzy boundaries that allow for occasional overlap and mixing (cf. Rosch 1978; Wolf 2005; Sinding 2010; Bruhn 2014). This fluid concept of genre is particularly suitable for poetry because there are no defining criteria for poetry, although certain features like relative shortness, verse structure, sound patterns (such as rhymes), metre, rhetorical figures and tropes, and a high degree of aesthetic self-referentiality are commonly associated with the genre. However, poetry has a rather weak potential for creating aesthetic illusion because the subject matter tends to be presented indirectly, whereas its counterpart, the novel, uses detailed settings, characters, and plot, to mediate an aesthetic illusion (cf. Müller-Zettelmann 2000: 73–138).

The transition space between poetry and prose narratives is richly inhabited, as there are novels written in verse and poetry that is decidedly narrative in character. One of the peripheral members of the prototypical category of poetry that inhabits this transition space is the subgenre of ballads. While exhibiting many prototypical features of poetry like verse structure, a stanzaic form, a regular metre, and end rhymes, ballads usually tell a story whose plot is restricted to one single event. In line with this, ballads typically define the lead-up to this event and its aftermath, the characters involved, and a setting. Like most prose narratives, they also make use of dialogue and a – traditionally impersonal – narrator. Therefore, ballads create a reasonably strong aesthetic illusion and their mix of poetic and narrative features makes them a particularly suitable form of poetry to embed in a novel.

The process of embedding, however, has certain effects on the poems and the novel. As the term 'embedded poem' suggests, the prose narrative is the dominant form to whose aesthetic illusion the poems can contribute in a meaningful way. This unification requires that the poems need to point outside of themselves, so self-referentiality is probably detrimental to the process of embedding. If integrated successfully into the narrative, the embedded poems may serve the "rhetorical and aesthetic principle of *variatio*, which makes the work as a whole more attractive to readers" because "the alternation helps to avoid fatigue" (Bauer 2013/2014: 177). With regard to the overall aesthetic illusion, poems may add to the description of characters, as in several Gothic novels (cf. Brown 2008: 115), or to the description of the setting. They may also create the illusion of an oral tradition, a major strategy in the fiction of Walter Scott (cf. Müller 2005: 178). In terms of supporting the plot, poems can be used to trigger, foreshadow, summarise, or reflect on plot events. They can be tied to a particular quest in the surrounding narrative, or they may serve as vehicles of central themes throughout the narrative.

Apart from the fertile intergeneric and intramedial transition zone between poetry and the novel, poetry and film also share similarities, particularly the aspect of acoustic performance and the affinity with music. Like literary narratives, film narratives create an aesthetic illusion with settings and characters and also follow a plot trajectory. Consequently, the above-mentioned functions embedded poems can assume for the plot in novels arguably apply to films as well.

However, film adaptations of novels are cases of "re-mediations," that is, "intersemiotic transpositions from one sign system [...] to another" (Hutcheon 2013: 16), and film as a medium has its own means of mediating a story. In contrast to literary narratives' reliance on verbal expression, film predominantly uses visual modes of expression such as light, colours, camera positioning, focus, and editing that channel the representation of the story. Such techniques often serve to alleviate the constraints of audiovisual representation. The sphere of the mind, for example, cannot be as easily penetrated in film as it is through the interior monologues or the free indirect discourse in a novel (cf. Hutcheon 2013: 14). Instead, film may use voice-overs to relate a character's thoughts (cf. Kuhn and Westwell 2012: 446–447), or close-ups of characters to hint at their internal processes (cf. Dix 2008: 24), but such internal phenomena are rarely verbally, and thus explicitly, phrased. While film may lack the literary techniques of representing consciousness, it has the advantage of acoustic representation and, more importantly, the incorporation of music which can be conducive to the representation of a character's internal processes, such as emotions. Whereas a poem is merely visually described as a song in a novel, film may offer a musical, and therefore audible, presentation of it, thereby endowing the poem with various social and communicative as well as individual and psychological functions of music (Bullerjahn 2001: 55–56) which literature can only describe but not deliver.

Analogous to the distinction between story and discourse, film music can, on the one hand, be used as part of the story level in the form of songs sung by characters in the scene or as sounds and music whose source is directly visible onscreen. On the other hand, the music and songs can be part of the mediation of the story. Among the various terms coined for these different mediations of music, the terms 'diegetic' and 'non-diegetic music' (Rabenalt 2005: 93) will be used in the following due to their close relationship to literary terminology. It should be kept in mind, however, that certain transition styles exist in which the diegetic music can move to the non-diegetic level in the form of instrumental themes or when a song sung by a certain character begins to be accompanied by non-diegetic orchestration (cf. Karlin and Wright 2004: 187; Rabenalt 2005: 95).

Even though film songs are often integrated into films for commercial reasons (cf. Bullerjahn 2001: 68; Karlin and Wright 2004: 443), any kind of film music is first and foremost functional within the film since "[i]t is a cardinal rule for the film composer that the visuals on the screen determine the form of the music written to accompany it" (Prendergast 2002: 227; cf. Bullerjahn 2001: 59). Due to its strong emotional impact, film music can be used for characterisation by metaphorically zooming into the character's head (cf. Karlin and Wright 2004: 63; 136–137). Similarly, leitmotifs, the repeated and variable connection of a specific piece of music with a character or a situation (cf. Weidinger 2006: 68), can be used to add an emotional dimension to a single character, or "[a]n entire group of people can become as one, representing the psyche of a single character" (Karlin and Wright 2004: 70). Moreover, music and songs may be used to evoke the setting, to convey the atmosphere, to solve a conflict, or to follow a plot line (cf. Bullerjahn 2001: 69–70; Karlin and Wright 2004: 81). In terms of dramatization, music is furthermore capable of manipulating the discourse time (cf. Bullerjahn 2001: 71), by, for example, underscoring analepses or prolepses in the narrative or by conflating simultaneously occurring events by means of song and the technique of montage.

The fact that the films to be analysed are adaptations based on the novels implies "repetition, but repetition without replication" (Hutcheon 2013: 7), and consequently possible deviations from the poems' form and functions can happen. For example, a different number of poems can be used in the film, as usually not all poems from the novel are used. Hutcheon stresses "the pragmatic necessity of cutting a sprawling novel to make it fit the screen in terms of time and space" (2013: 37), and many films are furthermore driven by "an unrelenting, forward-driving story" (Hutcheon 2013: 23) and might therefore favour poems that are significant to the plot. Another reason for omitting certain poems may be the overall tone of the adaptation, as in Jackson's *The Hobbit*, where the childish songs of the Elves and Goblins in Tolkien's novel would not fit the more epic character of the adaptation. Although it is beyond the scope of this paper to discuss the rationale underlying the selection or omission processes of all poems in the film adaptations, there is a noticeable reduction of poems from novel to adaptation in the theatrical version of Jackson's *Hobbit 1*, which contains eight of the narrative's 13 poems from beginning to end (although the Special Extended Edition has two more). Julian Eilmann has compiled a very useful and comprehensive overview of included and omitted poems in *The Lord of the Rings* adaptation (2013: 199–201), the like of which would also be interesting for the *Hobbit* films but has hitherto not been undertaken. In *Mockingjay 1*, the number of songs corresponds to the first part of Collins's book, as there is only one.

2 "Misty Mountains" in Tolkien's *The Hobbit* and Jackson's *The Hobbit: An Unexpected Journey*

In Peter Jackson's adaptation, the first snatches of "Misty Mountains" already occur in the prologue. The old hobbit Bilbo writes down his story and relates the fall of Erebor, the ancient kingdom of the Dwarves, and the coming of Smaug, the last dragon in Middle-earth, by means of voice-over narration while the story is shown on-screen. After the Dwarves' expulsion from Erebor, Bilbo says, the "young Dwarf-Prince took work where he could find it, labouring in the villages of men" in order to demonstrate how low the mighty people of Erebor had fallen. Bilbo then continues: "But always he remembered the mountain smoke beneath the moon, the trees like torches blazing bright. For he had seen dragon fire in the sky and a city turned to ash. And he never forgave and he never forgot" (*The Hobbit 1*, 2012).

Bilbo here uses lines of the poem "Misty Mountain" as it appears in the book in a slightly altered fashion: "The mountain smoked beneath the moon" is the first line of the ninth stanza in the original ballad and "The trees like torches blazed with light" is the last line of the seventh (Tolkien 2008: 20–21; lines 28 and 33). However, as they are detached from their poetic context and included in Bilbo's narration, they are hardly recognisable as ballad lines, but it could be assumed that an audience familiar with the text would recognise them. Due to the ballad's narrative mode, its lines easily accommodate Bilbo's narration. The grammatical and lexical changes are made necessary by the context of Bilbo's speech. One reason for choosing only these two unconnected lines in the ballad could be their strong imagery evoking the dragon without explicitly showing it. The entire sequence has a clear focus on Thorin and establishes him as a key character, the images of the two lines of the ballad appear to be engraved into his memory and fuel his desire to return and take vengeance.

In the book, there is no prologue because the story of the fall of Erebor is not told in detail but poetically summarised by the rendition of the ballad in Bilbo's parlour. Once the entire company is assembled there, it is Thorin who demands music and subsequently begins to play and sing "Misty Mountains" together with the other Dwarves (cf. Tolkien 2008: 18). The same scene occurs in the film. By means of a tracking shot, the camera approaches the company, creating the impression that the viewer is part of the congregation while the Dwarves hum in unison, supported by non-diegetic music. The next shot shows Thorin's firelit face in close-up, his eyes turned upwards as if he were lost in thoughts or memories, which evokes the prologue's use of the ballad. Then, he begins the song before he turns to his companions who join in, thereby emphasising Thorin's designated role as their leader.

Notwithstanding the similarities concerning the speech situation, the text of the poem differs considerably in length between book and film. In Tolkien's *The Hobbit*, the poem comprises ten quatrains with regular iambic tetrametre and alternate rhymes (cf. Tolkien 2008: 19–21). Not only is the stanzaic form evocative of the ballad but the first, fifth, and tenth stanzas are almost identical with only slight variation in their last lines, so that they can be considered a refrain to the entire poem. In addition, they structure the narrative of the ballad into three parts. The first stanza formulates the goal of travelling "far over the misty mountains cold / [...] / To seek the pale enchanted gold" (lines 1–4); stanzas two to four recount the life of the Dwarves before the arrival of the dragon and celebrate their unparalleled smithery (lines 5–16). Stanza five again repeats the goal of winning these treasures back (lines 17–20); stanzas six to nine narrate the calamitous arrival of the dragon, whose "ire more fierce than fire" destroyed nature, the human city in the "dale" (lines 22–32), and eventually the Kingdom under the Mountain from whence the Dwarves "fled their hall to dying fall" (line 35). The last stanza repeats again the purpose of the journey.

The narrative of the ballad is significant for the overall plot of *The Hobbit*. It relates the past history of the Dwarves: the loss of their home to the dragon. It expresses their present urge to commence the journey "ere break of day" in order to win back what is rightfully theirs, and anticipates the main future event of this journey – the confrontation between the Dwarves and the dragon. Thus the ballad can be said to exemplify the main plot in miniature, and the emotional motivation propelling the protagonists to their quest.

Particularly the last line, "To win our harps and gold from him," summarises the purpose of the quest. The gold and harps are important items of Dwarvish culture. Not only do they denote their obsession with metal and material wealth but the harp is also a symbol of their unique music and song tradition "unheard by men and elves" (line 24). It may not be a coincidence that Thorin, as the Dwarf prince, plays the harp himself (cf. Tolkien 2008: 19). Since the Dwarves have no difficulties joining into the song, "Misty Mountains" appears to be part of this poetic tradition. It is a song of exile in that the line "over the misty mountains" suggests a crossing of the dividing mountain range in Middle-earth and locates their exile home in the Blue Mountains in the far west, whereas the Lonely Mountain is situated in the far east. It furthermore encapsulates the Dwarves' yearning for their "ancient homes" (Tolkien 2008: 19), and the company around Thorin identifies with the collective lyrical subject that is expressed by the ballad's first person plural pronoun 'we.' Thus they appropriate the poetic desire of the ballad for their own purposes and try to make it come true.

The song also has a strong effect on Bilbo as it evokes "the love of beautiful things made by hands [...], a fierce and jealous love, the desire of the hearts of dwarves" (Tolkien 2008: 21). These lines attest to the power of music which is compared to "magic moving through him" (21) and enables Bilbo to gain insight into and adopt the Dwarvish mindset. As a consequence of this temporary shift in perspective, a previously unknown desire is kindled in the homely Hobbit "to go and see the great mountains, [...] and wear a sword instead of a walking-stick " (21). Although the thought of the dragon and the subsequent conversation with the company about the imminent journey frighten him, the longing for adventure is seeded in him by the song. Just before he goes to bed, he hears Thorin humming the first stanza, which eventually lulls him to sleep, subtly influencing his unconscious mind. On the next day he is whisked away to his life-changing journey with the Dwarves.

In the film, only two stanzas of the ballad are used, the refrain stanza and the seventh stanza. The reduction might be explained by the shorter time frame reserved for songs in the film, but, more likely, it is due to a shift in the narrative sequence. Not only has the account of the fall of Erebor already been related in the prologue, so that the audience already knows the background story of the Dwarves, but the planning of the journey in Bilbo's house also precedes the performance of the song in his living room. In the book, it is the ballad itself that first imparts the story of the Dwarves and the dragon to Bilbo and the reader. Hence, in the film, the lyrics focus on the purpose of the journey in the first stanza while the second stanza conjectures the looming danger of the dragon heralded by the "pines [...] roaring on the height" and "winds [...] moaning in the night" (lines 22–23), and equated with the destructiveness of a raging fire (lines 27–28). The two stanzas encapsulate the desire and the fears of the Dwarves concerning their quest, which is illustrated by their thoughtful gazes and the solemn atmosphere. Since their serious faces are illuminated by the firelight and the camera focuses on the cosy, domesticated fire in Bilbo's house during the line "the fire was red," stanza seven is particularly poignant as it juxtaposes the homely fire with the deadly and untamed fire of the dragon and adds to the effect of the song on Bilbo.

In the two previous scenes Bilbo confesses to Gandalf that he would not dare to join the adventure and Balin questions Thorin about the seemingly hopeless attempt to win back Erebor (cf. *The Hobbit 1*, 2012). Such doubts even among the Dwarves highlight the riskiness of the quest. For the Dwarves, their joint singing of the song and their standing up one after the other with their eyes set on Thorin amount to a ritual of devoting themselves to the quest and their leader. Bilbo, who is sitting in an adjacent room, is shown listening in silence but evidently full of thoughts. Interestingly, the first stanza of the film's version is identical to the stanza which Bilbo hears before he drifts off to sleep in the book, and the film scene similarly ends with the song fading out slowly. Cutting from the interior of Bilbo's home to a shot showing it from outside, the camera moves upward by means of a tilting shot and the viewer's gaze is drawn to the starlit sky signalling the late hour and approaching sleep. The next scene begins on the following day. Since Bilbo follows the Dwarves on their quest that day, it appears that his change of mind owes much to the influence of the song. As a home-loving Hobbit, he understands the Dwarves' pain of not having one and wants to help them win it back (cf. *The Hobbit 1*, 2012). Thus, the song has a psychological function in kindling a strong sympathy for the Dwarves' situation and turning Bilbo into a member of the company.

The emotional impact the poem exerts on Bilbo, the Dwarves, and probably also the audience, is increased by its performance as a song. In contrast to the book, in which the narrator concedes that the ballad "is like a fragment of their song, if it can be like their song without their music" (Tolkien 2008: 19), the film medium is able to endow the poem with music. With its "very minor moded tune with male voices" (Adams qtd. in "Songs" 2015) and its simple "folk song" structure (Longin qtd. in "Songs" 2015), it has a very solemn sound to it which Thorin actor Richard Armitage describes as "almost religious" and "very personal" when the "voices are blending" ("Songs" 2015). As the sequence is shown in slow-motion, the sombreness of the song is matched visually. The entire arrangement and tune resemble the major Dwarf tunes used in the film version of *The Lord of the Rings* and thus create a sense of coherence. The composers, Janet Roddick and Dave Long, wanted it to sound as if it was traditionally sung in large cavernous spaces ("Songs" 2015). These considerations reveal that the song is meant to reflect Dwarvish culture. In Howard Shore's score the tune is taken up and orchestral variations are added which again stress the idea of a traditional folk song's persistent and mutable character (cf. Adams in "Songs" 2015). These variations can be heard occasionally throughout the film, for example, in the scene where the Dwarves charge heroically against the Orcs and Wolves while their leader lies wounded and defenceless on the floor (cf. *The Hobbit 1*, 2012). The song thus attains the status of a leitmotif stressing the significance of the journey and Dwarvish heroism. Yet another version complete with different lyrics, performed and arranged by singer Neil Finn, accompanies the credits and has become a commercially successful song, sold and clicked numerous times on download portals and video platforms. Due to their audiovisual representation in the film, the original lines from Tolkien's book have reached a mass audience.

3 "Hanging Tree" in Collins's *Mockingjay* and Lawrence's *Mockingjay, Part 1*

Unlike the previous example, the text of "The Hanging Tree" is not reduced but used in its entirety in both the novel and the film version of *Mockingjay*. It consists of four stanzas that are almost identical except for the third line, which varies from stanza to stanza as indicated in the brackets below.

> Are you, are you
> Coming to the tree
> Where they strung up a man they say murdered three.
> (2nd stanza: Where the dead man called out for his love to flee.)
> (3rd stanza: Where I told you to run, so we'd both be free.)
> (4th stanza: Wear a necklace of rope side by side with me.)
> Strange things did happen here
> No stranger would it be
> If we met up at midnight in the hanging tree.
> \hfill (Collins 2010: 144–146)

The incremental repetition, the dialogue without answer, and the fact that these lines are the lyrics of a song with a tune "simple [...] and easy to harmonize to" (Collins 2010: 146) point to the ballad tradition, which is also substantiated by the fact that the ballad is part of a folk tradition in the book. The protagonist Katniss learns the song from her father who, as a miner and hunter, represents a deep connection to the land and its people but also the will to survive. In addition, he seems to preserve the tradition of stories and songs which he hands down to his daughter. Music in general, and "The Hanging Tree" in particular, instills the memory of her father. The first time Katniss sings the song in the book, she is in the forest – the old hunting spot where her father had taught her how to survive. Throughout the book, songs and music also have a therapeutic function because they aid Peeta's process of recovery and prevent Katniss from committing suicide (cf. Hanlon 2012: 63–67), but these instances and the resulting function are entirely missing from the film adaptation. In the epilogues of the book and the film *Mockingjay 2*, the concept of the folk ballad is taken up when Katniss sings Rue's lullaby (cf. Fitzgerald 2015), which Katniss had also learnt from her father, to her own children. Ballads and music are thus represented as integral parts of the cultural and communal heritage in the books and films.

In terms of content, the song seems to share affinities with the subgenre of murder ballads due to its emphasis on the hanging tree where a murderer is executed for his crimes (Burt 1958: xii). However, between stanzas two and three the "dead man" is replaced by a first-person pronoun, and the demand to the addressee to "wear a necklace of rope side by side" with the speaker marks a shift in perspective. The speaker and addressee become part of the ballad's diegesis. Katniss's own interpretation of the song in fact identifies the hanged murderer mentioned in stanzas one and two as the subject of the entire ballad calling out to his love to join him in death. While she had originally considered the murderer to be "the creepiest guy imaginable," her experiences in the arena along with the deaths and the living conditions under Capitol rule have made her more sympathetic towards him: "Maybe his lover was already sentenced to death and he was trying to make it easier. To let her know he'd be waiting. Or maybe he thought the place he was leaving her was really worse than death" (Collins 2010: 147).

These issues of love and death as an escape from a life worse than death haunt her throughout the book, particularly in the complicated love triangle between herself, Peeta, and Gale, who are both in love with her. Gale actually identifies with the ballad's speaker "still waiting for an answer" (152), and the last stanza comes to Katniss's mind when Peeta asks to be killed instead of running the risk to be captured by the Capitol. Finally, the song occurs again, though only the first two lines, when Gale confidently remarks that Katniss would surely kill him before the Peacekeepers could imprison him. Both repetitions of the song illustrate that Katniss is confronted with the question whether it is more merciful to have her lovers die than letting them "face the evil [...] in the world" (339). Towards the end of the narrative, the Peacekeepers do indeed capture Gale and he implores Katniss to kill him, which she fails to do. Similarly, Peeta is unable to let Katniss commit suicide and her hopes that Gale would kill her are thwarted after Katniss's assassination of President Coin. With hindsight, the song anticipates the moral dilemma Katniss herself comes to face in the course of the narrative. While Barbara Ching is right in claiming that "[t]he broken communal bonds we hear in collected ballads play out most suggestively in murder ballads" (2015: 319), Katniss, Gale, and Peeta eventually resist the fatalistic attitude of the ballad's protagonist by choosing not to let their lovers die.

In the film, the complicated relationships between Katniss, Peeta, and Gale are only subtly connected to the song. Katniss's interior monologue about her interpretation of the song is not represented in the film, and the song does not reappear in moments when a decision between life and death occurs. It is, however, present as an orchestral version in intimate moments between Peeta and Katniss when their relationship is negotiated. In this respect the song does become a leitmotif conveying Peeta's and Katniss's complicated relationship but it does not have the same implications as the repetitions of the song in the book.

The song also has a rebellious dimension to it. Not only does Katniss memorise the song in defiance of her mother but its content turns the Capitol's public death sentence by hanging into an autonomously chosen form of escape. The first occurrence of the song is also significant in that respect. Katniss sings it because Pollux, a member of her squad, asks her to sing to the Mockingjays around them. Pollux is a former Capitol slave whose tongue had been cut out, so he cannot sing anymore. As the song itself was also forbidden by the Capitol, District 12 was consequently robbed of an essential aspect of their cultural identity. Therefore, Katniss's performance becomes a powerful answer to the Capitol's banishment of song as an individual as well as a cultural form of expression. The association with folklore presents Katniss as part of this oppressed community and she becomes "a hunting, foraging, ballad-singing heroine" who "uses her celebrity and critical rural knowledge to spark a revolution" (Ching 2015: 306). Unsurprisingly, District 13 has her performance recorded to use it as footage for propaganda videos. However, in the book the video is never aired as such so that the song does not become an instrument of revolutionary propaganda.

In the film, by contrast, the song's decision between life and death is connected to the concept of revolution itself. Again the medium of film is able to turn the soundless lyrics of the book into an aural experience. The situation being almost identical to the book, Katniss begins to sing "The Hanging Tree" a cappella, which again points to the folk tradition. The simple structure and melancholic low-key tune composed by Jeremiah Fraites and Wesley Schultz and arranged by James Newton Howard match the sad but also eerie content. Schultz explains that the tune had "to be something that can be hummed or sung by one person [or] by a thousand people" and that "it's supposed to almost feel like a nursery rhyme [...] innocent, even though it has a really dark undertone to it" (qtd. in Caulfield 2015). Minor words had to be omitted for metrical reasons, such as 'up' in the last line, but most words are retained. In the course of the second stanza, the scene cross-cuts between the squad members' reactions, beginning with Gale's, who might at that moment be identifying with the murderer waiting for his beloved's answer though he remains silent. Cressida, Castor, and Messalla also look at Katniss with stern expressions. Pollux, whose initial smile has faded, lowers his gaze noticeably at the word "flee" – possibly because he is reminded of his own flight from the Capitol. All of these reactions are suggestive of personal memories triggered in each member of the crew who witnesses Katniss's performance. They highlight the song's potential as a platform for collective identification.

The third stanza is sung non-diegetically as it underscores the crew's departure from District 12 and Gale's ongoing contemplation of Katniss inside the hovercraft. The scene cuts to a meeting between Haymitch, Plutarch, and Coin watching propos of Katniss. Here, the fourth stanza is again part of the diegetic level because the trio can hear it accompanying the video they are watching. In the propo Katniss roams an utterly destroyed District before turning to the camera at the line "wear a necklace of rope side by side with me," which thus appears like a direct address of the potential viewer. Plutarch informs the others that "[t]hat line was originally 'a necklace of rope.' I had it changed to 'a necklace of hope'" because "so is war" (*Mockingjay 1* 2014). He justifies his ostensible manipulation of the song as conducive to the purpose of the revolution. In contrast to the book, the film reveals that the video with the song is broadcast into the Districts, so that it becomes a vehicle for revolutionary propaganda.

As a result, the sequence then cuts to a group of rebels who approach a dam that provides the Capitol's power supply in order to blow it up. Although the two stanzas of "The Hanging Tree" are used non-diegetically, it is implied that "The Hanging-Tree" has become a song of the masses because Katniss's voice is blended with and gradually drowned out by the choir and the orchestra. The rebels' steps match the song's rhythm and are magnified to imitate the sound of an army marching in unison. After the second stanza the singing stops but the orchestra continues as the scene cuts to a long shot of the dam, establishing it as the target of the rebels. Another cut to the dam's bridges places the viewer among the Peacekeepers by means of an over-the-shoulder shot (cf. Mercado 2010: 71). Once the rebels come into view, their diegetic shouts are heard but these shouts are simultaneously accompanied by a non-diegetic choir, giving the entire scene an almost spiritual quality. Many rebels are shot in the attack before they eventually gain ground and position the boxes. The ensuing explosion ends the song. Serving as the theme for a rebellious act of sabotage and the martyrdom of many rebels, the song clearly attains ideological importance in the film adaptation. It underlines the rebels' decision to support the revolution, even though it might result in their own deaths, rather than to succumb to a life of oppression under the totalitarian regime of the Capitol. As the film uses the technique of montage and the song to combine all these stages into a meaningful sequence, the discourse time becomes significantly shorter than the story time. The question asked over and over again in the song becomes a question of individual commitment to the cause of rebellion against the Capitol, and thereby expresses the major theme of the film in a nutshell.

Its suitability for a mass audience has eventually taken the song beyond the narrative and the closing credits of the film as it has become an international chart hit in many countries (cf. Caulfield 2015). Part of its success outside the narrative might derive from its potentially universal applicability. "Misty Mountains," for example, provides a clear reference to the fictional world of Middle-earth. The song is therefore more strongly anchored in its narrative context than "The Hanging Tree" with its more general lyrics. The latter exemplifies a step towards generic self-referentiality because it could be experienced without being necessarily associated with the narrative, and therefore it is accessible to an even larger audience.

4 Conclusion

The previous analyses illustrated that the incorporation of poems in novels and their respective film adaptation enables poems to point to aspects beyond their own poetic diegesis. While poetry's generic self-referentiality has to be somewhat compromised for the poems to be integrated into the narrative, the two examples show that poems can become conducive to the plot, the characterisation of individual characters and cultures, as well as to the overall themes of the narratives.

As adaptations, the two examples further show that the films use the adapted text in a creative manner. The functions of "Misty Mountains" in Tolkien's book are generally preserved in Jackson's film adaptation. While the reduction from ten to two stanzas in the film adaptation may have diminished the amount of historical and cultural information conveyed by the ballad in the book, these functions are transferred to the prologue and other filmic flashbacks. The ballad's more fragmentary use in the prologue and its turning into a full-scale song and musical leitmotif therefore heighten the ballad's significance for the overall narrative and increase the emotional impact on the audience. The therapeutic function of "The Hanging Tree" in the book is completely eliminated in the film, therefore the film adaptation more fully exploits the ballad's potential for a revolutionary anthem by having one of its lines changed considerably and by using it as a song and non-diegetic soundtrack to a heroic act of rebellious sabotage and martyrdom – a dimension that is only adumbrated in the book. Both ballads are thus presented as part of the diegetic poetic tradition of their fictional worlds and therefore clearly contribute to the creation of aesthetic illusion in the narratives.

In terms of poetry's representations and functions in written and audiovisual media, it can be concluded that novels tend to include a larger number and variety of poems whereas films often have to shorten or omit them entirely. Films, however, can exploit poetry's performative potential far better than written narratives. Due to their audiovisual representation techniques, they can actually represent songs as songs whereas the written medium can only describe them and give the lyrics. In that respect, the ballad seems a particularly suitable subgenre of poetry for embedding due to its inherent affinity to music and song. By endowing the lyrics with a tune and an orchestral arrangement, the poems enter the medium of music and film and thereby have an increased emotional impact on the audience, to which the commercial success of the songs beyond the films also testifies.

Regardless of their verbal or audiovisual mediation, the subtle references embedded poems can make to characters, plot events, or the mood and atmosphere of the surrounding narrative turn them into a third voice that complements those of the characters and the narrator. As poems in literary prose narratives, they thereby attain the potential to cross genre boundaries, and as full-scale songs in film adaptations they also overcome media boundaries.

Works Cited

Attebery, Brian. 1992. *Strategies of Fantasy*. Bloomington: Indiana University Press.
Baldick, Chris. 2008. *The Oxford Dictionary of Literary Terms*. Oxford: Oxford University Press.
Bauer, Matthias. 2013/2014. "Poetry in Fiction: A Range of Options". *Connotations* 23.2: 173–188.

Brown, Marshall. 2008. "Poetry and the Novel". In: Richard Maxwell and Katie Trumpener (ed.). *The Cambridge Companion to Fiction in the Romantic Period*. Cambridge: Cambridge University Press. 107–128.
Bruhn, Mark J. 2014. "Introduction: Integrating the Study of Cognition, Literature, and History". In: Mark J. Bruhn and Donald R. Wehrs (eds.). *Cognition, Literature, and History*. New York: Routledge. 1–14.
Bullerjahn, Claudia. 2001. *Grundlagen der Wirkung von Filmmusik*. Augsburg: Wißner.
Burt, Olive Woolley. 1958. *American Murder Ballads and their Stories*. Oxford: Oxford University Press.
Caulfield, Keith. 2015. "Jennifer Lawrence's 'The Hanging Tree': The Roots of 'The Hunger Games' Hit". Billboard. Billboard.com. http://www.billboard.com/articles/columns/chart-beat/6458119/jennifer-lawrence-hanging-tree-hunger-games-hit [accessed 2 February 2017].
Ching, Barbara. 2015. "Murder Ballads and Hunger Games: Re-Collecting Rural America". In: Antje Kley and Heike Paul (eds.). *Rural America*. Heidelberg: Winter. 305–325.
Clute, John, and John Grant (eds.). 1999. *The Encyclopedia of Fantasy*. New York: St. Martin's Griffin.
Collins, Suzanne. 2010. *The Hunger Games: Mockingjay*. New York: Scholastic.
Dix, Andrew. 2008. *Beginning Film Studies*. Manchester: Manchester University Press.
Eilmann, Julian. "Cinematic Poetry: J.R.R. Tolkien's Poetry in *The Lord of the Rings* Films". In: Julian Eilmann and Allan Turner (eds.). *Tolkien's Poetry*. Zurich: Walking Tree, 2013. 177–203.
Fitzgerald, Jon, and Philip Hayward. 2015. "Mountain Airs, Mockingjay and Modernity: Songs and Their Significance in *The Hunger Games*". *Science Fiction, Film and Television* 8.1: 75–89.
Hanlon, Tina L. 2012. "Coal Dust and Ballads: Appalachia and District 12". In: May F. Pharr and Leisa A. Clark (eds.). *Of Bread, Blood and the Hunger Games: Critical Essays on the Suzanne Collins Trilogy*. Jefferson: McFarland. 59–68.
The Hobbit: An Unexpected Journey. 2012. Dir. Peter Jackson. Warner Bros. Pictures.
The Hunger Games: Mockingjay Part 1. 2014. Dir. Francis Lawrence. Lionsgate Films.
The Hunger Games: Mockingjay Part 2. 2015. Dir. Francis Lawrence. Lionsgate Films.
Hutcheon, Linda, and Siobhan O'Flynn. 2013. *A Theory of Adaptation*. Oxon: Routledge.
Karlin, Fred, and Rayburn Wright. 2004. *On the Track: A Guide to Contemporary Film Scoring*. New York: Routledge.
Kuhn, Annette, and Guy Westwell. 2012. *The Oxford Dictionary of Film Studies*. Oxford: Oxford University Press.
Mercado, Gustavo. 2010. *The Filmmaker's Eye: Learning (and Breaking) the Rules of Cinematic Composition*. Oxford: Focal Press.
Müller, Wolfgang G. 2005. "The Lyric Insertion in Fiction and Drama: Theory and Practice". In: Eva Müller-Zettelmann and Margarete Rubik (eds.). *Theory into Poetry: New Approaches to the Lyric*. Amsterdam: Rodopi. 173–187.
Müller-Zettelmann, Eva. 2000. *Lyrik und Metalyrik*. Heidelberg: Winter.
Prendergast, Roy M. 1992. *Film Music: A Neglected Art*. New York: Norton.
Rabenalt, Peter. 2005. *Filmmusik: Form und Funktion von Musik im Kino*. Berlin: Vistas.
Rosch, Eleanor. 1978. "Principles of Categorization". In: Eleanor Rosch and Barbara B. Loyd (eds.). *Cognition and Categorization*. Hillsdale: Lawrence Erlbaum. 27–48.

Sinding, Michael. 2010. "Framing Monsters: Multiple and Mixed Genres, Cognitive Category Theory, and *Gravity's Rainbow*". *Poetics Today* 31.3: 465–505.
"The Songs of *The Hobbit*: Bonus Material". 2015. *The Hobbit: An Unexpected Journey*. The Hobbit Film Cast and Crew. Warner Brothers. DVD.
Todorov, Tzvetan. 1975. *The Fantastic: A Structural Approach to a Literary Genre*. Trans. Richard Howard. Ithaca: Cornell University Press.
Tolkien, J.R.R. 2006. *The Hobbit or There and Back Again*. London: Harper Collins, 2008.
Weidinger, Andreas. 2006. *Filmmusik*. Konstanz: UVK.
Wolf, Werner. 2005. "The Lyric: Problems of Definition and a Proposal for Reconceptualisation". In: Eva Müller-Zettelmann and Margarete Rubik (eds.). *Theory into Poetry: New Approaches to the Lyric*. Amsterdam: Rodopi. 21–56.

Jessica Bundschuh
Re-erecting Genre Distinctions?: The Sound Recordings of William Carlos Williams's *Paterson* and John Montague's *The Rough Field*

Abstract: Poetry recordings are often considered mere supplements to the visual, typographic poem. This chapter questions that claim, examining the effects of audio performances on generic boundaries in experimental works, such as William Carlos Williams's *Paterson* (1946–1958) and John Montague's *The Rough Field* (1972). In Williams's reading in 1947, he leaves out the prose passages, thereby undoing *Paterson*'s innovative weaving together of genres. An Irish contrast is Montague's performance of *The Rough Field* that leaves nothing out. Montague discovered "open-form" in *Paterson* and his bombastic performances are the result of that inspiration. This chapter considers how an audio recording presents a poet with a decision of far-reaching implications for the reader and listener: either harmonize the lyrical orality of the work with its narrative experimentation (as Montague does), or re-erect a generic boundary between poetry and prose, to juxtapose their relationship as typographic companions on the page (as Williams does).

Keywords: auditory, performance, typographic, oral, triadic line

1 The Voice of Textuality Sounded

Poetry recordings are often considered mere supplements to the visual, typographic experience of the poem on the page. As poet and critic Charles Bernstein argues in *Attack of the Difficult Poems*, "the a/oral dimension of the poem can't be split from the text 'itself,' even if it threatens to undermine the coherence of the poem by adding possibly new and incommensurable textual layers" (2011: 111). That is, as listeners of the poem read aloud, we witness its project *already* underway: "Textuality, sounded, evokes orality," contends Bernstein (2011: 105). The orality of the typographic poem is what enables it to be carried into the social realm:

> Poetry's social function in our time is to bring language ear to ear with its temporality, physicality, dynamism: its evanescence, not its fixed character; its fluidity, not its authority; its structures, not its storage capacity; its concreteness and particularity, not its abstract logicality and clarity. (Bernstein 2011: 105)

Thus, the performance of a typographic poem heightens the poem's materiality. The concrete particularity of language is of particular concern to both William Carlos Williams and John Montague, as their canonical book-length poems *Paterson* (1946–1958) and *The Rough Field* (1972) attest. Both poems are visually arranged with great care, with fragments of prose in reduced type collaged alongside verse, suggesting to the reader a particular acoustic approach to the written texts. In the following I will examine how an audio recording – recalling poetry's oral roots – presents a poet with a decision of far-reaching implications for the reader and listener: either harmonize the lyrical orality of the work with its narrative experimentation (as Montague does), or re-erect a generic boundary between poetry and prose, to juxtapose their relationship as typographic companions on the page (as Williams does).

Williams had tirelessly been working on *Paterson* for many years when he referred in 1951 to prose as "a load of ill-defined matter" (1954: 256); nonetheless, *Paterson* is his testament to a generic reconciliation of the narrative and lyric genres. In 1943, Williams, having compiled hundreds of pages of prose and verse, writes in a letter to Robert McAlmon: "I'm in the process of writing a book, the book I have contemplated doing for many years – prose and verse mixed" (1957: 216). In spite of his decade-long devotion to the work, Williams read publicly from the book-length poem (as opposed to the 1937 poem, "Paterson, episode 17," on which it is based) on only a few occasions. In his reading of the work on October 18, 1947 at the Library of Congress – the reading of greatest significance for this chapter – Williams chooses to leave the prose from the typographic version out of his reading. He thus orally reinstates a genre hierarchy, undoing one of the most innovative features of *Paterson*: the weaving together of genres. It is fitting that Williams, after a long estrangement, visits Ezra Pound in St. Elizabeth's Mental Hospital on this very day he first records *Paterson*. As Williams explains in his "Excerpts from a Critical Sketch" (1931), it was Pound's *Cantos* (1925) that suggested to Williams that he might integrate prose into his verse. All the same, for the recording in 1947, Williams decides to read only the verse passages of *Paterson*, leaving the prose unvoiced and resigned to the page.

An Irish contrast to Williams's reading of *Paterson* is John Montague's performance of *The Rough Field* that leaves nothing out. In the preface to the poem, Montague says he discovered his form in Williams's work: "I managed to draft the opening and the close, but soon realized that I did not have the technique for so varied a task" (2005: vii). Since Montague was living in the United States at the time, he discovered firsthand the ongoing "debate on open-form from *Paterson*" (2005: vii). Enacting the strategy of "composition by field" from Charles Olson's 1950 manifesto, "Projective Verse," and Williams's "The Poem as a Field of Action" (1948), Montague's bombastic, cacophonous performance of *The Rough Field* honors generic inclusivity.

2 Performing the Poem: It Must Be Heard

The divide between typography and orality is a long-standing Western myth. Ruth Finnegan contends that "[t]he written verbal formulation, something hard and permanent, appears as the essence, a notion further reinforced in a range of influential languages by the association of 'literature' with alphabetic writing (letters)" (2005: 165). Indeed, such a binary has misguidedly established a contrast between two

> types of social and cognitive organization, the one oral, communal, emotional, non-scientific, traditional, undeveloped, and primitive; the other literate, rational, scientific, individualistic, creative, civilized, Western, and modern. (Finnegan 2005: 167)

Even today, this binary tale persists, as Peter Middleton explains, rooted in the assumption that the transition from oral to written culture was irreversible, occurring gradually up to its culmination in the Renaissance, to make print dominant for the past four hundred years (1998: 272). This stereotype, however, disregards the widespread practice of 'listening groups' prevalent until World War I, which transmogrified into the contemporary poetry reading. Middleton asserts that "[s]ilent reading and reading aloud have been part of a single economy throughout history." In fact, "historians of writing and reading are finding evidence that supports the idea that orality and literacy are much more interdependent than has hitherto been supposed and poets have become less inclined to polarize orality and literacy in such value-laden terms" (1998: 273). A consideration of the interdependence between the poem on the page and the poem performed requires that we set aside the ill-fitting dichotomy between the typographic and the sonic.

Williams himself asserts the import of orality at the beginning of a reading at Harvard University on December 4, 1951. Before a live audience – amid a community of poetry enthusiasts – Williams proclaims that the poem must be read aloud to be fully experienced:

> Listen! Don't try to work it out. Listen to it. Let it come to you. Sit back, relax. Let the thing spray in your face! [laughs] Get the feeling of it. Get the tactile sense of something, something going on. It may be – that you will then perceive, have a sensation that you may later find will clarify itself as you go along. So that I say, don't attempt to *understand* the modern poem. *Listen* to it! And it should be *heard*. It's very difficult sometimes to get it off the page. But once you *hear* it, then you should be able to appraise it. In other words, if it ain't a pleasure, it ain't a poem. [laughs] All art is made to *please*! That's the way it approaches you. (Williams 1951)

Williams emphatically argues that the physicality of the poem comes to the fore as it is read aloud – and *heard*. Only then can it become a "pleasure" to the ear. Here, Williams radically asserts that understanding follows rather than precedes the auditory experience of the poem. In its sonic form, the poem becomes an active force capable of "approaching" the listener, who is, likewise, actively engaged. The "appraisal" of the poem, in such a context, begins with the coupling of mouth and ear, which allows it to return to its lyrical roots in music, as poet Donald Hall argues: "The poem is its sounds, and its sounds – mouth pleasures, dance pleasures – are the code which allows the mind to slip back into old and poetic ways of thinking: Ways of fantasy, ways of magic, transformation, metaphor, metamorphoses" (1978: 49). As such, the genre of poetry is inexorably bound to its auditory inscription. Former chairman of the National Endowment for the Arts, Dana Gioia, reinforces this claim:

> All poetic technique exists to enchant – to create a mild trance state in the listener or reader in order to heighten attention, relax emotional defenses, and rouse our full psyche, so that we hear and respond to language more deeply and intensely. (2015)

As an epic poem, a 'tale of the tribe,' *Paterson* is, by definition, performative in its dialogic nature, full of dissonant voices and multi-vocality. Thus, it is apt that a poem written about a community be shared in a communal, public setting – and this applies equally to Montague's *The Rough Field*. In the groundbreaking study *Orality and Literacy* (1982), Walter J. Ong suggests that when a speaker addresses an audience, they become a new community jointly: "There is no collective noun or concept for readers corresponding to 'audience.' [...] To think of readers as a united group, we have to fall back on calling them an audience, as though they were in fact listeners" (2002: 73). In the democratic setting of a public reading, the poem is transformed into an enactment of its form, just as the audience is transformed, through their engagement in joint or tandem listening, into a collaborative community. Similarly, in "The Law of Genre" (1980), Jacques Derrida contends that genres benefit from their intermingling as a larger community, testing and breaking down the boundaries between them. In deconstructionist fashion, he claims that within every categorization, like genre, there exists the possibility of subverting the very taxonomy on which it is built. Thus, the borders between genres (like those between the audience members as a poetry reading) remain open – what Derrida calls the "axiom of non-closure" (1980: 65). In *The Power of Genre*, Adena Rosmarin concurs that "[g]enres can never be perfectly coincident with texts unless we posit as many genres as texts" (1985: 45). Further, Rosmarin proposes that hybrid forms, like poems that integrate prose, are "obsessed with deciding [their] generic identity" (1985: 52), as we readily observe in both *Paterson* and *The Rough Field*.

3 Voicing Paterson's Triadic Line

Three and a half decades prior to Montague's composition of *The Rough Field*, Williams begins his 1947 recording, intended as part of an album, with a reading of three poems from three volumes (*The Wedge*, 1944; *An Early Martyr*, 1935 and *Adam & Eve & The City*, 1936), before moving to excerpts from book 1 and 2 from *Paterson*. When he finally reads passages from *Paterson* at the end of the recording session, what is remarkable is that he does not begin with book 1, but rather with book 2, doubling back to book 1 afterwards, as the second and third excerpts. His first selection – testifying to the flexibility of a text that need not be entered at the beginning – is the famous demonstration of the triadic line, an expression of his variable foot, which, as Williams describes it in a 1955 letter to John Thirlwall, is "at the base of our striving:" it is "the division of the line according to a new method that would be satisfactory to an American," "an instinctive approximation of the principle" of Einstein's relativism (1957: 335). Thus, Williams begins his reading of *Paterson* with the passage from book 2 that best exemplifies his prosaic invention of the variable foot:

```
The descent beckons
            as the ascent beckoned
                        Memory is a kind
of accomplishment
            a sort of renewal
                        even
an initiation, since the spaces it opens are new
places
     . . . . . . . . . . . . . . . . . . . . . . . . . . . . . . . . . . .
                        descent follows,

endless and indestructible (1992: 78–79)
```

Williams's choice to begin with book 2 could potentially suggest that his excitement over his variable foot – with a directness and spontaneity akin to a live conversation – exceeds that of his excitement about his innovation of integrating prose. However, rather than seeing these two instances of experimentation in *Paterson* as competing with one another, we would be better served if we read them as enablers of each other. Thus, we might recognize how they similarly rely on an auditory temporality to be fully felt as important contributions to *Paterson*.

Paterson testifies to Williams's fixation on the auditory texture of prosody. Five years after the recording at the Library of Congress, during a 1952 reading and lecture at Hanover College, Williams sets up his reading of the same "the descent beckons" passage with an address before an audience of university educators and students. Leading up to the brief, five-minute reading, Williams explains at length that a long poem like *Paterson*, wherein genres are not sealed off from one another, is a reflection of the mind; the poetic line freed from traditional meter in a greater approximation to prose, therefore, facilitates the opportunity for its listeners to align themselves with modernity.

A new measure, Williams enthusiastically proclaims, can open the mind of the listener to the possibilities of an expansive society, whereas "dead," conventional poetic meter keeps those who hear it locked in the past. At the end of his address, Williams declares to his audience that he will now share with them the "result of [his] Herculean labors," namely, the triadic line of *Paterson*, book 2, section 3, which – as opposed to iambic pentameter – his listeners should "give a damn about" (Williams 1952):

> This [poem I am about to read is] from a long poem called *Paterson*. [...] To give you an idea of a new *measure*, a new *way* of measuring the line. We're not stressing it. It makes it artificial. It throws you out of your life. You don't give a damn about it. You study it because you've got to study it. But it's *dead*! It doesn't concern *you*! It isn't the way you're measured on your *insides*! That's what the artist has to think of. (Williams 1952)

Williams was convinced that for those listening attentively to his morning address at Hanover College, his "new measure" could bring them in sync with their "modern" world (Williams 1952).

To make sure his listeners could visualize his triadic line – without the advantage of having the printed poem in front of them – Williams interrupts his reading mid-way through the third section, just prior to the famous descending passage. He explains in teacher-like fashion, "Now I might speak – give you a rough idea about the measurement. Don't try to count it as you would count ordinary poems, but just according to a pulse, beat, which *is* measurable by the way" (Williams 1952). Here, Williams emphasizes that he is concerned with a new approach to the genre of poetry; that is, he approaches his lyric orality by way of a muscular prose-like prosody that offers him the opportunity to expand the "field of action" in his long poem. Regardless, his lyrical line is *not* an example of free verse, which Williams had earlier explained in his address does not exist: "there must be measure," a "rhythmic integrity" (Williams 1952).

Many scholars of Williams's work find themselves perplexed by his triadic line. Marjorie Perloff, for instance, argues that "the three-step grid is an externally imposed geometric form, a kind of cookie cutter. [...] The locution of prose [is] forced into a triadic mold without sufficient attention to the relation between positioning and the line" (1996: 109). Likewise, Kingsley Weatherhead calls the variable foot a "contradiction in terms, like an 'elastic inch'" (1966: 121). In defense of Williams's prosody, poet Denise Levertov (1990), a close friend of Williams's for the last decade of his life, explains that we must approach the triadic line in terms of the ear rather than the eye, as most critics do, including Perloff. Levertov contends that it is this fixation on the typographic quality of the variable foot, with disregard to its sonic characteristics, which has prompted a misreading of Williams. That is, the variable foot is best approached temporally rather than spatially:

> Each segment of a triadic cluster is a foot, and each has the same *duration*. Thus, a foot (or segment) with few syllables, if it is to occupy the same amount of time as one with many, must by the reader be accorded, in the enunciation of those syllables, a slowness. [...] [S]o, in reading aloud a poem of Williams' written in this relative mode, the opening segment (many, or few-syllabled) is a determinant. As one moves through a poem, the consistency of *duration in time*, though not absolute, can be felt, registered, experienced [...] in much the same way that the consistency of traditional metric patterns is felt: as a *cohesive factor*. (1990: 143).

Similarly, T. Hugh Crawford assesses Williams's line in terms of its auditory duration: "the variable foot allows for compression and expansion of the line" (1996: 670). The triadic line is ideally suited for a live reading since it is bound to a specific historical moment and experienced as it unfolds line by line for the listeners, like a score of music. As a result, the auditory performance transforms the line, and the poem as a whole, allowing for multiple points of access:

> When a poem is read aloud, positions of identification and interpretation open up within the semantic space that are available to both individuals and the group. The performance occasion works as a model of civic or public space. (Middleton 2005: 32)

Following the arguments from Levertov and Crawford, then, the triadic line is not defined by a cookie-cutter pattern in our acknowledgement of its significant acoustic and temporal presence. That is, Williams's choice in his public readings and recordings of *Paterson* to repeatedly emphasize, even in an exclusionary manner, the auditory passage of "the descent beckons" should signal to us that the strength of the triadic line is most fully apprehended orally.

4 Voicing (or not) Paterson's Integration of Prose

Many critics of *Paterson* focus on the dichotomy between prose and verse by fixating onto the differences between the two genres. This fails, however, to acknowledge that the relationship between the two is more metaphorical than confrontational. Rosmarin's reading of genre via metaphor is useful for an investigation of such a hybrid text:

> For genre, like metaphor, is powerfully persuasive not only because it leads us to perceive similarity but because it leads us to perceive that similarity in the midst of and in spite of difference. (1985: 46)

Williams concurrently asserts in a 1948 letter to Tyler Parker the value of a metaphorical approach to inter-generic texts: "[Prose] is *not* an antipoetic device. [...] Poetry does not *have* to be kept away from prose as Mr. Eliot might insist, it goes *along with* prose" (1957: 263). Williams's staggering accomplishment of enacting this assertion by interlacing prose and poetry is not the primary reason *Paterson* may be deemed innovative, as Williams's celebration of the triadic line attests. And therein lies one of the reasons Williams likely chose *not* to record the prose passages. That is, he may not have wanted to pull the focus from his variable foot. Another possible motivation for Williams's decision not to read the prose passages *himself*, without any external readers on hand (in contrast to Montague), may have been the fear that he would have taken his typographically multi-vocal epic poem – with prose excerpts found and altered from a variety of desperate sources – and would have compressed and simplified it into a univocal poem of one reader.

In the second excerpt from the 1947 recording of *Paterson*, book 1, section 1, Williams establishes his key figure, Paterson, as a personification of the multi-vocal, gurgling setting of the poem and of William's birthplace: "Paterson lies in the valley under the Passaic Falls" (1992: 6). The giant, Mr. Paterson, "[e]ternally asleep" so that "[b]utterflies settle on his stone ear," "neither moves nor rouses," "though he breathes" (important in a poem that relies on breath for its prosody), "and the subtleties of his / machinations / [are] drawing their substance from the noise of the pouring river" (1992: 6). It is the water of the falls and the river that animate, though subtly, this sleeping giant. And it is the water, "[j]ostled" to "interlace, repel and cut under, / rise rock-thwarted and turn aside / but forever strain forward – or strike / an eddy and whirl" (1992: 7–8) that, like the wandering dreams of the giant, symbolize the interconnections between the verse and the prose drawn from Cubist-like found sources, such as newspaper accounts, histories, letters, and advertisements. In this landscape of energetic frenzy, the water of the falls is "a fury of / escape," "the air full / of the tumult and of spray" (1992: 8). Here verse co-exists, if uneasily, with background prose vignettes that ground the frothy, forward-hurrying verse.

In this excerpt from book 1 – as opposed to the excerpt from book 2 he first reads aloud – Williams leaves out of the audio recording numerous important prose passages. As a result, only readers, not listeners, learn about the pearl-gathering craze in the mid-nineteenth century that robbed Paterson of all its mussels (9); a local "monster in human form" who welcomed George Washington as a visitor (10); the 126–pound striped bass "pelted with stones by boys" until its death (11); the abuse of slaves and Indians in the area by the British Army (12); and, most famously, Mrs. Sarah Cumming's fall (intentional or not?) into the waterfall in 1812 (14) and the death of Sam Patch, who frequently leapt from a platform at the top of the falls – sometimes following a pet bear – only to disappear until the next season, his "body found frozen in an ice-cake" (1992: 16). The absence of these prose anecdotes from Williams's 1947 audio recording hinders the listener from making sense of the lines that appear in his third reading excerpt, from book 1, section 2, wherein he refers back to the prose from section 1, repeating even verbatim phrasing from the earlier newspaper account:

> Patch leaped but Mrs. Cumming shrieked
> and fell – unseen (though
> she had been standing there beside her husband half
> an hour or more twenty feet from the edge).
> :a body found next spring
> frozen in an ice-cake; or a body
> fixed next day from the muddy swirl –
> both silent, uncommunicative. (1992: 20)

What is also lost to the listener of Williams's 1947 recording is the significance of the thematic elements woven together. That is, by leaving the prose passages out of the recording, Williams fails to replicate orally the broken and jostled imagery of *Paterson*'s typographic presentation, wherein verse and prose share space as bedfellows on the page – and yet remain separate and distinct, "divorced," as Williams says, from each other. Typographically, Williams establishes this interchange through the fallen "bud," cut off from its source:

> a bud forever green,
> tight-curled, upon a pavement, perfect
> in juice and substance but divorced, divorced
> from its fellows, fallen low –
>   Divorce is
> the sign of knowledge in our time,
> divorce! divorce!
>   with the roar of the river
> forever in our ears (arrears)
> inducing sleep and silence, the roar
> of eternal sleep .. challenging
> our waking –. (1992: 17)
> ....
> a green bud fallen upon the pavement its
> sweet breath suppressed: Divorce (the
> language stutters). (1992: 21)

In this image, the stunted bud, "tight-curled, upon a pavement," is unable to mature into a blossom; as a result, "the / language stutters" and the "green bush sways [...] all of a piece," a separated whole. The inclusion of the prose passages in the recording would have offered readers a multi-vocal and experiential interaction with Williams's river, the currents roaring "brother to brother" (24) in "parallel but never mingling," "conversant with eccentricities / side by side" (25):

> .. a mass of detail
> to interrelate on a new ground, difficultly;
> an assonance, a homologue
>   triple piled
> pulling the disparate together to clarify
> and compress
> The river, curling, full. (1992: 19)

By funneling this passage into a subsequent prose letter from "T." Williams enacts the charged, incongruous and yet comingled energy of *Paterson's* setting through genre integration. In the letter, T. tells his addressee of his sister Billy, who "has been chopped on by the surgical chopper"; as he complains, "she has always been eccentric and wanted to boss," "slap[ping] her husband square in the face." Nonetheless, T. loudly brags that had she done that to him, he would have "knocked her so far she would not have got back up in a week" (Williams 1992: 26), suggesting in this domestic context yet another dynamic and fraught sibling relationship, a mirror of the "divorce" of currents flowing through

Paterson: "I told my buddie, in Hartford, she [the sister] was just like our landlady, THE PISTOL. He said he had a sister just like that" (1992: 26). In the absence of the prose letter about "T." and his abusive sister, the listener of Williams's recording correspondingly misses out on the generic sibling rivalry Williams so persuasively establishes typographically. As a literary device, metaphors are invitations to the reader to step up and establish a connection between discrete ideas or images. So, too, Williams's metaphorical handling of the genres of poetry and prose in the typographic version of book 1 – establishing the tone for the poem ahead – creates a mutually enriching, inter-generic relationship between them, even if it is also fraught with conflict and "divorce."

5 The Rough Field's Performative Exuberance

Montague's choice, in both oral and typographic presentations, to generically harmonize *The Rough Field*'s narrative experimentation with its lyricism can be felt in another hybridity it shares with *Paterson*, namely, in its desire to be simultaneously rooted and cosmopolitan. In a 1929 essay on Kenneth Burke, Williams declares – as he had in many other instances – his personal mantra that the local is the only universal:

> From the shape of men's lives imparted by the places where they have experience, good writing springs. One does not have to be uninformed, to consort with cows. One has to learn what the meaning of the local is, for universal purposes. The local is the only thing that is universal. (1954: 132)

Montague, likewise, "cosort[s] with cows" in situating his poem between two extremes: the Irish traditional attention to the local, and the internationalism shaped by an influence of American experimental poetry. In a 1972 print interview concurrent with the publication of *The Rough Field*, Montague asserts that

> the real position for a poet is to be a global-regionalist. He is born into allegiances to particular areas or places or people, which he loves, sometimes against his will. But then he also happens to belong to an increasingly accessible world. [...] So the position is actually local *and* international. (1979: 174)

Montague's practice of "global-regionalism" extends to his devotion to an American meter and syntax, modeled after Williams's *Paterson*. While studying at the Iowa Writers' Workshop in the mid-1950s, Montague became, as he describes in the essay "The Figure in the Cave," familiar with the work of "American poets, like those who I met in Iowa in the halcyon days of the Workshop, from Berryman to Dickey and Snodgrass, or much later in the releasing freedom of San Francisco in the sixties, with Snyder and Duncan and McClure" (1989: 17).

The result of Montague's hunt for the appropriate poetic form for *The Rough Field* is his combination of a series of lyrics stitched together with found prose, woodcuts, and archaic typography that inhabit the margins of the page, to create a distinctly unruly and variegated poetic sequence. In "A Note on Rhythm," Montague suggests how this merging of poetry and prose sets him apart from his Irish contemporaries:

> There is an inhibiting traditionalism in contemporary poetry on this side of the Atlantic which saps inventiveness. It is only a habit of the mind which makes us expect a poem to march docile as a herd of sheep between the fence of white margins. And what about all that waste paper, not reserved for silences but left fallow at the poem's edge? No farmer would allow such poor ploughing. [...] I feel words visually and musically. (1989: 48–49)

Indeed, Montague's typographic poem is anything but docile; he allows no white space to fall "fallow." In conceiving of the page as a literal *field* to harvest, making use of all the space available to him, Montague answers Williams's call to his audience at Hanover College in 1952: radicalize meter to radicalize society. Montague's economic use of every corner of the page suggests an archivist's efficiency, salvaging the snippets of history from placards to broadsides, letters, and graffiti scrawls.

Montague's spatial experimentation works in tandem with an auditory experimentation. In an October 1972 radio interview on RTÉ Radio One – a fortnight before the publication of *The Rough Field* – Seamus Heaney, as the interviewer, asks Montague about the technical difficulties he encountered in writing the book-length poem. Montague responds that he is most committed "technically" to metrical variety; in fact, he suggests that his readers approach *The Rough Field* as an "experimental novel" in which each "chapter," or section, has a meter tailored to its specific subject matter. The result, he argues, is that both the reader and the poet share, from one section to the next, "a continual technical excitement" (Montague 1972). In fact, the poem even includes – as its very last line – a metrical tribute to Williams's triadic line:

> to what is already going
> > going
> > > GONE. (2005: 83)

The poetic arc of *The Rough Field* is to return imaginatively to Ulster, to the old farm and countryside of Montague's youth, in order to recover a sense of identity and cultural meaning. Montague accomplishes a reconnection to this lost world by scouring the scars in the landscape for the culture and old language buried there. In the fifth section, "The Severed Head," Montague illustrates this process of recovery though the violent image of the "grafted tongue," the alien language that the Irish were forced to learn:

> (Dumb,
> bloodied, the severed
> head now chokes to
> speak another tongue –
> ....
> An Irish
> child weeps at school
> repeating its English.
> After each mistake
> The master
> gouges another mark
> on the tally stick
> hung about its neck. (2005: 39)

In the margins of the prior section, on the opposing page, a prose insert reads: "We have killed, burned and despoiled all along the Lough to within four miles of Dungannon ... in which journeys we have killed above a hundred of all sorts, besides such as we have burned, how many I know not." It is attributed to "*Chichester to Mountjoy, Spring 1607*" (Montague 2005: 38). In his typographical placement of poetic imagery alongside the prose of historical evidence, Montague invites his readers to approach each genre with new expectations, rooted not in generalizations, but rather in a localized and historical specificity. Such an approach to genre moves beyond a mere static taxonomy, signaling instead the dynamic transformation of an evolving text, as Jonathan Culler explains:

> A claim about a generic model is not an assertion about some property that all examples of the genre possess. It is a claim about fundamental structures that may be at work even when not manifest, a claim that directs attention to certain aspects of a work, which mark a tradition and an evolution, dimensions of transformation. (2015: 48)

By foregrounding each genre's ability to productively transform and comingle, one may better recognize that which poetry and prose fundamentally share.

Montague connects an Irish child weeping over "its" inability to "speak another tongue" (Montague 2005: 39) – including the child's own Gaelic name transliterated into English – to the insidious result: a master's forceful gesture of gouging a mark on a stick. Such violence memorialized in the lyric began long ago, as Montague reminds his readers through the violent prose dispatch from Sir Arthur Chichester, the lord deputy of Ireland from 1605 to 1616. In straddling both genres, Montague acts as the detached poet – a cultural anthropologist of Ulster – and as the lyricist who witnesses the indignity of the most vulnerable of Ulster's citizens. That is, Montague foregrounds the stuttering pupil of the past whose speech falters, and whose experience is ultimately transformed into the grandchild speaking in a ruptured Gaelic, rather than in a broken English:

> Decades later
> that child's grandchild's
> speech stumbles over lost
> syllables of an old order. (2005: 39)

In essence, Montague connects these differences through his experimentation across genre. The "grafted tongue" of the section epigraph lifted from an old Irish children's rhyme – "And who ever heard / Such a sight unsung / As a severed head / With a grafted tongue?" (Montague 2005: 31) – conveys the necessary presence of foreign materials, from leaf buds to prose passages, to create a prolific and grafted whole. Montague further emphasizes the need for interconnection in his arrangement of verse in two parallel narrow ribbons or columns of newspaper-like prose. As the genres exuberantly interact from one page or section to the next, they establish difference and connection, loss and affirmation, amid the poem's form and content – and this is equally true of the typographic and the auditory experience of the poem.

Montague's July 8, 1973 reading of *The Rough Field* was performed by many voices, including those of Montague and four other readers, one of them the preeminent embodiment of Irish literature himself, Seamus Heaney. The performance was presented by the British Irish Association at Round House, Chalk Farm, London and recorded by Claddagh Records; the readers were additionally accompanied musically by The Chieftains. (The poem had first been performed in Dublin at the Peacock Theatre in 1972.) More recently – in memory of Montague's death on December 10, 2016 – RTÉ Radio One aired another performance of *The Rough Field* on January 15, 2017, performed by three Irish actors: Gerard McSorley, Barry Cassin, and Fionnuala Flanagan. Both the 1973 and 2017 recordings are more akin to dramatic theatre plays than readings of a long poem. The performances are in no way subtle or nuanced; the voices and instruments, instead, remain deliberately fractured and discordant, interspersed with crowing roosters, snare drums, and clashing cymbals, all as auditory markers of fissure and dissonance at the heart of a local history.

Of course, it is unfair to suggest that the performances of *The Rough Field* are more accomplished auditory transcriptions of Montague's typographic poem than is Williams's audio recording of excerpts from *Paterson* in 1947, a solo recitation in a recording studio at the Library of Congress. Rather, to propose a performative contrast between Williams and Montague, as I have done in this investigation, is to bring into dialogue two ends of a spectrum: The first is a reading of a multi-generic work restricted to its lyric passages, signaling the poet's desire to pedagogically focus his listeners – relative newcomers to the complexities of the mid-century modern poem – on his innovative triadic line, instead of a lively juxtaposition between its lyric and narrative modes. The second is a reading of a likewise multi-generic work that potently enacts the diversity of Irish culture for a community caught in the violent throws of the 'Troubles.' Each poet seeks an approach – successfully or not – to most powerfully establish, from his perspective, a direct connection to that particular audience.

6 Conclusion: The Voice of Audio Recordings in a Digital Age

If we regard audio recordings as a critical component of a holistic investigation of poetic works, then we can approach the efforts of John Montague – and other poets who shape their audio performances as dynamic enactments of the typographic work – with greater appreciation. Further, we can recognize the weakness in recordings that pick and choose, cafeteria-style, the best or easiest bits of the poem, frequently dumbing it down for the audience present. Williams writes in a 1950 letter of his discomfort with reading poetry aloud in public "because of the mutual embarrassment that comes from trying to speak in public of a thing that by its very nature is intimately personal and needs to be warmed and loved to thrive as it should" (1957: 281). Williams makes a valid argument regarding the intimate nature of the poetic text, even if it "took the emergent college-reading platform to provide the social energy [Williams] needed to sustain himself as a modern poet" (Middleton 1998: 276). Yet the long-term value of incorporating the sonic experience of the poem into a discussion about the work's significance outweighs the short-term unease of bringing a poem into the potential cold of the reading hall or recording studio, even if, or especially if, the vocalizing poet, as Williams says, is tempted in reading aloud to "automatically select the obvious or pass quickly over a delicate, questionable passage" (1957: 281).

In the experimental works of Williams's *Paterson* and Montague's *The Rough Field*, we should be doubly committed to audio recordings that honor their generic complexity. In other words, in the way that both Williams and Montague typographically integrate narrative passages into their lyric prosody – while still celebrating the particulars of each – rather than relegating the prose to footnotes (as Eliot does in "The Waste Land"), so, too, should an approach to a typographic poem incorporate recordings that enable the alphabetic text to become a truly three-dimensional and temporal experience. Essentially, Williams and Montague make space for multiple genres in their long poems to establish a connection between discrete perspectives, both formal and thematic. Thus, they suggest that prose and poetry – the older sister to prose, as Pound liked to remind Williams (Williams 1957: 265) – exist along a single historical and literary continuum: a long-standing and cacophonous conversation made tangible in any audio recording and performance in which a full palette of typographic genres participate in the sonic transcription of the work.

Works Cited

Bernstein, Charles. 2011. *Attack of the Difficult Poems*. Chicago: University of Chicago Press.
Crawford, Hugh T. 1996. "*Paterson*, Memex and Hypertext". *American Literary History* 8.4: 665–82.
Culler, Jonathan. 2015. *The Theory of the Lyric*. Harvard: Harvard University Press.
Derrida, Jacques. 1980. "The Law of Genre". Trans. Avital Ronell. *Critical Inquiry* 7.1: 55–81.
Finnegan, Ruth. 2005. "The How of Literature". *Oral Tradition* 20.2: 164–187.
Gioia, Dana. 2015. "Poetry as Enchantment". *The Dark Horse* 35: 10–24. http://www.thedarkhorsemagazine.com/danagioiapoetrya.html [accessed 15 March 2017].
Hall, Donald. 1978. "Poems Aloud". *Goatfoot Milktongue Twinbird: Interviews, Essays, and Notes on Poetry, 1970–76*. Ann Arbor: University of Michigan Press. 49–50.
Levertov, Denise. 1990. "On Williams' Triadic Line: Or How to Dance on Variable Feet". In: James McCorkle (ed.). *Conversant Essays: Contemporary Poets on Poetry*. Detroit: Wayne State University Press. 141–148.
Middleton, Peter. 1998. "The Contemporary Poetry Reading". In: Charles Bernstein (ed.). *Close Listening: Poetry and the Performed Word*. New York: Oxford University Press.
Middleton, Peter. 2005. "How to Read a Reading of a Written Poem". *Oral Tradition* 20.1: 7–34.
Montague, John. 1972. "John Montague". *RTÉ*. RTÉ Radio One. http://www.rte.ie/culture/2016/1213/838637-on-john-montague-classics-from [accessed 10 February 2017].
Montague, John. 1979. "Global Regionalism: Interview with John Montague". *The Literary Review* 22:2: 153–74.
Montague, John. 1989. *The Figure in the Cave*. Dublin: Lilliput Press. 1–19.
Montague, John. 2002. *The Rough Field*. Claddagh Records. CD.
Montague, John. 2005. *The Rough Field*. Winston-Salem: Wake Forest University Press.

Montague, John. 2017. "The Rough Field." *RTÉ*. RTÉ Radio One. http://www.rte.ie/drama/radio/plays/2017/0118/845930-the-rough-field-by-john-montague [accessed 10 February 2017].

Ong, Walter J. 2002. *Orality and Literacy*. London: Routledge.

Perloff, Marjorie. 1996. "'To give a design': Williams and the Visualization of Poetry". *The Dance of the Intellect: Studies in the Poetry of the Pound Tradition*. Evanston: Northwestern University Press. 88–118.

Rosmarin, Adena. 1985. *The Power of Genre*. Minneapolis: University of Minnesota Press.

Weatherhead, A. Kingsley. 1966. "William Carlos Williams: Prose, Form, and Measure". *English Literary History* 33.1: 118–137.

Williams, William Carlos. 1947. "Reading at NBC Studios, Washington DC, for the Library of Congress Recording Laboratory". *PennSound*. PennSound. http://writing.upenn.edu/pennsound [accessed 10 February 2017].

Williams, William Carlos. 1951. "Reading and Commentary at Harvard University". *PennSound*. Pennsound. http://writing.upenn.edu/pennsound [accessed 10 February 2017].

Williams, William Carlos. 1952. "At the Conference of the Indiana College English Association, Hanover College, Indiana". *PennSound*. PennSound. http://writing.upenn.edu/pennsound [accessed 10 February 2017].

Williams, William Carlos. 1954. *Selected Essays*. New York: New Directions.

Williams, William Carlos. 1957. *The Selected Letters of William Carlos Williams*. Ed. John C. Thirlwall. Obolensky: McDowell.

Williams, William Carlos. 1992. *Paterson*. Ed. Christopher MacGowan. New York: New Directions.

Timo Müller
Poetry to Music: Gil Scott-Heron's Intermedial Performance Aesthetics

Abstract: Widely regarded as one of the most innovative African American artists of the mid-twentieth century, Gil Scott-Heron has variously been described as a poet, a musician, a performance artist, and a rapper avant la lettre. Rather than describing his art in conventional categories, this essay stresses the productive tensions created by his transgression of genre and media boundaries. Through a contrastive reading of his records *Small Talk at 125th and Lenox* (1970) and *Reflections* (1981), it traces the development of his aesthetics from a poetic toward a musical emphasis but shows that both of these influences are present throughout his work. The aesthetics Scott-Heron developed, the essay argues, is more thoroughly intermedial than previous accounts suggest. Rather than combining various media into an organic whole, his intermedial aesthetics foregrounds the conflictive yet creative process of negotiating their influences.

Keywords: Gil Scott-Heron, intermedial, performance, poetry, music

Gil Scott-Heron (1949–2011) is widely regarded as one of the most innovative African American artists of his time. His combination of poetry and music, of social activism and entertainment, made him a respected intellectual and a chart-breaking celebrity at the same time. Artists as diverse as Amiri Baraka and Jay Z acknowledged his influence on their own work and on the outlook of their generation (Toop 1984: 119; Baram 2014: 79). His most striking innovation was the intermediality of his aesthetics. Even more so than The Last Poets, a group of politically radical spoken-word artists associated with the Black Arts Movement, he brought together poetry and music. Rather than combining these media into an organic whole, this essay argues, Scott-Heron created a new art form that evolved throughout his career in response to artistic and institutional impulses. In broad terms this evolution led him from poetry toward music but remained suspended in between these categories, challenging their media and genre boundaries. By the time of his death, Scott-Heron was not only hailed as the "Godfather of Rap" but was said, perhaps more accurately, to have created his "own genre" (Tate 2016: 149). The following discussion offers a systematic account of his aesthetic development. It shows that Scott-Heron's work was more thoroughly intermedial than previous scholars have suggested, including those that discuss him as a performance poet. The essay identifies the main features of his intermedial aesthetics through a systematic analysis of his first record, *Small Talk at 125th and Lenox* (1970), and traces the development from poetry toward music by comparing that record with the later *Reflections* (1981).

While many scholars of African American culture have acknowledged Scott-Heron as an influential innovator, few have examined his aesthetics in any depth. The most extensive discussions of his work can be found in popular biographies and music histories. Scholarly debate, by contrast, has remained limited to brief comments and a handful of essays.[1] The first of these essays was the afterword to his collection of poems *So Far, So Good* (1990), contributed by the scholar Joyce Joyce, who situates Scott-Heron in the tradition of the Black Arts Movement and emphasizes his achievement as a poet rather than a musician. The first substantial discussion of his blurring of genre and media boundaries was Daniel Simmons's essay "His Revolution is Continued: Gil Scott-Heron's Relationship to Rap Music" (2007), which examines the accuracy of the "Godfather of Rap" designation. Tony Bolden pursues this strand of analysis in more depth in an essay entitled "Blue/Funk as Political Philosophy" (2008), which draws attention to the progressive politics not only of Scott-Heron's message but of his aesthetic strategies as well. By operating across media boundaries, Bolden argues, Scott-Heron's work shows that "separating orature from literature" is a "Eurocentric practice," whereas "Afrocentric art" draws on various textual and musical traditions at the same time (2008: 227–229). Most of the essay reads like a discussion of music-inflected poetry, however, as it reprints Scott-Heron's lyrics and analyzes them from a formalist point of view. While it arguably offers the most incisive scholarship on Scott-Heron published so far, Bolden's essay thus reflects the difficulties that Scott-Heron's intermedial aesthetics poses for conventional analytic categories.

Some of these difficulties can be avoided if this intermediality becomes itself the object of systematic analysis. The concept of intermediality was developed to account for works of art that, in one influential definition of the term, enact "a transgression of boundaries between conventionally distinct media."[2] This description certainly applies to Scott-Heron's work, and the conceptual framework developed around it arguably captures his aesthetics more accurately than

---

[1] For popular biographies see Goffe 2012; Baram 2014. For journalistic or essayistic pieces see Schiefer 2004; Hamilton 2011. Some scholarly publications mention Scott-Heron in passing (Greig 1999: 141; Conyers 2001: 193) or merely summarize previous discussion (Pfeiler 2003: 120–123).

[2] Wolf 2008: 19. Scott-Heron is discussed largely within conventional media boundaries by Woodson 1985; Massa 1999 (as a writer), Greig 1999, Lynskey 2010 (as a musician).

concepts such as live, slam, or performance poetry, which have also laid claim to his work. These concepts necessarily prioritize the word and fall short of capturing the importance of musical elements in Scott-Heron's performances. Where they attend to the interplay of different media at all, they focus on the interplay of the written and the spoken word.[3]

Most conceptualizations of performance poetry in the broadest sense, moreover, tend to assume that performance poets come into their own on the stage and record or print their work – if at all – once they have successfully performed it in a live setting. Usually developed with reference to slam poetry, these accounts stress the importance of bodily signifiers such as gestures and facial expressions, which do not apply on record or in print (Somers-Willett 2009; Bauridl 2013). Some extend this conceptual matrix to poets from the pre-slam area: Charles Bernstein, for example, argues that many poets of the 1960s effectively regarded public readings as rehearsals and accorded them a formative impact on their printed work (1998: 6). Scott-Heron, by contrast, wrote his poetry for the page first, then recorded it, and only began to prioritize stage performance once the popularity of his records drew sizeable audiences. As a result, his performance aesthetics is very different from the practiced expression of slam poets but also from the seamless blending of stage and page enacted by Allen Ginsberg and others of his generation.

This difference helps explain why most genre typologies of performed poetry fail to account for Scott-Heron's work. John Miles Foley, in his study *How to Read an Oral Poem*, distinguishes four types of oral poetry, including "oral performance," which does not involve any writing, and "voiced texts," which are written for performance (2002: 39). Since the latter category does not encompass readings of texts not originally intended for performance, as Foley emphasizes, most of Scott-Heron's work does not qualify as oral poetry and is excluded from the typology. The model presented in Martina Pfeiler's *Sounds of Poetry*, which foregrounds continuity from page to stage, seems able to account for Scott-Heron at first glance. It includes a category for "page-stagers," where

---

[3] See Novak 2011 on live poetry, Somers-Willett 2009 on slam poetry, and Bauridl 2013 on performance poetry. Novak addresses the "bimedial" quality of live poetry, by which she means the interplay of writing and speaking. Her discussion seems predicated to reading and listening rather than writing and speaking, however, which directs its focus to reception rather than mediality (50–51). – Performance poetry seems to have become the most widely used of these terms, though some poets and scholars have criticized it for "implying the separateness of oral and printed poetry" (Fowler 2016: 177 n1) and for stereotypically associating the poets, many of whom are people of color, with the former category (Sanchez in Joyce 2007: 108; cf. Medina 2001: xix).

the poet "writes but occasionally presents the written work at live readings in front of an audience" or in "studio recordings" (2003: 105; cf. 77–85). Like Foley, however, Pfeiler operates with a holistic notion of performance poetry as an organic, linear development from page to stage. Both models rely on an implicit notion of intentionality, assuming that the poetic text bears traces of the writer's intention to have the work performed. This is contradicted by the example of Scott-Heron's early work, which was written for the page and later adapted to performance.

These problems indicate that Scott-Heron's work is intermedial in a more radical sense than most of the work usually discussed under that label. Instead of blending different media into an organic whole (as in opera, for example) or transposing the work of art from one medium into another (as in film versions of novels), the spontaneous, unfinished quality of his work situates him in between the media of poetry and music (Rajewsky 2005; Wolf 2008). Judging from scholarly discussions of performed poetry, there seem to be only two ways of accounting for Scott-Heron's intermedial aesthetic: either to dissolve genre and media boundaries altogether and speak of a "continuum from 'unperformable' (e.g. visual poetry) to 'highly suitable for performance'" (Novak 2011: 57–58), or to define a separate category for it. Bob Holman (2002: 343–45) opts for the latter and introduces a category "Music and Poetry," which includes Scott-Heron, The Last Poets, Jayne Cortez, and Quincy Troupe. By including Cortez and Troupe, Holman approximates this category to conventional poetry readings with musical accompaniment and raises the question of how exactly music and poetry relate in these artists' work.

The vocabulary of intermediality studies allows for a systematic discussion of this question because it can account for both the differences and the similarities of written poetry, music, and the performance in which these media come together. It can also account for diachronic developments, for example from one medium to another or from monomedial to intermedial art. A thorough discussion of Scott-Heron's aesthetic arguably needs to take both of these perspectives into account in order to capture his development from page poet to recording artist and the interstitial quality his work acquired in the process. The remainder of this essay will explore both perspectives through a comparative close reading of *Small Talk at 125th and Lenox*, the first recorded performance of his poetry, and *Reflections*, a studio album professionally produced by the time he was widely recognized as a recording artist. In the earlier work both media, poetry and music, remain distinct, whereas the later album attempts to blend them into an organic whole. The comparison thus foregrounds the processuality of Scott-Heron's aesthetic, traces the productive exchange between two media, and offers a view into the making of multimediality.

For a systematic discussion of these questions Lars Elleström's theory of mediality offers a useful starting point. Elleström (2011) argues that media can be defined by five qualities: the material, the sensorial, the spatiotemporal, the semiotic, and, on a different logical level, the cultural conventionality of media distinctions. These qualities capture the synchronic and diachronic dimensions of Scott-Heron's aesthetic. The material of his art, for example, initially was the paper on which his poetry was published but grew to encompass the speaking and singing voice as well as musical instruments, with the latter acquiring an increasingly prominent role in the course of his career. While his early publications operated visually, the live performances added the aural sense, whereas the records through which most recipients became familiar with his work largely shed the visual component and foregrounded the aural. This distinguishes Scott-Heron's work from most contemporary performance poetry, which emphasizes visual elements such as the speaker's body, gestures, and clothing style (cf. Somers-Willett 2009).

The spatiotemporal dimension draws attention to a fundamental difference between poetry and music on the reception side. As theorists from Lessing (1984) to Joseph Frank (1945) have pointed out, poetry is a spatial art that can be apprehended as a whole and read in various directions. Music, by contrast, is a temporal art that unfolds in and relies on linear time. Performance is closer to music in this respect, an observation that helps explain several characteristics of Scott-Heron's performance pieces. In his early live performances, Scott-Heron shows himself aware of the spatial readings his poems require. Since the audience cannot go back over the piece nor study it closely enough to understand cross-references within it, Scott-Heron comments on particularly inventive elements several times in the live session recorded on *Small Talk*. In doing so, however, he makes use of the temporal quality of performance, which allows for spontaneous additions to and changes in the text. Such improvisation mainly occurs in between his pieces but rarely within them. Since Scott-Heron regarded himself primarily as a poet, he retained the concept of the poem as a stable artefact. The records of his live performances, and even more so the studio-produced pieces that predominated in his later career, effectively shifted his art back toward the spatial dimension. They allow readers to play the pieces repeatedly and to study them closely, which approximates the circumstances of reading a poem.

Lastly, Elleström's emphasis on the formative role of media conventions is valuable in that it foregrounds the most innovative aspect of Scott-Heron's work: his transgression, redefinition, and blurring of genre and media boundaries. His success in this respect is confirmed by the efforts of those in charge of categorizing artists: agents, promoters, and critics. The cover of *Small Talk*, his first record, prominently announces him as "A New Black Poet," the inlay features photographs of him singing and his percussionists at their instruments; the liner notes are by a jazz critic who describes him as a novelist, poet, composer, pianist, and student. The "interplay between music and writing" in Scott-Heron's work is "instructive," that critic continues, because it is representative of a tendency among younger artists to "leap across the old barriers between the different 'fields'" (Hentoff 1971). These comments are echoed by the first academic analysis of Scott-Heron's work, the abovementioned afterword to *So Far, So Good*, which describes the artist as "a poet, a novelist, a political activist, a composer, and a musician" (Joyce 1990: 74). In his memoirs, Scott-Heron recalls that he was widely regarded as a literary figure when *Small Talk* appeared but that critics soon began to ask whether the regarded himself as "jazz or poet or singer or ...?" (Scott-Heron 2012: 195). The album itself raises these questions because of its distinctive mixture of language, percussion, and music – in short, because of its intermedial aesthetics.

Small Talk at 125th and Lenox is a recorded version of pieces taken from Scott-Heron's poetry collection of the same title, which had appeared earlier that year. The album replicates the aesthetics of poetry and the communication strategies of the poetry reading in many ways. Scott-Heron introduces most of the pieces with a brief comment on sources and contexts. In these comments he refers to the pieces as poems, including those few in which he actually sings. With a few exceptions the pieces are taken over verbatim from the poetry collection, which shows in their structure, delivery, and composition. Most of the pieces, including the well-known "The Revolution Will Not Be Televised," "Brother," and "Whitey on the Moon," are free-verse poems with varying line lengths. They are structured to different degrees by the repetition of words or lines but do not follow any consistent metric, rhyme, or stanza patterns. The delivery is distinctly verbal. Scott-Heron prioritizes rhythm and message over intricate soundscapes. The percussion often reinforces the rhythm and message, for example by modifying the speed or volume, but the text determines its own rhythm without taking the beat of the percussion drums into account. In "Evolution," for example, Scott-Heron indicates the shift of mood between the spirited framing stanzas and the more reflexive ones in the middle by taking conspicuous breaks in the delivery and slowing down in the middle stanzas. The percussionists respond to his delivery and adapt their speed. Music plays a similarly subordinate role on the album. In the few pieces accompanied by instruments other than drums, the music is little more than background ornamentation.

The language is only intermittently shaped by sound elements like rhyme and onomatopoeia. Homophony is explored for its semantic rather than acoustic effects, and the pieces generally foreground semantic devices such as wordplay and polysemy. These often work better in writing, for example when Scott-Heron modifies "freedom" to "free doom" in "Comment #1," a song about the hypocrisy of American imperialism in the name of freedom. Many of the more intricate puns require careful reading, which explains his tendency to indicate them in performance. In "Brother" he criticizes the eponymous would-be black revolutionary, who seems more interested in excoriating fellow blacks than in fighting white racism, as following:

> Jumping down on some black men with both feet because they are after their B.A.
> But you're never around when your B.A. is in danger
> I mean your black ass

The idiosyncratic pun is difficult to understand even in writing, but in the relatively dense delivery of the performance piece it would probably go unnoticed by most listeners if Scott-Heron did not spell it out. While the explanation here belongs to the standard version of the piece, in "Omen" Scott-Heron spontaneously comments on the double meaning of the concluding words after performing the piece, which describes his vision of a black revolution against repressive state power.

> Washing away things that we didn't need to see
> Just like beer cans, peanut shells, and copies of the Daily News
> And then, laying there, bleeding like a stuck pig
> Was a stuck pig.
> Get the point?

The pun on "pig" – contemporary slang for police officers – brings the piece to an emphatic conclusion that blends in an almost surrealistic manner the dream vision of revolutionary chaos with a revenge fantasy widespread among urban African Americans of the time. Scott-Heron's comment to the audience, which elicits chuckles and affirmatives, reconnects the imaginary scene with the daily life of his listeners, who were suffering increasingly repressive police action in urban black neighborhoods.

Such spontaneous audience interaction only occurs in between songs, however. Scott-Heron maintains the boundary between poem and commentary familiar from conventional poetry readings. He remains faithful to the written text in his performances, sometimes changing the set list, as his band members recalled, but not the pieces themselves (Baram 2014: 132). He does improvise the stage banter in between pieces, which he keeps brief on the *Small Talk* recording but brought to considerable mastery in the course of his career (Baram 2014: 159). This makes it the more remarkable how strictly he enacts the distinction between the poem and its presentation. When an audience member completes he final pun of "Whitey on the Moon" on the *Small Talk* album – the speaker says he will send his medical bills to "whitey on the moon" since the government prioritizes space exploration over the basic needs of African Americans – Scott-Heron ignores the opportunity for audience interaction and pointedly protracts the end of the song in order to complete the line himself. Whereas most scholarship on performance poetry, and even more so on rap music, stresses the improvised, ephemeral quality of performance and its capacity to break open conventions of genre and thought (Shusterman 2004: 462), Scott-Heron presents his poems as artefacts whose shape remains unaffected by the circumstances of their performance – on an aesthetic level. On the level of message, by contrast, the shifting contexts reflected in his stage talk do modify the meaning and implications of his poems, for example by pointing to the persistence of the white racism criticized in his early pieces (Baram 2014: 132).

The extent to which this disconnect between poetry and performance still obtains on the *Small Talk* recording is illustrated by the address pattern of the poems. Whereas the stage banter directly addresses the audience, many of these poems feature an addressee as well but that addressee is never the actual audience of the performance session. Some pieces address a generic audience composed of either black or white people. "The Revolution Will Not Be Televised," for example, is a general critique of the widespread disinterest in revolutionary politics among African Americans, who are addressed from the very first line ("You will not be able to stay home brother") to the end ("The revolution will put you in the driver's seat"). The poem "Enough," by contrast, addresses white people who continue to ignore the history and persistence of white violence against African Americans. Other pieces have a more specific addressee, for example the abovementioned "Brother," which rebukes "you would-be black revolutionaries." These address patterns indicate that the pieces are not written primarily for successful performance but to create awareness among a broad range of recipients, many of whom could not be assumed to attend Scott-Heron's live performances.

The album was produced by music executives, however, who chose the live reading format to gauge the market potential for a studio album (Scott-Heron 2012: 157). While Scott-Heron regarded himself as a poet by vocation, he had been a singer and songwriter for some years by that point, and it was this occupation that first gave him an audience (Scott-Heron 2012: 109, 196; Baram 2014: 50–56). In his memoirs he occasionally mixes musical and literary terms when describing his work, as when he recalls that "Whitey on the Moon" was inspired by Langston Hughes's technique of "repeating the opening line of the poem [...] after the bridge-like middle section" (2012: 117). Against this background it is hardly surprising that *Small Talk* features various musical elements that go beyond a recorded poetry reading. Some pieces modify their speed or volume in a manner not reproducible on paper. In "The Revolution Will Not Be Televised" Scott-Heron speeds up gradually throughout the performance, while in "Omen" and "Evolution" he modifies the volume of his voice for intensification. Other pieces, such as "The Subject Was Faggots," heavily rely on percussion instruments to create a pressing rhythm that the printed words cannot evoke in the same manner.

These musical elements became more prominent on the albums Scott-Heron published at a remarkable rate throughout the 1970s. The best-known manifestation of this trend is the revamped version of "The Revolution Will Not Be Televised" that appeared on his second album, the studio-produced *Pieces of a Man*, in 1971. The new version features a bass line and flute accompaniment, which shifts the listening experience from the spoken word to the interplay of word and music. *Pieces of a Man* is generally more mainstream than *Small Talk* in that its political messages are couched in mellow soul-jazz tunes. This set the tone for Scott-Heron's albums of the 1970s and early 1980s, which were marketed as music records for a broader audience. With the exception of *The Mind of Gil Scott-Heron* (1978), which returned to the predominantly verbal delivery and heavily political content of *Small Talk*, these albums foregrounded pieces that followed the genre requirements of the radio-friendly song rather than the performed poem.

The instruments attain equal prominence to Scott-Heron's voice, in terms of volume but also of their overall contribution: there are long instrumental intros, outros, and solo passages. Scott-Heron's voice becomes mellower and more melodic, and some of the tracks feature disco-style background singing. Among the most palpable manifestations of the genre shift is the textual structure of these songs. The arrangement of lines and stanzas is much more regular than in Scott-Heron's early poetry, including the poems featured on the *Small Talk* album. Repetition continues to play a prominent role, but its role is no longer to accentuate the rhythm or give emphasis to individual lines. The rhythm is now determined entirely by the instruments, and the mellow sound discourages the sort of emphatic delivery that characterizes the *Small Talk* album. Repetition now occurs in a more regulated manner: in the shape of refrains or fade-out endings where the same line is repeated with diminishing rather than increasing emphasis.

These contrasts are brought out most clearly in *Reflections*, which appeared toward the end of Scott-Heron's most productive phase as a recording artist. The A side of the album features radio-friendly songs while the B side offers more complex pieces that blend the aesthetic of these songs with that of Scott-Heron's early performance poetry. The songs on the A side have a tight, regular stanza structure. They rely heavily on rhymes and the repetition of key words and lines. The contents are apolitical, focusing on personal stories such as love ("Morning Thoughts"), music ("Storm Music," "Is That Jazz?"), and family memories ("Grandma's Hands"). Their narratives are simple, focusing on a few memorable points or a clear storyline. The B side, by contrast, features forceful political messages on the deprivations of black urban life, on gun violence, and on political figures. Musical elements continue to play an important role. They determine the rhythm of the pieces, including the speed and pitch of Scott-Heron's delivery, which remain constant throughout the pieces where in his early performances he would have varied them to convey the urgency of the message. The three pieces on the B side negotiate the interplay of word and music in a different manner. They amount to a reverse summary of the development of Scott-Heron's aesthetic.

The first track, "Inner City Blues (Poem: The Siege of New Orleans)," maintains the musical quality of the A side. Although its message is one of direct social criticism – the beginning echoes "Whitey on the Moon" from *Small Talk* in its juxtaposition of space programs and poverty – this message is communicated in the blues style familiar from Marvin Gaye's version of the song, which Scott-Heron is covering. The blues style blunts the social criticism in several ways. It requires a mellower delivery than the sharp, pressing tone Scott-Heron used in comparable pieces on *Small Talk*; it foregrounds melody and instruments over the message; and it keeps the social criticism confined to short stanzas enclosed by the lamenting refrain. Halfway through the track, however, Scott-Heron inserts a passage of his own that counteracts the blues tendency of Gaye's original. The programmatically titled "Poem: The Siege of New Orleans" returns to the verbal delivery and consistently critical message of *Small Talk*. It reiterates Scott-Heron's points about the social exploitation of African Americans, the hypocrisy of consumer capitalism, and the need for solidarity and resistance. While the accompanying instruments remain prominent, "Poem" clearly foregrounds the spoken word and the political message it conveys.

The second track, "Gun," returns to a predominantly musical aesthetic. Scott-Heron's voice is less prominent, the message is somewhat redundant and drawn out by a long instrumental solo. The song criticizes increasing gun-ownership rates among urban blacks, pointing out that people are hurting one another rather than the political and economic elites that oppress them. The criticism remains implicit, however, and is brought across less forcefully than on *Small Talk*. Toward the end of the piece Scott-Heron uses the poetic device of onomatopoeia when he briefly imitates gun sounds, but he does so more tamely than for example Baraka in his recorded readings of "Black Art" (1966). The final track, "B Movie," demotes the musical accompaniment and returns to a distinctly verbal style. The message, a denouncement of the newly elected president Ronald

Reagan, is delivered in spoken words without constraints by the unobtrusive background beat. Yet "B Movie" does not attain the poetic quality of earlier pieces. The language is distinctly prosaic: it lacks the semantic density, carefully orchestrated sound, and inherent rhythm of Scott-Heron's early work.

Close analysis of Scott-Heron's intermedial aesthetics thus explains the difficulties critics have encountered in their attempts to categorize his art. Rather than developing a new art form that combines poetry and music into an organic whole, Scott-Heron's work explores the realm in between these media. It fosters tensions but also productive exchange between them. The result is an art of process rather than product, an art that expands and transgresses genre boundaries on both sides. Scott-Heron's performance pieces can be read as poetry and listened to as songs, but they resist reduction to or categorization as either of these genres. On the contrary, they encourage readers and listeners alike to become aware of the conventionality, and thus the artificiality, of genre and media boundaries.

Works Cited

Baram, Marcus. 2014. *Gil Scott-Heron: Pieces of a Man*. New York: St. Martin's Press.

Bauridl, Brigit. 2013. *Betwixt, Between, or Beyond? Negotiating Transformations from the Liminal Sphere of Contemporary Black Performance Poetry*. Heidelberg: Winter.

Bernstein, Charles. 1998. "Introduction." *Close Listening: Poetry and the Performed Word*. New York: Oxford University Press. 3–26.

Bolden, Tony. 2008. *The Funk Era and Beyond: New Perspectives on Black Popular Culture*. New York: Palgrave Macmillan.

Conyers, James L. 2001. "Africana Cosmology, Ethos, and Rap: A Social Study of Black Popular Culture". In: James L. Conyers (ed.). *African American Jazz and Rap: Social and Philosophical Examinations of Black Expressive Behavior*. Jefferson: McFarlane. 180–197.

Ellestrӧm, Lars. 2010. "The Modalities of Media: A Model for Understanding Intermedial Relations". In: Lars Ellestrӧm (ed.). *Media Borders, Multimodality and Intermediality*. Basingstoke: Palgrave Macmillan. 11–48.

Foley, John Miles. 2002. *How to Read an Oral Poem*. Urbana: University of Illinois Press.

Fowler, Corinne. 2016. "The Poetics and Politics of Spoken Word Poetry". In: Deirdre Osborne (ed.). *The Cambridge Companion to British Black and Asian Literature (1945–2010)*. Cambridge: Cambridge University Press. 177–191.

Frank, Joseph. 1945. "Spatial Form in Modern Literature: An Essay in Two Parts". *Sewanee Review* 53.2: 221–240.

Goffe, Leslie Gordon. 2012. *Gil Scott-Heron: A Father and Son Story*. Kingston: LMH.

Greig, Charlotte. 1999. *Icons of Black Music*. San Diego: Thunder Bay Press.

Hamilton, Jack. 2011. "Pieces of a Man: The Meaning of Gil Scott-Heron." *Transition* 106: 113–126.

Hentoff, Nat. 1971. "A New Black Poet: Gil Scott-Heron: Small Talk at 125th and Lenox". In: Gil Scott-Heron. *Small Talk at 125th and Lenox*. Flying Dutchman Records. CD.

Holman, Bob. 2002. "Performance Poetry". In: Annie Finch and Kathrine Varnes (eds.). *An Exaltation of Forms: Contemporary Poets Celebrate the Diversity of Their Art*. Ann Arbor: University of Michigan Press. 341–351.

Joyce, Joyce. 1990. "Gil Scott-Heron: Larry Neal's Quintessential Artist". In: Gil Scott-Heron. *So Far, So Good*. Chicago: Third World Press. 73–83.

Joyce, Joyce (ed.). 2007. *Conversations with Sonia Sanchez*. Jackson: University of Mississippi Press.

Lessing, Gotthold Ephraim. 1984. *Laocoön: An Essay on the Limits of Painting and Poetry*. Trans. Edward Allen McCormick. Baltimore: Johns Hopkins University Press.

Lynskey, Dorian. 2010. *33 Revolutions per Minute: A History of Protest Songs*. London: Faber & Faber.

Massa, Suzanne Hotte. 1999. "Gil Scott-Heron (1950–)". In: Emmanuel S. Nelson (ed.). *Contemporary African American Novelists: A Bio-Bibliographical Critical Sourcebook*. Westport: Greenwood. 416–420.

Medina, Tony. 2001. "Introduction". In: Tony Medina and Louis Reyes Rivera (eds.). *Bum Rush the Page: A Def Poetry Jam*. New York: Three Rivers Press. xix-xxii.

Novak, Julia. 2011. *Live Poetry: An Integrated Approach to Poetry in Performance*. Amsterdam: Rodopi.

Pfeiler, Martina. 2003. *Sounds of Poetry: Contemporary American Performance Poets*. Tübingen: Narr.

Rajewsky, Irina O. 2005. "Intermediality, Intertextuality, and Remediation: A Literary Perspective on Intertextuality". *Intermédialités* 6: 43–64.

Schiefer, Sylvia. 2004. "Americanisms under the Critical Eye of African-American Poet, Writer, Singer and Musician Gil Scott-Heron: The 'Movie' Poem". In: Michael Draxlbauer, Astrid Fellner, and Thomas Fröschl (eds.). *(Anti-)Americanisms*. Vienna: LIT. 224–231.

Scott-Heron, Gil. 1970. *Small Talk at 125th and Lenox: A Collection of Black Poems*. New York: World Publishing.

Scott-Heron, Gil. 1971. *Small Talk at 125th and Lenox*. Flying Dutchman. CD.

Scott-Heron, Gil. 1981. *Reflections*. Arista. CD.

Scott-Heron, Gil. 2012. *The Last Holiday: A Memoir*. Edinburgh: Canongate.

Shusterman, Richard. 2004. "Challenging Conventions in the Fine Art of Rap". In: Murray Forman and Mark Anthony Neal (eds.). *That's the Joint! The Hip-Hop Studies Reader*. New York: Routledge. 459–479.

Simmons, Daniel. 2007. "His Revolution Is Continued: Gil Scott-Heron's Relationship to Rap Music". *Griot* 26.1: 55–64.

Somers-Willett, Susan. 2009. *The Cultural Politics of Slam Poetry: Race, Identity, and the Performance of Popular Verse in America*. Ann Arbor: University of Michigan Press.

Tate, Greg. 2016. *Flyboy 2: The Greg Tate Reader*. Durham: Duke University Press.

Toop, David. 1984. *The Rap Attack: African Jive to New York Hip Hop*. Boston: South End Press.

Wolf, Werner. 2008. "The Relevance of Mediality and Intermediality to Academic Studies of English Literature". In: Martin Heusser, Andreas Fischer, and Andreas H. Jucker (eds.). *Mediality/Intermediality*. Tübingen: Narr. 15–43.

Woodson, Jon. 1985. "Gil Scott-Heron". In: Trudier Harris and Thadious M. Davis (eds.). *Afro-American Poets Since 1955*. Detroit: Thomson Gale. 307–311.

Nassim Winnie Balestrini
The Intermedial Poetry of Rap: Words, Sounds, and Music Videos

Abstract: Rap has been widely discussed as one of the central forms of expression within hip hop, but research on rap as a genre of poetry has been slow in entering literary scholarship. The essential function of a beat and, thus, a specific rhythmic structure as well as the frequent experimentation with rhyme makes rap a poetic genre, one that requires performances and recordings rather than printed formats for silent reading. Adding to the intermedial intertwining of the verbal/literary and the sonic/musical, music videos of rap songs have become staples in the production, distribution, and reception of the genre. With reference to two rap songs, Nas's "Wrote My Way Out" (music video, 2018) and K'naan's "Immigrants (We Get the Job Done)" (music video, 2017), audio versions of which were released as part of Lin-Manuel Miranda's album *The Hamilton Mixtape* (2016), this essay argues that rap research needs to take into account how medium-specific affordances of video/film interact with the verbal and sonic features of rap songs.

Keywords: Rap poetry, intermediality, rhyme, visualization, music video

The four basic elements of hip hop – MC-ing, DJ-ing, Bboying/breaking, and graffiti – comprise multiple media formats and sensorial modes: the sounds of words, beats, and music; the kinetics of dance; and non-kinetic visual representations. In practice, each of the four elements combines several modes of expression. Just as MC-ing – that is, rap – is based on performing a verbal text over a beat (and frequently over further musical elements), DJ-ing involves the transformation of audio recordings of music and spoken/sung words into creative tapestries that recombine music recordings and other sonic samples produced by the artist working the turntables. Bboying translates sound into physical movements, and graffiti transforms script into images whose meaning-making relies on verbal and visual semiotics. These building blocks of hip-hop artistic practice participate in the culture's fifth element: knowledge.[1]

---

[1] For introductions to the five elements, see – for instance – Price-Styles 2015, Johnson 2015, Miller 2015, Hansen 2015, and Gosa 2015. *The Cambridge Companion to Hip-Hop* (Williams 2015) contains such chapters on hip-hop basics but also widely expands hip-hop studies across multiple art forms and conceptual debates.

https://doi.org/10.1515/9783110594874-016

For the longest time, rap was studied and critiqued not as an artistic form or poetic genre but rather as one manifestation of the larger social project of hip hop. Comparable to lyrics in popular music in general, rap lyrics have not usually been perceived as poetry by readers/audiences that regard poetry primarily as a genre distributed in printed books and not in performances of popular music. Moreover, the word 'poetry' tends to imply the opposite of accessibility to readers outside academic contexts. As Adam Bradley puts it: "Rap is poetry, but its popularity relies in part on people not recognizing it as such. After all, rap is for good times [...] By contrast, most people associate poetry with hard work; it is something to be studied in school or puzzled over for hidden insights" (2017: xiv). At the same time, web forums like genius.com bespeak a burgeoning interest and willingness to communicate with other readers/listeners about the complexities inherent in – to them – highly enjoyable rap poetry, as commentators post their arguments about how to peel off layer after layer of possible meaning. Contributors to this website, which started as rapgenius.com and then opened up to tackling poetry of all kinds, take rap lyrics seriously as verbal texts that consist of multiple consciously and painstakingly composed levels of signification to be explored and debated through innumerable annotations by expert and amateur participants who have been creating a hypertextual variant of an annotated edition. A comparable impulse can be found in Jay Z's autobiography *Decoded*, which features a selection of his rap songs with his own annotations and which explicitly refers to, for instance, T. S. Eliot and other canonized American poets as reference points (cf. Balestrini 2015).

Despite persistent prejudices against rap as so-called popular music, a growing number of scholars has begun to appreciate rap lyrics as poetry: as a genre with its own stylistic and formal rules and as a genre that taps into various traditions of American poetry. Among these traditions, spoken-word poetry takes a prominent position, as do multiple "African American oral forms [...] such as the talking blues and oral storytelling"; jazz has also been seen as a precursor (Price-Styles 2015: 11, 14; cf. Bradley 2017: xxxii). This approach equips rap with a lineage that extends back to long-standing African American poetic forms and cultural practices. In any case, research on the embeddedness of rap in African American cultural traditions tends to emphasize the inseparability of everyday language, verbal poetry, and musical form. As Price-Styles argues, rap did not directly grow out of spoken-word poetry. Instead, it emerged from the simultaneity of MCs' verbal voiceovers with a DJ's turntablism, a method that originally fulfilled the practical purpose of working the crowd of dancers (2015: 13; see chapter 15 in this volume). Only when hip hop had become a widespread movement did innovation and diversification occur among rap artists – developments which resulted in growing overlap between formal features of spoken-word poetry and rap lyrics. Particularly poets linked to the Black Arts Movement (BAM), such as Amiri Baraka and Sonia Sanchez, have outspokenly stressed the artistic maturation of rap lyrics as showing the historical links between hip-hop culture and African American poetry since the 1960s (Prince-Styles 2015: 12–16; cf. Hoffmann 2013: 162; Smethurst 2012). These BAM poets sought widespread publication through newly emerging black presses. They also foregrounded the sonic features of their poetry in performance and by "encod[ing]" on the printed page "the politically discordant sounds of blackness" (Hoffman 2013: 170). Thus, it is not surprising that they would celebrate rap as a subgenre of oral poetry that has gained an immense audience.

Despite this dialogue between hip-hop artists on the one hand and authors who write in free verse and who revel in formal experimentation on the other, rap authors follow significantly different aesthetic paths than adherents of the Black Aesthetic and related schools of thought. In fact, rap closely adheres to some frequently derided features of poetry, particularly a specific number of stresses per line and the insistent focus on rhyme. Bradley, one of the most vocal defenders of rap as poetry, stresses the affinities of rap "to some of poetry's oldest forms, such as the strong-stress meter of *Beowulf* and the ballad stanzas of the bardic past." He argues further that "[r]ap's poetry can usefully be approached as literary verse while still recognizing its essential identity as music" (xvi; cf. 15–22). The latter argument also roots rap in poetry's ancient history of oral performance and its reliance on sound. The innovative element of rap resides in the *"dual rhythmic relationship"* (Bradley 2017: 6) between verbal rhymes and the beats over which the lyrics are voiced. Thus, the intertwining of musical/non-verbal and poetic/verbal sound provides the basis of rap's intermediality in performance and in recordings.

The centrality of rhyme in rap poetry led to a diversification of techniques that combine features of English-language poetry with features of African American oral poetry. As a result, the range of rhythmic forms expanded from doggerel and ballad meter to highly experimental multi-syllabic forms (Bradley 2017; Price-Styles 2015: 15; Kautny 2015: 102–103; Caplan 2014). Some rap has thus employed familiar lyrical formats in order to permit listeners to recognize when these very formats are not simply replicated and mastered but when they are adapted and manipulated for the sake of emphasis, innovation, or shocking effect. Furthermore, styles found in such musico-poetic forms have had an impact on how contemporary poets outside hip-hop culture write (see Caplan, Chapter 4).

In addition to the fundamental combination of music and poetry – both of which have sonic features, but convey them either non-verbally or verbally – rap frequently engages in further intermedial constructions of meaning. The words' ability to conjure up visual impressions becomes a marker of quality because a rapper successfully employs verbal power to take the listener on a mental journey. As Rakim raps at the beginning of "Follow the Leader" (Eric B. and Rakim 1988): "Follow me into a solo, get in the flow / And you can picture like a photo" and "I'm everlasting, I can go on for days and days / With rhyme displays that engrave deep as x-rays" (Eric B and Rakim). Thus, the flow of rap performance moves listeners toward more-than-common insight resulting from whatever the rapper's language elucidates. The verbal text may also evoke images through ekphrastic depictions of (often well-known) photographs and other visuals, through references to specific commercial products that assume emblematic functions, and through vivid narration of dramatic scenes in clearly delineated settings. A related approach is found in a narrative, plot-focused rap like N.W.A.'s "Fuck tha Police" (1988), whose different sections are presented by multiple rappers in order to create a verbal drama that parodies stock scenes in a court room: instead of imposing a "guilty" verdict on a racially profiled African American man, the song concludes with condemning a white policeman. In this example, the theatrical plot relies both on verbal and on other sounds.

In addition to elaborate stage shows during rap concerts that transform concept albums into full-length performances in front of crowds, fans consume rap and its poetic features through music videos, which, nowadays, are usually accessed online. The range of such music videos is extensive: among staple formats are those that capture stage performances, those that transfer performances into urban environments meant to look 'unstaged,' and those that follow film scripts in which the audiovisual components evolve alongside the verbal and musical features of the rap song and its beat.

In the following, I will discuss two examples of how the poetry of a rap performance figures in the respective companion music video published on YouTube and other platforms. Both songs are tracks on the *Hamilton Mixtape*, a 2016 album on which multiple artists present songs from Lin-Manuel Miranda's *Hamilton: An American Musical* (2015) and thematically related songs that were not part of the stage show. The first case study is Nas's song "Wrote My Way Out" (2016), which features Miranda, Aloe Blacc, and Dave East. The song focuses on how acts of writing positively affect both an individual's psychological well-being and the community in which s/he lives. More specifically, the song posits that writing in general and composing rap lyrics in particular are ways to escape dire socioeconomic circumstances. The emphasis on writing as a tool of self-liberation connects rap with African American life-writing traditions that stress the links between literacy (as well as education and knowledge in general) and freedom. The music video (2017) embeds the performance of the song into a larger framework that makes use of the medium-specific possibilities of filmed performance. The second example, "Immigrants (We Get the Job Done)" (2016), relies heavily on visual motifs to underscore a poetic text which addresses global, centuries-long histories of colonization, oppression, discrimination, and ethnic prejudice through a bilingual rap. The music video (2018) is the second instalment in Lin-Manuel Miranda's *Hamildrops*, a series of thirteen *Hamilton*-related music videos that have been released on a monthly basis since December 2017. In this video, the speed with which the camera moves through what comes across as a virtually endless succession of tunnel-like tight spaces and of predominately dark environments imitates and underscores the rapid-fire verbal presentation. Both case studies bespeak the urgency of including musical and visual (and, in particular, stage performance and music video) features in analyses of the genre of rap poetry. In other words, not only does the discussion of rap as poetry emphasize the intermedial characteristics of rap songs that rely on literary language and its sounds, but this genre is also closely tied to accompanying musical sounds and, more and more frequently, to audiovisual and filmic features in music videos that serve as crucial vehicles of performance and distribution.

"Poetry in Motion": Rhyme, Space, and Mobility

"Wrote My Way Out" features Nas, Aloe Blacc, Dave East, and Lin-Manuel Miranda. The rap song characterizes Miranda's wildly successful Broadway hit *Hamilton: An American Musical* as a project with which he intended to give rap an opportunity to prove its potential social role by connecting with the ur-American theme of overcoming obstacles through hard work and unrelenting willpower. On the one hand, the simile in Nas's opening line – "I picked up my pen like [Alexander] Hamilton" – establishes a link between George Washington's Secretary of the Treasury, whose success relied partially on his rhetorical and intellectual strengths, and the persona of this verse. Continuing the analogy, Nas casts his lyrical I as a "Street analyst" who possesses "No political power, just lyrical power." That the "just" is an understatement becomes clear through the spatial metaphors that celebrate the amazing achievements of the 'lyrical street analyst.' This poet manages to write his way "out" when he is confronted with the obstacles of "the world [having] turned its back on me" and with thus being "up against the wall." In addition to overcoming this sense of being encased and alienated, the speaker escapes a situation in which he lives without solid ground under his feet: he has "no foundation / No friends and family to catch my fall," descending fast with the evocatively swishing sound of the alliteration.[2] He reverses this "fall" by rising vertically and by becoming "black Elohim from the streets of Queens." This process of ascending is stressed by the assonance and by a reference to the biblical-sounding title of Nas's second album (released in 1996): "The definition of what *It Was Written* means / Know what I mean?"

The assonance highlighted in Elohim/streets/Queens recurs in Miranda's segment, which describes the courage necessary to acquire knowledge and to practice one's skills in an environment that foregrounds physical survival skills and denounces school-related learning: "I caught my first b**ea**tin' from the other kids when I was caught r**ea**din' / 'Oh, you think you smart? Blah! Start bl**ee**din'" (emphasis added). Possibly addressing critics who regard Miranda's use of rap in *Hamilton* as a reprehensible appropriation of hip hop for Broadway, the closing lines turn the entire song into a reckoning with what Miranda (and, presumably, his collaborators on this piece) regard as the purpose of rap: "Really, I saw like a hole in the rap game / So if I wanted to put my little two cents in the game, then it would be from a different perspective / (I wrote my way out) / I thought that I would represent for my neighborhood and tell their story, be their voice / In a way that nobody has done it / Tell the real story." Thematically, this poetological song focuses on the positive impact of working hard to become a poet, that is, on the benefits of practicing and of expertise both for the artist and for those on whose behalf he intends to speak. It also addresses the ups and downs of the genre by claiming that while a "hole" may indicate decay, it may also offer the opportunity to invest something (by inserting the metaphorical "two cents") or the opportunity to look through it. The song turns a tear in the fabric of rap into an opening which offers a new perspective on each respective artist's 'investment' into rap. It claims thus to be an honest form of poetic representation, which, as phrased here, is one version of the much-debated hip-hop ethos of 'keeping it real.' Either option could imply a "way out," thus relating back to the title and the chorus.

The lyrical personae introduced by the featured rappers/singers (verse 1: Nas; Chorus: Aloe Blacc; verse 2: Dave East; verse 3: Lin-Manuel Miranda) jointly characterize themselves as channels for something outside a specific individual life. At the same time, the stylistic differences between their performances showcase the versatility of rap songs. Nas's verse starts with a slant rhyme that combines a single word with a pairing of two words: "Hamilton" / "channel 'em." While his section does include other end rhymes, this is the

---

[2] Throughout the discussion, boldface letters in quoted passages from rap poems are added by the author for the sake of emphasizing specific sounds.

most memorable one both in form and in terms of its importance for the song's argument regarding the lyrical power and the expected impact of knowing how to use language for the sake of social change. Dave Eastxe "Dave East"'s verse narrates the familiar hip-hop story of a hustler who becomes a successful artist. The story culminates in the line: "This [is] poetry in motion, I'm a poet," which immediately segues into the chorus. Eastxe "Dave East"'s closing line thus blends right into the spatial imagery and the im/mobility discourse of the chorus, and it emphasizes that rap is a specific kind of poetry. Subsequently, performing in his typical fast-paced rapping style, Miranda quite overwhelmingly uses pair rhyme, complemented with assonance. Rapping at break-neck speed, he inserts an unusually large number of syllables between accents in the four-beat lines, as in the verses "Oversensitive, defenseless, I made sense of it, I pencil in / The lengths to which I'd go to learn my strengths and knock 'em senseless / These sentences are endless, so what if they leave me friendless?" Towards the end of his section, Miranda echoes Nas's earlier assonance in the sequence "Puerto Rican" / "leakin'" / "speakers" / "beacon." In these verses, Miranda first describes how his thoughts become audible in the form of rapped lyrics that are performed and amplified by loudspeakers; he then expresses the hope that his art may offer an encouraging "beacon" or "light when it's gray out." In addition to thus characterizing his lyrical I's motivation, the use of assonance creates an audible link between verse 3 and verse 1.

The polylogue of voices that present various narratives (intersecting through their shared focus on the impact of writing and through the chorus) and the centrality of assonance and pair rhyme illustrate the reliance of rap on performance and/or a sonic recording. Obviously, rap is, generally speaking, not consumed as printed text but rather as a combination of poetry and musical sound. In the age of YouTube and other online platforms, it is becoming more and more likely that a growing number of listeners is accessing rap primarily through music videos. This raises the question of how the medium-specific affordances of the music video as an audiovisual art form can contribute to the analysis of rap as poetry.

Music video research frequently focuses on the relation between music and visuals (see the short summary of the state of research in Vernallis 2013: 439, as well her own suggestions for a musico-visual poetics). Strikingly, the verbal components of the songs are not discussed as poetry. In the same vein, Hawkins enquires into how music and image contribute to "embodiment" or even "hyperembodiment" of the performing artist (Hawkins 2013). Voice quality, physical shape, and the representation of ethnicity play a role in Hawkins's analysis, whereas the lyrics are only important insofar as they contribute content and occasions for specific voice qualities and other sonic features. From the perspective of a literary scholar who works with cultural-studies approaches (for instance DuPlessis 2012), rap videos particularly offer themselves as crucial rather than simply contextual material for the study of poetry. When considering the practices of hip-hop consumers, it appears essential to consider how official videos by rap artists embed and interpret their poetic works.

The music video of "Wrote My Way Out" does not merely show the artists performing a song in the physical environment associated with the narrative about growing up in New York's inner-city projects or near George Washington Bridge. Instead, it visualizes the preponderance of words and of acts of writing in the song's theme and argument as well as the psychological and social impacts of believing in one's abilities as a writer and, more generally, as a person who works hard at mastering something. Furthermore, the music video adds extras who visually represent various groups of people in specific urban environments: a multi-ethnic array of children and adolescents in schools and gyms, as well as a group of children and youths who are dancing and moving along with the four male rappers. Even though, in parts of the video, scenes shift swiftly from sidewalks to private homes and other locations illustrative of the narrated content, the focus on writing and on serving a community through writing remains audible and visible throughout.

At the opening of the music video, feet moving on an urban pavement amidst sheets of paper swirling in the wind may seem to comment on a lack of street cleaning in poorer neighborhoods. When one considers the verbal text, however, this opening prefigures either metrical feet or, at the least, the notion of walking through the city and through life surrounded by one's own and others' verbal arts that may go unnoticed and literally trampled underfoot. The video includes images of young girls and boys of various ethnicities who look pensive, unhappy, hopeful, confident, or unsure in school settings. These settings with their predictable visual components – ranging from desks and lockers to lovingly decorated classrooms and gyms – frequently flaunt verbal expressions of appreciation and self-worth, be they displayed as a single motto in front of a teacher's desk or as a series of mottoes taped to the vertical front panel of the steps seen when ascending a staircase. Written words thus visually support the emphasis on writing as a way of becoming self-assured and of thinking beyond one's immediate, often socioeconomically restricted environment.

The adolescents whom we see in school-related settings silently underscore the song's verbal content and broaden its significance beyond the lives of the four rapper-singers. The highly choreographed representation of individual kids (some of whose clothing is made to look as if they lived in poverty) and of these kids as a group moving alongside the professional performers includes acts of ventriloquism. Shown individually and as a group, these children and adolescents mouth the words rapped/sung by the four rappers. Listeners thus see their lips move while hearing the respective rapper's voice. By intermedially blending the camera's focus on these representatives of the next generation with the audio-presence of the artists, the promise of working your way out of misery through the power of words assumes a multi-generational trajectory which shifts some of the focus away from the adults' stardom to a concern with posterity.

The music video visualizes the chorus's metaphors of being walled in, of being deprived of solid ground, and of escaping by moving heavenward. It does so not only in the sections in which these metaphorical descriptions are voiced. A sense of being hemmed in becomes a visual motif throughout the video. The young people who are depicted as being in a quandary about who they are and who they want to be are shown alongside walls or fences, in narrow spaces, or near structures that tower over them. In this sense, this visual motif matches the chorus's recurrence. In contrast to closed-in or street-level locales, the four rappers are located in an elevated place (as seen in relation to buildings and other structures in the background), and sometimes only the cloudy sky is seen around them. Filmic images of locations mentioned verbally, such as New York City projects and the George Washington Bridge, anchor the song in a specific time and place. The visuals include close-ups of well-known environments, of street signs, and the like. The 'word scenery' within the song-poem is thus transformed into corresponding images. Similarly, acts of writing are visualized by the rappers' hand movements, which imitate putting pen to paper, and by some of the adolescents inscribing the phrase "Wrote My Way Out" onto a classroom door window or on paved ground outside.

"Immigrants (We Get the Job Done)": Is There Light at the End of the Tunnel?

This second example from the *Hamilton Mixtape* includes sections in English and in Spanish performed by J. Period (Intro), K'naan (verse 1), Snow Tha Product (verse 2), Riz MC (verse 3), and Residente (verse 4). Moreover, the piece features a sample from the *Hamilton* song "Yorktown" and a chorus beginning with one of the signature verses of the musical: "Immigrants, we get the job done." The chorus then elaborates upon this verse and connects it with George Washington's statement, taken from the musical's "Yorktown" song, that winning the Revolutionary War does "not yet" mean that all newly minted Americans have attained freedom. While "Immigrants" makes use of poignant rhymes, these are outweighed by the thematic trajectory of reading the current immigration debate in light of the war for independence from Britain and of embedding U.S. history within a broader history of colonization and oppression. The central motif running through the verbal text is a visual one, which is enhanced by the images of the music video.

K'naan invites listeners to "see the world with new eyes" because the willingness to do so is a prerequisite for re-interpreting both history and the present. Accordingly, the music video walks the listener/viewer through images that such a new outlook will produce. In this sense, the music video constitutes an integral part of the song's poetic effect or at least something like a 'second' or 'parallel track' of the rap because it visually concretizes specifics that the lyrics only hint at but do not explicitly mention. As is the case with other rap music videos, the audiovisual version is not a post-hoc adaptation by other artists but rather part of the complex package of producing and distributing the song-poem – a package designed by the poet/s himself/themselves. At least some rap songs thus require the reader to be a listener and viewer in order to get a comprehensive sense of the underlying artistic conceptualization. As a consequence, scholars need to consider how this will affect the analysis of the poetic features of rap songs that are produced and distributed on albums and in music videos.

Showing a group of scared-looking listeners, J. Period's intro is heard as a disembodied voice in a radio broadcast humming with electric static. His words immediately characterize the quandary of the United States as an immigrant country in which "'immigrant' has somehow become a bad word." Followed by a sample from "Yorktown," the piece implies that the promise of the Revolutionary War has yet to be fulfilled. K'naan's nine-line verse revolves around two diphthong-based perfect rhymes and assonances: prepared by the reference to "Lady Freedom," he subsequently rhymes "brave," "graves," "waves" and "lives," "supplies," "eyes." This sequence highlights similarities between the watery graves both of slaves and voluntary immigrants of yore, and of contemporary deaths of desperate people who cross bodies of water in their attempt to reach the United States. References to the existential desire to survive ("lives") and to have enough to live on ("supplies") are then intertwined with the willingness to assume a new perspective. The metalevel of K'naan's verse telescopes history through emblematically expressed events and circumstances, and it puts the onus of change on people who should re-see and re-think flows of immigration.

This metalevel facilitates accessing the double meanings of the chorus. Immigrants do not simply work and do things, but they – as the plural lyrical 'we' confidently asserts – are propelling the revolutionary-era project of striving for liberty towards completion. The oft-repeated line "Look how far I come" with its clipped present perfect refers back to K'naan's injunction to see "with new eyes." It also ambiguously mentions geographical distance and, in a figurative sense, an awareness of historical/temporal distance and of achievement.

Snow Tha Product's verse, in turn, links up with the earlier parts of the song by depicting poor immigrants who are working for rich people and are vilified by racists that accuse them of laziness. The trope of seeing in the sense of understanding then morphs into the symbolic act of walking in someone else's shoes in order to get a sense of where they are coming from (in a denotative and a figurative sense). The culminating set of verses metaphorically merges the invisibility of illegal immigrants (no papers, no records) with their unacknowledged role in writing history: "We're America's ghost writers, the credit's only borrowed." The ghostwriter is hired because of her/his abilities as an author, but another person's name will be printed on the resulting book. This invisibility of the ghostwriter again invokes not seeing or not seeing correctly. The interspersed Spanish verses claim that something has been stirring and that some people have awakened to hitherto ignored realities, as if encouraging the invisible Spanish-language ghostwriters of the nation's history.

Instead of alternating between languages, verses 3 and 4 are written in English and Spanish respectively. Riz MC broadens the term "immigrant" to include individuals from former British colonies moving to London and contextualizes the current situation within this long history of colonization and concomitant wars. His tightly structured lines employ end rhyme and assonance, most intensely when the blood of the lyrical I's ancestors, which was shed in building palaces and government buildings in imperialist capitals, is compared to "the ink you print on your dollar bill, oil you spill / Thin red line on the flag you hoist when you kill." Flowing liquids also create internal coherence in Residente's verse, which references rivers as escape routes and water as nourishment for plants. Residente compares immigrants to plants deprived of water and stresses that they grow and pick the fruit that others consume. He concludes by repeating Riz MC's reference to representative buildings constructed by unappreciated immigrants and/or slaves. Echoing Riz MC further, Residente symbolically relates the act of building of a castle ("un castillo") to Mexico having been deprived of much of its territory and of its gold.

The tight intertwining of the song's segments through thematic strands and motifs synthesizes multiple voices into one coherent text with a clear argumentative trajectory. While the verbal text makes its gist very clear, the intermedial possibilities of the music video heighten the sustained focus on sense perception – and especially on visual perception. As may be expected, the video shows immigrants in occupations such as agriculture (especially fruit picking), the meat industry, the textile industry (the workers produce U.S. flags), janitorial services, and restaurant businesses (with the proverbial focus on dishwashing). The video thus presents people being underpaid and mistreated rather than ascending the social ladder. This panorama of images is, in itself, not remarkable. A much more crucial feature of this piece is the manner in which – analogous to the multiple levels of meaning and the various scales of historical time and geographical space in the lyrics – the visual motifs of the video support and drive home the emotional impact of the central metaphors and symbols.

Traveling dangerous paths on solid ground and on waterways, the flowing of blood and water, and the long-term global significance of these phenomena are visually rendered by showing immigrants and refugees either traveling and living mostly in semi-darkness or darkness, or waiting, moving, and working in tunnel-like, claustrophobic spaces. Many such scenes seamlessly transition from train cars (with or without windows) to subway cars, crammed workspaces, narrow hiding places, tight living quarters, air-raid shelters, and so on. By contrast, those immigrants who do not have to hide or who have not been arrested are first shown as sitting on a moving train, sadly observing what is going on inside the train, and then – in the final segment – as walking outside.

In the tunnel-shaped settings, the camera mostly moves forward very quickly, capturing glimpses of innumerable individuals and going past them. In the closing segment, a group of individuals appears to be walking deliberately towards the camera. Instead of being forced to sit in or on a train running along fixed tracks (like the ones with which the video opens), they now stride on their own accord *and* in a group that offers solidarity. Nevertheless, once the darkness has lifted a little, it becomes clear that they still are walking on and along train tracks. Just before this segment, which runs parallel to the credits, we see an image of planet Earth crisscrossed by a tight network of train lines full of moving trains. A section of "Yorktown" from the musical *Hamilton* then reconnects the final section with the opening of the song: winning the Revolutionary War did not grant freedom to all. Freedom is an ideal that has yet to be transformed into reality. All in all, these juxtapositions of forced and voluntary mobility visualize acts of assuming and changing one's perspective. They encourage 'seeing with new eyes'; they make concrete what the lyrics indicate, hint at, and imply.

Conclusion

As explained at the outset, rap is intermedial poetry based on the combination of performed words and a musical beat. This combination of verbal sound and semantics with non-verbal rhythm and sound integrates rap into the performative trajectories of, for instance, the Black Arts Movement and of other forms of poetry that require oral performance. The foregrounding of innovative rhyming techniques has become a hallmark of rap. The case studies discussed in this essay demonstrate some of the subtleties and intricacies that rap songs can contain – complexities that require poetic expertise in encoding and decoding levels of possible meanings. Furthermore, these works exemplify the embeddedness of rap in cultural traditions, in histories that go far beyond the contemporary local contexts of their genesis, and in transnational and multilingual networks.

The practice of making 'official videos' available on online platforms requires scholars to consider this audiovisual format not only in terms of studying the production, distribution, and reception of rap's verbal texts and its musical and sonic elements, but also in how this affects rap as a poetic genre. Researching visual elements in rap will also contribute to understanding visual features of hip hop in a wider sense: by interrogating the role of visuality in rap alongside its significance for graffiti, dance, theater, photography, fashion, album covers, and graphic design-based life writing (regarding the latter, cf. Balestrini forthcoming; Balestrini 2016; Balestrini 2015). So far, research on music videos has not considered rap as a poetic genre but has, instead, privileged intermedial linkages between images and music.

The case studies in this essay exemplify different ways in which visual elements reinforce and/or complement verbal and sonic features. In addition to showing the New York City neighborhoods and landmarks mentioned in the verbal text, "Wrote My Way Out" represents the poetological subject matter of the creative work of a rapper and depicts writing as a liberating force in a larger sense. This is achieved both through realistic details (e.g., children and adolescents in schools and gyms, on streets and stoops in specific neighborhoods) and through symbols (e.g., sheets of paper blowing by the wind, close-ups of walking feet, writing on highly visible surfaces like public places and classroom doors). By combining, on the one hand, a recognizable setting and performers in 'everyday' clothing (albeit stylized and consciously chosen for this effect) with, on the other hand, features that need to be read figuratively (such as children mouthing words sung by adults), the music video uses its medium-specific possibilities to emphasize the poetic qualities of the rap song. "Immigrants (We Get the Job Done)" relies on visual possibilities in a manner that enhances the narrative trajectory of the polyvocal verses and that allows the viewer/listener to experience the very process that the poem/song suggests as a possible step toward abolishing prejudices against immigrants: the willingness to see the immigration experience and so-called immigrants with new eyes. The fast-moving camera, the evocation of a claustrophobic tunnel, the multi-ethnic performers and innumerable extras, the contrast between enclosed and open spaces, the lack of light, and the symbolic representation of the globe covered by metaphorical 'trains' of swiftly moving people demonstrate that the impact of this song depends to a significant extent on the cinematic possibilities of music video. Ultimately, the immense popularity of music videos and their growing role in accessing rap songs necessitate conceptualizing rap as an intermedial genre of poetry that links literature, music, and audiovisual forms.

Works Cited

Balestrini, Nassim Winnie. 2015. "Strategic Visuals in Hip-Hop Life Writing". *Popular Music and Society* 38.2: 224–242. DOI: 10.1080/03007766.2014.994318 [accessed 5 December 2018].

Balestrini, Nassim Winnie. 2016. "Hip-Hop Life Writing and African American Urban Ecology". In: Catrin Gersdorf and Juliane Braun (eds.). *America after Nature: Democracy, Culture, Environment*. Heidelberg: Winter. 287–307.

Balestrini, Nassim Winnie. Forthcoming. "Intermedial Hip-Hop Life Writing". In: Justin D. Burton and Jason Lee Oakes (eds.). *Oxford Handbook of Hip-Hop Music Studies*. Oxford: Oxford University Press.

Bradley, Adam. 2017. *Book of Rhymes: The Poetics of Hip Hop*. New York: Basic Civitas.

Caplan, David. 2014. *Rhyme's Challenge: Hip Hop, Poetry, and Contemporary Rhyming Culture*. Oxford: Oxford University Press.

DuPlessis, Rachel Blau. 2012. "Social Texts and Poetic Texts: Poetry and Cultural Studies". In: Cary Nelson (ed.). *The Oxford Handbook of Modern and Contemporary Poetry*. Oxford: Oxford University Press. 53–70.

Eric B. and Rakim. 1988. "Follow the Leader". *Follow the Leader*. Genius Media Group. https://genius.com/Eric-b-and-rakim-follow-the-leader-lyrics. [accessed 5 December 2018].

Gosa, Travis L. 2015. "The Fifth Element: Knowledge". In: Justin A. Williams (ed.). *The Cambridge Companion to Hip-Hop*. Cambridge: Cambridge University Press. 56–70.

The Hamilton Mixtape. 2016. Various artists. Atlantic Records. CD.

Hansen, Kjetil Falkenberg. 2015. "DJs and Turntablism". In: Justin A. Williams (ed.). *The Cambridge Companion to Hip-Hop*. Cambridge: Cambridge University Press. 42–55.

Hawkins, Stan. 2013. "Aesthetics and Hyperembodiment in Pop Videos: Rihanna's *Umbrella*". In: John Richardson, Claudia Gorbman and Carol Vernallis (eds.). *The Oxford Handbook of New Audiovisual Aesthetics*. Oxford: Oxford University Press. 466–482.

Hoffman, Tyler. 2013. *American Poetry in Performance: From Walt Whitman to Hip Hop*. Ann Arbor: University of Michigan Press.

Jay Z [Shawn Carter]. 2011. *Decoded*. New York: Spiegel and Grau.

Johnson, Imani Kay. 2015. "Hip-Hop Dance". In: Justin A. Williams (ed.). *The Cambridge Companion to Hip-Hop*. Cambridge: Cambridge University Press. 22–31.

Kautny, Oliver. 2015. "Lyrics and Flow in Rap Music". In: Justin A. Williams (ed.). *The Cambridge Companion to Hip-Hop*. Cambridge: Cambridge University Press. 101–117.

K'naan, featuring Snow Tha Product, Riz MC, and Residente. 2016. "Immigrants (We Get the Job Done)". *The Hamilton Mixtape*. Atlantic Records. CD.

K'naan, featuring Snow Tha Product, Riz MC, and Residente. 2017. "Immigrants (We Get the Job Done)". *YouTube*. YouTube. https://www.youtube.com/watch?v=6_35a7sn6ds [accessed 5 December 2018].

Miller, Ivor. 2015. "Hip-Hop Visual Arts". In: Justin A. Williams (ed.). *The Cambridge Companion to Hip-Hop*. Cambridge: Cambridge University Press. 32–41.

Miranda, Lin-Manuel. 2015. "Yorktown (The World Turned Upside Down)". *Hamilton*. Genius Media Group. https://genius.com/Lin-manuel-miranda-yorktown-the-world-turned-upside-down-lyrics [accessed 5 December 2018].

Nas, featuring Dave East, Lin-Manuel Miranda, and Aloe Blacc. 2016. "Wrote My Way Out". *The Hamilton Mixtape*. Atlantic Records. CD.

Nas, featuring Dave East, Lin-Manuel Miranda, and Aloe Blacc. 2018. "Wrote My Way Out". *YouTube*. Hamilton: An American Musical. https://www.youtube.com/watch?v=_zhR6d6LDzM [accessed 5 December 2018].

N.W.A. 1988. "Fuck tha Police." *Straight Outta Compton*. Genius Media Group. https://genius.com/Nwa-fuck-tha-police-lyrics [accessed 6 December 2018].

Price-Styles, Alice. 2015. "MC Origins: Rap and Spoken Word Poetry". In: Justin A. Williams (ed.). *The Cambridge Companion to Hip-Hop*. Cambridge: Cambridge University Press. 11–21.

Smethurst, James. 2012. "'Internationally Known': The Black Arts Movement and U.S. Poetry in the Age of Hip Hop". In: Cary Nelson (ed.). *The Oxford Handbook of Modern and Contemporary Poetry*. Oxford: Oxford University Press. 639–54.

Vernallis, Carol. 2013. "Music Video's Second Aesthetic?". In: John Richardson, Claudia Gorbman and Carol Vernallis (eds.). *The Oxford Handbook of New Audiovisual Aesthetics*. Oxford: Oxford University Press. 437–465.

Williams, Justin A. (ed.) 2015. *The Cambridge Companion to Hip-Hop*. Cambridge: Cambridge University Press.

Julian Wacker
Grime Poetry: Black British Rap Lyric(s) in the Twenty-First Century

Abstract: The essay explores the relationship between grime, a black British genre of music, and contemporary spoken-word poetry in the UK. The first part adds to already existing research on the relationship between rap lyrics and lyric poetry, outlining several distinct features that contribute to the poetics of grime. Attesting to the density inherent to lyrical poetry, it proposes that grime negotiates the pressures and spatial densities experienced in marginalized estate spaces both thematically and formally. The second part then analyses how contemporary poets like Debris Stevenson, George The Poet, Isaiah Hull, and Caleb Femi find different, experimental entryways to borrow from and rework grime in their evolving forms. The essay also establishes vital links between dub poetry and grime poetry, understanding both as forms of protest lyric that give a voice to marginalized communities.

Keywords: grime, poetry, estate, urban, London

In their 2011 article "Stanzas on the Street: Is Grime Poetry?" journalists Omar Shahid and Robbie Wojciechowski follow the question why grime, a contemporary black British musical genre that uses rap techniques, is typically not considered poetry among the public. The debate whether rap can be regarded as poetry is anything but new. In the article, professor emeritus John Sutherland points to an "inherent snobbery" in dismissing grime from the genre of lyric poetry (Shahid and Wojciechowski 2011), which holds true for other rap genres such as U.S. hip hop as well. Voices from within the artistic community, however, point towards rap's – and consequently grime's – poetic potential. Including interviews with several influential grime artists, like Wretch 32 and Devlin, or spoken-word poets like Kate Tempest, the article shows that the artists themselves clearly locate their art in a poetic tradition. White grime rapper Devlin, for instance, compares himself to Shakespeare in that he touches on similar subjects as the famous bard which are, according to him, "just phrased in different ways" (Shahid and Wojciechowski 2011). Moreover, poet Kayo Chingonyi, winner of the prestigious Dylan Thomas Prize, has as of late revealed that he considers rap to be the most formalist poetry he was exposed to in his youth (Wroe 2018). Rap lyrics, according to Chingonyi, are hyper-metrical, the rhyme schemes are intricate and the levels of allusion, and allusive play, in the average rap song is staggering. When you put that against the work of more canonical poets I think there is a lot of kinship between people driven by an affinity with, and flair for, language. (Wroe 2018)

Taking these insights as a starting point, this essay does not provide a clear-cut definition of grime poetry. Rather, it engages with the various conversations between grime music and poetry along the following questions: can we read grime as poetry, and what are its possible poetic characteristics? And how then might we possibly distinguish it from 'grime poetry'? As part of this collection, the essay does not prescribe stable generic boundaries. Instead, it emphasizes crossovers and remediations as a central characteristic of grime culture.

Reading Grime as Poetry: Discussions from Both Sides of the Black Atlantic

To understand the poetics of grime, it is necessary to understand its history and cultural practices. Grime is a distinctly black British musical genre that originated in East London's council housing estates. It harks back to a fertile black British sonic history dating to the earliest forms of reggae and dub brought to the UK by Caribbean migrants in the late 1940s and 1950s. Grime artists would consume these genres in their parents' flats, often, as in the case of Wiley, listening to their fathers, relatives, and their friends making music together (Wiley 2018: 9–10; 39–41). When most of grime's pioneering artists were growing up in the 1990s, they were also immensely influenced by Europe's – and more specifically the UK's – vibrant electronic music scene. The aspiring musicians went to UK garage raves, some of them DJing there; they bonded over the melancholic yet energetic soundscape of jungle, black Britain's fusion of dub, breakbeats, and 2-step patterns. Yet, grime captures a moment in time when these youths did not feel included in the mainstream rave culture anymore. The 'no hats, no hoods' policy in the UK had barred many working-class youths from entering clubs only because of their street attire. Experimenting in their bedrooms with free music software like Fruity Loops or producing sounds on their PlayStations, these innovative artists from East London's social housing estates created with grime a counterpoint to UK garage's by then highly commodified, shiny, and increasingly exclusivist rave culture. This defiance, 'murking' in grime speech, is, for instance, tangible in Wiley's seminal track "Wot U Call It?" in which the MC mockingly invites his addressees to place his new sound in the hook: "What do you call it, garage? / [...] / What do you call it, urban? / [...] / What do you call it, two-step? / [...] / Tell us what you call it" (2004). Wiley's track captures the confident spirit of a time when grime was trying to emancipate itself as a genre in the fragmented landscape of British music shortly after the millennium.

Despite its strong ties to black British music, there is at least one defining feature that leads people to place it near U.S. American hip hop: the MC's rap techniques. Although grime draws on jungle, garage, dubstep, and drum 'n' bass in its instrumental repertoire, the rapping is certainly inspired not only by British rap but by its U.S. American sibling. Working against critics who tend to devalue rap's poetics because of an alleged lack of lyrical 'greatness,' recent scholarship has by now extensively explored the relation between rap and poetry (see chapter 16 in this volume). Two of the most sophisticated and insightful analyses can be found in Adam Bradley's *Book of Rhymes: The Poetics of Hip-Hop* (2009) and David Caplan's *Rhyme's Challenge: Hip-Hop, Poetry, and Contemporary Rhyming Culture* (2014). While for Bradley "[e]very rap song is a poem waiting to be performed" (2009: xi), Lars Eckstein finds in his work *Reading Song Lyrics* (2010) that "[l]yrics are not poetry, and their study therefore requires a different set of analytical tools from that which is conventionally applied to poetry" (2010: 23). Arguing for a "cultural rhetoric of lyrics", Eckstein points out, among his many findings, that

> lyrics are always 'actualised' in the sense that they are given the body of a voice and set in relation to musical sound. As a performance art, they are always 'situated', spatially, temporally, socially, physically and medially, in a particular arena in which they are performed. (2010: 30)

While the scope of this essay makes impossible a detailed engagement with Eckstein's analytical framework, it is important to keep in mind that rap lyrics and their cultural rhetorics crucially depend on said *actualisation* and *situatedness*.

One of rap's central defining features, according to Bradley, is its inherent *dual rhythmic relationship*. As such, rap "expresses itself most powerfully in the dual rhythmic relationship between the beat of the drums and the flow of the voice" (2009: 31). In contrast to poetry on the page, which is solely governed by the rhythm (and meter) of the language in its respective lines, an MC's distinct flow is thus not only shaped by the rhythmic structures of their utterances, "but by the audible rhythms of the track" as well (2009: 31). The MC's lyrics thus do not carry the full rhythm or meter alone; rather, "[t]he rhythm of rap's poetry ... is defined by that fundamental relationship between the regularity of the beat and the liberated irregularity of the rapper's flow" (2009: 34). Closely related to rap's rhythmic pattern is the second most prominent characteristic in rap, *rhyme*. Rhyme, for Bradley, "gives rap its song, underscoring the small but startling music of language itself" (2009: 49). Together with the beat, however, rhyme also "provides the necessary formal constraints on their potentially unfettered poetic freedom" (55). It is this tension between a form of poetic freedom and structural principles that assigns rhyme a central role in rap. The scholarly work of Bradley, Caplan, and others has stressed the poetic innovativeness of rap. Artists oscillate in their rhyming techniques between perfect and slant, end and internal, monosyllabic and multisyllabic, or even broken rhymes.

These observations on rhythm and rhyme as two central poetic features in U.S. American rap certainly hold true for grime as well. In fusing electronic beats and rap techniques, grime tracks encapsulate the same challenging dual rhythmic relationship. Grime artists also draw on distinct rhyming patterns as a key element in their lyrics. There are, however, several differences that result in grime's specific poetic characteristics as a rap genre. Overall, grime's beats are faster than those commonly found in American rap. This owes much to electronic music, with garage pounding around an average of 130 bpm, jungle between 150 and 200 bpm, and drum 'n' bass pulsating between 160 to 180 bpm. In a funny yet insightful anecdote, DJ and producer Plastician explains grime's typical 140-bpm rhythmic pattern with technicalities of its early DIY production: "The fact that Fruity Loops' default tempo setting was 140BPM may also have a lot to answer for" (Collins and Rose 2016: 37). The velocity of their musical arrangements also influences the speed of grime MCs, who typically rap faster than other rap artists. Grime has developed a 16-bar verse structure as its structural backbone – a "street stanza" as rapping poet and founder of The Hip-hop Shakespeare Company, Akala, calls it – as its main verse structure (Shahib and Wojciechowski 2011). Its beat, however, typically uses an 8- to 16-bar two-step arrangement that lacks regular four-to-the-floor bass-drum patterns and that has the bassline usually changing every eight bars. Instead of the bass drum, in grime the snare often dictates the track (Wiley 2018: 47).

Spreading across the UK from East London's council housing estates, grime not only often addresses the pressures of black life in marginalized inner-city spaces thematically, but poetry's inherent density finds specific expression in grime. Up to now, perhaps the most substantial insights into the relation between grime and poetry come from poet Kayo Chingonyi. Bringing together grime artists and spoken-word poets for the ICA symposium "The Poetics of Grime" in 2016, Chingonyi noted *monorhyme* as one central rhyme scheme in grime. Indeed, grime tracks often feature several passages in which all lines end on the same end rhyme (or use repetitive sounds). This is taken to the extreme in the following lines from Dizzee Rascal's track "Bop 'N' Keep It Dippin'" (2018):

Jack the lad (3)
Jack an' nab (3)
Had to snatch and grab (5)
I was black and sad (5)
Couldn't even catch a cab (6)
Sittin' in the pad (5)
Thinkin' I was bad (5)
Like a chav (3)

In this snippet, Dizzee Rascal combines several end and slant rhymes, resulting in a repetitive sound that stretches across a total of 31 lines. The individual lines consist of comparatively few syllables (three to six) through which they assume a hasty, yet punchy quality. In accordance with the track's fast rhythmic structure of 140bpm, this brevity lets the artist's voice race over the beat. At the same time, the brevity of the lines makes it hard to distinguish between possible external and internal rhymes. Monorhyme offers a possible reading as a poetic response, which channels the repetitiveness many grime artists encountered in their daily lives into a productive direction. Moreover, Lethal Bizzle's (formerly also known as Lethal B) grime anthem "Pow! (Forward)" (2004), for instance, makes bold use of onomatopoeia in its hook. 'Pow' here mimics the sound of a punch, creating a rawness through its formal characteristics that is often lauded in grime:

> Pow! Yeah I'm Leth to the B (7)
> Pow! I got the top grime dawgs with me (9)
> Pow! If you don't know about me (8)
> Pow! Yeah I'm–pow! Yeah, you know–pow! (8)

The anaphora across the different lines – slightly longer than Rascal's – lends each bar a bashiness that is followed by monorhymes at their end. In the last line, however, the characteristic "pow" is used in the form of both internal and external rhymes, evoking a faster beat (and punch) sequence.

These findings resonate with Chingonyi characterization of grime's poetics as "the music of alleyways, street corners, stairwells, concrete," which "sounds like it too" (2016). But how does grime sound like the concrete buildings it emerged from? Chingonyi provides a partial answer when he writes about Dizzee Rascal's track "Stop Dat" that

> Dizzee's bars are broken down into short, sharp bursts, like trainers hitting the pavement. There is serious intention there – he uses words that are made up of one or two syllables, and the last word in each line is accented in performance to make sure it finds its mark. The resulting sound is distinctive and punchy, and because Dizzee is warding off would-be assailants (lyrical and otherwise), he chooses words that sound like pre-emptive blows. (2016)

Adding to his observations, poetry's generic lyrical density and the larger cultural context that grime lyrics are embedded in provide productive leads. In grime, poetry's inherent semiotic and formal density meets a thematic negotiation of the pressures and densities of black life within estate communities. Twisting Chingonyi's image of the street corner, I propose that it is rather the idea of *being cornered* that sounds in grime. Grime's poetic form draws on a spatial and semiotic density that characterizes black life in marginalized inner-city spaces. This perhaps finds its most famous expression in the title of Dizzee Rascal's debut album *Boy in Da Corner*. As in the excerpt from "Bop 'N' Keep It Dippin'", Dizzee Rascal addresses the theme of density, of the pressures that influence black experiences in estate spaces, thematically on several of his tracks. His 2018 track "Everything Must Go," for instance, takes as its theme the continuous gentrification in London. These densities are not only addressed thematically but – as a form of poetry – find specific ways of expression in grime lyrics. Lethal Bizzle's punchy lines in "Pow!" speak to a similar notion, sonically breaking the confinements that are expressed elsewhere in the cypher – for example in Fumin's verse "How you gonna buss if there's no room?" (Lethal Bizzle 2004).

Although the scope of this essay forecloses an in-depth analysis of grime music video culture, in the accompanying music video Lethal Bizzle tries to smash the screen during his hook. Such fourth-wall breaks testify to the urge to break out of the video's dense setting – an estate disproportionally small in size for the rapping characters – and the restrictions associated with black life in inner-city spaces and the medium alike. However, notions of density in grime do not only capture pressures but also solidarity, bonding, and dwelling – or, in the words of music journalist Dan Hancox: "Grime was created in bedrooms – but not alone, or in isolation: it didn't allow for eccentric hermits, because the London it came from didn't either: boroughs of densely populated flats on densely populated estates, where a tower block is itself a kind of vertical community" (2018: 57). In grime, poetry's density finds specific expression in the predominantly short, condensed verses, its monorhyme scheme, and the velocity of both beat and rapping techniques. This is often fruitfully complemented by the lyrics' thematic focus.

As with rap and poetry, however, every genre brings with it its own variations. I would like to briefly mention Kano's "T-Shirt Weather in the Manor" (2016) as an example of grime's diverse songscape here. In the track, the narrator describes his upbringing in Manor Road, East London, and writes back to the typically grim accounts of estate life one often finds in mainstream media coverage through a portrayal of communal dwellings in the area. The song's arrangement lacks the aggressive-sounding instrumentals and heavy basslines listeners often encounter in grime tracks and instead foregrounds an upbeat piano melody. However, the song does not buy into overly romanticized ideas of multi-ethnic working-class life in London's marginalized inner-city spaces. Rather, in the song's last verse, Kano addresses the problems – for example shootings and drug dealing – that still haunt these communities from the inside. Using monorhyme in grime's conventional scheme, the lyrics, through intricate wordplay, describe an ambivalence central to living in these areas:

> But I just want the summer back how it used to be
> When Nanan had us eating toffee apples by the sea
> Or when we wore Moschino and were moving off key
> When our chips were down, they weren't beefing 'bout Ps
> The purest summers were those in the 90s
> '05 changed my life forever, it's bittersweet
> I've been riding that wave, still waters run deep
> No sand in the ends, still life is a beach
> And that's T-shirt weather in the manor, my friend

The narrator evokes the image of the sea as a site of nostalgic longing for family vacations and contrasts it with his own career as well as life in his neighbourhood later in the verse. The internal contrasts between "I've been riding that wave, still waters run deep" and "[n]o sand in the ends, still life is a beach" emphasize both the grimness and beauty of estate life. The phrase "life is a beach" also creatively alludes to and twists the popular expression 'life is a bitch,' further stressing the joys the narrator can find in his home, Manor Road, and thus in places associated predominantly with struggle and hardship. The last bar "And *that's* t-shirt weather in the manor, my friend" (emphasis added) highlights the importance of finding the silver linings in the duality of estate life, which is caught between grimness and beauty, between hope and struggle.

Since the early 2000s, grime has developed into a confident black British artistic form. It has developed its own poetic features that have attracted – and deserve – academic attention, beyond common reservations towards popular rap music. Despite the usual commodifications and appropriations that impact subversive subcultures, grime has kept its political spirit through its adolescence and today has grown into an artistic vehicle that assumes political significance. As a vital and diverse cultural current, grime reaches beyond itself and inspires filmmakers, novelists, and – significantly for this chapter – spoken-word poets, who find new forms of expression in grime.

Grime Poetry: Sampling, Instrumentalization, Theme

In recent years, several spoken-word poets who draw on and make use of grime in their poetry have come to the fore. Often, and much like grime music video, their performances are either subsequently distributed via YouTube or specifically produced to be promoted through the streaming platform. This section examines several different examples of performance poetry, all of which carry different implications for a possible genre of grime poetry. Deborah 'Debris' Stevenson's acapella performance of "Stop Dat" not only directly samples Dizzee Rascal's eponymous grime hit but reshapes the lyrics to address themes such as the importance of education and misogyny in a feminist act of rewriting. In "Grinding," George The Poet uses instrumentalization reminiscent of grime while self-consciously foregrounding the blurry relationship between grime and (grime) poetry. Isaiah Hull's 2016 performance of "What is Grime?" does not extensively use grime's formal characteristics but directly debates grime as a theme. Similarly, Kareem Brown and Caleb Femi use grime tropes in their poetry and negotiate themes closely associated with the music.

The poet who probably most overtly draws on grime as a vital source for her poetry is Deborah 'Debris' Stevenson. At the aforementioned ICA symposium, Stevenson described her own artistic process and her return to grime in striking metaphors:

> It felt like I had undergone this slight gentrification of myself by accident. [...] I felt like I needed to return to a lot of where I had come from, and part of that journey has been returning to grime infrastructually. [...] I feel like there is a reverence and a rage within it that I feel existed in spoken word when I started but has kind of evaporated in a way that I'm not as happy about. (ICA 2016)

Stevenson uses spatial metaphors for her own artistic transformations and evokes the idea of an infrastructure inherent to grime. With reverence and rage as central components of that underlying structure, she constructs her engagement with grime as a counterpoint to her own 'gentrification,' i.e. her own distancing from her former self. In that sense, Stevenson's return to grime is a metaphorical transformation towards herself as an estate. Through grime, she restructures herself from the debris that is left after she has torn down her gentrified self.

Stevenson's project "Poet in Da Corner," which premiered at London's Royal Court Theatre in September 2018, is inspired by Dizzee Rascal's seminal grime album "Boy in Da Corner" and is an act of creative rewriting or remediation. In one of the poems that have sprung from the project, "Stop Dat," Stevenson samples some lyrics and features of Rascal's track. Not only does the poem carry the same title as the grime song but Stevenson at several points directly writes back to Rascal's lyrics. Similarly intoned, her verses "So, stop dat, start dat, get dat (war)" (2018: 1:51-1:54) are heavily borrowing from Rascal ("Stop dat, start dat, get dat (what)") but are embedded in a feminist response to misogyny and the lack of faith in women's abilities. Prior to the warped lyrical sample, Stevenson criticizes the objectification of women at raves, concerts, or poetry gigs: "No, I won't twerk your crotch / no guestlist / raves as dry as air strips, skips, and chat shit" (2018: 1:43-1:50). The objectification she addresses also seeps through in the outro of Rascal's source track:

> Look, girls, ladies do the butterfly
> Shake your batty low, shake your batty high
> Don't ask me who, where, when or why
> Wanna see your batty rise high to the sky

Stevenson's subsequent verses, "[v]ibes in the air, man feel that (war) / Who said that I couldn't do that (war) / [...] / Trapped in a system (war) / So, I broke outta the system (war)" (2018: 1:51-2:06), in which the repetition of "war" produces a monorhyme, combine grime's characteristic defiance and her own biographical background to address the failures of the educational system for people who do not exactly fit into this system. Switching rhythms at several times in the acapella version of the poem and using intricate breaks that invite listeners to ponder on the message of her verses, Stevenson reworks some of grime's central features into a spoken-word form that, through its sampling and borrowings, translates Dizzee Rascal's song into grime poetry.

In his performance poem "Grinding," spoken-word poet, performance artist, and social commentator George The Poet interrogates the very boundaries between poetry and music, or, to be more precise, between grime poetry and grime. His 2015 live performance for Vevo UK opens with George chatting to the audience. His charismatic chatter is interrupted, however, by the signature iPhone ringtone. During what appears to be a phone call from a friend, George is warned of police in the venue, which is accompanied by blue strobe lights in the concert hall (2016: 0:08-0:33). This prelude can be read as alluding to the surveillance of grime concerts by the Metropolitan police and thus primes the audience that the following performance bears relations to grime. George's opening verse "See man driving a German whip" (2016: 0:34-0:35) is a direct quote from Meridian Dan's 2014 grime track "German Whip," which sparked a second wave of grime music in the UK. Already his second line, however, "See boy dem, I don't turn and dip" (2016: 0:36-0:37), is a departure from the original lyrics of the song. As it also slightly breaks with the rhythm of the source track, it indicates a novel trajectory while still paying homage to grime through the intertextual reference.

After verse eight, the iPhone ringtone is looped back into the performance with George rapping "Not to be seen, people never thought that I could make a poem a song / But I've been figuring it out as I'm going along" (2016: 0:48-0:52) over the loop. This couplet not only alludes to George's own artistic pallet, which includes spoken-word poetry as well as music, but self-reflexively interrogates the nature of "Grinding" as grinding along the continuum between (grime) poetry and grime. After the second eight verses, the drums kick in and add another layer to the performance's instrumentalization. Not only is it significant that the track – in a very scripted manner – pretends to make up its instrumental arrangement as George is rapping his verses, but the instrumentalization mirrors grime's typical 8-bar structure with new elements added every eight bars. Moreover, the instrumentalization – which adds in more electronic basslines and sound effects reminiscent of dubstep – is set to a tempo of 140 bpm. It evokes both the speed and the sonic make-up of most grime tracks, corresponding to George's vocal rhythm in the very beginning. Sticking to grime's common syllabic structure, George uses verses with approximately six to ten syllables, creating at times a double-time flow over the equally fast rhythmic structure of the beat.

What helps us to further contour a possible genre of grime poetry is a look back to the 1970s, arguably the dawn of a specifically black and Asian British music-poetry tradition. During these unsettled times for the black and Asian British communities, spoken-word artists like Linton Kwesi Johnson, Jean 'Binta' Breeze, and Oku Onuora would perform their poetry over Afro-Caribbean reggae and dub instrumentalizations. When Linton Kwesi Johnson first used the term 'dub poetry' in 1976, he was referring to himself and fellow dub lyricists as DJs-turned-poets who created "a new form of (oral) music-poetry" (Morris 1997: 66). 'Dub' refers to the technology used in 1970s reggae music, adding in and removing sounds, or dubbing words over the rhythm (see chapter 12 in this volume). As such, dub poetry, according to Mervyn Morris, can be described as a form of performance poetry usually (but not always) written in creole/patois and accompanied by a beat, "wherein the lyricist overdubs rhythmic phrases on to the rhythm background of a popular song" (Morris 1997: 66). There is a continuity between dub and grime poetry, with contemporary spoken-word artists increasingly speaking their rhythmic poetry over grime rhythms and beats. Stewart Brown moreover has pointed out that "the protest function, the duty of the poet to voice the concerns of the community" (1987: 52), lies at the very centre of dub poetry's politics. Similarly, grime artists like George The Poet and other poets considered below today act as social commentators and/or spokespersons on behalf of their respective (estate) communities. In the foreword to George's poetry collection, *Search Party* (2015), the director of Island Records, Darcus Beese, even brands him the new Linton

Kwesi Johnson – intelligent, eloquent, witty, and socially conscious. As George The Poet, according to Beese, is slowly taking over from Johnson – "It was as if the baton was being passed" (George The Poet 2015: 3) – it is certainly this protest function that equips grime poetry with the potential to become the twenty-first century equivalent to dub poetry.

In comparison to "Stop Dat" and "Grinding," poet Isaiah Hull, who was chosen to perform right before grime artist Skepta's set at Radio 1's 2016 Big Weekend, debates grime as a theme in his performance poem "What is Grime?" "I see grime as poetic," Hull said in an interview with *i-D* in 2017, with both grime and poetry drawing on the same skill set but taking different paths (Whitehouse 2017). His poem opens with the lines "What / What / What Is Grime?" (2016: 0:08-0:14). Through this repetition, the verse assume the quality of a chant. His repetition stresses the subsequent elaborations on the development of grime, also making use of monorhyme. While asking "what is grime?" several times throughout the poem, Hull makes sure to first play on the word 'grime' in the following stanza:

> Is dirt ingrained on the surface, or something?
> Emerging from London
> The hybrid of garage and jungle
> The microphone killer
> At a Saturday function   (2016: 0:17-0:26)

Although the exact origins of its usage remain obscure, in its musical context the word grime is often attributed to EZ, who would call tracks with very raw beats 'grimey' during his radio show on Kiss (Collins and Rose 2018: 77–78). Hull's verse "Is dirt ingrained on the surface, or something?" plays with the meaning of the word, often used to describe dirty surfaces, from the perspective of an intricate insider of the genre. Through its connection to London in the following lines, the bar also pokes fun at the assumption that grime music may foster violence or anti-social behaviour, both perceived as stains on British society from a neoliberal and conservative point of view. The corresponding lines "The microphone killer / At a Saturday function" here might refer to either the importance of grime at social gatherings on the weekend, or its role as a substitute for religion in the lives of many young people.

"What is Grime?" sketches a condensed history of the genre which is infused with other, more intimate accounts of the poet's own connection to the music. Shifty, Blizzard, and Hypes – Mancunian grime artists – are listed among arguably more influential figures from London such as Jammer, JME, and Ghetts. This decentralizes the music's common association with the capital – as does Hull's Mancunian accent – and pays attention to alternate voices of grime that have long emerged beyond the metropolis and continue to nourish young people with music from distinctly local surroundings. Isaiah Hull's first take on the commissioned poem was an intricate dedication to Manchester's grime songs that he would share with friends via Bluetooth – but he changed it to meet the expectation of the crowd and the event (O'Brien 2018). The question "What is Grime?" thus also addresses tensions and different branches within the genre; although Hull debates grime in this poem and makes the music its central theme, his poetry is far from being grime. Unlike George The Poet's "Grinding" or Debris Stevenson's Poet in Da Corner project, "What is Grime?" neither draws on grime instrumentalization nor does it heavily use common formal features we can find in the music.

As Isaiah Hull's poem shows, it is not only direct structural or sonic borrowings that allow for spoken-word poems to be read as grime poetry. Hull and other fellow artists like Kareem Brown and Caleb Femi draw on grime as a theme, use it as tropes in their poetry, or touch upon socio-political issues that are frequently negotiated in grime. For Brown's poem "I Know," according to Chingonyi, "grime has provided [Brown] with a means of looking at the world and writing about it" (2016). Chingonyi lists especially the focus on the "black male body under threat," the poem's "emphatic delivery," and the direct reference to the work of Skepta as examples of grime tropes in Brown's poem (2016). In his poem "Sunny D and Purple Stuff," Brown also, at least through word play, hints at grime. Interrogating the positionality of black men in Britain, the verses "My blackness will not stand ringside and wait to be tucked in / [...] / I'm like the men's toilets, expect me to be grimey, whatever building I'm in" (2017: 0:47-0:59) can be read as identifying the speaker with the empowering, self-confident identitiy politics of grime. By using metre reminiscent of grime as well as monorhyme, the poem simultaneously plays with notions of hypermasculinity often promoted in grime (cf. Boakye 2017), contributing to an artistic grime pallet that transcends such representations.

In comparison, Caleb Femi's poem "In Praise and In Defense of Giggs" provides a South London take on themes closely related to grime. Although Femi's poetry typically does not feature many rhymes and differs significantly from grime's poetics, his spoken-word videos address marginalization in South London, the troubles of young men, and the significance of grime and British rap at large for the country's youth. Femi's spoken-word praise of Giggs, a popular British road rapper who was convicted for alleged possession of a firearm and was acquitted on all charges after six months in prison, stresses Giggs's importance for the community in Pecknarm despite his controversial image, especially for young boys:

> Before you, boys from the Narm
> Were known for riding out, locking off shoobs

> And generally handing out bad days to anyone who wanted it
> And then you dropped Hollow Meets Blade
> And the glow of your music shrouded us
> Like the dankest dank everywhere we went   (2017: 1:00-1:15)

Giggs is seen here as someone whose music provides a protective and comforting gown for the teenage boys in Pecknarm. "Dankest dank" stresses the pride in the superb quality of Giggs' record and at the same time highlights its grittiness. As the poem closes with "Your voice more consistent and more present than some of our fathers" (2017: 2:28-2:34), it writes back to the alleged dangers of unstable fatherless families promoted in British public discourse and inscribes Giggs as a substitute father figure and role model for Pecknarm youth.

Conclusion: Evolving Forms

In acknowledging the inherent poetics of rap, this essay has offered readings of grime music as poetry. Working against stigmatizations of grime as lacking poetic quality, I have drawn on existing research to outline several of the formal and thematic features that may come to describe grime's specific poetics. However, as we have seen, the boundaries between grime and grime poetry are porous; cross-pollinations fertilize the creative relationship between grime music and emerging forms of grime poetry. Grime serves as an inspiring source for many contemporary poets, who borrow and rework common features of grime: brevity in verse, lines with many monosyllabic words, a high density of syllables overall, frequent use of monorhymes, instrumentalization with grime rhythms (sometimes with 8-bar arrangements), a thematic focus on the interplay between struggle and dwelling in estate communities. Grime poetry comes in many forms and, much like dub poetry, resists being tied to one single genre aesthetics. George The Poet's "Grinding" perhaps comes closest to the definition of music-poetry, which also applies to an extensive body of dub poetry. Debris Stevenson borrows from and remediates Dizzee Rascal's track "Stop Dat", while Isaiah Hull and Caleb Femi debate grime and associated issues thematically.

All of these examples make it clear that grime poetry captures a variety of evolving forms that spoken-word artists explore in the twenty-first century. The poets discussed in this essay or, to bring in another up-and-coming name, Kojey Radical, draw on grime as an inspirational source. Their influences, however, cannot just be tied back to grime. Grime poetry then describes experimental forms of poetry that borrow – either in form or theme – from grime, remediate it, or take grime as an entryway into other, new directions. Grime poetry thus also marks a significant return to rhyme in contemporary spoken-word poetry, which had increasingly distanced itself from overt use of rhymes schemes (see chapter 15 in this volume). What lies at the very center of grime and grime poetry is a political drive that has long transcended a specific black British experience alone. In twenty-first-century Britain, grime brings to the fore an empowering upheaval against the manifold forms of oppression and disenfranchisement of working-class communities in multi-ethnic estate spaces.

Works Cited

Boakye, Jeffrey. 2017. "Boys to Mandem: Grime and the Masculinity Barrier". In: Jeffrey Boakye (ed.). *Hold Tight: Black Masculinity, Millennials and the Meaning of Grime*. London: Influx Press. 355–361.
Bradley, Adam. 2009. *Book of Rhymes: The Poetics of Hip Hop*. New York: Basic Civitas.
Brown, Kareem. 2017. "Sunny D or Purple Stuff". *YouTube*. Sofar Sounds. https://youtu.be/lXtnpApLzYI [accessed 3 October 2018].
Brown, Stewart. 1987. "Dub Poetry: Selling Out". *Poetry Wales* 22.2: 51–54.
Caplan, David. 2014. *Rhyme's Challenge: Hip Hop, Poetry, and Contemporary Rhyming Culture*. Oxford: Oxford University Press.
Chingonyi, Kayo. 2016. "Bard In Da Corner: Drawing the Line Between Poetry and Grime". *Noisey*. Vice. https://noisey.vice.com/en_uk/article/6wqa3m/exploring-the-relationship-between-poetry-and-grime [accessed 3 October 2018].
Chingonyi, Kayo. 2018. "Kayo Chingonyi: 'The Most Formalist Poetry I have been Exposed to Is Rap Lyrics'". Interview by Nicholas Wroe. *Guardian*. https://www.theguardian.com/books/2018/may/28/kayo-chingonyi-poet-dylan-thomas-prize [accessed 3 October 2018].
Collins, Hattie and Olivia Rose. 2016. *This Is Grime*. London: Hodder & Stoughton.
Dizzee Rascal. 2018. "Bop N Keep It Dippin". *Raskit*. Universal Island Records. CD.
Eckstein, Lars. 2010. *Reading Song Lyrics*. Amsterdam: Rodopi.
Femi, Caleb. 2017. "In Praise and In Defence of Giggs". *YouTube*. Canvas. https://youtu.be/whOEN6B5mSg [accessed 3 October 2018].
George The Poet. 2015. *Search Party*. London: Virgin Books.
George The Poet. 2016. "Grinding (Live): Vevo UK @ The Great Escape 2015". *YouTube*. George The Poet. https://youtu.be/0XWuYaohlak [accessed 3 October 2018].
Hancox, Dan. 2018. *Inner City Pressure: The Story of Grime*. London: William Collins.
Hull, Isaiah. 2016. "What Is Grime? (Radio 1's Big Weekend 2016)". *YouTube*. BBC Radio 1. https://youtu.be/7_CL6c3qTXc [accessed 3 October 2018].
Hull, Isaiah. 2017. "'I Want More Difference in Poetry': 19-Year-Old Poet Isaiah Hull Contains Strong Language". Interview by Matthew Whitehouse. *i-D*. https://i-d.vice.com/en_uk/article/gy58nm/i-want-more-difference-in-poetry-19-year-old-poet-isaiah-hull-contains-strong-language [accessed 3 October 2018].

ICA. 2016. "The Poetics of Grime". *YouTube*. ICA. https://youtu.be/NvZwiwEwByM [accessed 17 October 2018].

Kano. 2016. "T-Shirt Weather in the Manor". *Made In The Manor*. Parlophone. CD.

Lethal Bizzle. 2004. "Pow! (Forward)". *Lethal Bizzle – Pow!* Relentless Records. CD.

Morris, Mervyn. 1997. "A Note on 'Dub Poetry'". *Wasafiri* 13.26: 66–69. DOI: 10.1080/02690059708589571 [accessed 24 September 2018].

O'Brien, Jennifer Lee. 2018. "Isaiah Hull, Poet". *The City Talking*. http://www.thecitytalking.com/isaiah/ [accessed 3 October 2018].

Shahid, Omar, and Robbie Wojciechowski. 2011. "Stanzas on the Street: Is Grime Poetry?". *The Guardian Online*. https://www.theguardian.com/music/2011/dec/15/grime-stanzas-on-the-street [accessed 3 October 2018].

Stevenson, Debris. 2016. "Stop Dat (Co-written with Jammz for Poet in da Corner)". *YouTube*. Sofar Sounds. https://youtu.be/OasNp7M6bDs [accessed 3 October 2018].

Wiley. 2004. "Wot Do U Call It?". *Treddin' on Thin Ice*. XL Recordings. CD.

Wiley. 2018. *Eskiboy*. London: William Heinemann.

Notes on Contributors

Nassim W. Balestrini is Professor of American Studies and Intermediality at the University of Graz, Austria, and Director of the Centre for Intermediality Studies in Graz (CIMIG). Her research interests include American literature and culture from the eighteenth through the twenty-first centuries, particularly adaptation and intermediality (as in her monograph *From Fiction to Libretto: Irving, Hawthorne, and James as Opera*, 2005, and in the edited volumes *Adaptation and American Studies*, 2011, and *Intermediality, Life Writing, and American Studies*, 2018, co-edited with Ina Bergmann), life writing, hip-hop culture, climate change drama, U.S. American and Canadian theater and performance, African American literature and culture, and the poet laureate traditions in the United States and in Canada.

Jessica Bundschuh is a lecturer in English Literatures at the University of Stuttgart, initially joining the faculty as a Fulbright Lecturer in American Studies and Culture. She has a Ph.D. in English Literature and Creative Writing from the University of Houston and an MFA in Creative Writing from the University of Maryland. She has published on such topics as contemporary American, Canadian, and Irish performance poetics and transnational, ekphrastic poetry. Her publications have appeared in *Poetics Today, The Paris Review, Columbia Review*, and *The Los Angeles Review*. Her current research project is on the politics of poetic form.

Katharina Engel is working on her Ph.D. on retellings in contemporary British performance poetry by women. Her research focuses on contemporary poetry, specifically spoken word, as well as on representations of gender and queerness in Anglophone Literatures. Until 2018 she worked as lecturer at University of Bonn; she also works freelance as dramaturg and event manager.

Rainer Emig is Chair of English Literature and Culture at Johannes Gutenberg University Mainz, Germany. He was educated at Frankfurt am Main, Warwick, and Oxford, and taught at Cardiff, Regensburg, and Hanover. His research focuses on nineteenth- to twenty-first-century literature and culture. His publications include *Modernism in Poetry* (1995), *W.H. Auden* (1999), and *Krieg als Metapher im zwanzigsten Jahrhundert* (2001) as well as edited collections on *Stereotypes in Contemporary Anglo-German Relations* (2000), *Ulysses* (2004), *Gender ↔ Religion* (with Sabine Demel, 2008), *Hybrid Humour* (with Graeme Dunphy, 2010), *Performing Masculinity* (with Antony Rowland, 2010), *Commodifying (Post-) Colonialism* (with Oliver Lindner, 2010), and *Treasure in Literature and Culture* (2013).

Astrid Franke is Professor of American Studies at Eberhard Karls University Tübingen. She received her Ph.D. from the John F. Kennedy Institute in Berlin and then worked as an assistant professor of American Studies at Johann Wolfgang Goethe University Frankfurt. Amongst her publications are *Keys to Controversies: Stereotypes in Modern American Novels* (1999) and *Pursue the Illusion: Problems of Public Poetry in America* (2010) as well as articles on pragmatism, African-American poetry, contemporary literature, and popular culture. As a member of the Collaborative Research Center "Threatened Orders," she has become interested in the conjunction of literature, unjust orders, and the surprising persistence of inequalities.

Elena Furlanetto earned her doctorate in American Literary and Cultural Studies from the Technical University of Dortmund in 2015 and currently works as a researcher and postdoctoral fellow at the University of Duisburg-Essen. She is the author of *Towards Turkish American Literature: Narratives of Multiculturalism in Post-Imperial Turkey* (2017) and a co-editor of *A Poetics of Neurosis: Narratives of Normalcy and Disorder in Cultural and Literary Texts* (2018). Her work in progress includes studies on the influences of Islamic mystic poetry on Walt Whitman, on Islamophobia and the popularization of Islam in the U.S., and on the Early American captivity narrative. Her research and teaching interests also include orientalism, postcolonial literatures, comparative empire studies, and poetry.

Patrick Gill is a senior lecturer at Johannes Gutenberg University Mainz, where he also received his Ph.D. He is the author of *Origins and Effects of Poetic Ambiguity in Dylan Thomas's* Collected Poems (2014) and co-editor of *Constructing Coherence in the British Short Story Cycle* (2018). He has lectured and published on English poetry from the Renaissance to the present day. His ongoing research is into the efficacy of literary form.

Kathrin Härtl is a postdoctoral researcher in the research group "Philology of Adventure" at LMU Munich. She studied English and German Literature at LMU Munich. Her Ph.D. thesis on "The Common Bond of the Sea. Derek Walcott and Joseph Conrad" was submitted in 2017 and will be published in 2019. She is currently working on her postdoctoral research project, "Transforming Victorian Adventure Writing: Modernist Urban Fiction and Postcolonial Rewritings." Her research focuses on Victorian and modernist adventure fiction as well as Caribbean poetry.

Michaela Hausmann obtained her Ph.D. at the University of Vechta on the topic of "Prosimetric Fantasy: The Forms and Functions of Embedded Poems in British Fantasy Narratives from the 1850s to the 1950s." She has taught seminars on English and American literature at the University of Vechta. Her research interests include fantasy literature, Romantic and Victorian literature, and urban poetry.

Stefanie John is a lecturer and postdoctoral researcher in the English Department at the Technical University of Braunschweig. In 2017, she completed her Ph.D. at the University of Münster as a member of the Research Training Group "Literary Form", funded by the German Research Foundation. Her doctoral thesis focused on Romantic legacies in contemporary eco-poetry and feminist poetry from Ireland, Scotland, and Wales. She has published essays on contemporary and Romantic poetry and on Romantic ideas of childhood. She co-edited a collection of essays on intersections of literary form and knowledge, *Formen des Wissens: Epistemische Funktionen literarischer Verfahren*.

David Kerler is a senior lecturer in English Literature at the University of Augsburg. His research focuses on postmodern literature and film, English Romanticism, and poststructural and cultural theory. He has lectured and published on intertextuality and (meta)hermeneutics in the contemporary novel (dissertation), trauma and/in literature, postmodern film (David Lynch; Game of Thrones), and Romantic poetry. Currently he is working on his habilitation, scrutinizing the nexus between archives, melancholia, and spectrality in English Romantic poetry (working title: "The Archive Fever of the Romantics: Melancholia, Archives and Spectrality").

Ewa Kołodziejczyk is Associate Professor at the Institute of Literary Research, Polish Academy of Sciences, Warsaw. She holds a Ph.D. (2005) and a habilitation (2016) in Polish Literature from the Jagiellonian University in Krakow. Her areas of interests are Polish-American literary filiations in twentieth century, archival research, and literary documentation. She is the author of two books and numerous articles with special focus on Czesław Miłosz's American themes. In 2011 she was a visiting fellow at Beinecke Rare Books and Manuscript Library, Yale University, and in 2013 at Columbia University, where she researched Miłosz's archives. In 2016, her monograph *Czesław Miłosz's American Years* was awarded the Tadeusz Kotarbiński Prize for the best monograph in the humanities in Poland. The book will be published in English by De Gruyter Open in 2020.

Annika McPherson is Junior Professor of New English Literatures and Cultural Studies at the University of Augsburg, Germany. Her research and teaching areas include postcolonial studies; theories, policies and literary representations of cultural diversity in comparative perspective; Caribbean, West African, South African, and Indian literatures in English; diaspora studies; as well as speculative fiction and Afrofuturism. Her most recent articles focus on postcolonial and decolonial patterns of critique and on Afropolitan aesthetics. Her current projects include a reconceptualization of the notion of 'neo-slave narratives' across genre boundaries, covering novels, short fiction, film, and TV as well as poetry, song, and sound.

Pierre-Héli Monot teaches Comparative Literature at LMU Munich. His first monograph, entitled *Mensch als Methode: Allgemeine Hermeneutik und partielle Demokratie*, was published in 2016 (Heidelberg). He was a Visiting Fellow at Harvard University (2012–2013) and is currently a Visiting Fellow at King's College London. His current work focuses on the poetics and politics of autonomy in the nineteenth and twentieth centuries.

Timo Müller is Professor of American Studies at the University of Konstanz, Germany. His research interests include modernism, poetry, environmental studies, and mobility studies. He is the author of *The Self as Object in Modernist Fiction: James Joyce Hemingway* (Königshausen & Neumann, 2010) and *The African American Sonnet: A Literary History* (UP of Mississippi, 2018), and editor of the *Handbook of the American Novel of the Twentieth and Twenty-First Centuries* (de Gruyter, 2017). His work has appeared in journals including *American Literature, Arizona Quarterly,* and *Twentieth-Century Literature*. He has held visiting fellowships at the British Library, Harvard, and Yale.

Julian Wacker teaches English, Postcolonial and Media Studies at the University of Münster, where he is also a Ph.D. candidate. His doctoral thesis focuses on space and identity politics in audiovisual grime culture and examines its remediation across different textualities, including British inner-city novels. Further research areas include black and Asian British film in the twenty-first century, music and literature, black (neo-)Victorian/Edwardian imaginaries, and Afropolitan writing. He published an interview with Chinese-Jamaican author Kerry Young titled "Outside the Boxes" (2017) in *Wasafiri*. A historical survey of black and Asian British popular texts is forthcoming from Cambridge University Press.

Index

Adaptation 2, 3, 48, 176, 196, 201, 204, 205
Adcock, Fleur 76
– "Ex-Queen Among the Astronomers, The" 76
Aesthetics 10, 17, 20, 65, 69, 74, 77, 125, 158, 174, 191, 227–229, 232, 237, 267
Affect 6
Agbabi, Patience 8, 155–169
– *Bloodshot Monochrome* 161, 166
– "Problem Pages" 166, 168
– "Prologue" 157–159, 168
– "Rappin It Up" 160, 161
– *R.A.W.* 160, 161
– *Telling Tales* 163, 169
– *Transformatrix* 157, 161, 162, 164–166, 168
– "Ufo Woman (Pronounced Oofoe)" 162
– "Word" 157, 159, 160, 161, 168
Aiken, Conrad 130
Al-Hallaj, Mansur 52
Alienation 36, 131, 135, 136, 162, 182, 243
Alighieri, Dante 143-145
– *Divina Commedia* 144
Allen, Lillian 174, 182
– "Nelly Belly Swelly" 182
Antiquity 1, 2, 101, 102, 140, 141, 144, 149
Architextuality 19, 23
Archive, Poem as 4, 17–26
Aristotle 2, 104
Auden, W. H. 65, 68
– *Orators, The* 68
Autobiography 7, 177, 183, 240

Bakhtin, Mikhail 2
Ballad 20, 76, 122, 123, 128, 191–194, 197–199, 201, 202, 205, 241
Baraka, Amiri 227, 236, 241
– "Black Art" 236
Barthes, Roland 2, 43, 110
Bayazid-e-Bastami 52
Bennett, Louise 21, 174
Beowulf 241
Bernstein, Charles 209, 229
– *Attack of the Difficult Poems* 209
Berryman, John 219

Black Arts Movement 227, 228, 241, 251
Black British 11, 156, 158, 177, 255–257, 261, 264, 268
Blake, William 17, 18, 71, 130, 131, 133
– "Sick Rose, The" 71
– *Songs of Innocence* 17
Blues 121, 122, 122n2, 160, 236, 240
Boland, Eavan 4, 31–40, 42, 44, 78, 79
– "After a Childhood Away from Ireland" 35, 36, 39
– "Mise Eire" 37, 38, 42
– "Outside History" 32
– "Woman Painted on a Leaf, A" 78
Bourdieu, Pierre 109
Braidotti, Rosi 162, 168
Brathwaite, Edward Kamau 74, 75, 143, 173
– "New World A-Comin'" 74
Breeze, Jean 'Binta' 8, 155, 156, 171, 172, 172n1, 173n1, 174, 176–179, 182–185, 264
– "Aid Travels with a Bomb" 172, 174
– "Can a Dub Poet Be a Woman?" 172
– "Dreamer" 172, 172n1, 176
– *Eena Me Corner* 176
– *Fifth Figure, The* 8, 171, 172, 177, 179, 182, 185
– "Mad Woman" 176
– "Riddym Ravings" 172, 176, 177, 183, 184
– "Song to Heal, A" 172, 173n1, 176
– "Testament" 183
– "To Plant" 174
– *Tracks* 173n1, 176
– "Where Have All the Dub Poets Gone?" 174
Broadway 243, 244
Brooks, Gwendolyn 114, 122–124, 125n3, 166, 167
– "Bronzeville Mother Loiters in Mississippi, A" 122
Brown, Kareem 182n4, 262, 266
– "Sunny D and Purple Stuff" 266
Browning, Robert 114–118, 123, 130
– "My Last Duchess" 114, 115, 118
Brunias, Agostino 177, 178
– *Dancing Scene in the West Indies* 177

https://doi.org/10.1515/9783110594874-019

- *Villagers Merry Making in the Island of St. Vincent* 177
Buddhism 70
Burke, Kenneth 219
Butler, Judith 159
Byron, Lord (George Gordon) 21

Capitalism 8, 99, 100, 102, 103, 108, 142, 236
Castoriadis, Cornelius 6, 99–103, 106–108, 110
Céline, Louis-Ferdinand 104, 104n2
Césaire, Aimé 143
Chapman, George 140
Chaucer, Geoffrey 156, 163, 164
- *Canterbury Tales* 163
- "Wife of Bath, The" 156
Chingonyi, Kayo 255, 258–260, 266
Christianity 51, 58, 70, 119, 121, 122, 144
Cicero 101
Clarke, Gillian 78
Class 5, 6, 58, 77, 103
Classicism 102, 134
Cognitive Theory 3, 193
Coleridge, Samuel Taylor 19, 41–43, 167
- *Dejection: An Ode* 42
- *Kubla Khan* 19
- "Rime of the Ancient Mariner, The" 41
Collins, Suzanne 10, 192, 192n1, 196, 200
- *Mockingjay* 10, 192n1, 192, 196, 200
Colonialism 5, 7, 8, 74, 75, 140–142, 144, 145, 173–175, 177, 178, 180, 181, 243, 248, 249
Communism 6, 100, 104, 105, 128
Contemporary Poetry 5, 65, 76, 77, 127, 131, 132, 156, 157, 167, 211, 220
Cortez, Jayne 76, 230
Crane, Hart 130
Culler, Jonathan 2, 33, 221
Cultural Memory 3, 20
Culture 1, 3, 4, 7, 8, 11, 18, 20–22, 32, 36, 39, 61, 65, 70, 75, 76, 99, 100–105, 107–110, 125, 128, 130–133, 137, 156, 161, 168, 171, 173–176, 178, 179, 184, 185, 200–202, 205, 211, 220–223, 228, 231, 239–241, 245, 251, 256, 257, 260, 261
Cummings, E. E. 130

Darwin, Charles 102
Davie, Donald 73
- "Remembering the 'Thirties" 73
Dawes, Kwame 158
de Man, Paul 110
Death 18, 27, 40, 48, 49, 52, 54–56 58, 63, 64, 76, 79, 116, 129, 161, 162, 165, 179, 201–203, 217, 222, 227
Decolonialism 5, 7, 8, 174, 175, 179, 184, 185
Deconstruction 7, 26, 162, 193, 213
Defamiliarisation 67, 75–77
Deleuze, Gilles 151
Democracy 6, 100–104, 106–110, 212
Derrida, Jacques 2, 4, 7, 18–20, 22–24, 26, 110, 193, 212, 213
- *Archive Fever* 18, 22
- "Law of Genre, The" 2, 19, 26, 212
Diaspora 8, 140, 142, 146, 156, 163, 172, 175, 176, 184, 185
Dickey, James 219
Digital Poetry 8
Divinity 49, 51, 55
Dizzee Rascal 258–260, 262, 263, 265, 267
- "Bop 'N' Keep It Dippin'" 258, 260
- *Boy in Da Corner* 260, 262
- "Everything Must Go" 260
- "Stop Dat" 259, 262, 265, 267
Documentary Poetics 118
Donne, John 83, 130, 143
Doolittle, Hilda 130
Drama 2, 66, 67, 113, 114, 128, 193
Dramatic Monologue 114, 116, 118, 119, 121, 123, 162, 177
Dreiser, Theodore 131
Dub Poetry 8, 155, 158, 171–176, 182, 184, 256, 264, 265, 267
Duffy, Carol Ann 76
- "Mrs Midas" 76
- "Scottish Prince, The" 76
Duncan, Robert 220

Edwardian Age 69
Einstein, Albert 213
Ekphrasis 21, 23, 25, 92, 116, 117, 242
Elegy 64, 142

Eliot, T. S. 64, 65, 67–70, 73, 74, 76, 77, 84, 86, 130, 133, 216, 224, 240
- "Boston Evening Transcript, The" 69
- *Burnt Norton* 69
- "Mr. Eliot's Sunday Morning Service" 69
- *Waste Land, The* 65, 67, 68, 70, 224
Elizabethan Love Poetry 23
Emerson, Ralph Waldo 47, 48, 106
Empiricism 5
Engels, Friedrich 100
Enlightenment 20, 49, 56, 128
Epic 2, 8, 67, 68, 128, 129, 139–149, 151, 152, 193, 196, 212, 216
Epigraph 118, 222
Eric B. and Rakim 242
- "Follow the Leader" 242
Escapism 33, 34, 44
Evaristo, Bernardine 155

Factionalism 20
Fantastic Literature 10, 191, 192
Femi, Caleb 262, 266, 267
- "In Praise and In Defense of Giggs" 266
Feminism 4, 7, 31, 32, 34, 38, 42, 43, 117, 156, 162, 166–168, 182, 262, 263
Ferlinghetti, Lawrence 68
Film 9, 10, 163, 191–205, 230, 243, 252, 261
Fin de Siècle 104
Flint, F. S. 66
Formalism 67, 109, 155, 228, 255
Fragmentation 19, 20, 24, 25, 64, 67, 68, 70, 72, 73, 75–77, 182, 199, 205
Freud, Sigmund 18, 76
Frost, Robert 130, 167
Froude, J. A. 141, 142

Gender 3, 5, 7, 8, 35–37, 39, 40, 42, 77–79, 108, 116, 118, 123, 124, 156, 164–166, 172, 174, 176, 184
Gender Studies 3, 7
Genette, Gérard 2, 19, 109, 123
George The Poet 262–267
- "German Whip" 263
- "Grinding" 262–267
- *Search Party* 264
Ginsberg, Allen 7, 127, 132, 135, 229

Gioia, Dana 212
Glissant, Édouard 146
God 49–53, 55, 56, 59, 60, 134
Graffiti 220, 239, 251
Grime 11, 164, 255–268

Haiku 129
Hall, Donald 212
Hamilton, Alexander 243, 244
Hamilton Mixtape, The 10, 242, 247
Hardy, Thomas 69, 84
Harrison, Tony 76
- "Kumquat for John Keats, A" 76
Hayden, Robert 114, 118–121, 123, 124, 125n3
- "Middle Passage" 118
- "Night, Death, Mississippi" 124
Heaney, Seamus 42, 220, 222
Hill, Geoffrey 73, 76
Hinduism 60, 139, 141
Hip Hop 3, 9, 160, 239–241, 239n1, 244–246, 251, 255, 257, 258
History 1, 3, 5–7, 11, 20–22, 24, 25, 32, 32n1, 33, 37–39, 42, 44, 51, 52, 61, 65, 69, 73, 78, 84, 99–103, 107, 110, 117, 118, 121, 123, 127, 132, 137, 145, 146, 150, 151, 164, 166, 171, 173, 177–179, 185, 198, 205, 211, 215, 220–222, 224, 234, 241, 248–250, 256, 265
Homer 140, 141, 143, 145, 148–151
- *Iliad* 141, 148
- *Odyssey* 140, 143, 148
Hopkins, Gerard Manley 63–65
- "In Memoriam" 64
- "Wreck of the Deutschland, The" 63
Hughes, Langston 234
Hughes, Ted 73, 74
Hull, Isaiah 262, 265–267
- "What is Grime?" 262, 265, 266
Hunt, Leigh 27
Hutcheon, Linda 160, 162, 196
Hybridity 2, 3, 7, 140, 166, 177, 213, 216, 219, 265

Identity 4, 19, 27, 27n3, 37, 40, 49, 59, 117, 118, 134, 137, 156, 159, 162, 164, 165, 171, 173, 182, 184, 202, 213, 220

Ideology 1, 3, 4, 8, 33, 35–37, 39, 44, 102, 103, 107, 141, 143, 144, 174, 204
Imaginary 50, 103, 233
Imagination 20, 25, 26, 33, 34, 40, 41, 56, 73, 131, 134, 160
Immortality 22, 50
Imperialism 3, 27, 141, 144–146, 151, 233, 249
Impersonality 73, 77–79, 194
Implied Audience 115
Implied Author 114, 116–118, 121, 122, 125
Individuality 2, 37, 38, 105
Innocence 17, 132, 177, 203
Intermediality 2, 3, 9–11, 192, 227, 228, 230, 232, 237, 241, 243, 247, 249–252, 256, 262, 263, 267, 268
Intertextuality 2, 19, 44, 143, 150, 151, 163, 167, 184, 263
Islamic Mysticism 52, 60
Isocrates 101

J. Period 247, 248
Jamie, Kathleen 4, 31–33, 39–44
– "Crossing the Loch" 40, 41
– "Meadowsweet" 42, 43
Jay Z 227, 240
Jazz Music 160, 232, 235, 240
Jeffers, Robinson 130
Johnson, Linton Kwesi 171, 174, 264, 265
Jonson, Ben 143
Jordan, June 166
Joyce, James 143

Kano 260, 261
– "T-Shirt Weather in the Manor" 260
Kay, Jackie 155
Keats, John 21, 33, 34, 37, 44, 73, 76, 77
– "Ode on a Grecian Urn" 21
– "Ode to a Nightingale" 34, 73
Kierkegaard, Søren 108
K'naan 247–249
Kojey Radical 267
Kristeva, Julia 2, 110

Larkin, Philip 5, 75, 83–95
– "And now the leaves suddenly lose strength" 92
– "Autobiography at an Air-Station" 89, 90, 92
– "Card-Players, The" 92–94
– "Flesh to flesh was loving from the start" 86
– "Friday Night in the Royal Station Hotel" 93, 94
– *High Windows* 84, 85, 93–95
– "Hotter shorter days arrive, like happiness" 92
– "II" 87
– "January" 92
– *Less Deceived, The* 84, 85, 89, 91
– "Money" 93
– *North Ship, The* 84, 85, 87
– "Spring" 90, 91
– "Street Lamps" 86, 87
– *Whitsun Weddings, The* 84, 85, 91, 92, 94
Last Poets, The 227, 230
Leśmian, Bolesław 133
Lessing, Gotthold Ephraim 231
Lethal Bizzle 259, 260
– "Pow! (Forward)" 259
Levertov, Denise 68, 215
Lewis, Cecil Day 67
– *Magnetic Mountain, The* 67, 68
Lindsay, Vachel 130
Lowell, Robert 130
Lukács, Georg 5
Lyric 1, 4, 6, 31–44, 50, 67, 84, 129, 137, 193, 210, 215, 219, 221, 223, 224, 255
Lyrics (Song) 182n4, 191, 199–201, 203–205, 228, 240–242, 245, 248, 250, 255, 257, 258, 260–263

MacLeish, Archibald 130
Magazine 8, 22, 32, 130, 167
Magical Realism 75
Maoism 110
Markham, Edwin 130
Marley, Bob 185
Marx, Karl 100
Marxism 5, 6, 174
Masters, Edgar Lee 130
Materialism 107
McAlmon, Robert 210

McClure, Michael 220
McGuckian, Medbh 78
McKay, Claude 104, 104n2, 106, 167
McLuhan, Marshall 11
Media 1–3, 8–11, 19, 21, 22, 24, 25, 70, 131, 134, 137, 162, 191, 194, 199, 203, 205, 227–231, 237, 243, 245, 251, 260
Mediality 9, 11, 192, 229n3, 231
Melancholy 122, 203, 256
Memoir 8, 172, 177, 181, 182
Memory 21, 24–26, 36, 40, 41, 72, 73, 124, 131, 133, 135, 179, 182, 183, 185, 197, 201, 221, 222
Metadiscourse 4, 22, 23
Metalanguage 4, 43
Metaphor 19, 23, 40, 42, 49, 54–56, 74, 78, 101, 108, 120, 132, 133, 135, 146–148, 151, 152, 160, 162, 168, 212, 216, 219, 243, 244, 247, 249, 250, 252, 262
Metapoetics 17, 23, 106
Metres, Philip 114, 118, 119, 121–123
– *abu ghraib arias* 118, 119, 121
Mignolo, Walter 174, 185
Miller, Henry 131
Miller, Kei 50n2, 175
Miłosz, Czesław 6, 8, 107, 127, 128, 129, 130, 130n1, 131, 132, 133, 134, 135, 136, 137
– *Ars poetica?* 133
– *Captive Mind, The* 128
– *City without a Name* 128
– *Daylight* 128
– *From the Rising of the Sun* 128
– "My Faithful Mother Tongue" 132, 135
– *Poem on Frozen Time, A* 128
– *Rescue* 128
– *Three Winters* 128
– *Treatise on Poetry* 128
– *Visions from San Francisco Bay* 131, 135
Milton, John 27, 83, 130, 135, 160
– *Paradise Lost* 135
Mimicry 141, 142, 144, 150
Miranda, Lin-Manuel 242, 243, 244, 245
– *Hamilton: An American Musical* 242, 243
Modernism 4, 5, 63, 64, 65, 66, 67, 68, 69, 70, 71, 72, 73, 74, 75, 76, 77, 78, 79, 83, 104, 105, 110, 128, 129

Montague, John 10, 209, 210, 211, 212, 213, 216, 219, 220, 221, 222, 223, 224
– *Rough Field, The* 10, 209, 210, 211, 212, 213, 219, 220, 222, 223, 224
– "Severed Head, The" 221
Moore, Marianne 66, 67, 130
– "Nevertheless" 66
Morgan, Edwin 72, 73
– "Strawberries" 72
Morrison, Toni 179
– *Beloved* 179
Music 9–11, 33, 35, 41, 66, 77, 118, 122, 122n2, 157, 160, 172–176, 178, 179, 182, 184, 185, 191, 192, 194, 195, 197–199, 201, 205, 212, 215, 227–232, 234–237, 239–243, 245–252, 255–267
Musical 247, 250
Mutabaruka 171, 174
Mystical Poetry 50, 60
Mysticism 4, 47–50, 52, 55, 60, 61

N.W.A. 242
– "Fuck tha Police" 242
Nabokov, Vladimir 115
– *Lolita* 115
Narratology 6, 113, 114, 125n3
Nas 242–245
– "Wrote My Way Out" 242, 243, 246, 247, 251
Neoclassicism 20
New Apocalypse 86
New Criticism 2, 33n1, 107, 109
Nichols, Grace 143
Nobel Prize 128, 139, 143, 146
Novel 2, 5, 7, 9, 10, 49, 113, 115, 177, 191–196, 200, 204, 205, 220, 230, 261

Ode 20, 66, 128
Olson, Charles 68, 211
– "Projective Verse" 211
Onomatopoeia 25, 41, 157, 232, 236, 259
Onuora, Oku 171, 174, 175, 264
Oppen, George 6, 104–110
– "Of Being Numerous" 104–107, 110
– *This in Which* 109

Oppression 122, 202, 204, 236, 243, 248, 268
Orality 156–158, 167, 209–212, 215, 240, 241, 251, 264

Palimpsest 24, 129, 179, 181, 183
Pantheism 49, 53
Parody 4, 70, 76, 128, 166
Pearse, Patrick 37
Performance 2, 3, 8, 10, 122, 139, 140, 142, 148, 155–161, 164, 167, 168, 172, 174, 176, 177, 179, 194, 199, 202, 203, 205, 210–212, 215, 222–224, 228–231, 233–237, 239–247, 250, 251, 257, 259, 262–265
Performance Poetry 2, 158–160, 164, 168, 176, 229–231, 234, 235
Perspective 3, 5–8, 10, 19, 26, 40, 42, 43, 108, 114, 117, 118, 121, 124, 125, 129, 159, 160, 166, 198, 201, 223
Petrarchism 85
Philosophy 106, 107, 134, 137
Placedness 49, 60
Pluralism 4
Poetic Persona 4, 48, 49, 52, 60, 159, 163
Politics 1, 4–8, 11, 20, 21, 31–33, 35, 38–40, 42–44, 60, 67, 68, 75, 77, 99–102, 104–108, 110, 127, 137, 156, 160, 167, 168, 171, 173, 179, 181, 185, 227, 228, 232, 234–236
Postcolonialism 3, 4, 7, 31, 34, 74, 141, 144, 156, 175, 184
Postmodernism 2, 3, 8, 77–79, 128, 133, 155, 156, 159–164, 166, 168, 174, 175
Poststructuralism 2, 18, 109, 159
Pound, Ezra 64, 66–69, 76, 77, 130, 143, 210, 224
– *Cantos* 67, 68, 210
Pragmatism 102, 106
Print Culture 4, 18, 21–23, 26
Propaganda 167, 202, 203
Prose 2, 8, 10, 32, 39, 68, 72, 75–77, 129, 137, 166, 167, 172, 177, 181, 193, 194, 205, 210, 213–222, 224, 237
Prosody 214–216, 224
Psychoanalysis 18
Psychology 85, 110, 134, 195, 199, 242, 246

Ramanujan, R. K. 74, 75
– "Self-Portrait" 75
Ramayana 139–142, 146
Ramleela 139, 140, 143
Rap Music 10, 11, 157, 160, 164, 227, 228, 234, 239, 240, 241, 242, 243, 244, 244n2, 245, 246, 247, 248, 250, 251, 252, 239–252, 255–258, 260, 261, 264, 266, 267
Realism 5, 105, 192n1, 251
Reality 7, 49–53, 59, 60, 84, 93, 118, 131, 135, 184
Reed, Henry 69, 70
– "Chard Whitlow" 69
Reggae 173–176, 184, 256, 264
Religion 20, 51, 52, 58, 60, 83, 100, 105, 119, 125, 131, 151, 200, 265
Renaissance 5, 43, 117, 166, 211
Residente 247, 249
Revolutionary War 247, 248, 250
Rhyme 25, 33, 37, 41, 43, 64, 66, 68, 71, 73, 75, 84, 118, 158, 160, 184, 193, 194, 197, 203, 222, 232, 235, 241–245, 247–249, 251, 256–263, 265–268
Rhythm 2, 64, 66, 75, 122, 147, 148, 157, 158, 160, 173, 176, 180, 203, 215, 232, 235–237, 241, 250, 257–259, 263, 264
Riz MC 247, 249
Rodney, Walter 174
Roethke, Theodore 130
Romance (Genre) 20
Romanticism 3–5, 9, 17, 19, 20, 20n2, 22, 27, 31–44, 71, 73, 76, 78, 83, 116, 117, 134, 150, 193
– Post-Romanticism 38, 39, 42, 43
Rukeyser, Muriel 113, 118
– *Book of the Dead* 113, 118
Rumi 4, 48–55, 57–61
– *Divani Shamsi Tabriz* 59
– *Fihi ma Fihi* 55
– "Universal Man" 52, 53

Sanchez, Sonia 229n3, 241
Sandburg, Carl 130
Science Fiction 5, 192n1
Scott-Heron, Gil 10, 227–237
– "B Movie" 236, 237

- "Brother" 232–234
- "Enough" 234
- "Evolution" 232, 235
- "Grandma's Hands" 236
- "Gun" 236
- "Inner City Blues" 236
- "Is That Jazz?" 236
- *Mind of Gil Scott-Heron, The* 235
- "Morning Thoughts" 236
- "Omen" 233, 235
- *Pieces of a Man* 235
- *Reflections* 10, 228, 230, 232, 235
- "Revolution Will Not Be Televised, The" 232, 234, 235
- "Siege of New Orleans, The" 236
- *Small Talk at 125th and Lenox* 10, 228, 230–236
- *So Far, So Good* 228, 232
- "Storm Music" 236
- "Subject Was Faggots, The" 235
- "Whitey on the Moon" 232, 234, 236

Semiotics 239
Sexuality 118, 133, 156, 165, 172, 176
Shakespeare, William 1, 25, 77, 83, 119, 130, 141, 143, 160, 166–168, 255
- *Hamlet* 1
- *Tempest, The* 119, 141

Shapiro, Robert 130
Shelley, Percy Bysshe 4, 17, 18, 20–27
- "Ozymandias" 4, 17, 18, 20–27

Sidney, Sir Philip 83
Slam Poetry 157, 164, 229
Slavery 120, 171, 178, 180, 182
Smartt, Dorothea 155
Smith, Charlotte 26, 27, 83
- *Elegiac Sonnets* 27

Smith, Michael 171
Snodgrass, W. D. 118, 122n2, 219
- *Fuehrer Bunker, The* 118, 122n2

Snow Tha Product 247, 249
Snyder, Gary 220
Socialist Realism 107, 128
Sonnet 3–5, 18–20, 22–27, 83–91, 93–95, 143, 156, 165–168
Sonnet Sequence 143, 166
Spatial Turn 3

Spoken Word 10, 155–158, 175, 229, 235, 236, 240, 241, 255, 258, 261–264, 266–268
Stalinism 107
Stein, Gertrude 67
Steinbeck, John 131
Stevens, Wallace 130
Stevenson, Deborah 262, 263, 266, 267
Structuralism 2
SuAndi 155, 156
Sufi 4, 47–50, 52–58, 60, 61
Sufi Poetry 4, 47–50, 52, 54–56, 58, 60, 61
Sufism 48–50, 53, 61
Surrey, Earl of (Henry Howard) 83, 166
Sweeney, Matthew 177
Swift, Jonathan 76
- *Gulliver's Travels* 76

Tempest, Kate 255
Temporality 18, 23, 24, 26, 134, 210, 214
Tennyson, Alfred 40, 64, 68
- "Crossing the Bar" 40

Terza rima 25, 144
Theology 51, 52, 137
Thomas, Dylan 70–72, 84
Thomas, R. S. 69
- "View from the Window, The" 69

Thoreau, Henry David 48
Tolkien, J. R. R. 10, 191, 192, 192n1, 196–198, 200, 205
- *Hobbit, The* 10, 192, 192n1, 196–198
- *Lord of the Rings, The* 200

Tragedy 1, 2, 64
Traherne, Thomas 130
Transcendence 4, 5, 31, 33, 49, 55, 131, 134
Transcendentalism 47, 61
Transmediality 10
Trauma 64, 114, 180, 182, 184
Trope 49, 56, 105, 141, 149, 193, 249
Troupe, Quincy 230
Typography 8, 89, 93, 118, 121, 209–211, 215–217, 219, 220, 222–224

Unreliability 40, 114–117, 119, 120, 122

Verse Foot 213–216, 246
Victorian 4, 64, 69, 76, 117

Violence 6, 221–223
Virgil 141
– *Aeneid* 141

Walcott, Derek 8, 74, 75, 139–152, 175
– *Another Life* 150
– "Antilles, The" 139, 142
– "Caribbean, The" 142
– "Figure of Crusoe, The" 150
– "Homecoming Anse La Raye" 140
– *In a Green Night* 143
– "Muse of History, The" 143
– *Omeros* 8, 139, 141, 143–152
– "Sea Grapes" 146
– "Tales of the Island" 143
Washington, George 217, 243, 247
Whitman, Walt 4, 6, 47–61, 99, 102, 104–110, 113, 127, 130–132
– *Leaves of Grass* 4, 47–50, 105
– "Out of the Cradle Endlessly Rocking" 55, 56
– "Passage to India" 48
– "Persian Lesson, A" 48
– "Salut au Monde" 48
– "Song of Myself" 48, 50–55, 58–60, 113
Wiley 256–258
– "Wot U Call It?" 256
Williams, William Carlos 10, 68, 104, 104n2, 130, 209–220, 223, 224
– "Excerpts from a Critical Sketch" 210
– *Paterson* 10, 209–214, 216–219, 223, 224
– "Poem as a Field of Action, The" 211
Woolf, Virginia 120
– *Mrs. Dalloway* 120
Wordsworth, William 24, 31, 33–35, 37, 40–42, 83, 160, 167
– "Lines written a few miles above Tintern Abbey" 34
– "Song" 34
World War I 65, 211
World War II 68, 69, 72, 130
Wyatt, Thomas 83

Yeats, W. B. 69, 73, 76, 130, 143

Zephaniah, Benjamin 171, 172, 174

www.ingramcontent.com/pod-product-compliance
Lightning Source LLC
Chambersburg PA
CBHW031801220426
43662CB00007B/489